I0895590

Studies in Eighteenth-Century Culture

VOLUME 35

Studies in Eighteenth-Century Culture

Volume 35

Co-Editors

Jeffrey S. Ravel
Massachusetts Institute of Technology

Linda Zionkowski
Ohio University

Editorial Board

Andrew Curran
Wesleyan University

Lisa Freeman
University of Illinois at Chicago

George Justice
University of Missouri

Lawrence Klein
Cambridge University

Rebecca Messbarger
Washington University in St. Louis

Kathleen Wilson
Stony Brook University

Studies in Eighteenth-Century Culture

Volume 35

Published by The Johns Hopkins University Press for the American Society for Eighteenth-Century Studies

The Johns Hopkins University Press
Baltimore and London
2006

© 2006 American Society for Eighteenth-Century Studies
All rights reserved.
Printed in the United States of America on acid-free paper.
9 8 7 6 5 4 3 2 1

The Johns Hopkins University Press
2715 North Charles Street
Baltimore, Maryland 21218-4363
www.press.jhu.edu

ISBN 0-8018-8416-0
ISSN 0360-2370

Articles appearing in this annual series are abstracted and indexed in *Historical Abstracts* and *America: History and Life*.

Contents

Editor's Note

The American Society for Eighteenth-Century Studies held its first meeting in 1970, and the first volume of *Studies in Eighteenth-Century Culture* appeared the following year. Both ASECS and *SECC* are now well into their second generation, and the continuing vitality of both the Society and the journal attests to the durability of the enterprise inaugurated thirty-six years ago. This sense of continuity became apparent to me when, having agreed to a two-year stint as editor, I discovered that my undergraduate mentor, Harry C. Payne, had edited *SECC* volumes 10, 11, and 12. Hank graciously agreed to write a reader's report for this volume, thereby renewing his involvement with the journal he had edited a quarter of a century ago.

Volume 35 begins with an eloquent tribute to this theme, the intergenerational solidarity of our Society. At the 2004 annual meeting in Boston, the ASECS Women's Caucus organized a roundtable to honor the career of Professor Madelyn Gutwirth, one of the Caucus' founding mothers. Reproduced here in slightly altered versions are the warm testimonies delivered at that occasion by scholars and friends who have profited over the years from Professor Gutwirth's insightful scholarship and tireless promotion of women in the academy. Collaborators from across her career, including two ASECS presidents, discuss the importance of Gutwirth's teaching and organizational activities, as well as the foundational significance of her work on Germain de Staël and representations of women during the Old Regime and the French Revolution. In a moving, humorous response, Gutwirth celebrates the improved position of women in our Society today, but also cautions against complacency.

While the Society occasionally takes time to acknowledge its past, and thereby assesses its present state and plots its future paths, we also keep our attention focused on the subject that brings us together: the diverse people and practices of eighteenth-century Europe, and the broader world with which Europeans interacted in this period. The remaining eleven contributions to this volume display the usual mix of intellectual vibrancy and interdisciplinary acumen that characterize our collective endeavors. Ellen Malenas and Vanessa Smith take us beyond Europe's geographical borders, to the Caribbean and the South Pacific, respectively, to examine the often fraught encounters of English and French men with peoples and cultures different from their own. Malenas offers a reading of a journal written in the early nineteenth century by West Indies plantation owner, and conflicted abolitionist, Matthew Lewis; she highlights Lewis' use of different genres within the journal to assuage his guilt over the material prosperity he enjoyed in Britain as a result of Caribbean slave labor. Smith scours the pages penned by European visitors to the South Pacific for discussions of breadfruit, a plant native to the South Pacific that, at least in the minds of eighteenth-century European voyagers, resembled flour-based bread when cooked. She ably contrasts European and South Pacific dietary uses and cultural perceptions of breadfruit, and returns us briefly to the Caribbean to examine the unfavorable reception in the British West Indies to the plant's importation.

Back in the British Isles, Mark Blackwell re-examines John Locke's *An Essay Concerning Human Understanding*, a work labeled the "Bible" of the Enlightenment in these pages ten years ago by Katharine Morsberger.[1] Blackwell's exegesis of this text stresses that Locke's understanding of the self may not have been as unitary or monolithic as recent literary critics have asserted. Fraser Easton is also concerned with representations, and misrepresentations, of the self, in the context of newspaper accounts of female cross-dressers in eighteenth-century Britain. Easton discovers that the press valorized women who dressed as men to engage in "heroic" military activities, while it excoriated those who hoped to pursue same-sex relationships under male guise. Dianne Dugaw has previously considered representations of "warrior women" in popular British ballads; here she joins with Amanda Powell to study the way in which women poets in England and the Hispanic world fashioned Sapphic identities through parodies of Petrarchan poetic conventions. These meditations on the pliability of the eighteenth-century self, in theory, in practice, and in verse, highlight the diversity of eighteenth-century studies approaches to a fundamental topic in the Western tradition.

While Europe's others and its own diverse selves are relatively recent preoccupations in the field, Robert Dimit takes a fresh look at a topic that predates the Enlightenment by approximately two millennia: rhetorical conventions. His study of aposiopesis, a device in which the speaker or author breaks off a sentence already begun ("Why, you...I oughta...."), ranges from Dryden and Racine to Sterne and Wordsworth in an effort to understand the eighteenth-century creation of a "language of the passions." Ryan Hanley, like both Dimit and Blackwell, re-examines a well-known topic, in his case anti-theatricalism, from a new perspective. Although

Adam Smith was an avid theatergoer, Hanley notes, he shared Jean-Jacques Rousseau's doubts about the public utility of the playhouse. While many of the period's stage theorists enthusiastically trumpeted the didactic possibilities of the stage, both Smith and Rousseau, in similarly pragmatic ways, argued that the theater might at best have a palliative effect on a polity already corrupted by unregulated commercial and sexual desires. Anne Vila also calls our attention to the stage through her study of representations of the *philosophe* in early eighteenth-century French theater. At this juncture, particularly in Philippe-Néricault Destouches' popular 1727 play *Le Philosophe marié*, French playwrights began to abandon a centuries-old tradition of lampooning the supposed pedanticism and sexual inadequacies of intellectuals. Instead, the French stage played host to a new vision of the intellectual that emphasized his ability to combine intellectual engagement with virtuous, love-based marriage; in so doing, it may have helped to prepare a modern notion of the intellectual that allows for both meaningful public engagement and private satisfactions.

One French intellectual whose public engagements both before and after 1789 have long provided important insights is Louis-Sébastien Mercier, republican, playwright, dramatic theorist, and perhaps the original *flâneur*. Joanna Stalnaker reads his pre- and post-revolutionary descriptions of Paris, the *Tableau de Paris* and *Le Nouveau Paris*, for the ways in which the experience of revolution changed one acute observer's relation to the late eighteenth-century urban landscape. In a sense, Stalnaker uses Mercier to study how a modern city becomes "indescribable." Danielle Bobker is also concerned with the changing relations between motion and perception afforded by eighteenth-century developments. Turning her attention to Laurence Sterne's *A Sentimental Journey*, she focuses on the spaces of sociability created by the carriages that Sterne's Yorick inhabits in the text. These rolling salons create new social possibilities, and new discomforts, for Sterne's fictional characters as well as for leisured Europeans of the period. The volume concludes with Dan Edelstein's genealogy, from the late eighteenth century down to the mid-twentieth, of a "hyperborean Atlantis," situated not in the middle of the Atlantic but somewhere in the arctic north. Jean-Sylvain Bailly, the late eighteenth-century originator of the idea, built on the Enlightenment conceit of diffusionism, which argued that all human culture has a single, originary source (in this case the lost civilization of Atlantis). Edelstein traces the idea through to the writings of the late nineteenth-century pseudo-social theorist Madame Blavatsky, where the Atlantis of the North took on heavily racialized overtones that were subsequently picked up by Nazi propagandists, and Hitler himself, in the

1930s. The echoes of the eighteenth century that reverberate across generations are not always melodious.

In closing, I would like to thank the many people whose voices have come together to orchestrate this volume. I am heavily indebted to my predecessor, Catherine Ingrassia, for her wise advice, and to Linda Zionkowski, my co-editor, for her sage counsel throughout the editorial process. The members of the editorial board, Andrew Curran, Lisa Freeman, George Justice, Lawrence Klein, Rebecca Messbarger, and Kathleen Wilson, worked diligently to help evaluate the five dozen submissions we received. Vickie Cutting, in the ASECS office, and Myrta Byrum, at The Johns Hopkins University Press, saw the volume through to press with professionalism and patience. James Nadeau, a graduate student in the Comparative Media Studies Program at MIT, served as an editorial assistant. Finally, as a learned Society we owe a great debt collectively to the scholars who submitted their work to *SECC* for publication, and to the readers who responded to their scholarship. The fine essays that appear in these pages stand in for the many fruitful dialogues occasioned by this volume of *SECC*; these engagements crossed disciplines, traversed geographical borders, and, of course, united generations.

Jeffrey S. Ravel
Massachusetts Institute of Technology

NOTES

1. Katharine M. Morsberger, "John Locke's *An Essay Concerning Human Understanding:* The 'Bible' of the Enlightenment," *Studies in Eighteenth-Century Culture* 25 (1996): 1–20.

Studies in Eighteenth-Century Culture

VOLUME 35

ASECS Women's Caucus Roundtable: The Career and Work of Madelyn Gutwirth

INTRODUCTION

KATHARINE JENSEN

To help mark its thirtieth anniversary (officially celebrated in 2005), the Women's Caucus of the American Society for Eighteenth-Century Studies (ASECS) wanted to honor one of its most renowned senior scholars, Madelyn Gutwirth. The essays that follow were originally presented in a plenary session at the 2004 annual meeting in Boston. Each participant focused on a particular aspect of Gutwirth's life, work, or method, and together the presentations, now essays, portray a woman whose ground-breaking scholarship changed the shape of several fields. Yet it is also clear that the conditions under which Gutwirth was able to accomplish such remarkable work, especially during the early part of her career, were far from supportive of women scholars, much less of feminist ones. By honoring Madelyn Gutwirth at its plenary, the Women's Caucus hoped we would also reflect on where women and feminist scholars were thirty years ago and where we are now. The essays collected here, punctuated by Gutwirth's own contribution, offer the same opportunity for reflection.

In her opening essay, Janet Whatley reminds us that Gutwirth's career as a tenured professor (1969–1991) was spent at West Chester University, where she taught eight courses a year, ranging from elementary French language to twentieth–century literature. Gutwirth herself indicates that before being hired at West Chester, she taught part-time at three different institutions (1958–1966). Despite this itinerancy and demanding teaching load, not only did she manage to do research and to publish, she also founded the Women's Studies Program at her home institution and served ASECS and the Modern Language Association in a number of capacities. As Whatley remarks, Gutwirth's concern to bring about a more just and compassionate academe, so evident in her commitment to professional service, also informs her scholarship.

For example, her 1978 book on Germaine de Staël, the first extensive study in English, is as notable for its empathic portrayal of a complex personality as for its rigorous analysis of Staël's works. Karyna Szmurlo highlights Madelyn's innovative assessment of Staël, whom critics had previously judged an insignificant writer, as a powerful model of resistance, both in her life and in her writing, to woman's domestic role in the eighteenth century. As Sarah Maza further notes, one of Gutwirth's keenest insights comes from using allegory to reveal the significance of Staël's depictions of both self and heroine as the ancient sybil. Being seen as vessels of divine truth, rather than speaking it in their own voices, worked to legitimate these women's genius at a time when feminine genius was considered anathema.

Identifying the rich interdisciplinary method that characterizes Gutwirth's scholarship, an interweaving of literature, history, art history, and psychoanalysis, Maza underscores one of the historical–theoretical aspects of the book on Staël. By illustrating how this writer acted out her various national identities (Swiss, Dutch, French), Gutwirth shows how nationalism is a gendered construction. Indeed, this insight anticipates a current cross–disciplinary preoccupation, the performative nature of the self.

Gutwirth's ability to anticipate trends in cultural analysis is nowhere more apparent than in her 1992 *Twilight of the Goddesses*. As Madeleine Dobie shows, in this monumental study, Gutwirth explores gender as a category always in flux; she understands culture as a process of displacement and compensation. Examining literary, political, and visual representations in relation to social history, Gutwirth dispels the long-held myth that eighteenth-century France was a woman's paradise. For example, the market women's march on Paris, which led to an assault on the queen, reveals a female misogyny meant to express solidarity with men through a demonstration of national loyalty and feminine purity. Gutwirth thus demonstrates how dominant behaviors and discourses pitted women against one another.

In more recent work on Beaumarchais's Figaro trilogy, as Carol Blum points out, Gutwirth explores a variety of themes through the figure of the foundling. These include ambivalent attitudes in late eighteenth-century France toward sexuality, women's role in family life, familial vs. public investments in the child, and individual freedom as emblematized by the illegitimate child's right to be integrated into society.

This issue of integration leads to one of the questions Gutwirth, in her closing essay, asks us to ponder. To what extent, in the last thirty years, has feminist scholarship been successfully integrated into academic society? The overt resistance Gutwirth faced in graduate school and the more genteel resistance of ASECS to feminist questioning prior to the founding of the Women's Caucus are, by and large, behind us. Yet despite the vast productivity of feminist scholars since the 1970s, Gutwirth reminds us that we are in the midst of a backlash that we must resist. She challenges us to develop more adequate frameworks, through cross-national and cross-disciplinary collaborations, in order to extend the racial and gender analyses we have already developed in eighteenth-century studies.

OVERVIEW OF THE CAREER OF MADELYN GUTWIRTH

JANET WHATLEY

People who are relatively new to the profession may not realize just how different eighteenth-century studies today are from what they were in the 1950s and 60s. The texts we now teach in readily available editions, including *Lettres de Mistriss Henley, Lettres d'une Péruvienne,* or *Ourika*, were not considered part of the curriculum a generation ago.

Madelyn Gutwirth's work brought into intellectual discourse not only women writers of the eighteenth century but also the realities of women's lives: childhoods in poverty or wealth, adolescence, virginity, marriage, pregnancies desired or undesired, breastfeeding, aging. Such themes, now to be found in abundance as subjects of dissertations, of scholarly books and articles, were all but unthinkable when Madelyn was beginning her work.

Gutwirth received her B. A. in 1948 from Brooklyn College, and her Ph. D. in 1958 from Bryn Mawr College, where she studied with Margaret Gilman, Jacques van den Heuvel, Ted Morris, and Germaine Brée. Her teaching career includes appointments at Haverford, Bryn Mawr, Swarthmore, and the University of Pennsylvania Graduate School. She has been a full professor at West Chester University in Pennsylvania, during which time she produced much of the rich body of work that we now recognize as indispensable. With Marcel Gutwirth and John Spielman she published a textbook of cultural documents that I still reach for frequently: *Sources et reflets de l'histoire de France.*[1] She wrote many articles and papers on Germaine de Staël, but also published on Rousseau, Isabelle de Charrière, Laclos, Don Juan, *The Magic Flute,* the theatre of Marie-Joseph Chenier, and the rhetoric of Revolutionary hymns. She cast a wide net over the literature and culture of the late eighteenth century, with Staël as her anchor; her book *Madame de Staël, Novelist: The Emergence of the Artist as Woman*, appeared in 1978.[2] Madelyn was producing all this work not in a research university; she was teaching, year in and year out, eight courses a year, including everything from elementary and intermediate French to Marivaux, Giraudoux, Sartre and Camus.

Meanwhile, she was serving the profession as President of the Northeast Modern Language Association, chairing the Modern Language Association (MLA) Commission on the Status of Women, and working on the MLA committee on Academic Freedom. In 1986 she organized and chaired the French Eighteenth-Century Literature meeting, one that some of us remember vividly because it was an occasion to take stock of the development—indeed the transformation—of the eighteenth-century canon. It constituted a collective *prise de conscience* of the newly-recognized place of women's writing. In 1991 she edited with Avriel Goldberger and Karyna Szmurlo a collection of essays, *Germaine de Staël: Crossing the Borders*.[3]

In 1992 she retired (although that hardly seems the right word) as Professor Emerita from West Chester. That was also the year that saw the publication of one of her most powerful and influential books: *The Twilight of the Goddesses: Women and Representation in the French Revolutionary Era*.[4] This work traces the image of women from the era of the aristocratic "goddesses" of the rococo salons, precariously licensed to think and speak as cultural agents, through the period of the French Revolution, with its paradoxes of unleashed energies and patriarchal constraints on women's expression and participation.

Her productivity since that time has been equally astonishing: more than two dozen articles and papers presented at the major conferences on the eighteenth century and Romanticism, including work on Beaumarchais and "Family Values," on the *Encyclopédie*, and on the historiography of the Revolution. In 1996 she and Carol Blum offered an NEH Summer Seminar for College Teachers, "Women, Marriage, Sex, and Reproduction in Eighteenth-Century France: A Multidisciplinary Inquiry." Her tireless generosity has brought her to public libraries, art museums, senior centers, and even a correctional institution, where the audience evinced a lively curiosity about Enlightenment attitudes toward race, liberty, and equality. She has shared her love of literature and the history of cultures, as well as her urgent sense of their relevance to the lives of her listeners, with all these elements of her community.

Madelyn Gutwirth has received many awards and honors, which I could list here. But there is a kind of recognition that does not show up on a CV: that which resides in the minds of our students. I was talking recently with a colleague who has taught a course on Romanticism for many years. He has always had his students read Staël, especially *Corinne*; Madelyn Gutwirth's work served, in his words, as "a guiding light," one that fired them to write in turn their own essays and honors theses on Staël. ("You *know* her?" another student said to me recently, with wonder.) In a sense, Madelyn gave the English-speaking world Germaine de Staël. It is not that work on Staël in English was nonexistent before her book. There was, in fact, a big and popular biography: J. Christopher Herold's *Mistress to an Age*.[5] But hers was the first extensive work in English to bring real imaginative sympathy to the study of Staël; without either condescension or idealization, Madelyn Gutwirth wrote elegantly of that capacious mind and personality with an ardor and generosity truly befitting her subject. This was the gift recognized not only by the community of scholars but also by our students as they try to grasp the basic elements of cultural history. We, and they, have also seen how Madelyn's empathetic recreation of the human strivings and struggles of the past connects with her concern for justice, comprehension, and compassion in the here and now.

While it is hard, ultimately, to do justice to the impact of Madelyn's work, I do wish she could have seen the expression on the face of an M.A. student, working on the theatre of the Revolution, who came into class recently. She had just begun to read *The Twilight of the Goddesses*. "My God, there is so much in it!" she exclaimed. "I can't wait to get back to it!" Our sentiments exactly.

RECLAIMING GERMAINE DE STAËL

KARYNA SZMURLO

Madelyn Gutwirth's work has been instrumental not only in bringing to the attention of the American academe the illustrious, yet too long neglected, woman writer of postrevolutionary France, Germaine de Staël, but also in nurturing her fellow scholars. I had the good fortune to meet Madelyn in the late 1980s while still teaching at Rutgers University. Madelyn and I, together with Avriel Goldberger, organized the first international Staël conference on the American continent: "Germaine de Staël: Crossing the Borders." Our efforts resulted in a volume in which, indeed, borders were crossed: geographical, because we succeeded in reuniting three generations of researchers from both sides of the Atlantic, and above all, methodological, for the volume became a breakthrough in new approaches to Staël's work.

An event of this magnitude would not have been possible without the groundwork Madelyn Gutwirth provided in her pioneering study *Mme de Staël, Novelist: The Emergence of the Artist as Woman*, which incited the outburst of feminist interpretations over the next two decades.[6] Gutwirth wrote *Mme de Staël, Novelist* to dissent from the view of authorities who had banished Staël's fiction from the list of authors to be read; for generations, work on Staël indulged primarily in the scandals of the private life of Necker's daughter. Her study belongs, as Nancy Miller proclaimed after its publication, "to the new literary history of feminist scholarship: a revision of the canon with sympathetic and deliberate attention to the female artist." [7] In an assessment of her own efforts today, Madelyn goes further in emphasizing the transformative objectives of her work. By a feminist challenge she understands not only changing the past but also altering the future perception of history. Her crusade to dismantle the long held myth of the eighteenth-century cult of women and to unmask the social failure of their aspirations originates in "Staël's strong arraignment against the men of her time," who "since the Revolution, had found it useful to reduce women to the most absurd mediocrity."[8]

At many levels of Staël's thought Gutwirth found her own fascination with the dichotomy of stasis and movement. Her best pages depict this tension: talent versus society, voice versus silence, Sybils versus Madonnas. They also unveil how Staël represents women's ambitions through images of closure, how she destabilizes the esthetics of cameos and friezes, typical of Empire art, or distorts the static neoclassical forms through flowing lines of the Romantic style. Madelyn Gutwirth lent new life to a marginalized proto-romantic writer waiting to be moved out of the shadow of her famous male contemporaries, Chateaubriand, Constant, and her own father, Jacques Necker. Through a meticulous demonstration of Staël's pursuit of passion and accomplishment against paternal prohibitions, against the repressive tides of society, and against the exile imposed by Bonaparte, Gutwirth restores Germaine de Staël as a symbol of resistance to woman's domestic role in the eighteenth century. Furthermore, Gutwirth's treatment of Staël's novels, in particular her passionate chapters on Corinne's fury inherited from the Racinian Phedra or on Corinne's prophecies of women's ability to change the world, endow Staël's fiction with mythic dimensions unperceived by generations of critics.

Gutwirth draws heavily on the comparative, inclusive methods embodied in Stael's life. Banished from Paris, Staël organized at her family estate in Coppet, Switzerland, a multinational circle of literary and political dissidents. Probing Staël's limitless connections, Gutwirth structures her own study as a dialogic interdisciplinary enterprise. A polyphony of voices from the long eighteenth-century participate in her reconsideration of the female genius, its genesis and development. As the door to Jacques and Suzanne Necker's Parisian salon opens, we see the precocious Anne-Louise Germaine surrounded by the best minds of the Enlightenment: Diderot, Voltaire, Condorcet, Grimm, Marmontel, Mme Geoffrin, Buffon, Hélvetius, the abbés Raynal, Thomas, and Galiani. The quest for the origins of the young prodigy's "singularities" leads Gutwirth to explore the mother/daughter rivalry for the affection of the idolized Jacques Necker, and the child's attempts to surpass the expectations of the famous father who openly disapproved of feminine self-expression. The schismatic figure of parental love and reprimand, warmth and coolness, presence and absence, so intensely inscribed in Gutwirth's critical apparatus, echoes her own personal experience. To her own adoring father, Louis Alexander Katz, who did not hesitate to verbalize his disappointment in not having a son, Madelyn would dedicate her second book, *The Twilight of the Goddesses,* to provide a regenerative aspect to his painful legacy.[9] It is clear that from her earliest youth, she had felt a stubborn protest against the female condition.

An attuned listener, Gutwirth also detected in Staël a rebellion kindled by the paradoxes of the maternal voice. Suzanne Curchod Necker, a cultivated Protestant bred on Rousseau, tirelessly enlightened the mind of the daughter to prepare her for the role of a learned yet submissive wife. As Gutwirth argues in a hermeneutic dissection of Staël's own assessment of Rousseau, Germaine, after years of ambivalent feelings toward her own mother, dared to respond critically to Rousseau's views on women.[10] Defying the dutiful Mme Necker, who had to abandon her own literary aspirations at the firm request of her beloved husband, Germaine became a disquieting example of sexual mobility, of a ruthless pursuit of happiness and of intellectual freedom.

Gutwirth's decisive research depicts the affiliations of transhistorical and transpatial values. In her readings, Staël regains a prestigious place in the account of literature by women, in particular, Margaret Fuller and many others of Anglo-American heritage.[11] Furthermore, Gutwirth demonstrates, often through early nineteenth-century iconography, how Staël transmits the Romantic ethos: enthusiasm, excess, passions, melancholy, and Ossianic mists. The crossing of geographical and temporal borders in Gutwirth's critical itinerary suggests new dimensions to Staël's work: the woman writer can bridge, in a positive way, Enlightenment, Revolution and Romanticism; she can adapt the past to the new era of spiritual awakening. For example, Gutwirth sees a parallel between Staël's espousal of the idea of progress, inherited from Condorcet and William Godwin, and her theory of novelistic practice. Despite the darkest irrationalities of the Terror, Staël consistently supported the concept of perfectibility, while also believing in the Christian catharsis of suffering as a ground for the moral advancement of humankind. She acclaimed the novel as the art of the future, capable of rehabilitating readers from passions and pain.[12] This mixture of past and future, the haunting presence of lost generations and prophecies so masterfully presented in Gutwirth's works, situates Germaine de Staël as a precursor of the influential movements predominantly reserved for male thinkers: nineteenth-century European idealist historiography and North American transcendentalism.[13]

Gutwirth's scholarly career is an outstanding act of generosity and courage toward the subject of her study and toward the profession. The prestige of her work as well as tireless efforts to promote Staël research earned her the friendship and collaboration of Simone Balayé, recently deceased dean of Staël studies in Europe and the long-term president of the Parisian *Société des études staëliennes*. In recognition of Gutwirth's contributions to the field, the *Société* has granted her membership on its Honorary Board, limited to the foremost scholars of our time. More recently, in *Cahiers staëliens*, the official journal of the French society, Madelyn delivered a comprehensive analysis of Staël studies in the United States during the second half of the twentieth century.[14] In this critical review, she emphasized the explosion of gender studies since the 1970s and the differences between European and American scholarship; she also commented on the growth of comparative studies due to the translation of Staël's works and to major conferences. In this extensive yet self-effacing account, Madelyn did not mention the fact that the majority of American contributions would not have come into existence without her own militant activism in the field.

A result of her labor, the Society for Staël and Coppet Group Studies (USA) was founded and given status as a new affiliated group at the annual ASECS meeting in New Orleans in 2001. Its new name, "Germaine de Staël Society for Revolutionary and Romantic Studies," reflects the group's intention of welcoming more researchers whose scholarly work crosses the boundaries between academic disciplines. With its own publication channels in the future, it will be the most appropriate forum for the demonstration of our different feminist and internationalist tendencies surveyed so well by Gutwirth. It will also provide a forum for the polemics and controversies in which Madelyn Gutwirth excels. She stands ready to reprimand those who, ignoring the last two decades of research, still try to judge Germaine de Staël according to the long-held attitudes of the past. Like her European counter-part, Simone Balayé, whose "generosity was demanding and friendship jealous" toward those who could not understand Staël, Madelyn Gutwirth does not easily forgive reactionary attacks against her exegete.[15] In these matters, Madelyn's generosity changes to the aggression of the Racinian Phedra, as we witness it in her article "Taking *Corinne* Seriously" published in *Signs* in reply to Ellen Moers' mocking attitude toward Staël. More recently, P. N. Furbank's "Call Me Madam," an openly misogynous review of Staël's first novel, *Delphine*, provoked Gutwirth's passionate rebuke in *The New York Review of Books*.[16] Indeed, without Madelyn Gutwirth's exceptional impact and enthusiastic involvement, the field of Staël studies would be lacking vitality and excitement.

MADELYN GUTWIRTH, HISTORIAN

SARAH MAZA

My title alludes both to Madelyn Gutwirth's celebrated book on Germaine de Staël, and to my desire to claim at least part of Gutwirth and her work for my own discipline. I first encountered Gutwirth's work in the mid 1980s, when I was casting around to write a commissioned paper on women in Napoleonic France—a subject on which the bibliography was then pretty much non-existent. I happened upon Gutwirth's *Madame de Staël, Novelist* and read it in one sitting: not only was it a life-saver for what I was writing, it also suggested illuminating ways in which literary biography could connect with socio-political history. Long before questions about gender and the construction of nationhood, about the role of female allegories in political culture had become central issues for historians, Gutwirth placed such matter at the center of her study of the life and writing of a cosmopolitan and intensely political woman. In so far as such distinctions make any sense at all, Gutwirth is as much a historian as a literary critic.

Part of my fascination with Gutwirth's Staël book came from the fact that I knew little about its protagonist, and discovered her in Gutwirth's pages. Madame de Staël was not the bluestocking harlot I had encountered in the dismissive allusions of other (mostly male) scholars.[17] But she was not the girl next door either, and Gutwirth did not try to make her that. Germaine was certainly smart, bold, and creative, but also in many ways an insecure, self-absorbed and self-dramatizing diva. (I have encountered a number of Germaines in academia, and was relieved when I finally met Madelyn to discover that she was emphatically not one of them). The author's fine balance of empathy and distance was one of the things that drew me into the book in the first place.

But the book also opened up themes which uncannily anticipated much of the gender and cultural history of the following decades. Some of the book's motifs partook of classic 1970s feminism: this was the story of a woman who wrote at a time when women's words were considered too insubstantial to consign to paper, and upper-class women in France were supposed to speak wit rather than substance. Madelyn's account of Germaine's account of Corinne—a cascade of women "creating" one another—sounded post-sixties themes about the silencing of women and the need to find one's voice. But Gutwirth's deep command of cultural history, evident in the book's many and varied illustrations, lifted the matter well out of the realm of cliché, weaving family history and psychology together with the largest themes of revolution, war, and nationalism. Germaine de Staël's parents were Swiss, her husband Swedish, her lover and country of residence French. Staël, Gutwirth argued, understood the articulation of personal and political freedom, and in the aftermath of Napoleon's plunder of Italy she cast an Italian woman as the heroine of her most famous novel, *Corinne, or Italy*.

Gutwirth's approach in the book suggested that the history of women, mostly conceived at the time as straightforward social history, must also incorporate the study of archetypes and allegories. Most strikingly, she pointed out that Germaine de Staël cast both herself and her most famous heroine as the ancient sybil, the possessed priestess. Gutwirth's poignant insight was that the sibyl was at the time "one of the few licit figures of female genius, even though she represents possession by the inchoate power of power of prophecy" (174). Women like Germaine and her heroines found it easier to claim access to truth if they were not speaking but spoken through.

Gutwirth's *Madame de Staël* was the first book in which I saw the images that were later to become ubiquitous, of women being beaten in the streets of revolutionary Paris alongside representations of female allegories of the

Revolution; it was the first book in which I encountered the names of prominent female revolutionaries like Olympe de Gouges and Théroigne de Méricourt, names which did not yet appear in books about the French Revolution. This was also, long before anyone began dropping the name of Benedict Anderson, a book about the gendered construction of nationalism. It played, along with Staël's novels, on gendered allegories of nationhood. It posed the question of how a cosmopolitan woman was to understand her life in the context of Europe's emerging modern nations. In showing how Germaine acted out her various national identities in her own life and through those of her characters, Gutwirth's study also anticipated that most recent of historical themes, the constructed and performative nature of the self. That this book was conceived and written in the 1970s and before is, to my mind, remarkable. Reading it in the mid 1980s, I caught a glimpse of the riches that were within the reach of historians if they paid attention to the work of certain literary scholars.

Madame de Staël, Novelist pointed logically towards a larger study of cultural constructions of womanhood in the age of revolution. Madelyn Gutwirth produced that synthesis in 1992 with her masterwork (to date), *The Twilight of the Goddesses*, a typically rich brew of literature, history, art history and psychoanalysis. Just as Germaine de Staël espoused and then subverted the role of polite salonnière, *Twilight of the Goddesses* lays waste to the cliché of the Age of Enlightenment as the golden era of refined womanhood. Its title cleverly points both to the historical fate of princesses and salon ladies at century's end, and to the demise of a nostalgic, pastel-hued vision of eighteenth-century femininity. In this stunning survey of womanhood in contexts ranging from village life to literature and philosophy to street politics, Gutwirth restores the maidservant and the wet-nurse, the harpy and the medusa, to their rightful place alongside the mistress and the salonnière.

Throughout her career, Madelyn Gutwirth has tackled the themes of cultural history, bringing to them insights inaccessible to most historians. What historian, for instance, could describe as she does the deep ambivalence about children in eighteenth-century culture, a context in which children were loved far more in theory than in practice? Children were evicted from the picture even as they were idealized, Gurtwirth has argued, most recently in an illuminating article on Beaumarchais's Figaro trilogy.[18] Typically, Gutwirth brings forth not just the usual information about Rousseau's contradictory behavior, but the demographers' figures on illegitimacy and child abandonment. Once human life became an end in itself, she suggests, family relations were eroticized, making children into troubling sexual presences like Chérubin in *The Marriage of Figaro*, or those swarms of menacing putti in rococo paintings. In the eighteenth-century demographic regime too many children were surviving to compete with their fathers for their mothers' breasts.

These are just a few examples of Madelyn Gutwirth's method, a combination of literary, historical, iconographic and psychoanalytic approaches that prefigured and still represents the best in interdisciplinary work in the humanities. Gutwirth's interest in psychoanalysis and in public mythologies of family life made her a natural interlocutor for Lynn Hunt in the 1990s, after the publication of Hunt's *The Family Romance of the French Revolution*, and led to a friendly debate in the pages of *French Historical Studies*.[19] In response to a provocative defense of disciplinarity by Hunt, Gutwirth wrote that yes, we do come from disciplinary families whose values we espouse: "But sometimes we notice that our own families don't know as much as we once thought they did. We meet other families and are amazed at what they have to teach us, even about solving problems our own family has trouble grappling with."[20] Madelyn Gutwirth has spent her career (so far) roaming into the disciplinary company of strangers who have become her friends, and we in turn have learnt much from her intellectual daring and gregariousness. I am certain that I speak for many historians when I say how glad I am that Madelyn Gutwirth's family romance led her wandering off towards my own tribe.

THE CRITICAL METHOD OF MADELYN GUTWIRTH

MADELEINE DOBIE

Madelyn Gutwirth's long career as a scholar and teacher allows her to articulate the cultural memory of the field and the profession. When she discusses the status of gender-based studies of the eighteenth century, or the place of women in the contemporary academy, Gutwirth draws on her own broad experience of scholarly life, both before and since the advent of feminism. At the 2001 annual meeting of the American Society for Eighteenth-Century Studies, Gutwirth warned against taking the changes that have occurred in scholarship and academic culture over the last three decades for granted. She spoke as a pioneer, reminding younger scholars that the historical and theoretical questions that are now explored so fruitfully, and the equal treatment of women scholars that we have come to expect, are rather recent developments. This cautionary outlook is also shaped by Gutwirth's scholarship; it reflects her view of the eighteenth century as time in which women's rights were debated and in some measure secured, only to be swept away in the backlash of the Revolution. Underpinning this transhistorical feminism are several important philosophical postulates: the perception of gender as a tendentious category that is always in flux, and the conviction that culture rarely advances in a progressive fashion toward the resolution of conflict. Both perceptions are central to Gutwirth's most influential study, *The Twilight of the Goddesses*.

Scholars who are productive over a long period often become identified with the ideas and methods of a particular era. Madelyn Gutwirth is one of the striking exceptions, a scholar whose work has kept pace with, and indeed helped to shape, new trends in literary analysis. This dynamism is particularly evident in *Twilight of the Goddesses*. Whereas in her earlier books, Gutwirth approaches the question of women's place in eighteenth-century France through a study of the *œuvre* of a woman writer, Germaine de Staël, in *Twilight of the Goddesses*, making creative use of recent critical theory, she explores gender as a relational phenomenon, a fluid category shaped in the mould of representations.

Twilight of the Goddesses is divided into two parts. The first half examines gender and culture in the latter half of the eighteenth century, while the second explores the unprecedented momentum brought to gender relations during the revolutionary period. The mast of works on eighteenth-century culture address only one of these periods; in fact, this separation constitutes something of a fracture within the field. Writing against the grain of this division, Gutwirth examines the gendered reconstruction of the nation during the Revolution from an historical perspective that reaches back as far as the comedies of Molière. She posits a deep continuity between the anxiety toward the participation of women in public life discernable in many Enlightenment texts, and the ultimate denial of political rights to women during the Revolution. However, *Twilight of the Goddesses* does not plot eighteenth-century history as a linear course culminating in this negative outcome. Structurally, the book is of a series of thematically organized chapters, each divided into short subsections or vignettes that center on a key historical date, the reading of a text or painting, or a deft biographical sketch. This aggregate composition supports an overall account of culture as multilayered, overdetermined and unstable, always on the move but not always moving in a single direction. One advantage of this organization is that it allows for a zoom-lens technique, as the narrative shifts between the presentation of social, political, and demographic data, and close readings of canonical works. Throughout the study, historical context illuminates texts and canvases without crowding them, and correspondingly, analyses of art and literature shed light on the rhetorical dimension of social, political and scientific discourses. A similar point may be made of the biographical sketches—of Rousseau, Épinay, Condorcet, and Marie-Antoinette, among others—scattered throughout the book. Gutwirth's writing is empathetic. Perhaps because she worked for many years on a single writer, she is able to establish intuitive, psychological connections to her eighteenth-century subjects. In these sketches, however, the life is never allowed to dictate the work. Rather, *Twilight* traces a series of causal volutes in which biography and creativity are delicately shown to be at once autonomous and intertwined.

Although she stops short of arguing that history amounts to the history of representations, Gutwirth emphasizes that historical interpretation must attend closely to the tenor of representations, whether rhetorical or visual, political or aesthetic. *Twilight* cross-examines different modes of representation: literary fiction, political polemic, visual art, and revolutionary festivals, among other media. Particularly important to the book's argument is Gutwirth's description of a shift in French iconography from the anecdotal preoccupation with pagan goddesses that is characteristic of the rococo, to the allegorical deployments of female figures to embody abstract ideals that abounded during the Revolution. The book's final figure, Ingres's striking early drawing, *The Wounded Amazon*, eloquently conveys this trajectory in gender relations: the deliberate foreclosure of women's right to play an heroic, or indeed any visible role, in the public life of the nation.

This is not the place to debate the pros and cons of interdisciplinary writing, or Gutwirth's particular practice of cultural cross-referencing, an issue raised in some reviews of *Twilight of the Goddesses*. I would like to observe only that in this study visual symbols are never reduced to statements of ideology, or treated as surrogate texts. Gutwirth is attentive to the aesthetic qualities and formal properties of visual art, and sensitive as to the limits that impose themselves when we travel outside our field of specialization.

Twilight is a deeply skeptical book. Gutwirth is suspicious of any representation, past or present, that portrays eighteenth-century France as a woman's paradise. She sniffs out residual gallantry in claims that rococo art, the Enlightenment salon, or libertine literature reflect women's agency or desire in an uncomplicated way. Approaching culture as a field of displacement and compensation, Gutwirth is always on the lookout for the trap concealed in any apparent advantage accorded to women. This skepticism extends even to the feminocentric plot-lines of novels, including novels by women, that have been received with enthusiasm by other feminist readers. For Gutwirth, prevailing discourses all too often pitted women against each other, impeding the growth of real networks of female solidarity.

Conflict among women occupies center stage in Gutwirth's account of the events of 5–6 October 1789, when a group of market women marched from Paris to Versailles to petition for bread, and ended up leading an assault on the person of the queen. As Gutwirth observes, this attack, which involved a rejection of Marie-Antoinette's self-representation as a devoted mother (she appeared before the women on the king's balcony holding her children by the hand, only to be ordered to send them back inside and come out alone), reflects animosity toward a privileged woman who had escaped the lot of much of her sex, as well the internalization of a widespread discourse about women: "what the men hated the women had to hate with an inflated venomousness. . . . To despise the "Austrian Whore" became for women a sign not only of national loyalty but also of personal purity (243).

As this passage suggests, Gutwirth's skepticism is aligned with concern for the experiences of the whole range of social classes. *Twilight* repeatedly proposes that the intellectual brilliance of the Enlightenment should not be divorced, as it is in many studies, from the everyday realities of poverty, famine, poor work conditions, and along with gendered reproductive issues, including the abandonment of infants, the wet-nursing industry, the staggeringly high rate of infant mortality. In this vein, Gutwirth argues that the breast fetish of the period, the discursive and iconographic preoccupation with nursing and motherhood spearheaded by Rousseau, should be read against the backdrop of the array of social problems tied to reproduction. Gutwirth's sketches of the lives and careers of key figures such as Madame de Tencin, her *fils naturel*, Jean Le Rond d'Alembert, and Jean-Jacques Rousseau, offer concrete illustrations of how the material realities of pregnancy and child abandonment intersected with the literary and political discourses of the age.

Twilight of the Goddesses examines a vast array of primary sources, and also synthesizes a wide range of secondary literature. With an intuitive sense of the emergent trends in eighteenth-century studies, Gutwirth often cites articles that appeared ahead of major books, or conference papers that had an obvious future. She is a equally attentive to French and English-language sources, a critical bilateralism that is quite rare. She draws on an impressive range of theoretical writing: Gadamer on the historical interpretation of aesthetic experience; Freud, Kofman, Horney and other psychoanalytic thinkers on sexual difference; Bourdieu and Sahlins on the anthropology of gender. This turn to theories formulated in relation to different social and historical contexts reflects the fact that, although the enquiry of *Twilight* is firmly anchored in eighteenth-century France, the play of representations that it describes resembles, with important differences, the gender debates of other times and other places. Combining anthropological and historical consciousness, Gutwirth notes succinctly in this vein that dichotomies such as female/male, nature/culture, private/public, family/society, body/mind, passion/reason "occur with nauseating repetitiveness," yet "not as static categories, but along a continuum of possibilities" (116).

Any project of the scope and ambition of *Twilight* will inevitably generate critical responses. As I have suggested, not all readers have embraced its interdisciplinary method. Nor have all scholars agreed with the largely pessimistic account of Enlightenment and Revolution that Gutwirth lays forth. Lynn Hunt, for one, perceives in the radicalism of the Revolution a less vicious curtailment of women's rights, and a stronger prospect for the emergence of feminism. She and Gutwirth, in company with other respected scholars, have vigorously debated the Revolution's meaning for women, its relationship to gender politics in the eras that preceded and followed it, and women's participation in and resistance to revolutionary debate, legislation and ritual. For my part I find it difficult to agree fully when Gutwirth writes, in reference to the novels of Isabelle de Charrière, "Charrière's world is still an aristocratic and provincial one, where the woman's struggle is vain, her defeat foreordained." I find there to be greater optimism in Charrière's writing, and perhaps find more cause to hail the positive achievements of her age. This said, I also recognize that the overall pessimism concerning the direction of gender politics that is articulated in *Twiligh*t bespeaks Gutwirth's underlying belief in an ideal equality of the sexes toward which women and men can only continue to strive. In other words, Madelyn Gutwirth's militancy in relation to the present stands in counterpoint to her apparent pessimism regarding the past. In this spirit it seems appropriate for me to conclude with the short but moving final paragraph of *Twilight of the Goddesses*: "The women of history, too, survived the French Revolution, in and in spite of men's representations of them. For while their struggle to alter men's consciousness of their reality had met with pitiless civil and moral retribution, their resilience was imperishable" (385).

IN RETIREMENT

CAROL BLUM

I've had the good fortune of knowing Madelyn Gutwirth and Marcel for a number of years, both through her writings and through our encounters at ASECS, EASECS and NEASECS meetings. We really became friends however when they and I were spending the Fall of 1993, in Paris. We ran into each other in the *Bibliothèque nationale*; when Madelyn asked me what I was doing, I told her my husband had just died and I had no idea what I was doing, and she said, "Well, tonight you're having dinner chez Georges with us." And so we did. It was immensely comforting to have her and Marcel's warm presence that difficult autumn, as we shared meals, trips to the theater and as always, great eighteenth-century talk. Her superb book, *Twilight of the Goddesses*, had just appeared, and we were able to explore the ideas she discussed, as I learned more about the shadowy other side of the Enlightenment. Madelyn's book was, and still is, a wonder to me; I remain amazed by the immense range of materials she has assimilated and woven together into such a powerful demonstration of the complexities of being a woman in eighteenth-century France, a subject not unrelated to being a woman anywhere, anytime.

A few years later we decided that it would be wonderful to see if we could get National Endowment for the Humanities (NEH) funding for a summer seminar. In the summer of 1996 I had the pleasure of codirecting an NEH Summer Seminar for College Teachers, "Women, Marriage, Sex, and Reproduction in Eighteenth-Century France: A Multidisciplinary Inquiry" with Madelyn. She and Marcel rented a little house in Stony Brook for the six weeks and we worked with a super group of participants, fourteen women and one courageous male, who remarkably kept his equanimity throughout the whole experience. It gave me the feeling for Madelyn's superlative gifts as a teacher as well as a scholar, or rather the intimate connection between the two activities when they work together as effectively as they do for Madelyn. I remember watching her and listening to her that summer, as she interwove her own vast store of knowledge about the eighteenth century and women's rocky road through it, with the texts we were reading and the participants' own contributions, questions and responses. The dynamics were terrific, as occasionally happens in life, even among specialists in French literature. The pleasure of teaching in tandem with someone like Madelyn was one I had never had before; the synergy was so energizing that it has stayed in my mind with a particular warmth, a little grace period of an inestimable privilege of the academic life.

At the 1999 ISECS meetings in Dublin, Madelyn presented a paper for our section on "Population anxiety: family, reproduction and demographics in eighteenth-century France," which came out last year in *Studies on Voltaire and the Eighteenth Century* in the section loosely labeled "Demography." In this paper Madelyn explores Beaumarchais' Figaro trilogy, *Le Barbier de Seville*, *Le Mariage de Figaro* and *La Mère coupable* as they reflect the changing attitudes and ambivalent values in the last decades of the eighteenth century towards the couple, marriage, sexuality and the child. Madelyn makes a remarkable argument in this paper about the peculiar role of the foundling in late eighteenth-century France, talking about a host of rankling issues: the rights and wrongs of sexual drives; people's affiliative needs, allegorically localised to the mother-child bond; the public's versus the family's interest in and responsibility for the child; the character of marriage; women's role in family dynamics; and centrally, individual freedom, as posed primarily by the right of what the French called the 'natural' child to become integrated into the social body. Madelyn points to the era's impulse to shed constraint as symbolized by the campaign against binding infants: "infants are to be delivered of their ancient swaddling clothes," and their mothers are admonished "to discard their deforming stays and stylishly crippling shoes." Madelyn shows how at the same time as the corsets and swaddling clothes were being routinely denounced, a doctrine of family togetherness was gathering steam, offering a rigid moral code to insure the right functioning of what was really a bourgeois family structure: virtuous couple, responsible patriarch, submissive wife, children enmeshed in filial duty. In her subtle analysis, these theses are shown to clash and combine, without achieving any real synthesis in the context of Revolutionary society. Beaumarchais' plays, encompassing the period from 1784 to 1792, unite the joyous hedonism of the liberated Enlightenment, especially in the person of Figaro himself, and the emerging, neo-Rousseauvian cult of fertile domesticity, exemplified by a new kind of couple, the egalitarian, hard-working Suzanne and Figaro, who are compared to the dominating Count and his submissive wife.

But as Madelyn points out, while the theme of the family haunts the three plays, in reality all the mating results in no real family life. Figaro finally gets his mother and father back in a bitter-sweet parody of family reunion, Suzanne and Figaro are not seen to become parents, and while the count and Rosine eventually reproduce, it is each on their own recognizance, his illegitimate daughter and her illegitimate son further complicating matters by falling in love. Just as Rousseau's homages to family happiness, Julie and Emile, end in shattered couples, Beaumarchais' productions push toward a family perfection that eludes his characters until the very unconvincing, contrived ending of the third play, where the infidelities and mutual rage of the noble couple are plastered over, as the curtain falls. Recently I used Madelyn's adroit analysis of this tangle in terms of the historical context of debate over 'family values' to teach one ultra-bright young woman in a sort of tutorial about Figaro. One night we went into New York to see the City Center Opera's performance of *Le Nozze di Figaro*, and I was thinking of the blessed, unforeseeable connections forged by research, writing, and teaching in literature, history, art and music, as well as (who knew?) demography! Now Madelyn has spoken to yet another bright young person, bringing new perspectives into the mind of *la génération courante*. She shows the fluidity of Enlightenment associations, not only between theater and music but between art and political agenda, political agenda and conscious or unconscious primitive sexual fears and wishes, roiling libido and science, public policy, and personal struggles, all of which lead back to the eighteenth century's most gripping literature. I am deeply grateful for the original, foundational understanding of the eighteenth century that Madelyn has brought us in her many writings, as I am for the gift of her friendship.

RESPONSE

MADELYN GUTWIRTH

I simply can't convey adequately my astonishment at the news that The Women's Caucus had decided to devote a session to my career. It's something I'd certainly never dreamed of, out there in my Philadelphia suburb. Fortunately, I've gotten used to the idea. By now I've entered into a phase of distinct cheerfulness over having lived into the 21st century and my 79th year, beyond a number of equally meritorious colleagues, so as to see it happen.

So I thank the Women's Caucus and *Studies in Eighteenth-Century Culture* heartily for this honor. I'm especially grateful to the distinguished contributors to this tribute, not merely for their overgenerous remarks. I deeply admire each one of them for her curiosity, incisiveness, independence, and breadth as a scholar, as well as for her willingness to share in this rite. Each of them has elaborated so searchingly and rewardingly on various aspects of my work that even I understand it far better than before. I'm grateful to each of them for such flattering attentiveness. I want particularly to acknowledge my debts to those with whom I've collaborated fruitfully over the years: Karyna Szmurlo, my companion in furthering Staël Studies on this continent, for her astute, persistent, and devoted efforts; Carol Blum, for inviting me to share in teaching the wonderful NEH Summer Seminar for College Teachers, "Women, Marriage, Sex, and Reproduction in Eighteenth-Century France: A Multidisciplinary Inquiry" we held at Stony Brook in 1996; and Avriel Goldberger, my beloved graduate school friend, who took on her fine translations into English of Staël's *Delphine*, *Corinne*, and *Dix-années d'exil*, in part out of sisterly solidarity.

When I joined ASECS in the 1970's, there simply was no such organism as the Women's Caucus. In speaking to several age cohorts younger than myself, I feel a need to specify why it was thought necessary to form one. What was then the situation, for both eighteenth-century scholarship on women, or for women scholars?

In those days, this society, though some of its male members might or might not be matey with minority members of the opposite sex, retained very much the aura of a men's club, sometimes gracious, sometimes distinctly cool, to women interlopers. The Age of Reason, it was felt, was serious and philosophical; scholarly in an *Altgermanisch*, nineteenth-century mode, not totally unsuitable for an occasional female scholar, but she would have to maintain a jocular mien and, certainly not dream of upsetting established canonic saws, categories, or practices. A sample of this last, especially discomfiting to me today, is my lack of success when petitioning for special sessions: first, for one to explore reactions to Carol Blum's groundbreaking *Rousseau and the Republic of Virtue*; and then, after Gloria Flaherty's premature death, for a session celebrating the career of this former president of ASECS. Both were esteemed by program committees to be "out of bounds."

Already in 1967 the second twentieth-century feminist wave had begun to bathe the feet of ASECS. Marlene LeGates, for example, published an article entitled "The Cult of Womanhood in Eighteenth-Century Thought" in *Eighteenth-Century Studies* that year. And of course some female colleagues more than held their own. They might occasionally even preside over it, as did Patricia Spacks, or Gita May. But they knew themselves to be exceptions. Few members, particularly among women, specialized on women writers, artists, or thinkers, or on gender issues. By 1974, however, the women's movement had blown such wind into our sails that a whole new cohort of excellent scholars were making a distinctly greater impact on eighteenth-century studies. A set amongst them felt impelled to solidify our entry in materially greater numbers by establishing the Women's Caucus.

The Caucus has always had a dual purpose: to foster the aim of enriched scholarship on women via its special sessions and its graduate student essay awards; and to have a continuing care to guard the hard-won advance of eighteenth-century women scholars' careers in academe.

It's tempting, almost too vulgarly tempting, for me to try to recreate and denounce the professional atmosphere I hoped to enter at the outset of my own career. When, in 1948, I married a man, Marcel, who went to teach in suburban Philadelphia, I entered Bryn Mawr College for graduate study. In an initial interview, my distinguished woman professor of Old French, who was married, told me that being married as I already was was alright, even a good thing, but that if I were to have children, I would of course have to give up plans for a teaching career. She also told a classmate with luxuriantly long wavy chestnut hair that she'd never get any place professionally unless she cut it. This classmate, strangely enough, dropped out after a year. Being already from childhood a person with feminist leanings, I expressed to my professors a desire to write my dissertation on a woman writer. To my surprise, they were distinctly cool to this notion, though eventually it was Prof. Margaret Gilman who proposed Germaine de Staël to my attention. Far from fostering the careers of young women, Bryn Mawr at that date hired each and every year a dashing young man, freshly graduated from France's *Ecole Normale* or from Yale, to instruct the little band of maybe eight of us women.

As to my professors, the brilliant Germaine Brée went on to a distinguished enough career at NYU, the University of Wisconsin, and finally Wake Forest University. But the Ivy League she would surely have graced, as at least the peer of any of her male contemporaries, never enrolled her to teach in any of its faculties. Yet today several Ivies are presided over by this improbably competent sex.

To compare great things to small, akin to that perennial exile Germaine de Staël who referred to hers as a "miserable gypsy life," I part-timed at three different local institutions before gratefully finding asylum and tenure at West Chester University. I must also salute the several support groups I joined in the '60's, in one of which I made a lifetime friend of Rusty Shteir. Such groups, like the Caucus itself, provided the sustenance of solidarity to the aspirations of a generation of women. Other friends of my youth, who, like me, were thought of in our social circles as just "faculty wives," ended up achieving academic careers that certainly seemed to us in the 1960's beyond the realm of possiblity. Each of us felt a trepidation that women now, happily, face far more rarely, since our careers were wrested from what we strongly suspected was an overwhelming likelihood of failure. The more's the miracle we celebrate today.

Nowadays we guard our professional gains with sobriety, but without benefit of the double-edged rancor that fuelled our first efforts. But it is of the broader Caucus issue of our understanding of women's configuration in the eighteenth-century that I want to speak a bit more fully.

The tie that links my book on Germaine de Staël with the later *Twilight of the Goddesses* is Staël's own remark in *On Literature* that Karyna has referred to, that "since the Revolution men had found it politically and morally useful to reduce women to the most absurd mediocrity." Staël thereby presented me with an intriguing mystery, virtually untapped as such, that could only begin to be unraveled by delving for evidence into areas that literature alone could not wholly divulge. Janet, Sarah, and Madeleine have all referred to my recourse to interdisciplinarity. When I turned to it, it was because that is the way I always taught. Like many in my generation, to whom the then ambient notion of *Kulturgeschichte* was congenial, I used history and the arts to ground students' perceptions of literature in the aesthetics and politics of the target mentality. My teaching, since 1971, of the basic interdisciplinary Women's

Studies course, intensified my embrace of this method. I knew I was treading on dangerous ground in bringing it with me into print in *Twilight of the Goddesses*, but tenured and not expecting elevation except, perhaps, to Heaven, I had nothing to lose but face by making errors of judgment. So I enjoyed the liberation of roaming away from my literary base, and was rewarded by the cordiality of historians, and especially of art historians, who didn't find it aberrant that someone "outside" their field should be fascinated by it. Like one of those dry magic flowers that gain color and density once immersed in water, the dip into disciplines new to me, like medical history, fashion, demography, and even the anthropology Madeleine alluded to, renewed and opened out everything I was trying to explore about changes in gender relations in latter eighteenth-century France.

Not long ago in an issue of the *Times Literary Supplement*, Michael Londry quoted from a recently recovered commonplace book this remark by a late eighteenth-century woman: "That a woman should dare to have any thoughts that wander beyond the scanty Limits allow'd her by the other Sex, she knows will be consider'd by those haughty Monopolizers of all Sense and knowledge, as the highest presumption,/ she therefore resolves so cautiously to conceal her Treason that it shall never break out into any overt act . . ." (3/5/14). This eighteenth-century speaker's reference to a need to be covert in her Treasons inspired two reactions in me: the first, intense relief that our own thoughts no longer require such tyrannous inner censorship. But the second was how much of such caution respecting our own Treasons still hobbles us.

Our scholarship on women and gender has been virtually prodigious, so much having been achieved in the space of thirty years. But we've moved into an age of misogynistic backlash which threatens to weaken our nerve. As we scan course syllabi and professional journals, we have to admit that canonic structures, despite important emendations, still basically persist.

I'm fully aware what bad form it has become to speak of master narratives. Yet I appeal to you all: As we look about us in the world we live in, we are witness to the dynamism of women. Yet the bigotries of the categories we continue to employ in recording culture may well serve to falsify future accounts of our age just as they have done in the past. We now realize how wholly the suppression of issues of gender has served to mask cultural memory. When the record we're transmitting of the past is so deeply defective, surely it must be vitiating to our comprehension of the present.

The so-called Age of Reason, so dominant in the intellectual world I entered as a student, has suffered a kicking around from virtually every quarter in recent years, as none of us needs to be reminded. However, as German novelist Peter Schneider has observed, one of that age's most valuable formulations, one that allows us to reconstruct Enlightenment infinitely, was that of human fallibility.[21] Feminist scholars have not lagged in their critiques. In fact, they're illustrating handsomely how it was rather Unreason that then governed gender relations, no less than it does in our own time. But Reason's misappropriation of gender issues in the age that produced our secular modern societies is an Achilles Heel that dampens Reason's prestige in the present. This is why new paradigms of Enlightenment that might melt our rigid categories seem to me so necessary.

Many among us are attempting precisely to uncover them. It cannot suffice us to merely add female presence into the mix, since to do so will always only constitute it as a reflection. What we need are more adequate frameworks that incorporate the eye-popping and mind-blowing racial and gender critiques we've developed over the years. The Women's Caucus, with its built-in cross-national and disciplinary membership might foster more extended and speculative efforts with collaborative, longer-range projects. Such a widened spectrum of vision of the past must inform the broader and deeper Enlightenment of the future.

Allow me a last simile. I've been thinking of women's place in cultural memory as akin to an Engulfed Cathedral. In the Breton myth, the Cathedral of Ys lies under the sea, rising through morning mists into visibility by daylight, but lapsing back into invisibility with the day's ending. We've brought our cathedral up out of the depths where it can now be seen, glittering in the sunlight, but we haven't yet secured its structure from engulfment when the dark sets in.

I can only wish to each of you a joy similar to that I felt in waging, through scholarship, the struggle to keep its structure in view.

Thank you all, panelists and readers, for this gratifying tribute, to me and to our Caucus. It's been a terrific victory as a collaborative, ever-renewing effort. Long may it flourish, at least until we ourselves have decided its job is finished.

NOTES

1. Madelyn Gutwirth, Marcel Gutwirth, and John P. Spielman, eds., *Sources et reflets de l'histoire de France* (New York: Oxford University Press, 1972).

2. Madelyn Gutwirth, *Madame de Staël, Novelist: The Emergence of the Artist as Woman* (Urbana: University of Illinois Press, 1978).

3. Madelyn Gutwirth, Avriel Goldberger, and Karyna Szmurlo, eds., *Germaine de Staël: Crossing the Borders* (New Brunswick, N.J.: Rutgers University Press, 1991).

4. Madelyn Gutwirth, *The Twilight of the Goddesses: Women and Representation in the French Revolutionary Era* (New Brunswick, N.J.: Rutgers University Press, 1992).

5. J. Christopher Herold, *Mistress to an Age: A Life of Madame de Staël* (Indianapolis: The Bobbs-Merrill Company, Inc., 1958).

6. The year 1987 was exceptional in Staël studies: Avriel Golberger published her translation of *Corinne, or Italy* (New Brunswick, NJ: Rutgers University Press) and Vivian Folkenflik completed the first English "general reader," *An Extraordinary Woman: Selected Writings of Germaine de Staël* (New York: Columbia University Press). Two revisionist studies also appeared: Charlotte Hogsett's, *The Literary Existence of Germaine de Staël* (Carbondale-Edwardsville: Southern Illinois Press) and Marie-Claire Vallois's, *Fictions Féminines: Mme de Staël et les voix de la Sibylle* (Stanford: Anma Libri). Other important North American publications that feature chapters on Staël and her work include Carla Peterson's *The Determined Reader: Gender and Culture in the Novel from Napoleon to Victoria* (New Brunswick, NJ: Rutgers University Press, 1986); Nancy Miller's, *Subject to Change: Reading Feminist Writings* (New York: Columbia University Press, 1988); Joan DeJean's *Fictions of Sappho 1546–1936* (Chicago, London: University of Chicago Press, 1989); Doris Kadish's *Politicizing Gender: Narrative Strategies in the Aftermath of the French Revolution* (New Brunswick NJ: Rutgers University Press, 1992); and Margaret Waller's *Male Malady: Fictions of Impotence in the French Romantic Novel* (New Brunswick, NJ: Rutgers University Press, 1993).

7. Nancy K. Miller, *The French Review* 53.5 (1980): 745.

8. "Changing the Past: A Feminist Challenge," *Eighteenth-Century Studies* 28.1 (1994): 30.

9. Introduction, *The Twilight of the Goddesses: Women and Representation in the French Revolutionary Era* (New Brunswick, NJ: Rutgers University Press, 1992), xxi.

10. "Mme de Staël, Rousseau, and the Woman Question," *PMLA* 86.1 (1971): 100–09.

11. For a continuation of this vein of research see Linda M. Lewis, *Germaine de Staël, George Sand, and the Victorian Woman Artist* (Columbia, MO: University of Missouri Press, 2003) and Karyna Szmurlo, ed. *The Novel's Seductions: Staël's Corinne in Critical Inquiry* (Lewisburg: Bucknell University Press, 1999).

12. "Germaine de Staël on Fiction, Power and Passion," *Bulletin for Research in the Humanities* (February 1986): 242–54.

13. See the most recent research of Kari Lokke, "Children of Liberty: Idealist Historiography in Staël, Shelley, and Sand" *PMLA* (May 2003): 502–20; and Kurt Mueller-Vollmer's "Staël's Germany and the Beginnings on an American National Literature" in *Germaine de Staël: Crossing the Borders*, 141–58; as well as his most recent groundbreaking study, "Cultural Mediation as Innovation: The Incongruous Presence of Germaine de Staël in the United States (1805–1880)" in *Madame de Staël und die internationalität der Europaïschen Romantik* (Göttingen: Verlag, 2003), 111–34.

14. "Simone Balayé et les études staëliennes aux Etats-Unis," *Cahiers staëliens* 54 (2003): 61–71.

15. From Michel Delon's memorial minute, *Revue d'histoire littéraire de la France* 404 (2002): 699–700; translated by Madelyn Gutwirth for the Society for Staël and Coppet Group Studies (USA) at http://www.clemson.edu/caah/languages/stael.

16. "Reader Comment: Taking *Corinne* Seriously: A Comment on Ellen Moer's *Literary Women*," *Signs* 25. 3 (2000): 895–900; and "Allowing for Mme de Staël," *New York Review of Books* 43. 7 (April 18, 1996): 68–9, a letter on P.N. Furbank's "Call Me Madame," *New York Review of Books* 42. 20 (December 21, 1995): 64–7.

17. For several decades the standard biography of Staël in English was one whose title highlighted Staël's "scandalously" active sex-life over her intellectual accomplishments: J. Christopher Herold, *Mistress to an Age: A Life of Madame de Staël*.

18. Madelyn Gutwirth, "Revolution and Family Values: Beaumarchais' 'Trilogy'", *Studies on Voltaire and the Eighteenth Century* 2003 (1): 221–41.

19. Lynn Hunt, *The Family Romance of the French Revolution* (Berkeley: University of California Press, 1992); Madelyn Gutwirth, "Sacred Fathers, Profane Sons: Lynn Hunt's French Revolution", *French Historical Studies* 19 (2): 261–76.

20. Gutwirth, "Sacred Fathers", 275. Gutwirth was reacting to Lynn Hunt's "The Virtues of Disciplinarity," in *Eighteenth-Century Studies* 28 (Fall 1994): 1–7.

21. "Separated by civilization," International Herald Tribune -The IHP Online, www.oht.com/articles/513613.html.

Reform Ideology and Generic Structure in Matthew Lewis's *Journal of a West India Proprietor*

ELLEN MALENAS

> He said that kindness was the only way to make good negroes, and that, if *that* failed, flogging would never succeed; and he advised me, when I found my negro worthless, 'to sell him at once, and not stay to flog him, and so, by spoiling his appearance, make him sell for less; for blacks must not be treated now, massa, as they used to be; they can think, and hear, and see, as well as white people: blacks are wiser, massa, than they were, and will soon be wiser.' I thought this fellow himself was a good proof of his assertion.[1]

The advice transcribed above is from a slave waterman to Matthew Lewis. Its rhetorical virtuosity in blending threat and submission distills in this one small moment the most salient issues, economic and moral survival, explored in the *Journal of a West India Proprietor.* The text is primarily concerned with consciously promoting a reform agenda that attempts to mitigate suffering and cruelty on plantations while maintaining the institution of slavery. The *Journal* is a nexus for issues of race, gender and imperialism, but has received surprisingly little critical attention; most existing criticism positions the text in relation to aesthetics, surveillance and punishment, space, and issues of translation.[2] My study examines the political implications of the text's generic strategies and explores how these generic strategies catalogue interior struggles between idealism and self-interest.

Lewis's position toward slavery is complex and deeply ambivalent. He inherited two Jamaica plantations, Cornwall and Hordley, and roughly 413 slaves total. He owed his privileged lifestyle, complete with liberal education, to the system of absentee landlordism, yet abhorred the "execrable slave trade" and the abuse of slaves. Like many late eighteenth and early nineteenth-century intellectuals, his public statements reveal a rift between his political, anti-emancipation stance and his philosophical commitment to ideas of liberty and individual freedom.[3] Lewis maintained that the slaves' lives were much better than the ones they would have experienced in Africa, but that the middle passage and the "seasoning" period (the first three years in the colonies) were cruel and inhumane.[4] Lewis's conflicted position about slavery as an institution, however, was radically different from most of his planter-peers who viewed his attempts to ameliorate slaves' conditions as subversive and illegal. Lewis believed that by instituting reform and by being an engaged, benevolent master, he could alleviate the slaves' suffering during their "inevitable" servitude, while at the same time continuing to produce immense profit for himself. Thus, he supported legislation to abolish the slave trade in 1807, but did not support the abolitionists' drive for emancipation concurrent with the *Journal*'s drafting. Understanding Lewis's position is further complicated by the groundswell of anti-slavery sentiment in England between the *Journal*'s drafting before emancipation and its publication concurrent with emancipation. Lewis offered the first half of the *Journal* to Murray for publication in 1815. Lewis's main biographer, Lewis Peck, suggests that the reason it was not published was Lewis's demand of £2000 for the manuscript. Peck was partly correct, because Murray bought the manuscript from Charles Greville for only 400 guineas in 1834. However, as Peck also notes, Greville comments shrewdly in his diary that "it is the right moment for publishing them now that people are full of interest about the West India question."[5] Murray's desire to publish was most likely due to a combination of the right price and renewed interest in the conditions of West Indian slavery pre-emancipation. How emancipation would have affected the contemporary reader's reaction to the *Journal* is unclear. Although the legislation was enforced by 1834, emancipated slaves in the West Indies were still required to serve out a forced six-year "apprenticeship" to their former masters; slaves in India, Ceylon, and St. Helena were still legally in bondage; and the British government was ineffectual in quelling the illegal slave trade that continued from West Africa.[6] Given these circumstances, Lewis's documentation of reforms would have continued to be extremely relevant to the British public even after the 1833 legislation was passed.

From a historical standpoint, Lewis's anti-emancipation position was both logically suspect and psychologically untenable. The institution of slavery was incompatible with Lewis's vision of humane stewardship, partly because he lacked control over abusive slave-master relations on other plantations. At the same time, he became frustrated by the slaves' response of "ingratitude" and their active resistance to his reforms. He faces both stylistic and pragmatic problems in the text: how does an author promote an ideological agenda which is so quick to provoke criticism; how does the planter navigate the roadblocks to his reforms and then relate those navigations in his account?

I suggest that Lewis promotes his difficult, sometimes logically untenable position and maintains a stable narration by manipulating genre. Some of these generic changes within the text are immediately recognizable, such as Lewis's insertion of poems or song lyrics offset on the page. Other instances in the text that I call shifts in genre require further explanation. Although these moments in the text could be labeled changes in tone, I specifically use the term genre. When we think of a passage as generically specific, it evokes aspects of the passage less apparent than when it is classified under the umbrella term "journal entries." Labeling a passage as a discrete genre highlights the ways in which that passage resonates with other works within that genre, allowing the critic to interpret the passage in innovative ways. Generic classification then functions as an interpretive tool, rather than an elaborate taxonomy, where the most salient aspect of the text is the purpose for which it is being used, rather than its formal similarities to other texts of the same category. Thomas Beebee's suggestion that "generic differences are grounded in the 'use-value' of a discourse rather than in its content, formal features, or its rules of production,"[7] is central to this method of interpretation. In a similar vein, my method also draws from Adena Rosmarin's work on the rhetorical and pragmatic theory of genre, where generic classification is used specifically for critical interpretation, argument and analysis.

> [Pragmatic theory] places constitutive or constructive power in the genre, and defines the genre neither "historically" nor "theoretically" but in terms of its use in critical explanation. The genre is the critic's heuristic tool, his chosen or defined way of persuading his audience to see the literary text in all of its previously inexplicable and "literary" fullness and then to relate this text to those that are similar or, more precisely, to those that may be similarly explained.[8]

Alastair Fowler also refutes the idea that genre theory's main purpose is as a system of classification. "When we investigate previous states of the type, it is to clarify meaningful departures that the work itself makes. It follows that genre theory, too, is properly concerned, in the main, with interpretation. It deals with principles of reconstruction and interpretation and (to some extent) the value of meaning. It does not much deal with classification."[9] Classification should widen opportunities for analysis through explicit and implied comparisons among types.

In this essay, I discuss Lewis's use of generic strategy in a song, a recipe, and a long poem. These three examples illustrate how genre allows Lewis to advocate a fractured position and contain the anxieties concomitant with that position. These chosen genres do not constitute an exhaustive list of Lewis's variations, yet the insertion of song lyrics or poetry is common and consistent throughout the journal.[10] In terms of Lewis's reform program, I argue that genre functions in two ways in the *Journal.* First, Lewis manipulates genre for the purpose of pressing his agenda for humane stewardship. The text repeatedly attempts to rehabilitate the institution of slavery through exploiting the conventions of several genres. Lewis inscribes these generic variations under the auspices of the "private" journal to prove that slavery is neither morally wrong nor dehumanizing when properly managed.

As the narrative progresses, the *Journal*'s generic strategy is complicated further by the author's recognition of the possible limitations of an ideological reform agenda predicated upon humanizing a brutal economic and political system. To resolve this dilemma without destroying the integrity of the overall conservative argument of the text, Lewis uses his second generic strategy, where verse functions as a structure of containment for the issues that were most problematic in his amelioration plan: family, authority, sexuality, commerce and ethics.

Genre and the Case for Humane Stewardship

First offered for publication in 1817, at a critical period of debate about slave emancipation in the West Indies, the *Journal* was always intended to be a public document supporting an anti-emancipation view.[11] The choice of the journal as primary genre is significant because it functions as both a personal account and a political tract, making open reference to abolitionist discourse. Lewis's contemporary reader would have been exposed to frequent parliamentary and public debates led by William Wilberforce over emancipation, as well as abolitionist pamphlets and poetry written by prominent figures such as Hannah More and William Cowper. At the same time, Creole planters and absentee landlords defended their economic rights through the Society of West India Planters and Merchants in an equally public venue. Lewis's public relationships with both planters and emancipationists were strained by his position of compromise. Privately, Lewis's anti-emancipation stance was at odds with his social circle, as Lord Holland, who is the "Reporter" of the abolitionist African Institution group Lewis regularly attacks in the *Journal*, was a close personal friend.[12] The multiple layers of tension Lewis experienced (within his peer group, within himself, and with the reading public) create a specific tone in the *Journal*. He distances himself from the distasteful realities of Jamaica through irony and humor, while at the same time indulging in highly sentimental discourse to frame his relationships with the slaves. The jarring juxtaposition of these narrative elements results in an equivocal tone in which it is often unclear what Lewis's attitude toward any specific event is. This obfuscation of feeling and motivation points to Lewis's own internal conflict about his position as both reformer and slave owner and his desire to hide his true feelings and motivations in a setting where his ideologies were in conflict with his planter peers.

Lewis had many compelling reasons for choosing an indirect mode to express his viewpoint, and he most successfully argued the complexities of his fragmented position within the inclusive and fluid generic nature of the journal. A public journal is a slippery document; it suggests "private" thoughts exposed for public view. In arguing for stewardship of the slavery institution, Lewis uses the journal format to his advantage by framing his ideological agenda as both personal opinion and feeling. The reader then becomes a privileged viewer of ostensibly private thoughts, making these thoughts more immediate and persuasive than they otherwise would be. Lewis could have easily and quickly written an anti-emancipation pamphlet or published a lecture, as so many others did, but the *Journal* would have been less rhetorically successful operating under the stylistic constraints of a pamphlet.[13]

Like the Bakhtinian concept of the novel, the journal is generically imperialistic.[14] It can incorporate many other genres and break in and out of short generic digressions. The reader winks at the awkward shifts between genres and the suspect political sentiments in a journal because the journal is a "private" document and therefore not subject to the same literary or political scrutiny as other genres.[15] However, Lewis exploited the cover of "privacy" associated with the journal genre to make anti-emancipation arguments safely.[16] Within the larger framework of the journal, Lewis's text uses the strengths of different genres (the emotional evocation of poetry, the everyday concreteness of a recipe) to push his point about humane stewardship. The generic shifts in the journal are abrupt; each anecdote, joke or poem rarely takes more than one page. However, collectively these moments make a powerful case that slave life is not oppressive if properly managed by a benevolent master.

Lewis's recipe for the cane-piece cat (a euphemism for a dish made of rat) typifies a small generic digression that functions as a strong anti-emancipation argument when viewed collectively with other digressive moments. The recipe passage is also exemplary of Lewis's peculiar tone in the *Journal*. It has moments of intense irony and multiple layers of meaning juxtaposed with a straight narration of facts, making it particularly difficult to gauge Lewis's attitude towards the meal. However, the passage's main ideological thrust is to show the palatable nature of slave food using a narrative style similar to passages where Lewis earnestly describes Creole cuisine. The recipe is generically important because recipes represent specific and practical details of everyday life. Detailed descriptions of food preparation are concrete, lending Lewis's account of the cane-piece cat an air of authenticity where a simple descriptive statement of its flavor would be suspect.[17] The cane-piece cat recipe, its inclusion and Lewis's diction in reviewing the dish, has a strong ideological purpose in support of slavery. He uses the recipe genre to show, rather than tell, that the slaves' food was not unhealthy or substandard.

> To fill up my list of Jamaica delicacies, I must not forget to mention, that I did my best to procure a Cane-piece cat roasted in the true African fashion. The Creole negroes, however, greatly disapproved of my venturing upon this dish, which they positively denied having tasted themselves; and when, at length, the Cat was procured, last Saturday, instead of plainly boiling it with negro-pepper and salt, they made into a high seasoned stew, which rendered it impossible to judge of its real flavour. However, I tasted it, as did also several other people, and we were unanimous in the opinion, that it might have been mistaken for a very good game-soup, and that, when properly dressed, a Cane-piece cat must be excellent food.[18]

Rats were common pests in the sugar cane fields, and because of their plentitude, the Ibo slaves used them to supplement their diet. Eating rats was perceived as a form of degradation; the higher status Creole or Jamaican-born slaves would not eat them. Although Lewis tries many types of food during his visit, the choice of the cane-piece cat is significant because it was not something that other whites would have eaten.

His reference to the cane-piece cat as a "delicacy" is intentionally ironic. Yet, because Lewis includes the cane-piece cat in his "list of Jamaica delicacies," he rhetorically groups it with other actual delicacies he has previously described in detail such as black crabs, the ring-tailed dove, and the mountain mullet. To be defined as a delicacy, a dish need not be pleasurable to eat; it need only be choice and expensive. This ironic labeling (the rat is neither choice nor expensive; their infestation of the cane fields made them both free and plentiful) and grouping slave food with the master's expensive food suggests that both slave and master enjoy luxurious cuisine. In reality, slaves worked all day in the cane fields, but were expected to provide their own food from provision grounds (except for a small allowance of salt-pork or other protein sources which they were given.[19]) Most likely, the cane-piece cat was a response to deprivation and a way of utilizing a readily available source of protein.

The Creole's unwillingness to serve the rat to Lewis "roasted in the true African fashion" proves that the meal was most likely unpalatable. His lack of "authentic" experience is important because of the conflation he makes between his experience of the cane-piece cat and his slaves' experience of it. Not knowing its true flavor, he persists in his supposition that cane-piece cat is a desirable meal. He goes so far as to personally attest that he and others believed "it might have been mistaken for a very good game-soup" and "*must be* excellent food." Lewis's description of the cane-cat as "excellent" and a dish similar to one an English country squire might order supports his anti-emancipation agenda. His argument that the conditions of slavery are humane is reinforced through his use of the recipe genre, complete with spices and methods of cooking, which gives the reader a concrete example that slave provisions are wholesome and delicious. Lewis represents eating rats not as a condition of starvation, but yet another example of the Africans' delightful and amusing culinary eccentricities which Lewis, as a moonlighting ethnographer, is happy to document. The text is filled with these insidious small generic digressions, posing as slices of life, which imply through concrete examples that slave life is not unduly harsh.

Small examples such as the recipe reinforce the sustained message of longer entry sequences. Entries from 15 March to 26 March 1816 show how Lewis interweaves small generic digressions and follows generic threads to strengthen his anti-emancipation argument. In these eleven days, he uses song lyrics, court reports, jokes, and anecdotes to argue that humane stewardship can preempt slave uprisings. Some of these generic strategies arise as a response to the complex power struggles between absentee landlords, Creole planters, and slaves occurring at the time.

On 15 March, Lewis relates how a magistrate of the assize court accuses him of "calling the peace of the island into question" by subverting Jamaican slave laws through the reforms he has instituted on his plantation. The Creole planters view the reforms on Lewis's Cornwall estate as "over indulgences," and they resent Lewis's intercession to plead clemency on behalf of their own slaves. The planters see his reforms as encouraging revolt by making planter authority appear weak, while Lewis views the reforms as a guarantee of the slaves' loyalty through good treatment. His conviction is severely shaken during these eleven days, and he manages the expression of his fear by manipulating a series of genres.

On 16 March, Lewis relates the discovery of an alleged plot by the slaves of the neighboring parish of St. Elizabeth's to "murd[er] all the whites on the island." Lewis narrates these entries with characteristic irony and a comic sense of distance (he calls the plotted massacre a "grand fete") and never links the Creole planters' suspicions of his reforms and its relation to the discovered rebellion. Yet, a palpable tension arises in the narrative between both Lewis and his slaves and Lewis and his fellow planters that jeopardizes his reform project during these crucial days.

Although Lewis maintains to his fellow planters that good treatment guarantees loyalty, he begins to fear that his slaves' overt expression of affection for him is false. He expresses doubts that his reforms have engendered loyalty or gratitude and guaranteed his safety as he had hoped. (Throughout the text, Lewis relates news reports of other plantations where masters had been poisoned or had their throats cut.) He writes that the insurrection was planned on the estate of Lord Balcarras "where the overseer is an old man of the mildest character and the negroes had always been treated with peculiar indulgence."[20] Rather than address his concerns about reading the slaves' attitude toward him directly, Lewis uses a combination of genres and an ironic, humorous tone to deflate the sense of mounting threat. He does not respond to the escalating tension with deductive claims in favor of his reforms or against the "crack-down" mentality of his fellow planters; remarkably he never directly addresses the planters' charges or his fear of rebellion. Instead, he uses a combination of songs, anecdotes, court reports, and jokes to dispel fears of further uprisings and convince the reader that his humane treatment of the slaves has guaranteed his own safety.

This generically fractured response to both his fears and the planters' charges is much more effective than a logical, direct argument. The reader (and Lewis) know from the experience of Lord Balcarras's overseer that benign treatment does not guarantee safety. An overt statement that Lewis's reforms protect him would ring false. Instead, Lewis gives very specific, personal testimony of the slaves' regard for him through a sequence of song lyrics transcribed in the slaves' own words as proof of their loyalty, or at least their apathy, which will supposedly guarantee Cornwall's stability.

Lewis's transcription of song lyrics is a compelling generic strategy for proving that the slaves have a positive attitude towards him. Songs have been historically linked with emotional authenticity, especially in slave culture. In *The Souls of Black Folk*, W.E.B. Du Bois argues that slave songs reveal thoughts, emotions, and intentions that have no other socially acceptable outlet:

> What are these songs, and what do they mean? I know little of music and can say nothing in technical phrase, but I know something of men, and knowing them, I know that these songs are the articulate message of the slave to the world. They tell us in these eager days that life was joyous to the black slave, careless and happy. I can easily believe this of some, of many. But not all the past South, though it rose from the dead, can gainsay the heart-touching witness of these songs. They are the music of an unhappy people, of the children of disappointment; they tell of death and suffering and unvoiced longing toward a truer world, of misty wanderings and hidden ways.[21]

Du Bois argues that both the negative and positive valences of slave songs were viewed as authentic. This stamp of emotional authority is particularly important for Lewis's inclusion of song lyrics in the *Journal*. Rather than merely telling the reader that his slaves view him as liberator and benevolent master, which would seem suspect, he has the slaves report these sentiments directly, using a genre perceived as coming "from the heart." However, Lewis interprets the songs on the most superficial level, ignoring the inexpressible undercurrent of "unvoiced longing toward a truer world" in which they would have the political power to voice their desires openly. He presents only the literal meaning of the songs as authentic, ignoring any allegorical significance that contains dissent. His relation of the songs illustrates the rising mood of crisis between whites and slaves, while at the same exculpating Lewis from any participation in that crisis, because he presents them as straightforward declarations of intention.

Songs in this context and culture are not only emotionally authentic, but they also function as proof that a condition exists. Lewis introduces this idea when he describes the evidence used to convict the so-called "King of the Eboes" of plotting the massacre.

> [The insurgents] had elected a King of the Eboes, who had two Captains under him; and their intention was to effect a complete massacre of all the whites on the island; . . . On their trial they were perfectly cool and unconcerned, and did not even profess to deny the facts with which they were charged. Indeed, proofs were too strong to admit of denial; among others, a copy of the following song was found upon the King, which the overseer had heard him sing at the funeral feast, while the other negroes joined in the chorus:—
>
> SONG OF THE KING OF THE EBOES
> Oh me good friend, Mr. Wilberforce, make we free!
> God Almighty thank ye! God Almighty thank ye!
> God Almighty, make we free!
> Buckra in this country no make we free:
> What Negro for to do? What Negro for to do?
> Take by force! Take by force!
> CHORUS
> To be sure! To be sure! To be sure![22]

The court presented the above song, among others, as evidence of the King of the Eboe's guilt.[23] The songs are such an authentic expression that they serve as "proofs [which] were too strong to admit of denial." Lewis views the expressed desire for freedom in song as tantamount to the motivation to take that freedom through violence. There is no separation between lyrical expression and action. Lewis's and the court's evidence for this man's guilt is not a smoking gun, but a song.

This powerful perception of song as fact becomes more important to Lewis when his name appears in subsequent versions of this song, along with his emancipationist nemesis Mr. Wilberforce. Lewis believes that his inclusion functions as proof that the slaves view him as a hero and liberator. On the same day that Lewis transcribes the "Song of the King of the Eboes," he mentions the first report of his name being included and celebrated in the song. His position as a planter makes this inclusion embarrassing, even if he is secretly pleased at his notoriety. He dismisses the report suggesting, "if there be any such song (which I do not believe), I certainly never heard it."[24] But the plan for massacre scares him, so his need to believe in his inclusion in the song becomes stronger by the next entry.

Three days later, on 25 March, Lewis expresses anxiety for his own safety in an indirect, sentimental prose lament where he charges the slaves with "selfishness" in securing their own self-interest before serving his.[25]

> The negroes certainly are perverse beings. They had been praying for sight of their master year after year; they were in raptures at my arrival; I have suffered no one to be punished, and shown them every possible indulgence during my residence among them; and one and all they declare themselves perfectly happy and well-treated. Yet, previous to my arrival they made thirty-three hogsheads [of sugar] a week. . . during this last week they have managed to make but thirteen. Still they are not ungrateful; they are only selfish: they love me very well, but they love themselves a great deal better.[26]

The shift from the song lyrics to the prose lament is important, because it marks his move from an ironic tone to an immediate, emotional expression about the slaves whose attitudes most affect him. This prose lament highlights the conflict between Lewis's attempt at benign rule and the slaves' desire for freedom. Lewis has found that his attempts to use incentives and a gratitude-debt model to procure forced labor, instead of the cart-whip, lower productivity and unravel community order.

The reforms' failure to procure the slaves' goodwill, coupled with Lewis's loss of authority, cause him to fear for his safety. Will the slaves "take by force" the freedom the "buckras" refuse them? More important, does his potential inclusion as a liberator in this song of freedom place him outside the grouping of "buckras" and immunize him from the threat of insurrection? The locus of tension stems from whether the slaves' desire for freedom outweighs any bonds of affection they might feel for Lewis. His plaintive tone in the prose lament implies that he must solicit their labor rather than demand it. The threat of rebellion has tipped master-slave power relations, and Lewis seems both frustrated and emotionally hurt by the slaves' implied threat. This passage shows how closely linked expressions of power and sentimental discourse are in his conception of the master-slave relationship.

Lewis's expression of doubt suggests that his reforms have brought negative economic consequences without security from revolt. In reality, of course, Lewis is the "selfish" one, living off the proceeds of slave labor. However, his charge of selfishness is a tacit acknowledgment of the slaves' very natural self-interest. "They love me very well, but they love themselves a great deal better" means that whenever Lewis's agenda is contrary to the slaves' self-interest, he runs the risk of having his throat cut or dinner poisoned.

A system predicated upon forced labor cannot be humanely managed with success. When a master keeps a slave against his will, it is impossible to expect cheerful acquiescence. Although Lewis never states this fact, he becomes increasingly aware of it, and the fractiousness of his combination of genres increases. Throughout these journal entries the insertion of serious subjects, such as the rebellion and murder trials, are spliced into humorous anecdotes and quotidian details of housekeeping with an unsettling result that mirrors the rising tension of the plantation.

Lewis is losing both economic and physical security, but his journal relates a second song as proof of his invincibility. Just as the "Song of the King of the Eboes" functions as empirical proof of the slave's guilt in plotting a massacre, the songs the slaves sing about Lewis prove his innocence. The day after his prose lament, Lewis returns to the subject of his inclusion in the Eboe King's Song in greater detail.

> Young Hill was told at the Bay this morning that I make a part of the Eboe King's song! According to this report, 'good King George and good Mr. Wilberforce' are stated to have 'given me a paper' to set the negroes free (i.e. an order), but that the white people of Jamaica will not suffer me to show the paper, and I am now going home to say so, and 'to resume my chair, which I have left during my absence to be filled by the Regent.' Since I heard the report of a rebellious song issuing from Cornwall, I have listened more attentively to the negro chaunts; but they seem, as far as I can make out, to relate entirely to their own private situation, and to have nothing to do with the negro state in general. Their favorite, 'We varry well off', is still screamed about the estate by the children; but

> among the grown people its nose has been put out of joint by the following stanzas, which were explained to me this morning. . . .
>
> Hey-ho-day! Me no care a dammee (i.e. a damn,)
> Me acquire a house, (i.e. I have a solid foundation to build on,)
> Since massa come see we—oh!
> Hey-ho-day! Neger now quite eerie, (i.e. hearty,)
> For once me see massa—hey-ho-day!
> When massa go, me no care a dammee,
> For how them usy we—hey-ho-day![27]

The alleged content of the lyrics sets up the English-subject Lewis in opposition to the Creole "buckra" planters and aligns him with English abolitionists and the figure of the "good king" George. That he is viewed as an English liberator, and not a Creole planter, implies some measure of safety from an uprising. However, Lewis is still suspicious of the slaves' expression of affection and feels unsure how to read their speech.[28] Instead, he suggests a different song popular at Cornwall as evidence of their complacency with their own situation. Although he reports that the song is disliked by the older, more loyal slaves, these lyrics sidestep the issue of loyalty to Lewis. They suggest that if slave loyalty fails, his safety will still be secured by the apathy induced by his benevolence. Good treatment may not create goodwill, but it certainly will produce complacency. The recognition that the slaves' self-interest, their "private situation," takes precedence over any other concern quells Lewis' fears of revolt. Lewis is clearly invested in the reader understanding this diffusion, because he takes the trouble to translate the Creole dialect so the reader clearly comprehends the song's meaning. (Notice that he does not translate the "King of the Eboes," its menacing content being all too clear.) The song attests that the master's reform has brought "a solid foundation to build on," and that the slaves have become apathetic: "me no care a dammee." Instead of gratitude, it is apathy that comforts and protects. The song as evidence of this fact works beautifully. Rather than arguing his position vis-à-vis the slaves, which can never really be known, he has them testify to it in their own words, which he translates to suit his purpose.

To complement this diffusion strategy, Lewis then quickly shifts to a comic anecdote about the slaves' fear of his stuffed alligator, suggesting life on the plantation is fun. But the laughter subsides when he abruptly concludes the 26 March entry, demarcated from the joke with only a "*", with the following court report: "On the other hand, the King of the Eboes has been hung at Black River, and died, declaring that he left enough of his countrymen to prosecute the design in hand, and revenge his death upon the whites."[29] The songs reinforce

Lewis's argument for the reform agenda, because he is able to interpret this "emotionally authentic" generic expression to suit his purpose. Yet the end of the entry leaves the reader in doubt. Who will revenge the death of the King of the Eboes and, most important to Lewis, upon *whom*? This abrupt reversal of genre, from joke to grim news report, shows that even as Lewis pushes his agenda, he grapples to represent expressions of doubt.

Genre as Containment Strategy

While the insertion of a joke or the evidence of song lyrics diffused everyday tension within the *Journal*, Lewis's anxieties about issues of dominance, commerce, sexuality, family, and ethics give rise to more elaborate structures of containment. Chief among these containment strategies is the inclusion of the long poem, "The Isle of Devils."[30] His reforms, which failed to produce an economic benefit, are geared toward ameliorating his sense of collusion in the crimes of slavery. However, the reforms result in limited or no effect as either a good example (to other planters) or a model for an improved method of humane stewardship (for the slaves). He tries to express these concerns without disrupting the anti-emancipation argument of the *Journal* by encapsulating all of his doubts and fears in the long poem digression.

"The Isle of Devils" previously had a private function, as part of Lewis's personal papers, but on the return journey, he chose to place it before the public by transcribing it into the 10 May 1816 entry of the *Journal*. One can only speculate why Lewis chose to include this strange, nightmare vision, which threatens to subvert the careful progress narrative he has plotted about the amelioration of plantation life.[31] The untenable nature of his position becomes too unbearable not to be expressed, yet by cordoning off this expression of anxiety from the rest of the text, he is able to contain the subversive power of its message.

Lewis's choice of a long, narrative poem is particularly suited for the exploration of colonial anxieties. Like his romantic contemporaries, Lewis could use the long poem's capacity for extended character development, elaborate structures of feeling, and detailed description, to create the kind of nightmare world emblematic of his anxieties. More important, the narrative poem has an advantage over the lyric poem, because its length allows Lewis to explore the complexities and ambiguities of slave-master relationships that cause the most discomfort.

The first poem Lewis writes after leaving Jamaica on 1 April shows the lyric's limitations for exploring fully his Jamaican experience. The poem

"Yarra" features a female slave speaker giving good wishes to her departing master. As the lyric is generally confined to the single subject, there is no capacity within the structure for Lewis to explore the speaker's ambivalence about the master's departure or any other negative articulation. The result is a pap that absolves the absentee landlord/master of moral responsibility in his slave's suffering.

> And sure, the thought will bring relief,
> What e'er your fate, wherever rove you,
> Your wealth's not given by pain and grief,
> But hands that know, and hearts that love you.[32]

Including the poem in the *Journal* may have served to diffuse some of the immense guilt Lewis experienced about the source of his livelihood. However, Yarra's absolution contradicts what Lewis's experience in Jamaica has taught him: that his wealth *is* created by pain and grief, and the hands that know (and work) are not necessarily connected to devoted hearts. Lewis's development of the long narrative poem, in contrast to the lyric, will provide the framework for exploring both his and his slaves' ambivalence towards their positions of power and resistance. Because the long poem can stand alone, it can be hermetically isolated from the rest of the narrative's progressive argument.

The way Lewis introduces the poem reflects his desire to isolate it from the rest of the text. Like other generic shifts in the *Journal*, most of the lyric poems are transcribed without any type of preamble. (see Fig. 1) Lewis tells a story or defines a sea term, and then follows with a poem. The reader's only clue of the generic shift is the way that verse lines are offset on the page. However, before transcribing the long poem, "The Isle of Devils," Lewis makes a disclaimer:

> During the early part of my outward-bound voyage I was extremely afflicted with sea-sickness. . . I actually brought up almost a thousand lines, with rhymes at the end of them. Having nothing better to do at present, I may as well copy them into this book. Composed with such speed, and under such circumstances, I take it for granted that the verses cannot be very good; but let them be ever so bad, I defy anyone to be more sick while reading them than the author himself was while writing them."[33]

Lewis's assertion of authorial modesty (that the verse is so bad it might make the reader sick) is a common rhetorical disclaimer. Yet, the suggestion that boredom is his motivation for including the poem seems specious, given that he was a prolific writer of lyrics throughout the first three legs of his

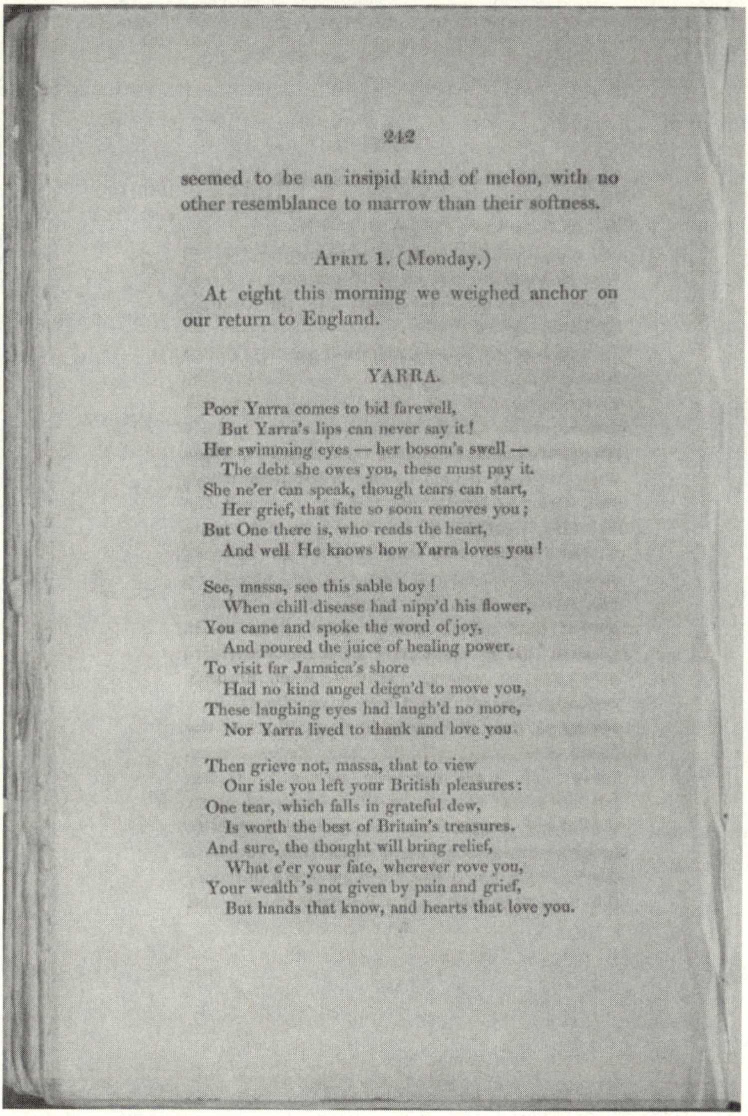

242

seemed to be an insipid kind of melon, with no other resemblance to marrow than their softness.

April 1. (Monday.)

At eight this morning we weighed anchor on our return to England.

YARRA.

Poor Yarra comes to bid farewell,
  But Yarra's lips can never say it!
Her swimming eyes — her bosom's swell —
  The debt she owes you, these must pay it.
She ne'er can speak, though tears can start,
  Her grief, that fate so soon removes you;
But One there is, who reads the heart,
  And well He knows how Yarra loves you!

See, massa, see this sable boy!
  When chill disease had nipp'd his flower,
You came and spoke the word of joy,
  And poured the juice of healing power.
To visit far Jamaica's shore
  Had no kind angel deign'd to move you,
These laughing eyes had laugh'd no more,
  Nor Yarra lived to thank and love you.

Then grieve not, massa, that to view
  Our isle you left your British pleasures:
One tear, which falls in grateful dew,
  Is worth the best of Britain's treasures.
And sure, the thought will bring relief,
  What e'er your fate, wherever rove you,
Your wealth 's not given by pain and grief,
  But hands that know, and hearts that love you.

Figure 1. *Journal of a West India Proprietor*. PZ2 .L494, Sadleir-Black Collection of Gothic Novels, Special Collections, University of Virginia Library. (London: John Murray, 1834)

journey. He invokes the common Romantic strategy of suggesting that the poem was composed in delirium, yet the meaning of his verse differs from his Romantic contemporaries' writings about slavery.[34] Of course, there are many abolitionist poems by figures such as More and Cowper that use the emotional capital of poetry and an overtly sentimental tone to evoke compassion for and identification with African slaves. There are also politically oriented lyric poems, like Wordsworth's "Toussaint L'Ouverture," which use the trope of slave rebellion to show a common fraternity among men or to draw a parallel between wage labor in England and the slavery of the West Indies. The only contemporary examples of long poems on the subject of slavery with a mythical or magical tone are Blake's "Daughters of Albion" and "America a Prophecy." Those poems, which depict master-slave rape and advocate violent slave revolution, do very different ideological work than Lewis's "Isle of Devils." Unlike Blake's poems, "The Isle of Devils" attempts to create a rhetorical safe-space for anxieties to erupt in order to contain them, so that Lewis can continue with his progressive tale of reform.

Rather than a trifle, written in sickness and transcribed in boredom, "The Isle of Devils" encapsulates Lewis's anxieties about miscegenation and his complicity in slavery and its inherent violence. Throughout the *Journal*, Lewis includes lyric poems on small quotidian subjects, such as a flying fish.[35] However, the shift here to the long, narrative poem signals a containment strategy, where psychologically unpalatable subjects can be explored through fantasy and under the guise of verse.

The poem tells of a beautiful Portuguese woman, Irza, and her nightmare experience on the Isle of Devils. As Lewis makes clear during the onset of the sea journey to Lisbon, Irza and her cousin-lover, Rosalvo, represent the aristocracy of the imperialist project:

> The viceroy's countless wealth that vessel bore:
> In heaps there jewels of various dyes,
> Ingots of gold, and pearls of wondrous size;
> And there (two gems worth all that Cortez won)
> He placed his angel niece and only son.[36]

The precious stones on the ship bound for the imperial center mirror Lewis's own position at the time the poem is transcribed as he returned to London with his imperial booty intact. When the ship is purposefully wrecked by the "Tempest Fiend" and Irza floats upon the shore of the Isle of Devils, the poem begins its metaphorical exploration of guilt and punishment.

About to be eaten by dwarves, she is saved by a monster "black as the storm." One would expect that this Caliban-esque "monarch-demon" would represent the allegorical slave, and that Irza, whose whiteness is metaphorically fetishized throughout the poem, would represent the planter class. However, the poem is particularly striking because the roles of master and slave are constantly re-negotiated.[37] Irza and the monarch-demon appropriate both roles at different moments in the text. This blurring of racial identities reflects Lewis's constant renegotiation of power relationships and roles with his own slaves. His ability to command labor is tenuous at best; thus, he and other planters were in the strange position of attempting to exact labor without provoking rebellion.

The roles of master and slave in the long poem depend on personal attributes and loci of power, not upon skin color. When the monarch-demon first appears, Lewis describes him as noble and imposing, an almost a courtly figure who rescues Irza.

> On *her* he gazed, and gazed so fixed, so hard,
> Like knights of bronze some hero's tomb who guard.
> Bright wreaths of scarlet plumes his temples crowned,
> And round his ankles, arms, and wrists were wound
> Unnumbered glassy strings of crystals bright,
> Corals, and shells, and berries red and white.[38]

The demon-monarch offers slavish devotion and protection from the dwarves if she will marry him. But unlike the comely knight, the poem describes the demon-monarch as "all shagged with hair, wild, strange in shape and show," and Irza shudders in disgust when she looks at him. Her disgust elicits a sullen response from him, as he becomes both obsequious and threatening at the same time. He is willing to lay his power at her feet for her condescension, as if he is complicit in her understanding that he is a lower beast, despite his immense physical power.

> Back fled the maid in terror; but her fear
> Was needless. Humbly, slowly crept he near,
> Then kissed the hearth, his club before her laid,
> And of his neck her footstool would have made:
> But from his touch she shrank.[39]

His position, of both subservience and menace, is quite similar to Lewis's experience of his own slaves. Lewis's use of the image of the demon-monarch inviting Irza to step on his neck recalls both Friday's devotion to Crusoe and an earlier moment in the *Journal* where the slaves kiss Lewis's feet as he prepares to leave. "[W]hen I came down the steps to depart, they crowded about me, kissing my feet, and clasping my knees, so that it was with difficulty that I could get into the carriage. And this was done with such marks of truth and feeling, that I cannot believe the whole to be mere acting and mummery."[40] Lewis half-heartedly interprets the slaves' sign of total submission and devotion as genuine. However, he would hardly need to mention the genuflection's authenticity after such a demonstration if he did not doubt its veracity. Returning to the poem, the speaker suggests that "her fear/was needless," but Irza has much to fear from this seemingly submissive demon, just as Lewis does from his seemingly submissive slaves. The demon-monarch is both a knight and a slave, and Irza's position of safety in relation to him is by no means guaranteed.

Irza sees the demon-monarch's protection as the lesser of two evils (the dwarves have already scratched and bitten her), so she tacitly agrees to be his "wife" when she accompanies the demon-monarch to his (oddly beautiful) grotto homestead. The marriage is in name only; the demon does not demand conjugal affection, only her companionship. His slavish yet menacing devotion continues as "ne'er had a nymph an humbler slave" and "so *she* found but pleasure, *he* was pleased," but he is in constant physical control. He simultaneously embodies both the slave and the master role at this point. His reactions to Irza's pleasure or displeasure are like Lewis's own experience of his slaves; their affection cheers him immensely and their emotional transitions he credits to his own frowns or smiles. "My own heart . . . seems to expand itself again in the sunshine of the kind looks and words that meet me at every turn, and seem to wait for mine as anxiously as if they were so many diamonds."[41]

Despite this sentimental vulnerability, the demon-monarch occupies the place of master in his constant surveillance designed to keep his prize by force.[42] The couple lives this way for one year, after which time the demon kills Irza's lover (who miraculously was also shipwrecked) and rapes Irza during her grief-stricken swoon. The result is a monstrous child which resembles its "sable sire" and disgusts Irza. Here, the demon-monarch appropriates the role of the master, destroying the bonds of affection between Irza and Rosalvo, taking her sexually by force, and propagating his offspring by exploiting his physical control over her. The rape of female slaves by masters and overseers was so common Lewis could not have been unaware of it. The product of that sexual violence was in evidence everywhere, as the Creole slave population became increasingly biracial.[43] These children then became the "property" of the slave-master. Rape not only served as a means of dominance and sexual pleasure for masters, but it also benefited them economically by increasing their stock of slaves. These children, just as much the master's offspring as the whites who resided in his household, were legally and in practice treated as slaves.[44] Lewis's poem reflects this historical reality. Irza shudders with horror when she comes in contact with the demon-monarch and when she suckles their child; she has no interest in raising him. Despite the child's genetic relation to Irza, she disowns him based on his physical similarity to the father.

When Irza disowns the child, the demon-monarch switches power relationships again. He becomes more like the raped slave-woman, who claims her child despite its origin in violence. When he realizes Irza hates the child, he breast feeds it himself. The demon-monarch's possession of male genitalia and female breasts is another aspect of this poem in which racial, social, and sexual identity is constantly in flux.[45] For the remainder of the poem, "round his neck" this "shaggy offspring" clings, imaginatively creating the demon-monarch as a simian or marsupial-like mother. But the monster literally re-appropriates his masterly phallus. After months pass, he drugs and rapes Irza again. This time the resulting child is so white that "through his fine skin the blood was seen to play," and Irza is unambivalently delighted with him. The speaker describes the child as "in small the model of her beauteous self" with "that skin than down of swans more smooth and white." Thus, Irza becomes like the historical slave master, who recognizes only the white offspring who reflects back his own racial image. Imagining that love for the white child will keep her on the island, the monster no longer confines Irza, and she escapes with a passing ship of monks. The monks convince Irza that both children are abominations and should be left behind, because the product of miscegenation can only be evil.

Realizing she is gone, the demon-husband dashes out the brains of the "angel" child as she watches from the ship; she continues her escape, convinced by the monk's arguments. In desperation, he holds up the demon-child and flings himself off the cliffs into the sea, charging her with ingratitude. His final speech, which is all articulated with his looks and gestures, rather than words, is verbalized by Lewis as follows:

> Look, mother, look! This babe is still your child!
> With him all social bonds you break,
> Scorn'd and detested for his father's sake:
> My love, my service only wrought disdain,
> And nature fed his heart from yours in vain!
> Then go, Ingrate, far o'er the ocean go,
> Consign your friend, your child to endless woe!
> Renounce us! Hate us! Pleased, your course pursue,
> And break their hearts who lived alone for you![46]

In his final moments, the demon-monarch eloquently expresses his fraught position as both master and slave. Like Lewis, the demon-monarch sees himself receiving a negative return for all of his careful solicitation of Irza. At the same time, he is like the slave accepting and resenting his position of inferiority and powerlessness to keep what he desires. Outside of his physical control, Irza can only be manipulated by the demon-monarch through the invocation of gratitude, similar to Lewis's attempts to invoke debt and gratitude once the cart-whip is abolished. Here, the roles of master and slave become conflated. As such, this passage, and Lewis's description of the Isle of Devils, articulates his anxiety about his role in the imperial project. These lines, in contrast with the soothing message of the "Yarra" poem, show the ominous side of Lewis's attitude towards slaveholding and his anxiety over the failure of his reforms. Near the poem's conclusion the speaker suggests that Irza's sense of complicity in her rape and abandonment of her children are a "fancied crime" and that she deserves no penance. Yet, as with all containment strategies, a happy ending that embraces the idea of absolution cannot serve as antidote to the troubling issues brought up within the narrative.

On the surface, the poem deals with the racist tropes of the monstrous birth resulting from miscegenation and fears about black masculine rage and sexuality. On a deeper level, this poem is about Lewis. He is the mother who has rejected his creation as an abomination, the colony that permits slavery, and hastens away, knowing that tragedy will ensue. At the same time, he is the demon-monarch who, unable or unwilling to use physical force to compel his will, must resort to the feeble hope of inducing guilt and a sense of gratitude to secure his physical and economic security. The charge of ingratitude is aimed at himself, as Lewis's family has lived off the proceeds of the plantation but cannot bear to be confronted with its realities. It is significant that Lewis transcribes this poem on returning to England, where he rejects his own Isle of Devils but not its capitalistic offspring. Lewis encapsulates these sources of guilt and psychological conflict in a poem which serves as a contained confession and absolution of his sins as slave owner.

Beyond its dramatization and containment of Lewis's guilt, "The Isle of Devils" is prophetic, in that Lewis behaves just as his fictional mother did when he inspects his other plantation, Hordley, on his second visit. When Lewis arrives at Hordley, he does indeed encounter an "Isle of Devils." Unlike Cornwall, Hordley is in a remote part of the island, requiring many river crossings to encounter. Its isolation, like the island, is one of the conditions which has allowed it to be run inhumanely, and Lewis finds a veritable hell when he arrives. Lewis had hoped that, like Cornwall, Hordley could be easily reformed to his humanistic sentiments with some cosmetic changes. He is soon disabused of this notion:

> What with the general clamour, the assertions and denials, the tears and the passion, the odious falsehoods, and the still more odious truths, and (worst of all to me) my own vexation and disappointment at finding things so different from my expectations, at first nearly turned my brain; and I felt strongly tempted to set off as fast as I could, and leave all these black devils and white ones to tear one another to pieces, an amusement in which they appeared to be perfectly ready to indulge themselves.[47]

Finding his scheme to humanize Hordley impossible, Lewis abandons his abomination/creation, the plantation. In his haste to run away, he finally claims the position of Irza who sees inevitable tragedy for her offspring when she leaves, yet is compelled by psychological survival to abandon them. Finding reform impossible, his only option is to distance himself both rhetorically and generically by containing his anxieties within the poem. Soon after his Hordley experience, Lewis dies of yellow fever on his ship returning to England. Unable to preserve his "babies," the projects of reform on the plantation, his grief and torment may well have contributed to the illness which resulted in his death.

NOTES

An early version of this paper was presented at the March 2004 American Society for Eighteenth Century Studies annual conference in Boston. I would like to thank Paul Hunter, Patricia Spacks, and Cynthia Wall for their input and assistance in developing this essay, as well as Sarah Hagelin, Samara Landers, and Andrea Stevens for reading and contributing to multiple drafts.

1. Matthew Lewis, *Journal of a West India Proprietor,* ed. Judith Terry (Oxford: Oxford University Press, 1999), 102–3.

2. Elizabeth A. Bohls, "The Planter Picturesque: Matthew Lewis's *Journal of a West India Proprietor,*" *European Romantic Review* 13.1 (2002): 63–76; Keith Sandiford, "Monk Lewis and the Slavery Sublime: The Agon of Romantic Desire in the *Journal,*" *Essays in Literature* 23.1 (1996): 84–98; Maureen Harkin, "Matthew Lewis's *Journal of a West India Proprietor*: Surveillance and Space on the Plantation," *Nineteenth Century Contexts* 24.2 (2002): 139–150; Lawrence Needham, "Goody Two-shoes/Goosee Shoo-shoo: Translated Tales of Resistance in Matthew Lewis's *Journal of a West India Proprietor,*" in *Between Languages and Cultures:*

Translation and Cross-Cultural Texts (Pittsburgh: Pittsburgh University Press, 1995), 103–118.

3. For a discussion of Wordsworth and Coleridge's ambivalent attitudes toward abolition and emancipation see Marcus Wood, "Slavery and Romantic Poetry," in *Slavery, Empathy and Pornography* (Oxford: Oxford University Press, 2002), 181–254; Helen Thomas, "Romanticism and Abolitionism: Mary Wollstonecraft, William Blake, Samuel Taylor Coleridge and William Wordsworth," in *Romanticism and Slave Narratives: Transatlantic Testimonies* (Cambridge: Cambridge University Press, 2000), 82–124.

4. Lewis locates the suffering of slavery to these limited time periods, what he calls "unavoidable hardships," and suggests that those born into slavery suffer less than the English working class. Lewis further argues that "their greatest fear is the not having a master whom they know," and that should slavery be abolished, the slaves would be incapable of self-governance and self-sustainment. Lewis, *Journal,* 46, 55, 65–6.

5. Charles Greville. 26 June 1833. *The Greville Memoirs*, ed. Henry Reeve (London: Longman, 1896), 2:384.

6. Harry Harmer, *The Longman Companion to Slavery, Emancipation, and Civil Rights* (Harlow, England: Longman, 2001), 75–78.

7. Thomas O. Beebee, *The Ideology of Genre: A Comparative Study of Generic Instability* (University Park, PA: The Pennsylvania State University Press, 1994), 7.

8. Adena Rosmarin, *The Power of Genre* (Minneapolis: University of Minnesota Press, 1985), 25. See also Peter Medway, "Fuzzy Genres and Community Identities: The Case of Architecture Students' Sketchbooks," in *The Rhetoric and Ideology of Genre* (Creskill NJ: Hampton Press, 2002), 123–155.

9. Alastair Fowler, *Kinds of Literature: An Introduction to the Theory of Genres and Modes* (Oxford: Clarendon Press, 1982), 38.

10. Other important generic variations within the text more closely related to the *Journal*'s alternate function as a travel narrative include the ongoing glossary of sea terms and island dialect. These ethnographic details are so profuse in the *Journal* that Judith Terry includes a glossary in the Oxford edition for Lewis's references to plant and animal life. Another ongoing generic variation is Lewis's insertion of "nancy-stories" or folktales. For an excellent discussion of the ways in which Lewis's relation of the nancy-story "Goosee Shoo-shoo's true and marvelous history of a lilly nigger-man born without a 'ed" functions as a moral of plantocracy, teaching slaves to find protection under authority, see Needham, "Goody Two-shoes," 103–118. In this article, Needham shows another valence of Lewis's difficult position in the contact zone as he attempts to function as an ethnographer of slave stories. He argues that Lewis's relation of the tales both represents colonialist ideology and unwittingly reproduces inherent aspects of the performance which subvert that discourse.

11. Judith Terry, introduction to *Journal of a West India Proprietor* by Matthew Lewis (Oxford: Oxford University Press, 1999), x.

12. Lord Holland, unlike Lewis, was both an abolitionist and an emancipationist. However, despite his political beliefs, Lord Holland owned two Jamaica plantations, Friendship and Greenwich, during his ongoing work as Reporter for the African

Institution. Friends with common interests, Lewis and Holland had made plans for reform on the four plantations together, which Lewis was charged to enact. These contradictions in Holland's behavior indicate how complex the social and political issues surrounding slavery were in Lewis's circle. Terry, Introduction to *Journal*, xvi.

13. Lewis's *Journal* is particularly inter-generic in comparison with other famous journals or reflections of the same period, such as *Lady Nugent's Jamaica Journal* and William Beckford's *A Descriptive Account of the Isle of Jamaica*. For example, Lady Nugent's *Journal* was specifically meant as a private document. It is most concerned with the day-to-day activities of a governor's wife and household. Any indication of political, cultural or agricultural conditions appears only in relation to these private concerns. Beckford's case is more complicated in that he is writing from the Fleet prison, attempting to leverage some gain off his knowledge of the island. Some of his generic deviations, like his inclusion of multiple tables, are more formal. In addition, the *Description*'s inclusion of anecdote or picturesque description, comprising long segments of text demarcated by large spaces on the page, is much less fractious than Lewis's.

14. Here I am specifically referring to Bakhtin's argument that the novel uses and dominates other genres: "The novel parodies other genres (precisely in their role as genres); it exposes the conventionality of their forms and their language; it squeezes out some genres and incorporates others in its own peculiar structure, reformulating and re-accentuating them." Mikhail Bakhtin, "Epic and Novel: Toward a Methodology for the Study of the Novel," in *Modern Genre Theory,* ed. David Duff (Harlow: Longman, 2000), 71.

15. Steven Kagle suggests that "there is no such thing as a totally private diary" and that all "diarists envision an audience for their entries" even if that audience is some type of future or idealized self. Steven Kagle, *Early Nineteenth Century American Diary Literature* (Boston: Twayne, 1986), 5. The dual private/public aspect of diaries is not specific to the *Journal.* Rather, what I argue is that Lewis exploits this aspect of diaries for his own purposes.

16. The strategy of using the journal format to avoid social censure is also used in a later journal of interest, Frances Anne Kemble's *Journal of a Residence on a Georgia Plantation* published in 1863. Kemble's journal details horrific instances of abuse on her husband's Georgia plantation under the guise of letters written to a friend in the North. Her utilization of the journal genre in describing slavery turned public opinion against Britain's support of the Confederacy. Interestingly, she used the same format as Lewis for completely opposite ideological ends. Kagle, *Diary Literature*, 60.

17. The description of the cane-piece cat follows the format of late eighteenth-century cookbooks, where specific measurement amounts are infrequent and the instructions take the form of a prose paragraph. For examples see *The Accomplished lady's delight in cookery; or, the complete servant's-maid's* [sic] *guide*, 1780?, <http://galenet.galegroup.com/servlet/ECCO> (13 January 2005); Martha Bradley, *The British housewife: or, the cook, housekeeper's, and gardiner's companion*, 1760?, <http://galenet.galegroup.com/servlet/ECCO> (13 January 2005).

18. Lewis, *Journal*, 147.

19. For an in-depth account of labor and agricultural conditions on plantations during this period see B.W. Higman, *Slave Population and Economy in Jamaica 1807–1834* (Cambridge: Cambridge University Press, 1976).

20. Lewis, *Journal*, 137.

21. W. E. B. Du Bois, *The Souls of Black Folk*, 1903, <www.bartleby.com/114/> (22 June 2004).

22. Lewis, *Journal*, 139.

23. The conviction of the King of the Eboes is particularly troubling in relation to the presentation of evidence. Lewis does not question why slaves, who lived in a mostly oral culture, would carry copies of song lyrics on their person. This discrepancy between oral culture and the production of written evidence suggests that the evidence may have been fabricated to prove empirically the existence of a song which was only overheard and not recorded in any way.

24. Lewis, *Journal*, 138.

25. I specifically use the term "prose lament" to highlight aspects of this passage that treat Lewis's sense of personal loss and a loss of status (specifically as a master to be obeyed and as a financially solvent plantation owner) that is the definitive feature of a lament. *ThePrinceton Handbook of Poetic Terms*, ed. Alex Preminger (Princeton: Princeton University Press, 1986), 112. Also, it is worth noting here that a lament need not be in verse; the sentiment of the passage outweighs formal considerations. *Literary Terms, A Dictionary*, eds. Karl Beckson and Arthur Ganz, 3rd ed. (New York: Noonday Press, 1989), 139.

26. Lewis, *Journal*, 141.

27. Lewis, *Journal*, 142.

28. For an extended discussion of Lewis's struggle to interpret Creole speech and body language see Ileana Rodriguez, "Apprenticeship as Citizenship and Governability," in *The Latin American Subaltern Studies Reader*, ed. Ileana Rodriquez (Durham: Duke University Press, 2001), 341–366; Donna Heiland, "The *Unheimlich* and the Making of Home," in *Monstrous Dreams of Reason: Body, Self and Other in the Enlightenment* (Lewisburg: Bucknell University Press, 2002), 174.

29. Lewis, *Journal*, 143.

30. "The Isle of Devils" has a complex, transatlantic publication history. It was composed on Lewis's first voyage to Jamaica between 8 November 1815 and 1 January 1816. However, Lewis transcribed it into the *Journal* during his first return voyage to England on 10 May 1816. After his death in 1818, the poem was published independently in Jamaica in 1827. In 1834, the poem was included in the first edition of the *Journal* published in England. See "note on the text" in Lewis, *Journal*, xxxv.

31. Other critics have theorized on the inclusion of the poem. Donna Heiland argues that the poem acts as a double to the prose entries, bringing into relief the gothic elements of Lewis's journalistic entries. D.L. MacDonald suggests that the poem is an allegorical frame for the impressions of plantation life recorded in the main document. D.L. MacDonald, "The Isle of Devils: The Jamaican Journal of M.G. Lewis," in *Romanticism and Colonialism: Writing and Empire 1780-1830* (Cambridge: Cambridge University Press, 1998), 193–194.

32. Lewis, *Journal*, 148.

33. Lewis, *Journal*, 159.

34. For an extended description of the Romantic poets' treatment of the subject of slavery and an extended interpretation of the poems I mention here see Wood, "Slavery and Romantic Poetry" and Thomas, "Romanticism and Abolitionism."

35. For a reading of the allegorical implications of some of these lyrics, see D.L. MacDonald, "The Isle of Devils," 193–94.

36.Lewis, *Journal*, 163.

37. MacDonald suggests "the demon-king of the poem is clearly a black slave, as recreated by the guilty and fearful fantasy of a white slave owner." MacDonald, "Isle of Devils," 192. Heiland also discusses the ways in which the demon-monarch and Irza can function as both colonizer and colonized, especially the ways in which this duality contributes to the *Journal's* sense of the uncanny. Heiland, "*Unheimlich*," 177. I argue, however, that it is precisely Lewis's confusion about which subject should appropriate which role, or if those roles can even be separated from one another, which is seminal to the demon-king's horrible aspect.

38. Lewis, *Journal*, 169.

39. Lewis, *Journal*, 169.

40. Lewis, *Journal*, 147.

41. Lewis, *Journal*, 59.

42. For a full treatment of the bilateral function of surveillance in the *Journal* see Maureen Harkin, "Surveillance and Space," 139–150.

43. Orlando Patterson, *Slavery and Social Death: A Comparative Study* (Cambridge MA: Harvard University Press, 1982), 206, 229, 260–61.

44. For an in-depth discussion of the link between female slaves' agricultural and sexual labor see Jennifer Morgan, "The Breeding Shall Goe with Their Mothers: Gender and Evolving Practices of Slave Ownership in the English American Colonies," in *Laboring Women: Reproduction and Gender in New World Slavery* (Philadelphia: University of Pennsylvania Press, 2004), 69–106.

45. Donna Heiland suggests that the demon-monarch's erroneous belief that he can control Irza through the duties of motherhood represents Lewis's own frustration at his inability to police the slaves' mothering techniques and raise the birth lists. Heiland, "*Unheimlich*," 180. If we take this allegorical representation further, the demon-monarch's desire to suckle the child himself would replace the slave mother with Lewis as the "father" and primary caregiver to the progeny of his plantation.

46. Lewis, *Journal*, 181.

47. Lewis, *Journal*, 231.

Give Us Our Daily Breadfruit: Bread Substitution in the Pacific in the Eighteenth Century

VANESSA SMITH

British voyagers and travelers, since their first taste of it in 1686, have perceived the *uru*, both practically and rhetorically, as a substitute. (fig. 1)[1] Although the earliest account of the fruit is found in the records of Mendana's voyage to the Marquesas in 1595, the Spanish sources do not make the analogy with bread that was to characterize its description in English, focusing instead on local nomenclature and modes of preparation: "it is eaten many ways, and by the natives is called white food."[2] William Dampier, by contrast, who sampled it in Guam, claims credit for giving the fruit its catachrestic English name breadfruit. His description of it, in his 1697 account, accumulates similes announcing its status as bread substitute. Dampier writes:

> The Bread-fruit (as we call it) grows on a large Tree, as big and high as our largest Apple trees. It hath a spreading head full of branches, and dark leaves. The fruit grows on the boughs like Apples: it is as big as a Penny Loaf when Wheat is at 5 shillings the Bushel. It is of a round shape, and hath a thick tough rind. When the fruit is ripe it is yellow and soft; and the taste is sweet and pleasant. The Natives of this Island use it for bread: they gather it when full grown, while it is green and hard; then they bake it in an Oven, which scorcheth the rind and makes it black: but they scrape off the outside

Figure 1. "The Bread Fruit" from John Ellis, A *Description of the Mangostan and the Bread-fruit...*(London 1775). Reproduced by permission of the Mitchell Library, State Library of New South Wales.

> black crust, and there remains a tender thin crust, and the inside is soft, tender and white like the crumb of a Penny Loaf. There is neither seed nor stone in the inside, but it is all of a pure substance like Bread; it must be eaten new; for if its kept above 24 hours, it becomes dry, and eats harsh and choaky; but 'tis very pleasant before it is too stale. The fruit lasts in season 8 months in the year, during which time the Natives eat no other sort of food of Bread kind.[3]

Dampier makes an anachronistic claim for the fruit, one epitomized in the name he gives it, that "the Natives of this Island use it for bread." The implication is that the man-made European staple is the standard to which the Pacific fruit aspires. For Dampier, and many that come after him, the breadfruit is always already bread substitute. Even if Dampier is referring to bread as staple, its sandwiching here between two references to the Penny Loaf indicates that the generic food-staff is only recognized in foodstuffs seen to approximate to the loaf of bread. Yet for Pacific islanders the breadfruit was not always primary staple, and where it served as such, was not customarily prepared in a bread-like mode. This essay is concerned with a British rhetorical insistence on the fruit's bread-like qualities, and on the implications this has for other dominant and conflicting images of the Pacific islands, as Edenic or savage, that shaped early European representation and exploitation of the islands and their resources.

The composite descriptions of the fruit that emerged from Anson's 1740-1744 voyage around the world suggest a struggle for dominance between the two halves of breadfruit's emerging metaphoric equation. In Richard Walter's official 1748 account a clear distinction is drawn between its fruity characteristics and its appropriation by the English as bread substitute. Walter writes, "There were besides guavoes, limes, sweet and sower oranges, and a kind of fruit, peculiar to these Islands, called by the *Indians Rima*, but by us the *Bread Fruit*, for it was constantly eaten by us during our stay upon the Island instead of bread, and so universally preferred to it, that no ship's bread was expended during that whole interval;" he draws upon vegetable, rather than farinaceous analogies in attempting to convey the breadfruit's taste: "[when green] its taste has some distant resemblance to that of an artichoke bottom [...] As it ripens it grows softer and of a yellow colour, and then contracts a luscious taste, and an agreeable smell, not unlike a ripe peach."[4] The official account was however pre-dated by a number of other publications that impressed the breadfruit upon the metropolitan imagination as natural bread substitute. John Philips's 1744 account simply interpolated a version of Dampier's description: once again segueing from apple to bread, implicitly accessing the ready symbolism of fall and redemption. This was further accentuated in Philips's text by the locating of the providential breadfruit in a brief recuperative pause within a narrative of intense physical suffering. The crew arrived at Tinian much debilitated by disease: "we sent on shore 54 sick men, wrapped up in their hammocks and placed them in the tents our men had provided, several of them not being able to stir hand nor foot, they were so excessively afflicted with the scurvy; and this day eight of our men died." Yet no sooner have the breadfruit and other fruits of the island begun to offer some relief, then they are visited by a different plague:

> Our felicity however was not of a long continuance, for we now began to be pestered by flies, which afterwards encreased to that degree, that if we shot a bullock and skined him, and let the carcase lie but one day, it would be almost devoured by them; nay, as soon as we took a piece of boiled beef out of the pot and set it on the table, it was so covered with them, that we could scarce tell whither [sic] we had meat or flies before us, and we could not put a bit of it into our mouths without having a great number of them upon it, which was very disagreeable sauce.[5]

A distinction is drawn between the vegetable products of Tinian, and in particular the vegetable staple breadfruit, which are restorative, and the equally providential meat supply found on the island, which is quickly tainted and invites vermin. The affliction, as depicted by Philips (the flies are made less of in Walter's account, which emphasizes the paradisal aspects of the island and consciously downplays the "circumstances in which it is defective"), recalls the punishment dealt to those Israelites who complained of their diet of manna in the wilderness and craved meat.[6] Numbers 11:4-8 records: "And the mixed multitude that was among them fell a lusting: and the children of Israel also wept again, and said, Who shall give us flesh to eat? [...] our soul is dried away: there is nothing at all besides this manna, before our eyes. And the manna was as coriander seed, and the colour thereof as the colour of bdellium. And the people went about and gathered it, and ground it in mills, or beat it in a mortar, and baked it in pans, and made cakes of it[.]" God promises to deliver a surfeit of flesh "until it come out at your nostrils, and it be loathesome unto you" (11:20), and causes quails to rain into the camp, "And while the flesh was yet between their teeth, ere it was chewed, the wrath of the Lord was kindled against the people, and the Lord smote the people with a very great plague."(11:33) Analogies between breadfruit and manna, the providential supplement, were later explicitly drawn in missionary literature from the Pacific.

Two other early accounts of Anson's voyage expand the variety of food comparisons attributed to the breadfruit. Pascoe Thomas writes:

> The Method of using the Bread-fruit is either by boiling or roasting it, and so dress'd it is pretty much like common Potatoes in Taste. The *Spaniards*, I am told, slice it, and expose it to the Sun, and when baked thereby to a Crispature, reserve it as Biscuit, and say it will bear long keeping when so prepared. The same Fruit, when grown ripe, is delicious to the Palate; and when mix'd with Lime or Orange-Juice, makes a grateful Tart, not unlike to Apple-sauce.[7]

Thomas displays a kind of scorbutic connoisseurship, figuring forth a range of delicious substitutions the breadfruit enables.[8] A similar culinary range is displayed by the authors of the *Navigantium atque itinerantium bibliotheca*, who conjure up the breadfruit, within their account of Anson's voyage, via a series of comparisons that invoke varying and regional subsistence resources and tastes: "pretty Loaf, with a tender yellow Crust," "new-bak'd Roll," "potatoe-bread made in the *West* of *England*," "the pleasantest Rusk."[9] Yet while these texts appear to be groping for ways to specify the taste of a fruit via a comparison with bread, they are effectively describing an approximation to bread from the world of fruit: although bread is ostensibly the vehicle and fruit the tenor in these metaphoric equations, bread is in fact the reality to which the fruit testifies.

James Cook is perhaps the most explicit subsequent exemplar of this tendency, writing in a letter of 1771, "Loaves of Bread, or at least what serves as a most excellent substitute growes here in a manner spontaneously upon trees."[10] The combined accounts of Cook's first voyage initiate a more extensive parsing of the breadfruit's symbolic and material connotations. Joseph Banks, in a letter to Count William Bentinck written in 1773, figures a fruit that purportedly frees cultures from the necessity to labour:

> In the Island of Otaheite where Love is the Chief Occupation, the favourite, nay almost the Sole Luxury of the inhabitants; both the bodies and souls of the women are modeld into the utmost perfection for that soft science Idleness the father of Love reigns here in almost unmolested ease while we Inhabitants of a changeable climate are Obligd to Plow, Sow, Harrow, reap, Thrash, Grind Knead and bake our daily bread and Each revolving year again to Plough, sow &c &c subject to Famine if the sun should parch or the rain should drench our superficial crop these happy people whose bread depends not on an annual but on a Perennial plant have but to climb up and gather it ready for baking from a tree which deep rooted in

> the Earth scorning equaly the influence of summer heats or winter rains never fails to produce plenty what a proportion of spare time must these people have when one of them by planting 4 breadfruit trees a work which cannot last more than an hour does as much for his generation as a European who with yearly returning toil cultivating corn for his family and this Leisure is given up to Love[.][11]

Where a series of demanding tasks must be performed for the European to extract sustenance from the recalcitrant corn, the breadfruit keeps not just the women of Tahiti but by implication the entire population in a state of effeminate passivity. Harriet Guest has observed, regarding representations of Tahitian physique from Cook's second voyage, that "the Society Islanders are perceived to be feminized to a degree that gives the Europeans a kind of right to exploit them, as though that were a natural masculine prerogative."[12] The depiction of the breadfruit as easily cultivated staple, a lazy alternative to the labor intensive production of bread, is, I would argue, a critical aspect of this representation.

The notion of breadfruit as effortlessly produced is enabled by the depiction of the tree as hyper-fruitful. In the four years that passed between Banks's visit to Tahiti and the penning of his letter to Bentinck, Banks had shaved six trees from the Tahitian subsistence crop: his journal lists ten trees as an appropriate number to ensure the sustenance of a Tahitian family.[13] This gap between the immediate and retrospective accounts is exemplary of the way in which a European discourse of Pacific plenty served to exaggerate images of labor free abundance derived from the voyage accounts.[14] If this was a discourse, then, produced primarily in the metropole rather than the islands, it surely gained force from the contrast it offered to the scarcity and attendant social discontent that characterized bread politics in the years leading up to the first British and French voyages to Tahiti. As Walter Shelton, George Rudé, Thomas Ashton and Richard Sheldon have all shown, the eighteenth century was one of chronic English food rioting.[15] Shelton's particular focus is on the waves of hunger rioting in southern England in 1766, the year before Wallis's *Dolphin* laid claim to Tahiti ('King George's Island') for George III. The popular disturbances were, he argues, caused by high food prices, coinciding with the movement of wheat to ports. "Middlemen" — grain merchants who added another tier to the ladder of bread production, and whose forestalling, regrating and engrossing were repeatedly subject to prohibition— emerged as figures of particular opprobrium. In this climate of what Shelton unequivocally refers to as *English Hunger*, the breadfruit must surely have come to represent a particularly piquant alternative staple. Its encounter with the British imagination coincided with fierce debate over the Corn Laws, and the competing claims of the international grain trade and domestic subsistence. In his analysis of scarcity tracts of the 1760s, Richard Sheldon notes that, among other causes, "luxury and conspicuous consumption of new goods were held responsible for all the symptoms of national decline including rising food prices and the increasingly rebellious mood of the poor."[16] Breadfruit, in Banks's letter, troubles the distinction between luxury and subsistence: it is figured as the staple of the luxuriant.

In the contentious fifth chapter of *The Wealth of Nations*, Adam Smith cites the value of corn as universal regulator of the price of commodities, arguing that "the nature of things has stamped upon corn a real value which cannot be altered merely by altering its money price." Corn attains this value because of its status as the laborer's primary means of subsistence. The value of corn is always measured by the quantity of labor, "whether liberal, moderate, or scanty," that it can maintain in any particular setting. "The real value of every other commodity," Smith writes, "is finally measured and determined by the proportion which its average money price bears to the average money price of corn."[17] As Glenn Hueckel points out, corn achieves this special status for Adam Smith as "a proxy unit."[18] By virtue of its status as staple, it becomes the closest measurable unit to determine the otherwise inexact and variable value of labor. Smith's early exegete Comte Germain Garnier spells out the intricate relationship between the staple and the labour required to make it palatable:

> The value of growing wheat results as much from the industry of the reaper who gathers it in, of the thrasher who separates it from the chaff and straw, of the miller and baker who convert it successively into flour and bread, as it does from that of the ploughman and of the sower [...] The earth furnished the means of wealth; but wealth itself cannot possibly have any existence, unless through that industry and labour which modifies, divides, connects, and combines the various productions of the soil, so as to render them fit for consumption.[19]

Garnier's list of labourers required to produce the daily loaf reinstates those very tasks that Bank's breadfruit renders redundant. In Banks's metaphorics the breadfruit, as substitute for bread, also becomes a substitute for labor. Labor cannot be measured in Tahiti by the proxy unit of the staple, because the breadfruit does away with the labor of its production: with all those various verbs that in Banks's letter testify to the relationship between corn and work within European societies. This understanding of the breadfruit as obviating labor only emerges once breadfruit has been drawn into a discourse on the

Edenic island that follows upon the European discovery of Tahiti. As we saw, when Dampier named the breadfruit, he invoked a very specific loaf to describe this new fruit: one weighed and valued within the current English market, "when Wheat is at 5 shillings the Bushel." No conflict registers in this representation between the identification of the new staple and existing equations of value. But Banks's metaphors effectively figure the breadfruit as the antithesis of the European staple. It offers subsistence unhinged from labor.

A kind of counterpoint to this, however, is provided by the figuration of the breadfruit, along with the coconut, as a tree of consummate utility. Many authors move from a discussion of the breadfruit as food staple to cataloguing the uses of each part of the tree. Such descriptions accommodate an implicit notion of thrift, of an economy that does not countenance waste, that works against the depiction of indolently sensual Tahitians. Parkinson, botanical illustrator on Cook's first voyage, perhaps initiates this tradition, observing that "The leaves of this tree are very useful to wrap fish and other eatables in, when put into the oven to be baked. Of the wood they build canoes, and make several sorts of utensils; and of the bark of young plants of it, which are raised on purpose, they make very good cloth[.]"[20] Parkinson's description of the tree incorporates depiction of Tahitians as cooks, sailors, carpenters, cultivators and weavers, creating an impression of complex occupation rather than sensual lassitude. The notion of the useful tree was developed by missionaries in the Pacific, who employed the breadfruit as object-lesson. Informative articles in such missionary publications as *The Saturday Magazine* and *Missionary Sketches* drew on accounts by early missionaries, and in particular the detailed ethnography of William Ellis's *Polynesian Researches* (1829), to cite the breadfruit in support of a Providential thesis: "it is scarcely possible for a Christian to behold it without increasing convictions of the wisdom and benevolence of the Most High, and a fresh motive for gratitude to Him."[21] However the breadfruit and other flora of Tahiti also contributed to a confounding sense of Tahiti as earthly paradise. Ellis writes: "Amid the unrestrained enjoyment of a bounty so diversified and profuse, it is hardly possible to suppose that the divine Author of all should neither be recognized nor acknowledged; or, that his very mercies should foster insensibility, and alienate the hearts of the participants in his bounty."[22] Such conclusions are resisted in the *Missionary Sketches*' troping of the breadfruit, which moves determinedly from the Tahitian tree to

> another tree infinitely more valuable—the "Tree of Life"—whose leaves are for the healing of the nations; another fruit [...] the fruit of the Spirit—the fruit unto holiness, and the end everlasting life. There is another bread, more valuable than that bread which a

> bountiful Providence furnishes, without care or labour, to the South Sea Islander from the prolific tree— or that manna which the Isrealites did eat in the wilderness, [...] even the true bread from heaven— "the bread of life".[23]

In its symbolic and practical fertility, its capacity for metaphoric and metonymic proliferation, the breadfruit begins to evince a supplementarity more Derridean than dietary. Yet this quality too underlines the anachronism of the fruit's identification as bread substitute: the "natural" fruit exposes a lack in what we have identified as the paradoxically man-made original. Parkinson seems alert to a potential for the breadfruit to supplant bread, suggesting that, when baked, it "appears very inviting, more so than the finest loaf I ever saw; [...] it tastes very farinaceous, and is, perhaps, the most agreeable and best succedaneum for bread ever yet known, and, in many respects, exceeds it."[24] However this notion of the breadfruit as substitute that exceeds conceals a competing story, of the breadfruit as poor substitute, which I want to bring into focus in the second half of this essay. I will look at two stories in which the breadfruit figures as surrogate, which might seem immediately to serve as allegories of the good and bad substitute, although they also highlight some of the desires and contradictions that lie behind the British identification of breadfruit as ersatz.

Breadfruit Sacrament: Symbolism and Corporeality

As I have mentioned, missionaries such as William Ellis were perplexed by the theological contradiction that the breadfruit seemed to represent: the bounty it appeared to confer upon unappreciative heathens. In an act of both practical necessity and pointed symbolic appropriation, the first missionary party to arrive at the Society Islands, on the *Duff* in 1797, used wafers of breadfruit to celebrate the sacrament. In a communal diary held in the Mitchell Library in Sydney, the missionaries recorded that

> [Bro. Cover] administered the Sacrament, Bros. Eyre, jefferson & Lewis, assisting. This opportunity was comfortable and refreshing to most of us, and we doubt not but it was the first time that the breadfruit of Otaheite, was used as a symbol of the broken body of our Lord, and received in commemoration of his dying love.[25]

The occasion was redescribed in official accounts of the missionary voyage, such as Thomas Smith's *History of the Missionary Society* and James Wilson's *Missionary Voyage*, where the conscious symbolism of the missionaries' syncretic gesture is reiterated.[26] Much is made, in turn, of the responsiveness of the Tahitians to the ceremony, Wilson writing, for instance, that "Mánne Manne [the chief] was present during the whole service, and very attentive, particularly during the administration of the Lord's supper; he placed himself in the circle with the brethren, and when they passed him he shifted his situation farther on, in hopes of partaking with them."[27] The breadfruit, familiar to the Tahitian as comestible, lures him inside 'the circle' of meaning which has been created for it by the missionaries' ritual: a circle reminiscent of those feasts and *kava* ceremonies into which Europeans were regularly incorporated when making contact with Polynesians. The significant difference here, however, is that the appropriation of breadfruit as host makes bad hosts of the missionaries: Mánne Manne is at once invited into and forced to experience his exclusion from the ceremony, and the fruit which has hitherto represented easy bounty becomes in this context the symbol of election. The eucharist is, of course, always and inherently a substitute: the wafer standing in for the body of Christ, as representation in the Protestant tradition, and by transubstantiation in the Catholic tradition.[28] When the breadfruit, with its own complex symbolism of fall and redemption, is in turn made to substitute for the wafer, an inevitable degree of additional self-reflexivity invests the ritual of the sacrament. Hence, perhaps, the metonymic slippage of the missionaries' formulation when describing the occasion: "it was the first time that the breadfruit of Otaheite, was used as a symbol of the broken body of our Lord." Body and bread seem literally to merge, the desire to assert the breadfruit's substitutability (in particular here its capacity to break like wheaten loaf) unintentionally implying a version of transubstantiation.

Yet the willingness of the *Duff* missionaries to perceive breadfruit as surrogate host is also an index of their Protestantism. During the period of Pacific exploration it was an integral part of the investiture of an English sovereign that they profess belief that "in the sacrament of the Lord's Supper there is not any transubstantiation of the elements of bread and wine into the body and blood of Christ at or after the consecration thereof by any person whatsoever."[29] This "Royal Declaration" was an explicit repudiation of Catholicity, and was also variously referred to as "the King's Protestant Declaration" or "the Declaration against Transubstantiation." The *Duff* missionaries' relatively straightforward substitution of breadfruit for sacramental wafer, then, suggests something not only about the cultural context in which these London Missionary Society members found themselves in the Pacific, but also the British cultural context from which they had emerged. As I have emphasized, it is British voyagers and explorers who focus upon and explore the poetics of the *uru* as bread substitute. Spanish explorers prior to

Dampier did not seize upon the metaphor, and early French commentators such as Bougainville, his botanist Commerson, and Diderot in his *Supplement*, though keen to develop metaphors of Tahiti as *Nouvelle Cythère* and earthly paradise, did not find a place for the breadfruit within this symbolic economy, simply mentioning it among Tahitian food plants, where Dampier's term translated as *le fruit à pain*.[30] Perhaps the legacy of an alternative acceptance and rejection of the doctrine of transubstantiation is evident in the cultural differences between the breadfruit poetics of Catholic and Protestant European nations. Steven Laurence Kaplan makes this connection in a different context in his comprehensive study of the bread politics of France, when he focuses on the refusal of Parisians prior to the Revolution to accept ersatz or supplemented loaves. Discussing Antoine-Augustin Parmentier's "efforts to circumvent the extraordinarily conservative disposition of Parisians in particular and of the French in general ('impassioned ignorance and ridiculous prejudice') by presenting the potato as a friendly farinaceous vegetable to be used in (procrustean) bread," Kaplan adduces the Catholic communion's investment of bread with "a powerful and miraculous spirituality." He concludes that the parallels between everyday bread breaking and the Eucharistic model may have reinforced a popular belief that "food acquired providential power and status only when it took the form of bread." As Kaplan points out, anything other than wheaten bread was an unacceptable eucharistic substitute in the Catholic service: "nonwheaten bread could not be validly consecrated, in the eyes of the church."[31] His description of the rejected potato as "friendly farinaceous vegetable" supplement recalls the identification of the breadfruit as benign vegetable substitute for bread in the accounts of British explorers.

The Tahitian originary myth of the breadfruit both reiterates and inverts the eucharistic symbolism. Ellis records a "traditionary legend," which tells that at one time the people of the Society Islands had fed on *araea*, or red earth. A couple had a son of delicate constitution, who could not eat the earth, and the father prayed to '"die, and become food for our son."' As Ellis narrates:

> In the evening he called his wife to him, and said, "I am about to die: when I am dead, take my body. Separate it, plant my head in one place, my heart and stomach in another, &c. and then come into the house and wait. When you shall hear at first a sound like that of a leaf, then of a flower, afterwards of an unripe fruit, and subsequently of a ripe round fruit falling on the ground, know that it is I, who am become food for our son."[32]

Ellis claims he has provided only a "brief outline" of the legend, which he dismisses as the likely invention of "some priest, to uphold the influence of the gods," noting however that:

> The origin of the coca-nut, chestnut, and yam, are derived from similar sources; the coca-nut having grown from the head of a man, the chestnut from his kidneys, the yams from his legs, — and other vegetable productions from different parts of his body. [33]

Although, like the story of the last supper, this is a tale of sacrifice commemorated, Ellis would be the last to recognize parallels between the myths of pagan and Christian priests. But perhaps what he is taking issue with here is in fact an absence of explicit symbolism, rather than a competing Tahitian symbolics: with the literalism of a tradition that has specific body parts rendered as specific foods; with its synaesthetic materialism, the red earth consumed, the accelerated life-cycle of the tree heard before it is seen or felt, the weight of ripening fruit falling on the ear rather than into the hand. An alternative Hawaiian version of the breadfruit legend has the fruits as not the head but the testicles of the dead father:

> This new kind of tree attracted the attention of many of the lesser Hawaiian gods. They tried to eat it raw but it was unpalatable. It was delicious when roasted. Kane and Kanaloa, two important gods, were told about this wonderful new food. They replied that the gods were eating the testicles of a dead man. The gods were disgusted and began vomiting [...] Breadfruit trees sprang up from their vomit and this is why breadfruit trees are so plentiful on Hawaii.[34]

The Polynesian legends of the breadfruit, unlike the Christian ceremony of the Eucharist, incorporate images of decay and abjection as elements of a mythology of renewal.[35] The refusal of British observers to acknowledge this element of abjection within their developing mythology of the breadfruit is a theme I will return to later in this essay.

Slavery's Staple: Breadfruit in the Caribbean

The second breadfruit story I want to recall here is the completion, in the *Providence* and *Assistant*, of William Bligh's commission to transport the breadfruit to St Vincent and Jamaica to supplement the diet of plantation slaves. (Bligh's first attempt was of course the thwarted *Bounty* voyage, which took place at the very time that Kaplan's revolutionary crowds were refusing to accept substandard bread in Paris).[36] A number of important books in recent years have analyzed the significant role played by the transportation and cultivation of plant specimens within the broader culture of eighteenth- and nineteenth-century European imperialism, and Bligh's breadfruit voyages are regarded as significant chapters in this history.[37] However my focus here is on the tenuous status of breadfruit as ersatz: an aspect that has evaded comment in discussions of what Richard Grove terms "green imperialism," perhaps because it highlights a moment of pause and resistance within the narrative drive of this account of cultural exchange.

The plan to transfer breadfruit plants to the islands of St. Vincent and Jamaica was promoted by Joseph Banks, by then head of the Royal Society, at the instigation of local planters.[38] Their petition was supported by botanist John Ellis, who wrote a pamphlet in 1775, the title of which, *A description of the mangostan and the bread-fruit: the first, esteemed one of the most delicious, the other, the most useful of all the fruits in the East Indies: to which are added, directions to voyagers, for bringing over these and other vegetable productions, which would be extremely beneficial to the inhabitants of our West India islands*, underlines the utilitarian emphasis of this breadfruit project. (fig. 2) Ellis cited Mendana, Dampier, Anson and Cook as early promoters of the supplementary value of the breadfruit, as well as the German-Dutch naturalist Rumphius, who had mentioned the breadfruit in his *Ambonese Herbal*. Although Rumphius was completing the *Herbal* around the time that Dampier was in Guam naming the breadfruit, it was only published between 1741 and 1750, due to Dutch apprehensions "that there were various items in these botanical writings which might have been of interest to the competition."[39] Ellis's citation, in a proposal to use breadfruit as slave subsistence within the British empire, belatedly confirms this suspicion. He quotes Rumphius on the breadfruit: "It affords a great deal of nourishment, and is very satisfying, therefore proper for hard-working people; and, being of a gentle astringent quality, is good for persons of a laxative habit of body."[40] Rumphius's insistence on the appropriateness of the breadfruit to the working diet contrasts with Banks's later effusions on the breadfruit as staple of an indolent Tahitian race, which are of course more immediately ironized by Banks's own promotion of the breadfruit as dietary supplement of indentured laborers.

Bligh's breadfruit commission in this sense stands as an attempt to bring the elusive breadfruit within the logic of political economy: to make the fruit submit to evaluation as a proxy for the most extreme and exploitative labor. And the discursive struggle this involves is registered in the unstable representation of the "bread" of breadfruit in the documents surrounding the voyage, as alternatively simply staple, or substitute. Banks's "Instructions" to the Gardeners on the *Providence*, which recommend the collection of other Tahitian farinaceous roots and fruits in addition to the breadfruit, as supplements for the West Indian diet, imply that the concern is simply to provide an adequate diet of starch for plantation workers: "You will also take charge of some plants of the sweet Plantain, called Meia, the apple or Avee, the root called Peah, of which the Islanders make a kind of Pudding, & the very large Yam which is of a better kind than any in the West Indies [...]."[41] I would nonetheless argue that a retained sense of the breadfruit as bread-like, rather than simply farinaceous staple, was necessary for the promotion of both the utility and benevolence of the project to British patrons. Hence the mixed metaphors of Bligh's initially jubilant letter to Banks, as he approached St Helena in late 1792 pending the completion of his fraught and extended breadfruit mission. He begins, "I give you joy of the success of your Plants. [...] I most sincerely pray you live to hear they flourish, and know Thousands are fed with their Fruit." Although Bligh refers to the breadfruit as plant and fruit, the image of the feeding of thousands invokes the gospel's loaves. Yet some pages further on in the same letter, once he has attained St Helena, a hint of disappointment emerges, as Bligh faces the possibility, even before he reaches the West Indies, that the ersatz will be rejected: "We have planted ten fine Plants, two sickly ones, & one of every other kind of Fruit we have on board. [...] but I am told the Yamstooks (as the people born in the Island are called) care little for what I have brought them with such pains & trouble."[42] Here Bligh figures himself as a bathetic Noah, whose ark brings one of each self-propagating fruit and sickly as well as healthy breadfruit, not to an empty and sin-freed world but to an unappreciative and scornful populace.

Four years later, Alexander Anderson, the superintendent of the botanical garden at the Caribbean island of St Vincent, wrote Banks the following mixed report of the success of the breadfruit transferal:

> The Bread fruit thrives (if possible) better than in its native soil, all the trees in the Garden are full of fruit in all stages; they have been bearing constantly for 18 months past, and I find that being in possession of 3 or 4 Trees, there will be a succession of fruit the year round. There are many varieties of shape as well as size, they are exceedingly good boiled or sliced & toasted the same as Bread, and they make the finest pudding I ever tasted, I give the fruit to everyone here, and send them to the different Islands, but strange to tell, there are some people who undervalue such a valuable acquisition, & say they prefer a plantain or a Yam. But, however, these are only some self conceited & prejudiced Creoles, and you

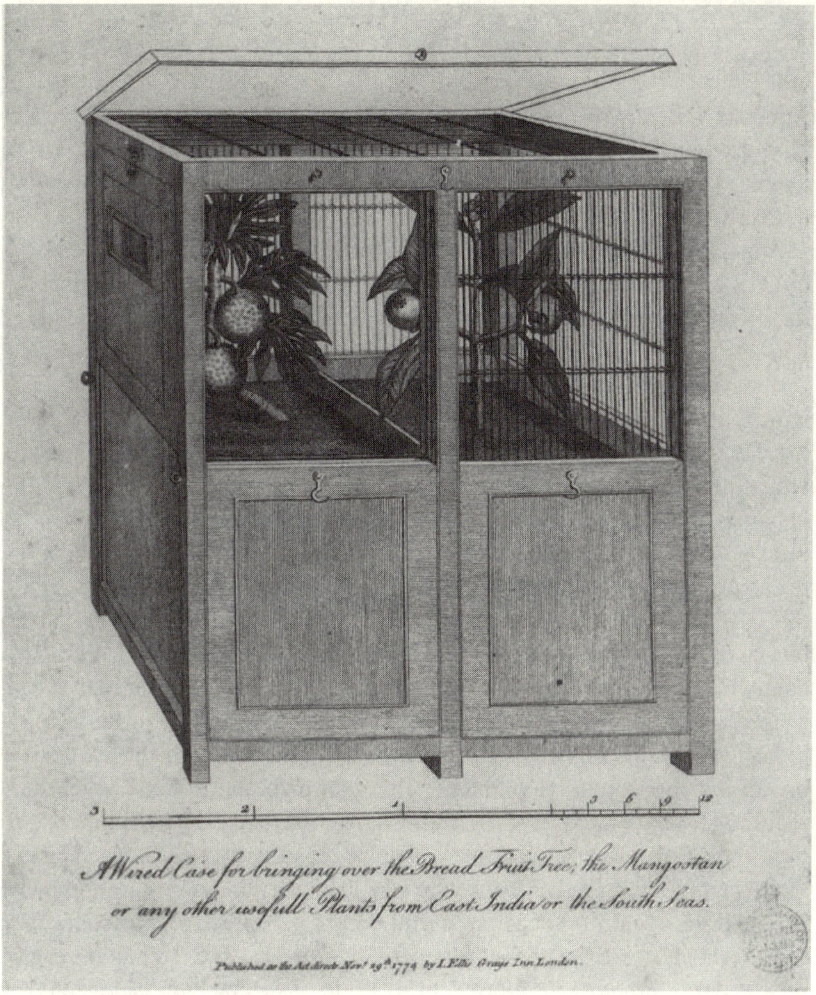

Figure 2. "A Wired Case for bringing over the Bread Fruit Tree; the Mangostan or any other useful plans from East India or the South Seas" from John Ellis, A *Description of the Mangostan and the Bread-fruit...*(London 1775). Reproduced by permission of the Mitchell Library, State Library of New South Wales.

> well know that many despise these things, tho' useful, they have had no hand in obtaining.[43]

Anderson's reversion to the notion of the breadfruit as bread substitute at this point, rather than simply farinaceous supplement, is telling. In the face of Creole rejection of the fruit, he invokes associations of English comfort foods: toast and pudding. Highlighting issues of taste (their preference for yam and plantain over ersatz bread) Anderson seeks to expose the Creoles as the real ersatz here: poor copies of whites, whose tastes are not informed by the kinds of recognitions that enable true Englishmen to identify the bread within the fruit. Yet at the same time the rebellion of taste causes a telling reversal of master/slave roles in this passage. By rejecting the bread proxy, which, as we have seen, is in political economic terms the proxy for labor itself, the Creoles take on autocratic attributes of self-conceit and prejudice, while the benevolent aristocracy that has supported the breadfruit mission becomes in turn a collective of laborers, who have turned their "hands" to procuring an item deemed worthless by the finicky and, by implication, relatively indolent Creoles.

Anderson's renewed emphasis on the status of breadfruit as substitute in the face of its rejection by the local community in St Vincent, draws our attention once again to the particular English investment in depicting the fruit as bread-like. In fact, the Creoles might be said not to fail a taste-test, but rather to draw attention to a hoax. For what they had been brought was not like bread, but rather a staple closer to the yam or plantain with which they legitimately compared it. The breadfruit, as it featured most prominently in the diets of Polynesians, had never resembled bread. And this was ascertainable from the more directly descriptive texts of some of the same explorers who invested such rhetoric in the representation of it as pre-lapsarian loaf. Thus Joseph Banks, who elsewhere figured the breadfruit as bread of paradise, also refers in his *Endeavour* journal to a "sour paste," which he eventually confesses is the product of a breadfruit that is seasonally restricted:

> As I have mentioned Sour paste I will proceed to de[s]cribe what it is. Bread fruit by what I can find remains in season only 9 or 10 of their 13 months so that a reserve of food must be made for those months when they are without it. To do this the fruit is gathered when just upon the point of ripening and laid in heaps where it undergoes a fermentation and becomes disagreably sweet; the core is then taken out [...] and the rest of the fruit thrown into a hole dug for that purpose generaly in their houses; the sides and bottom of which are neatly lind with grass; the whole is covered with leaves and heavy stones laid upon them. Here it undergoes a second

> fermentation and becomes sourish in which condition it will keep as they told me many months. Custom has I suppose made this agreable to their palates tho we dislikd it extreemly, we seldom saw them make a meal without some [of] it in some shape or other.[44]

The fact that this "sour paste," or *mahie*, appears at every meal suggests not only that the sense of breadfruit as boundless in supply is dependent on its capacity for preservation rather than its constant availability, but also that its preferred mode of preparation in Tahiti is far from bread-like. This is confirmed by numerous early sources and oral histories, where detailed descriptions are provided of the consumption of either breadfruit or taro staples as *poi*.[45] Eating *poi* involved a dexterous wrapping of gooey matter around the fingers and its swift transition to the mouth. In the circle of *poi* consumption, in contrast to the missionaries' circle of sacramental breadfruit consumption that I discussed earlier, it is typically Europeans who are shown up by their inability to mimic Polynesian etiquette.

In its Polynesian modes of preparation, just as in its Polynesian mythological figuration, the breadfruit repeatedly illustrates a capacity to collapse European oppositions: between nourishment and pollution, use and waste, luxury and necessity. James Morrison, one of the *Bounty* mutineers who remained at Tahiti and was eventually recaptured, and who wrote an account of his time in Tahiti, narrates such an ambivalent breadfruit story:

> In the time of Gathering in the Harvest of Bread for Store they make an Oven in which they Bake 15 or 20 Hundred weight of Bread which when baked becomes sweet like gingerbread, of this they make a sweet pudding, and on this the Children (Male & Female of or belonging to the family who make it) Feast while it lasts, which is generally six weeks or two months—during which time they are kept Covered from the sun and are restricted within their respective bounds which are houses fenced round in square[s] for that purpose —and at the end of that time they are liberated but are so fat that they can scarce breath and some are Weeks before they can Walk to any distance. During this time they loose the Tand Collour of their skin and assume their own natural one which is agreeably fair & Clear, but are so tender that the sun scalds them as fast as it would the Fairest European and those who expose themselves to the Weather soon alter their Complexion.[46]

In Morrison's proto-ethnography, preparation for scarcity becomes confounded with celebration of abundance, and feaster becomes the object of the feast. Some years before the Grimm brothers penned their dark tale of hunger, satiety and child abandonment, Morrison's account of children plumped and tenderized in pens until their skins resemble Europeans', on a diet of gingerbread-like breadfruit, sublimates fears of cannibalism into a tale of vegetarian gluttony.

As Banks's description of *mahie* indicates, European accounts tend to focus less on their writers' lack of skill in manipulating the sticky breadfruit prepared by their Polynesian hosts, than in their distaste for its mode of preparation. And the West Indian Creoles' rejection of the breadfruit is not so much a rejection of the proffered bread substitute as a mirroring of this distaste. There is something excremental in the European depiction of *mahie*, dug from pits in the ground rather than plucked from a tree; paste rather than bread. The breadfruit transferred to the West Indies purportedly as an excess: the product of that botanical luxuriance that Banks suggested made Tahitians an idle and sensual populace, is exposed, as Bataille would surely have had it, in this excrementality, and comes to represent a loss. The gift of the staple is rejected by the local palate, its Caribbean recipients refusing to affirm the benevolence of the botanical donation.

The elision of the link between taste and labor, a topic of nascent political economic concern in the eighteenth century, finds both text and refutation in the breadfruit. Boswell recounts the following exchange with Johnson:

> BOSWELL 'I am well assured that the people of Otaheite who have the bread tree, the fruit of which serves them for bread, laughed heartily when they were informed of the tedious process necessary with us to have bread;— plowing, sowing, harrowing, reaping, threshing, grinding, baking.' JOHNSON 'Why, Sir, all ignorant savages will laugh when they are told of the advantages of civilized life. Were you to tell men who live without houses, how we pile brick upon brick, and rafter upon rafter, and that after a house is raised to a certain height, a man tumbles off a scaffold, and breaks his neck, he would laugh heartily at our folly in building; but it does not follow that men are better without houses. No, Sir, (holding up a slice of a good loaf,) this is better than the bread tree.'[47]

Johnson counters Boswell's acceptance of travelers' claims that fruit is comparable with loaf, by drawing attention to the values that inform apparently visceral preferences of taste: the inevitable slippage that occurs between lip and cup, between taste in the mouth and fashionable taste. Johnson wishes to dispute the elevation of purportedly "savage" over "civilized" life-styles that the promotion of the breadfruit implies. Yet he does this by re-inserting labor into the equation. Where Boswell, following Banks, seeks to inflate the symbolic value of the fruit by making it a token of a pre-lapsarian plenitude, Johnson, in the mode of Comte Garnier, implies that bread is worth more than breadfruit because of, rather than despite, the labor that has gone into its production. Johnson, like Banks, subtly infers a connection between breadfruit and a life of idleness: bread and houses are signs on the other hand of a society based in masculine labor rather than feminine lassitude. For Johnson, the taste for bread over breadfruit indicates a cultivated palate precisely because of the value bread attains from the process of its production; a value that is only ever implicit in the 'good loaf', but requires articulation once comparison with a Pacific fruit threatens to erase it altogether.

NOTES

This essay is a revised version of a paper delivered at The American Society for Eighteenth-Century Studies 35th Annual Meeting, Boston, 24–28 March 2004. It is dedicated with great affection to the memory of Tony Tanner, who chivvied me to write about breadfruit.

1. *Uru* is the Tahitian word for the tree named by Parkinson *Artocarpus altilis*, and known as *ulu* in Hawaii and Samoa, *kuru* in the Cook Islands, and *mei* in the Marquesas, Tonga, and Gambier Islands. Diane Ragone, "Ethnobotany of Breadfruit in Polynesia" in *Islands, Plants, and Polynesians: an Introduction to Polynesian Ethnobotany*: 203–220, Paul Alan Cox and Sandra Anne Banack, eds. (Portland, Oregon: Dioscorides Press, 1991), 203–4.

2. James Burney, *A Chronological History of the Voyages and Discoveries in the South Sea or Pacific Ocean Part II from the year 1579, to the year 1620* (London, 1806; reprint Amsterdam: N. Israel, 1967), 146. The analogies used to describe the fruit in the Spanish account are primarily fructuous: "it grows to the size of a boy's head; when ripe, it is of a light green colour; but of a strong green before it is ripe: the outside or rind is streaked crossways like the pine apple; the form is not entirely round, but becomes narrow towards the end; the stalk runs to the middle of the fruit, where there is a kind of web: it has neither stone nor kernel, nor is any part unprofitable except the rind which is thin: it has but little moisture; it is eaten many ways, and by the natives is called white food: it is well tasted, wholesome, and nutritious; the leaves are large, and indented in the manner of those of the West India Papaw tree." Burney, *Chronological History*, 145–146. Burney refers to this description of the breadfruit, taken from Figueroa's 1613 *Hechos de D. Garcia. Marq: de Cánete* (Madrid 1613), as "the earliest description which can with certainty be attributed to the Bread fruit." It was probably compiled from the papers of the Portuguese navigator Pedro Fernandez de Quiros, who took command of the voyage after Mendana's death.

3. William Dampier, *A new Voyage round the World* (London: James Knapton, 1697), 296–7.

4. [Richard Walter and Benjamin Robins], *A Voyage round the World in the years MDCCXL, I, II, III, IV by George Anson*, Glyndwr Williams, ed. (London: Oxford University Press, 1974), 281.

5. [John Philips], *A Voyage to the South-Seas And to many other Parts of the World Performed from the Month of September in the Year 1740, to June 1744, by Commodore Anson, In his Majesty's Ship the Centurion, Having under His Command The Gloucester, Pearl, Severn, Wager, Trial, and two Store-Ships. By an Officer of the Fleet*. (London: A Merryman, 1744), 142,145–6.

6. [Walter and Robins], *Voyage round the World*, 284.

7. Pascoe Thomas, *A True and Impartial Journal of a Voyage to the South-Seas, and Round the globe, In His Majesty's Ship the Centurion, Under the Command of Commodore George Anson* (London: S. Birt, J. Newbery, J. Collyer, 1775), 167–168.

8. I have adapted this term from Jonathan Lamb's engrossing discussion of "scorbutic nostalgia," and in particular the exaggerated sensory appreciation shown by those afflicted with scurvy, including members of Anson's expedition. Jonathan Lamb, *Preserving the Self in the South Seas 1680–1840* (Chicago: University of Chicago Press, 2001), 114–131.

9. [John Harris], *Navigantium atque itinerantium bibliotheca; Or, A complete collection of voyages and travels*, John Campbell, ed. (London: Printed for T. Woodward, A. Ward, S. Birt, D. Browne, T. Longman, R. Hett, C. Hitch, H. Whitridge, S. Austen, J.Hodges, J. Robinson, B. Dod, T. Harris, J. Hinton, and J. Rivington, 1744–48), 351. I am grateful to Glyn Williams for directing me towards this source. It is this description, the most forcible in its range of bread, as opposed to fruit, similes, that was incorporated by John Ellis from among the Anson literature in his *Description of the Mangostan and the Bread-fruit* (1775), which promoted the transfer of the breadfruit as bread substitute to Britain's West Indian slave plantations.

10. James Cook, *The Voyage of the Endeavour 1768–1771*, J. C. Beaglehole ed. (Cambridge: Hakluyt and Cambridge University Press, 1955), 507.

11. Joseph Banks, *The Endeavour Journal of Joseph Banks 1768–1771*, J. C. Beaglehole, ed., 2 vols. (Sydney: Angus and Robertson, 1962), 2: 330.

12. Harriet Guest, "Cook in Tonga: terms of trade," in *Islands in History and Representation*, 93–115, Rod Edmond and Vanessa Smith, eds. (London: Routledge, 2003), 105.

13. Banks's Journal account of the breadfruit, which favours prelapsarian over libertine metaphorics, reads: "In the article of food these happy people may almost be said to be exempt from the curse of our forefather; scarcely can it be said that they earn their bread with the sweat of their brow when their cheifest sustenance Bread fruit is procured with no more trouble than that of climbing a tree and pulling it down. Not that the trees grow here spontaneously but if a man should in the course of his life time plant 10 such trees, which if well done might take the labour of an hour or thereabouts, he would as compleatly fulfull [sic] his duty to his own as well as future generations as we natives of less temperate climates can do by toiling in the cold of winter to sew [sic] and

in the heat of summer to reap the annual produce of our soil, which when once gathered into the barn must again be resowd and re-reapd as often as the Colds of winter or the heats of Summer return to make such labour disagreeable." Banks, *Endeavour Journal*, 1: 341; compare Cook, *Voyage*, 121.

14. The particular audiences of the two texts must however also be taken into account: as Banks notes at the top of the Letter to Bentinck, "This letter was wrote at the request of Count Bentink [sic] while I was in Holland 1773. who desired something of the kind to amuse the Princess of Orange." Banks, *Endeavour Journal*, 2: 330. His account of feminized and luxuriating Tahitians is produced, then, for a feminine aristocratic reader.

15. Walter J. Shelton, *English Hunger and Industrial Disorders: A Study of Social Conflict During the First Decade of George III's Reign* (London: Macmillan, 1973), 21; George Rudé, *The Crowd in History: A Study of Popular Disturbances in France and England 1730–1848* (New York: John Wiley, 1964), 33–46; Thomas Ashton, *Economic Fluctuations in England, 1700–1800* (Oxford: Clarendon Press, 1959), 159; Richard Sheldon, "Bread Politics and Political Economy at the Accession of George III," paper delivered at the session *Of Bread and Corn: dialogue sur le blé* at The American Society for Eighteenth-Century Studies Thirty-Fifth Annual Meeting, Boston, 24–28 March 2004, 204–247. For the French side of this history see Steven Laurence Kaplan's discussion of cereal dependence in Old Regime Europe: "No issue was more urgent, more pervasively felt, and more difficult to resolve than the matter of grain provisioning." Steven Laurence Kaplan, *Bread, Politics and Political Economy in the Reign of Louis XV*, 2 vols. (The Hague: Martinus Nijhoff, 1976), xvi.

16. Sheldon, 'Bread Politics', 211.

17. Smith, Adam, *An Inquiry into the Nature and Causes of the Wealth of Nations*, 2 vols. (Chicago: University of Chicago Press, 1976), 20.

18. Glenn Hueckel, "On the "Insurmountable Difficulties, Obscurity, and Embarrassment" of Smith's Fifth Chapter" *History of Political Economy* 32:2 (2000): 321.

19. Ian S. Ross ed., *On the Wealth of Nations: contemporary responses to Adam Smith* (Bristol: Thoemmes Press, 1998), 206–207.

20. Sydney Parkinson, *A Journal of a Voyage to the South Seas in his Majesty's Ship the Endeavour: Faithfully Transcribed from the Papers of the late Sydney Parkinson, Draughtsman to Sir Joseph Banks, Bart. In his Expedition with Dr. Solander round the World* (London, 1884; reprint London: Caliban Books, 1984), 46.

21. *Missionary Sketches* (1831), liii.

22. William Ellis, *Polynesian Researches, during a residence of nearly six years in the South Sea islands*, 2 vols. (London: Dawsons of Pall Mall, 1967) 1: 379.

23. *Missionary Sketches*, liii.

24. Parkinson, *Journal of a Voyage*, 45.

25. "Communal Diary," Papers of Rev. Thomas Haweis, *A Collection of 38 Draft Letters and Manuscripts many of which are in hand of the Rev. Thomas Haweis, dealing with the early missions to the South Seas, and including diaries*

sent by the missionaries to the London Missionary Society. Mitchell Library, Sydney, ms 4910X 1,2.

26. Surprisingly, no mention of the breadfruit sacrament is made by Sujit Sivasundaram in a recent article which labors the metaphoric parallels between Pacific missionaries' evangelical rhetoric and natural historical discourses of cultivation. Sujit Sivasundaram, "Natural History Spiritualized: Civilizing Islanders, Cultivating Breadfruit, and Collecting Souls" *History of Science* 39 (2001): 417–43.

27. Rev'd. Thomas Smith, *The History and Origin of the Missionary Societies; containing faithful accounts of the voyages, travels, labours, and happy results of the various missionaries who have been sent out for the purposes of evangelizing the heathen, and other unenlightened nations, in different parts of the habitable globe*, 2 vols. (London: Thomas Kelly, 1838), 21; James Wilson, *A Missionary Voyage to the Southern Pacific Ocean, performed in the years 1796, 1797, 1798, in the Ship Duff, commanded by Captain James Wilson* (London, 1799; reprinted New York: Frederick A. Praeger, nd), 81.

28. Miri Rubin, *Corpus Christi: The Eucharist in Late Medieval Culture* (Cambridge: Cambridge University Press, 1991), 1.

29. P. J. Fitzpatrick, *In Breaking of Bread: the Eucharist and Ritual* (Cambridge: Cambridge University Press, 1993), 1.

30. Louis-Antoine de Bougainville, *Voyage autour du monde par la frégate la Boudeuse et la flûte l'Étoile* (Paris: Éditions La Découverte, 1997), 150.

31. Steven Laurence Kaplan, *The Bakers of Paris and the Bread Question 1700–1775* (Durham and London: Duke University Press, 1996), 23–24, 31.

32. Ellis, *Polynesian Researches*, 381. Compare P. J. Wester, "The Breadfruit: a plea for the preservation of varieties" *Journal of Heredity* 13.3 (March 1922): 129; Gerrit Parmile Wilder, *The Breadfruit of Tahiti*. (Honolulu: Bishop Museum Press, 1928), 8–9; Rangone, "Ethnobotany," 216.

33. Ellis, *Polynesian Researches*, 381.

34. Fornander, quoted in Ragone, "Ethnobotany," 217.

35. For an extended discussion of the varied cultural relationships between pollution and the sacred, see Mary Douglas, *Purity and Danger: An Analysis of Concepts of Pollution and Taboo*. (Harmondsworth: Penguin, 1970).

36. Jocelyn Dunphy, "Insurrection and Repression: Bligh's 1790 *Narrative of the Mutiny on Board H.M.Ship Bounty*" in *1789: Reading Writing Revolution: Proceedings of the Essex Conference on the Sociology of Literature, July 1981*, Barker, F. et al. eds. (Colchester: University of Essex, 1982), 281–2.

37. Richard Grove, *Green Imperialism: Colonial Expansion, Tropical Island Edens and the Origins of Environmentalism, 1600–1860* (Cambridge: Cambridge University Press, 1995); Richard Drayton, *Nature's Government: Science, Imperial Britain, and the 'Improvement" of the World* (New Haven: Yale University Press, 2000); David Philip Miller and Peter Hanns Reill eds. *Visions of Empire: Voyages, Botany, and Representations of Nature*. (Cambridge: Cambridge University Press, 1996); Nigel Rigby, "The Politics and Pragmatics of Seaborne Plant Transportation, 1769–1805" in *Science and Exploration in the Pacific: European Voyages to the*

Southern Oceans in the Eighteenth Century, Margarette Lincoln ed. (Suffolk and Rochester, N.Y.: Boydell and Brewer, 1998), 81–100.

38. Alan Frost, *Sir Joseph Banks and the Transfer of Plants to and from the South Pacific 1786–1798* (Melbourne: The Colony Press, 1993), 38.

39. Rumphius, *The Poison Tree: Selected Writings of Rumphius on the Natural History of the Indies*, E. M. Beekman ed. and trans. (Amherst: University of Massachusetts Press, 1981), 10.

40. John Ellis, *A description of the mangostan and the bread-fruit: the first, esteemed one of the most delicious, the other, the most useful of all the fruits in the East Indies: to which are added, directions to voyagers, for bringing over these and other vegetable productions, which would be extremely beneficial to the inhabitants of our West India islands* (London: Printed for the author, and sold by Edward and Charles Dilly, 1775), 12–13.

41. Frost, *Sir Joseph Banks*, 53. Richard Drayton suggests that the breadfruit was intended as both supplement and substitute: "breadfruit [...] was meant to provide food for the slaves, supplementing plantains and cassava, and replacing the flour which American independence now made foreign." Drayton, *Nature's Government*, 114.

42. Frost, *Sir Joseph Banks*, 54, 58. The origin of the name 'Yamstooks', which seems redolent of an alternative preferred staple, is perhaps implied in Richard Grove's meticulous account of St Helena's early deforestation. Grove writes: "The yam, a staple food in the colony, especially for the slaves, and imported, like the slaves, largely from the Gold Coast, required large amounts of irrigation water for successful cultivation. Despite this, the plant was referred to in 1699 as 'to be looked upon as the main stuff.'" Grove, *Green Imperialism*, 108.

43. Frost, *Sir Joseph Banks*, 60.

44. Banks, *Endeavour Journal*, 1: 344; compare Cook, *Voyage*, 122.

45. David Malo, *Hawaiian Antiquities: Mo'olelo Hawai'i*, Nathaniel B. Emerson, trans. (Honolulu: Bishop Museum Press, 1997), 43; Teuira Henry, *Ancient Tahiti*, (Honolulu: Bishop Museum Press, 1928), 40.

46. James Morrison, *The Journal of James Morrison, Boatswain's Mate of the 'Bounty',describing the mutiny and subsequent misfortunes of the mutineers, together with an account of the island of Tahiti* (London: The Golden Cockerel Press, 1935), 213–14.

47. James Boswell, *Life of Johnson* (Oxford: Oxford University Press 1980), 538.

The People Things Make: Locke's Essay Concerning Human Understanding and the Properties of the Self

MARK BLACKWELL

> *Self* is that conscious thinking thing, (whatever Substance, made up of whether Spiritual, or Material, Simple, or Compounded, it matters not) which is sensible, or conscious of Pleasure and Pain, capable of Happiness or Misery, and so is concern'd for it *self*, as far as that consciousness extends.
>
> —John Locke, *Essay concerning Human Understanding* (1690–1706)[1]

> Mr. *Locke*'s Opponents needed but to examine, calmly and impartially, whether the declaring that Matter can think, implies a Contradiction; and whether God is able to communicate Thought to Matter.
>
> —Voltaire, *Letters concerning the English Nation* (1733)[2]

One of Citibank's recent television campaigns peddles the company's fraud-protection services by depicting identity-theft victims speaking in the voices of their impersonators. The advertisements construe the crime as a form of body-snatching, or at least as an uncanny assumption of another's buying power, and thus remind viewers that the virtual marketplace of credit cards and Internet shopping offers consumers opportunities to consume even as it simultaneously renders buyers vulnerable to possession; one's identity, the ads threaten, may circulate as freely as the goods one purchases. The humor of the commercials is conveyed through unlikely juxtapositions of class, age, gender, and ethnicity that tend to minimize the risk that identity theft poses to the victim's core selfhood. No one who knows these people, the ads suggest, could possibly confuse them with the disembodied, usurping voices speaking through them. Yet viewers are left with a disquieting sense that their identities are somehow vulnerable, prey to "unbodied spirits" that lurk online or in unmarked vans parked near ATMs. Identity is but another type of commodity, a thing of which one may be dispossessed.

Though identity theft of this sort is a peculiarly modern phenomenon, it nonetheless resonates with the distinctive conceit of numerous canonical eighteenth-century English fictions, including *Moll Flanders* (1722) and *Tom Jones* (1749), texts predicated on their title characters' tendency to lose themselves and assume the identities of others. Scholars eager to tell a particular story about attitudes toward human identity in the eighteenth century often invoke John Locke's *Essay concerning Human Understanding* (1690–1706) as one of the forces shaping the novelistic presentation of self in the period. Ernst Cassirer long ago touted Locke as the "guide and master" of eighteenth-century psychology, and more recent historians and critics have cited the *Essay* in order to explain the increasing importance of the freestanding individual and the psychological self in Enlightenment writing.[3] Thus, Ian Watt conjures Locke's authority in order to provide a philosophical basis for the novel's "truth to individual experience" and its "particularizing approach to character," while Hans Aarsleff credits Locke with inspiring the novel's "new intimacy and even inwardness in the conception and portrayal of character."[4] Indeed, Locke's influence is especially crucial to the magisterial "rise-of-the-novel" thesis sketched by Watt, though the outlines of that thesis can perhaps be traced as early as Voltaire's *Letters concerning the English Nation* (1733). Voltaire distinguishes the romance-writing philosophers of previous generations from Locke, who offers what Watt might describe as "a full and authentic report of human experience": "Such a Multitude of Reasoners having written the Romance of the Soul, a Sage at last arose, who gave . . . the History of it. Mr. *Locke* has display'd the human Soul, in the same Manner as an excellent Anatomist explains the Springs of the human Body. . . . He takes an Infant at the instant of his Birth; he traces, Step by Step, the Progress of his Understanding."[5] Voltaire construes the *Essay* as a sort of bildungsroman of human understanding.

However, Watt's compelling, still-influential story of prose fiction's growing emphasis on the "anatomy" of the individual character depends on a rather narrow reading of Locke's *Essay*, especially of its groundbreaking account of personal identity. Voltaire himself alludes to Locke's theory of identity-in-consciousness when he suggests that Locke's attention to the particularity of his own experience renders his "history" persuasive: "Above all, he consults himself; the being conscious that he himself thinks."[6] Yet Voltaire also recognizes the challenge of Locke's theory, namely, how radical it is for Locke to allow that matter might think or that beasts might have "a spiritual Soul," and how unsettling are Locke's identity puzzles, which posit reassignments of identity even more unlikely than those imagined by the writers who pen Citibank's advertising copy.[7] This essay proffers an alternative account of Locke's theory of personal identity and, ultimately, of the legacy of that theory for the history of prose fiction in eighteenth-century England. Popular eighteenth-century redactions of Locke reveal that his *Essay* inspired not only stories of autonomous, psychologically complex characters whose distinctive lives take shape in logically coherent narratives, but also episodic, patchwork tales of objects and animals that erode the distinctions between humans and their things and thus challenge the cohesion, the individuation, and the interiority considered the hallmarks of the novel as a genre. The person's troubled relationship with its properties was a Lockean legacy at least as important to his literary successors as psychological complexity and individual autonomy.

Locke's chapter "Of Identity and Diversity," first included in the 1694 second edition of *An Essay concerning Human Understanding*, articulated the long eighteenth century's best-known theory of personal identity. As Michael Ayers notes, Locke's attention to the problem of personal identity was almost certainly inspired "by the doctrine of the resurrection of the body, the topic of considerable controversy at the time," and his theory was intended to settle the matter by providing a new way of thinking about the connection between the deceased and the resurrected body, offering consciousness as an alternative to both sameness of corporeal substance (the notion that identity is preserved at resurrection because all the particles of the natural body are reassembled) and sameness of immaterial substance (the notion that identity is maintained because the soul that animated the deceased body is transferred to the reconstituted body).[8] The resurrection-controversy context reminds us that, from the start, the challenge facing Locke centered on the relationship between the self as a coherent moral agent and its physical embodiment, a relationship complicated not only by the body's tendency to change—to shed hair and nails, to lose teeth, to age—but also by the thorny problems of corporeal dissemination and reconstitution that issue from the corpse's susceptibility to decay. In *Locke and the Scriblerians*, Christopher Fox has traced the ways in which Locke's theory of personal identity, despite its effort to put paid to that theological controversy, instead inspired heated debate, particularly during the first fifty years or so after its initial publication.[9] Indeed, Locke's theory unwittingly resurrected the controversy about the self's relationship to its material properties.

Locke famously identified neither the soul, nor the body, nor "the unity of one continued life" as the guarantor of unique selfhood, settling instead on consciousness as the sine qua non of personal identity. For Locke, consciousness, the reflexive awareness that one is thinking, subtends the self. Charles Taylor terms this theory of self-regard "the perfectly detachable consciousness," arguing that it fosters disengaged subjects who take an instrumental stance to their feelings, thoughts, and desires. For Taylor, this detachment from human qualia, from what John Searle calls "the special qualitative feel" of each person's conscious perceptions, proceeds from Locke's problematic assumption that "something we call consciousness or self-consciousness could be clearly distinguished from its embodiment."[10] Taylor notes that this "philosophy of disengagement and objectification has helped to create a picture of the human being . . . from which the last vestiges of subjectivity seem to have been expelled. It is a picture of a human being from a completely third-person perspective. The paradox," Taylor continues, "is that this severe outlook is connected with, indeed, based on, according a central place to the first-person stance. Radical objectivity is only intelligible and accessible through radical subjectivity."[11] An unstated implication of Taylor's thesis is that the radical subjectivity we associate with the novel is only intelligible and accessible through radical objectivity. In his chapter on "Private Experience and the Novel," when Watt notes that novel readers "get inside [the] minds as well as inside [the] houses" of their favorite characters, he clearly means to emphasize the importance for prose fiction of what he calls "private and egocentric mental life," "the processes that occur in the individual consciousness."[12] Yet "getting inside their minds" is perhaps little different from entering their houses. In a process Catherine Gallagher has fruitfully explored in *Nobody's Story*, readers furnish their minds with characters' thoughts and experiences, engaging in readerly acts of appropriation made easier by the fact that the feelings and things owned by fictional characters belong to "nobody" in particular.[13] All readers, and perhaps all Lockean persons, share Moll Flanders' attitude toward others' property.

Taylor, for one, insists that the capacity to alienate emotions, thoughts, and possessions is not peculiar to novelistic characters. The disengaged subject of Locke's philosophy, Taylor notes, treats every experience as one "which could just as well have been someone else's," and Locke himself took seriously the possibility that someone else's experiences might be passed off as one's own.[14] Locke asks

> whether the consciousness of past Actions can be transferr'd from one thinking Substance to another. I grant, were the Consciousness the same individual Action, it could not: But it being a present representation of a past Action, why it may not be possible, that that may be represented to the Mind to have been, which really never was, will remain to be shewn. And therefore how far the

> consciousness of past Actions is annexed to any individual Agent, so that another cannot possibly have it, will be hard for us to determine . . . [T]hat which we call the *same consciousness,* not being the same individual Act, why one intellectual Substance may not have represented to it, as done by it self, what it never did, and was perhaps done by some other Agent . . . will be difficult to conclude from the Nature of things.[15]

Indeed, Locke suggests not only that another's consciousness can be appropriated, but that one's own can be estranged: "For whatsoever any Substance has thought or done, which I cannot recollect, and by my consciousness make my own Thought and Action, it will no more belong to me, whether a part of me thought or did it, than if it had been thought or done by any other immaterial Being any where existing."[16] How can one be certain that one's consciousness has not been counterfeited, tampered with, or imported when consciousness of past actions is, in theory, fabricable, transferrable, and effaceable? The very repetition of the lexical pairs "thought or done," "thought and action," and "thought or did" bleaches the particularity from any single mental event and makes plausible the notion that the contents of our minds are interchangeable. Lockean consciousness both provides the basis for personal identity and allows for the possibility that identity may be alienated and assumed at will.

Consider Locke's well-known example of the cobbler's body animated by the soul and consciousness of a prince. "[S]hould the Soul of a Prince," Locke writes

> carrying with it the consciousness of the prince's past Life, enter and inform the Body of a Cobler as soon as deserted by his own Soul, every one sees, he would be the same Person with the Prince, accountable only for the Prince's Actions: But who would say it was the same Man? The Body too goes to the making of the Man, and would, I guess, to every Body determine the Man in this case, wherein the Soul, with all its Princely Thoughts about it, would not make another Man: But he would be the same Cobler to every one besides himself.[17]

Locke's puzzle is intended to reinforce the distinction between "man" and "person" upon which his definition of personal identity depends. As John Yolton has pointed out, personal identity is deeply personal in Locke's *Essay*, for the "first-person awareness of my actions . . . is the basis of moral responsibility" and "constitutes my identity as a person, my personal identity, my 'personal self'. A self can only be personal."[18] Nonetheless, Locke seems uneasy about disembodied consciousness, about the detachment of moral responsibility from the bodies that have discharged a person's actions. He raises difficult questions about the relationship between personal identity and the social ascription of identity based both upon social rank and upon the recognizable, physical features of "men."[19] Indeed, Locke's distinction between the outward trappings characteristic of the man, including behavior and body, and the morally accountable, wholly personal core of the self means that society has but an obscure window upon the moral obligations and deepest feelings of its members, and thus that its systems for assigning blame and meting out justice are necessarily uncertain. Lockean consciousness makes interiority, the inward "truth" of one's individual identity, disturbingly inaccessible to others.[20]

Locke's awareness of the potential conflict between the "personal self" and the social imputation of identity provokes his wry observation that the prince's soul, "with all its Princely thoughts about it," will nonetheless seem a cobbler in everyone else's eyes and will be treated accordingly. Here Locke betrays his understanding of the complex relationship between interiority and the material signifiers of identity, between the self-awareness of the person and the social expectations foisted upon the man. The prince, Locke recognizes, has clearly lost more than his title, yet the whole point of this example of corporeal transfer is to make bodies just another property to be exchanged, appropriated, or lost, without consequences for our core selfhood. Locke's treatment of the body in the *Essay* is on this point consistent with his discussion of property in the second of his *Two Treatises of Government*, wherein Locke maintains that "every Man has a *Property* in his own *Person*" as well as in the "*Labour* of his Body, and the *Work* of his Hands," thereby implying a potential equivalence between the body and those things it appropriates, all of which may be considered the properties of the self.[21]

Michael Ayers insists that much of Locke's discussion of personal identity depicts a consciousness which spontaneously recognizes objects as its own rather than deliberately assimilating them in a process something like Lockean labor. According to Ayers, consciousness is for Locke an unintentional or natural (and in that sense, unconscious) acknowledgement of one's thoughts and actions rather than a considered selection of them akin to the mixing of work with land involved in property ownership.[22] The prince's consciousness, in other words, cannot but register the experience of the new perceptions it receives via the body and circumstances of a cobbler, "[f]or the Objects of our Senses do, many of them, obtrude their particular *Ideas* upon our minds, whether we will or no."[23] Our consciousness, and thus our personal identity, is held hostage by corporeal hosts that nevertheless bear no essential relation to it.

Yet Locke's insistence on the disembodiment of consciousness, on its blank and passive registration of impressions, is surely at odds with the cognitive dissonance and material disappointment he expects the newly incarnate "cobbler" to feel. For Locke, the cobbler's body, or any other body, for that matter, is immaterial to the person of the prince, but a theory of personal identity insensitive to the prince's subjective experience of loss and disorientation seems terribly impoverished, stripped like the prince himself of the very qualities which make selfhood both familiar and valuable. Consciousness's habitual absorption of experiences cannot continue uninterrupted and unexamined when faced with the prince's experience of incongruity.

Locke's winking anticipation of the rude awakening that awaits the prince demonstrates his awareness of the powerful influence that our properties have upon us. Locke recognizes that the objects we own become infused with identity just as the body does—that, in Jonathan Lamb's phrase, "things take a human print"—so that their loss affects our sense of self.[24] Moreover, he understands that property in turn puts its stamp on humans, that clothes and possessions do indeed make the man and may perhaps come to seem as integral to one's sense of self as the body. Though ostensibly intended to illustrate Locke's distinction between person and man, the cobbler-prince puzzle might make us wonder whether persons can be absolutely divorced from the specific forms and circumstances of their embodiment.[25]

The complicated question of consciousness's relation to the body and to its properties in the *Essay* was anticipated in Locke's earliest definition of personal identity, sketched in a journal entry over a decade before the publication of the chapter "Of Identity and Diversity": "Identity of persons lies not in haveing the same numericall body made up of the same particles, nor if the minde consists of corporeal spirits in their being the same. But in the memory and knowledge of ones past self and actions continued on under the consciousness of being the same person whereby every man ownes himself."[26] From the start, Locke grounded personal identity in the conviction that one "ownes" one's varied mental and physical actions. "Ownes" here seems to mean "acknowledges" in the sense of both "recognizes" and "takes responsibility for." But it also connotes property ownership, hinting that persons must take possession of themselves and thus that they are both subjects and objects of self-making actions. Hence Zachary Mayne's description of self as "the Subject, as well as the Object of *Consciousness*" in his "Essay on Consciousness" (1728).[27] Our owned actions comprise us, yet we constitute ourselves by performing an act of self-possession called consciousness. In the words of Horkheimer and Adorno, "the all-powerful self becomes mere possession—abstract identity."[28]

Early imaginative responses to Locke seize on this vision of the self as a strange amalgam of possessor and possession, or even as a possessor constituted solely by his possessions. Eustace Budgell's *Spectator* No. 578 (August 9, 1714), for example, invokes contemporary controversies about personal identity ("There has been very great Reason, on several Accounts, for the learned World to endeavor at settling what it was that might be said to compose *personal Identity*") and offers a single-paragraph recapitulation of Locke's definition of self as the preface to a story derived from *The Persian Tales*.[29] Budgell recounts the story of Prince Fadlallah, who falls under the spell of a young dervish. Won by the conversation and "[a]bilities of this stranger," Fadlallah offers him "the first Posts in his Kingdom," but the dervish modestly declines, "as having made a Vow never to accept of any Employment, and preferring a free and independent State of Life to all other Conditions." Hunting alone with Fadlallah one day, the dervish reveals that he possesses "the Power of reanimating a dead Body, by flinging my own Soul into it" and subsequently demonstrates his skill by leaving his own body and reviving a dead doe. Thereupon he offers to teach his secret to the king, who no sooner accepts and throws himself into the deer's body than the dervish shoots "his own Soul into the royal Corps" in order to assume the identity of the king.[30] Fadlallah flees into the forest, and later takes on the body of a bird in order to avoid the dervish-king's decree that all deer be killed. While the usurper enjoys Fadlallah's kingdom and wife, Fadlallah is reduced to a life as his queen's favorite nightingale, then as her lapdog. He is finally able to quit this humiliating condition when the dervish decides to entertain the queen by inhabiting the nightingale which Fadlallah had abandoned to become a dog. Fadlallah swiftly recaptures his lifeless body and kills the bird-cum-dervish.

If the story of Fadlallah speaks to contemporary issues deriving from Lockean consciousness, it undoubtedly serves as a cautionary tale, warning of the dangers of what Martinus Scriblerus calls an "individual self-moving, self-determining principle."[31] Possessing but a "lively and entertaining . . . Turn of Wit" and "preferring a free and independent State of Life to all other Conditions," the dervish poses a threat to the kingdom even before his fantastic deceit begins.[32] The formal possession of Fadlallah's body brings fully to light the sinuous power of the dervish's charms by explicitly enacting the transfer of identity that his creeping influence over the king adumbrated. The story's central conceit merely distills the less-than-fantastic tale of an able, ambitious, independent young man who uses his skills to make inroads upon the power and identity of his social betters. The particular threat held out by the dervish proceeds from his inaccessible interiority, his indifference to social and political obligations, and the remarkable personal mobility suggested by his ability to "throw" his soul. The dervish is the quintessential disengaged subject, detached from the world he inhabits even to the point of being able to shake off his flesh and assume another identity. As Taylor puts it, "[r]adical disengagement opens the prospect of self-remaking."[33] Furthermore, the dervish's core self remains obscure. The mobility of his "unbodied spirit" casts doubt on his "true" social and corporeal identity and further illustrates how hidden from view his inner self is, perhaps intimating that he possesses no interiority, no core person distinct from the trappings he puts on.

Exactly how disturbing is this insight about the inaccessibility or absence of another's interiority may be measured by the inconsolable affliction of Queen Zemroude once the deception has been revealed to her and her true husband restored. The narrator attributes Zemroude's persistent melancholy and untimely death to an "extream Delicacy" about her unwitting adultery.[34] But perhaps Zemroude's capacity to doubt the evidence of her senses has expanded inordinately, to the point where she cannot be certain whom or what to believe. Zemroude had direct, compelling physical evidence of the king's apparent continuity during the entire time the dervish animated his body. Even if she believes Fadlallah's explanation, it must offer her little comfort concerning either her skills as a judge of others' true selves or the depth of her relationship with her spouse. For her, even the authentic Fadlallah was little more than a body in royal clothes "fill[ing] the Throne and Bed" of the king.[35] If this story is intended to exemplify the relationship between consciousness and the body, the person and the man, then it depicts Lockean consciousness as a medium for forms of identity exchange in which bodies are taken up and discarded like commodities, yet are nevertheless the only available indices of the self.

Similar questions are raised in one of Matthew Prior's *Dialogues of the Dead*, between "Mr John Lock and Seigneur de Montaigne." The imagined meeting quickly pits traditional familially and socially determined notions of identity against Locke's vision of the self as simple consciousness:

> *Lock.* . . . I should judge You to be Michael Montaigne.
> *Montaigne.* Seigneur de Montaigne, if you please, Knight of the Order of St. Michael, and some time Mayor of Bordeaux.
> *Lock.* Yes, Sir, I know your Person by your insisting so much upon Your Titles, and I find the same strain run with a most voluble impetuosity almost thro every Chapter of your Book; As you see the Simplicity of my mind in my very Title page, where I only call my Self John Lock, Gentleman.[36]

Montaigne's identity is culled from his engagement in various systems of social and political authority, as member of the Montaigne family, knight of a particular order, and mayor of a certain city. Even his Christian name, "Michael," seems less an individual appellation than a sign of his ties to the "Order of St. Michael" and to the politico-religious hierarchy that establishes his aristocratic pedigree. John Marshall has likewise insisted on the importance of John Locke's status as a gentleman to his moral and social thought, noting that Locke "published his works as 'John Locke, Gent.'" and that he depended on "networks of beneficence and gratitude."[37] Yet Prior depicts a Locke who invokes the simplicity of an individualizing first name as a means of distinguishing himself from the title-dependent Montaigne. Indeed, the word "Self," capitalized according to period conventions for substantives, mirrors the position of "Seigneur" in Montaigne's name and thus hints, perhaps unintentionally, that the term functions for Locke as an alternative title of honor. Of course, Locke's insistence on another title, "Gentleman," undermines the distinction from Montaigne that he seems intent on asserting. Prior thereby underscores a contradiction between Locke's professions of simple, unique individuality (Self) and his implication in the webs of dependency discussed by Marshall (Gentleman).

Like his name and, by extension, his identity, Montaigne's work is but a "compilation" borrowed from classical authorities: "The best one can do is but to compose," Montaigne tells Locke; "I hope you do not pretend to create."[38] Locke, however, claims to "spin my Work out of my own Thoughts" and contends that, even when he happens to cast his "Web upon other Mens Textures," he "make[s] the Work my own, by not knowing it was theirs."[39] The passage echoes Jonathan Swift's well-known distinction between Ancient bee and Modern spider in *The Battle of the Books* (1704). Like Swift's spider, Prior's Locke treats writing as an act of personal "invention," but as Montaigne points out, his individual creativity becomes indistinguishable from that mercenary expropriation of others' ideas called plagiarism:

> In the bounding our Estates, we are pretty partial to our Selves; our Neighbor's Acre on the left hand, if taken in, would make our garden on that side, Square . . . Tho here the Civil Power has already determined what is ours and what is not. But as to the extent of our Knowledge, . . . we take all that comes fairly in our way, and either think it Originally our own, or at least not trouble our Selves whose it was before it came into our Possession. As to your Self, Mr. Lock, you have either Copied pretty servilly from your Predecessors or happened not only upon their Thoughts, but their Method.[40]

Montaigne suggests that Locke's work, like his property and his very identity, has been inherited—or stolen—from previous owners. Locke counters that consciousness of ownership (or, rather, willful obliviousness to others' ownership) *is* ownership: "I make the Work my own, by not knowing it was theirs. What ever may have been written by others, if I have not read their Books, what I write is as much my own Invention as if no Man had thought the same thing before me." Prior perhaps has in mind a particular description of consciousness in the *Essay*: "That with which the *consciousness* of this present thinking thing can join itself, makes the same *Person,* and is one *self* with it, and with nothing else; and so attributes to it *self,* and owns all the actions of that thing, as its own, as far as that consciousness reaches."[41] The capacity of a grasping consciousness to "join itself" to actions, thoughts, and memories, without regard to the physical bodies that experience them, is equivalent to the unacknowledged assimilation of others' ideas which Prior associates with Locke. For Prior, reading and writing serve as crucial metaphors for this expropriative power to forge one's identity by assimilating another's property. His dialogue thus strangely complements Gallagher's thesis about the literary "nobody" and perhaps suggests an alternative interpretation of the dervish's ability to inhabit others' bodies as an allegory of reading.

The most interesting imaginative refractions of Locke come in the it-narrative, whose popularity crested during the third quarter or so of the eighteenth century. By ascribing Lockean personhood to animals and objects, such works exploited Locke's distinction between person and man. They likewise explored the implications of Locke's theory of property, which inadequately distinguished the human body from the properties it owns. As, in the words of an unsympathetic reviewer, "a cluster of little stories, without connection or dependence" and "utterly destitute of novelty," such fictions also challenge the traditional boundaries of the character-driven, causally oriented novel.[42] The narrator of Charles Johnstone's *Chrysal* (1760–65), for instance, a gold coin that passes from hand to hand, is a Lockean person endowed with a consciousness that permits it access to its own experiences while also providing it the power "of entering into the hearts of [its] immediate possessors . . . and there reading all the secrets of their lives."[43] The distinction between consciousness and its objects, between possessor and possessed, and ultimately between Chrysal's personhood and that of its owners becomes fuzzy indeed. In Chapter Three, for example, Chrysal's own voice fades into "The history of Traffick" recounted in its own words: "My name is *Traffick;* I was the only son of a wealthy merchant in *London.*"[44] Chrysal's story constitutes its identity, and that story is a hodgepodge of others' stories, its voice an assembly of others' voices.

Among the best examples of these confusions comes in Chrysal's description of an early encounter with its first possessor's "spirit of consciousness, which you call the self": "I found the spirit very busy . . . She was running over a number of *niches,* or impressions, on the fibres of the brain, some of which I observed she renewed with such force, that she almost effaced others, which she passed over untouched, though interspersed among them."[45] After explaining to Chrysal that the ridges on the brain are "made by a communication of the impressions made on the senses by external objects," the self explains that by "touching these marks, on this material substance the brain, [she] can raise *ideas* in the immaterial mind":

> my whole employment, and end of being, is to touch them over, and acknowledge their acquaintance thus; without my doing which, a man would no longer continue the same person, for in this acquaintance, which is called *consciousness,* does all personal identity consist . . . this man . . . as I am his *self,* I shall henceforth, for conciseness and perspicuity, call *my self.*[46]

Johnstone registers his debt to Locke in a footnote, and his strange juxtaposition of the mechanistic and material (brain, fibers, niches, the exertion of force) and the immaterial (mind, spirit, the raising of ideas), together with the comic difficulty of locating the self in this passage, reveals his awareness of the confusing ramifications of Locke's theory for our ideas about both identity and narrative. The self is "the spirit of consciousness," a tireless laborer coursing over the grooves of the brain. The self is also the byproduct of consciousness' tedious work of connection, for as the spirit itself reminds us, only "in this acquaintance, which is called consciousness, does all personal identity consist." And the self is the man, the body in which these activities take place. Johnstone clearly separates the spirit of consciousness from consciousness itself through the distinction between agent and action, but he also underscores the difference between the spirit of consciousness and the body by gendering the former female ("she") and the latter male. Johnstone understands the complexity of Locke's distinctions in the chapter on identity well enough to offer a parodic rewriting of them.

Like the spirit of consciousness, Chrysal moves from owner to owner, tracing over the various impressions in the minds of those possessors and assimilating them. Chrysal is, in fact, a patchwork of the various selves it temporarily "becomes." It assumes their identities, forging these distinct consciousnesses into the larger, more comprehensive narrative acquaintance that constitutes both its own tale and its own personhood. Indeed, Johnstone offers social as well as metaphysical and physiological analogues for the billiard-ball experience of Lockean identity in his meticulous explanation of the textual history of Chrysal's manuscript, which relies upon the hackneyed conceit of the found text. *Chrysal*'s publisher purports to have discovered the first page of the manuscript serving "instead of a plate" to hold the butter of a family in whose cottage he has taken shelter from an unexpected shower of rain.[47] Multiplying contingencies seems to be the point of these details; only because of the rain did the publisher chance to stop at the cottage, and only because he happened to catch the cottagers at tea has the makeshift butter plate attracted his attention. The moment recalls the impromptu and unlikely association of city dwellers forced indoors by rain in Jonathan Swift's "A Description of a City Shower" (1710): "Here various Kinds by various Fortunes led, / Commence Acquaintance underneath a Shed."[48] Swift's poem depicts people who, despite the interruption in their personal routines and their forced and temporary "acquaintance," find themselves unable to interact freely with one another. They focus on things in order to bide their time until the storm passes, pretending to cheapen goods or call a coach, or using an oiled umbrella to avoid interruptions and untoward chance encounters. Like the image of the river of filth with which the poem ends, these people share much in common, brought together both by a local event (the shower) and by the shared, confluent course of human destiny. But like the poem's "Filth of all Hues and Odours," they nonetheless remain atomically distinct even in their common purposes, "seem[ing] to tell / What Street they sail'd from, by their Sight and Smell."[49] Humans' connections to both the things they own and the things they discard are closer and more telling than their relationships with each other, though both seem equally adventitious.

Like the damp and lonely strangers peopling Swift's poem, *Chrysal*'s publisher ruminates alone while his hosts enjoy breakfast:

> I had leisure to reflect on the advantages of commerce, which thus, in a manner, joins the opposite extremities of the earth, by bringing their products together: at the same time, that the variety in the equipage of the tea-table, or indeed, stool, on which "there was nothing of a piece," suggested a just ridicule on the vanity of luxury.
>
> This last reflection was extended to all the pursuits of man, on the sight of a piece of written paper, that served instead of a plate to hold their butter,—"Who knows (thought I) but the writer of this bestowed time and care upon it, and promised himself both profit and fame, in reward of his labour?"
>
> This thought prompted curiosity to look at the paper, which, by this time, was scraped quite clean. I therefore, after a few words of conversation, to introduce my request, desired leave to see it . . . when I was surprized to find my conjectures, as I imagined, confirmed, by its appearing to be part of some regular work.[50]

As the publisher fails to see, his unexpected encounter with his hosts, their superficial relations with each other, and the profound differences between them signaled, for example, by their different notions of the paper's value serve as another instance of the contingent juxtaposition of "opposite extremities" fueled by commerce. The mismatched tea service, like the unlikely group gathered around it, functions as an emblem of the bric-a-brac identity characteristic of a commercial society. Commercial activity seems merely to fragment purposeful human achievements, circulating their shards as a jumble of odds and ends, as the discordant "equipage of the tea-table" and the buttered remnants of "some regular work" reveal. Indeed, the difficulties the publisher faces in acquiring the pieces of the manuscript and in stitching those fragments together serve, like Chrysal's own adventures in commercial exchange, as an allegory of modern identity formation. The history of the manuscript thus becomes, like the history of Chrysal, the story of the Lockean person as a congeries of others' properties. The publisher's discovery of something more compelling, more alive in a greasy scrap of paper than in his human breakfast companions, his sense that an inanimate object may offer the best access to another human subject, resonates both with the distinctive conceit of the it-narrative as a genre and with the disengaged subjectivity fostered by Locke's account of personal identity.

In a later it-narrative, Helenus Scott's *Adventures of a Rupee* (1782), it is the pawnshop rather than the fragmented manuscript that prompts reflections on the self's relationship with its properties. Characters pawn possessions that represent their social identity and stolen goods mingle with objects invested with sentimental value. A soldier missing his legs and a boy who has sold his teeth pass through the shop.[51] Whenever the rupee expects the story of one of these humans to be of sufficient interest, it may dispatch the spirit of "Ductility" to mount the brain and read the impressions left there by sensations:

> One of my subordinate spirits immediately mounted his cella turcica by my command, from which spot the brain above may be seen marked with impressions, like the figures on a celestial globe. These impressions are nothing but the scratches made by objects which have been presented to the senses, and of which memory makes use in her operations. By reading these, we can discover all the transactions of any consequence in which a man has been engaged. I say of any consequence, for the less material impress with so little force, that the marks they leave, are in time entirely obliterated.[52]

For Scott, the material mind is a kind of pawnshop, a storehouse for things impressed with human significance, a record of the "transactions" in which one has engaged. Such a mind resembles the bodies of the soldier-amputee and the gap-toothed boy, forever marked by their own transactions with the world. Or perhaps it is the objects themselves, worn by human use, that resemble the brain distressed by its encounters with the material realm. Consciousness is ductility, a plastic capacity to constitute itself by claiming its own or another's things. In it-narratives, as in one perhaps tendentious reading of Locke, those things do not simply have the power to make persons; they have the capacity to *be* persons.

In the context of Julien Offray de La Mettrie's *L'homme machine* (1748) and of mechanical contrivances such as Jacques Vaucanson's duck and Pierre Jaquet-Droz's female harpsichordist, which seemed to confound the animate and the inanimate; in light of the philosophical controversies about the capacity of matter to think registered in my epigraphic citation of Voltaire; and in a culture in which goods were circulating in unprecedented numbers, it is perhaps unsurprising that there developed a vogue for stories narrated by self-reflective coins, garrulous embroidered waistcoats, and status-conscious sedan chairs.[53] As "intelligent Agents capable of a Law, and Happiness and Misery," such discursive objects and their brethren (pins, watches, corkscrews, whipping tops) qualify as Lockean persons and challenge the distinction between dumb materiality and a characteristically human interiority.[54] The evidence of it-narratives and of the sentimental fictions with which they were contemporary suggests that conceptual boundaries separating humans and objects were not securely established during the Enlightenment. Such narratives also remind us that early novels chronicle the externalities determining identity (Crusoe's "old hutch" filled with "provisions, ammunition, and stores"; Pamela's bundles of clothes; Tom Jones' bank bills) as assiduously as they recount the development of characters with inner lives.[55]

NOTES

A shorter version of this essay was read at the first of two panels entitled "The People Things Make" during the 2004 ASECS meeting in Boston. Thanks to Lynn Festa for organizing those sessions and for supplying their catchy title. In the spirit of Prior's Locke, I have made that title my own.

1. John Locke, *Essay concerning Human Understanding*, Peter H. Nidditch, ed. (Oxford: Clarendon, 1975), 341, 2.27.17.
2. Voltaire, *Letters concerning the English Nation* (London: C. Davis and A. Lyon, 1733), 101.

3. Ernst Cassirer, *The Philosophy of the Enlightenment*, Fritz C. A. Koelln and James P. Pettegrove, trans. (Princeton: Princeton University Press, 1951), 17.

4. Ian Watt, *The Rise of the Novel* (Berkeley: University of California Press, 1957), 13, 18; Hans Aarsleff, "Locke's Influence," *The Cambridge Companion to Locke*, Vere Chappell, ed. (Cambridge: Cambridge University Press, 1994), 262–63.

5. Watt, *Rise,* 32; Voltaire, *Letters*, 98.

6. Voltaire, *Letters*, 98.

7. Voltaire, *Letters*, 68.

8. Michael Ayers, *Locke: Epistemology and Ontology*, 2 vols. in 1 (London: Routledge, 1993), 2:256.

9. Christopher Fox, *Locke and the Scriblerians: Identity and Consciousness in Early Eighteenth-Century Britain* (Berkeley: University of California Press, 1988).

10. Charles Taylor, *Sources of the Self: The Making of Modern Identity* (Cambridge, Mass.: Harvard University Press, 1989), 159–60, 172. On qualia, see John R. Searle, "The Mystery of Consciousness," *The New York Review of Books* 42.17 (1995): 61.

11. Taylor, *Sources*, 175–76.

12. Watt, *Rise*, 175, 177.

13. Catherine Gallagher, *Nobody's Story: The Vanishing Acts of Women Writers in the Marketplace, 1670–1820* (Berkeley: University of California Press, 1994), 167–74.

14. Taylor, *Sources*, 162.

15. Locke, *Essay*, 337–38, 2.27.13.

16. Locke, *Essay*, 345, 2.27.24.

17. Locke, *Essay*, 340, 2.27.15.

18. John Yolton, *Locke: An Introduction* (New York: Blackwell, 1985), 30.

19. Or perhaps between personal identity and Althusserian "interpellation." The prince is in the odd position of being conscious of his "hailing," of what Paul Ricoeur neutrally describes as the formation of a "subject who has been made responsible by the expectation of the other." See Louis Althusser, "Ideology and Ideological State Apparatuses (Notes towards an Investigation)," *Lenin and Philosophy,* Ben Brewster, trans. (New York: Monthly Review, 1971), 170–77, and Paul Ricoeur, *Oneself as Another,* Kathleen Blamey, trans. (Chicago: University of Chicago Press, 1992), 168.

20. For Locke, of course, language is intended to publicize interiority: "Man, though he have great variety of Thoughts . . . yet they are all within his own Breast, invisible, and hidden from others . . . it was necessary, that Man should find out some external sensible Signs, whereby those invisible *Ideas* . . . might be made known to others" (*Essay*, 404–5, 3.2.1). But Locke's well-known chapters on "the Imperfection of Words" (*Essay*, 475–90, 3.9) and "the Abuse of Words" (*Essay*, 490–508, 3.10) bear testimony to his persistent concern about how reliably language signifies one's own—and others'—deepest thoughts and feelings.

21. John Locke, *Two Treatises of Government*, rev. ed. (New York: Mentor, 1965), 328–29.

22. Ayers, *Locke*, 2:266–68.

23. Locke, *Essay*, 118, 2.1.25.

24. Jonathan Lamb, "Modern Metamorphoses and Disgraceful Tales," *Critical Inquiry* 28.1 (2001): 147. Also consider Vico's account of the origin of fables, and ultimately of poetic monsters and metamorphoses: "since the nature that we know best consists in our own properties, men attribute to things that are insensate or inanimate, movement, sense and reason, which are the most luminous labours of poetry" (*The First New Science*, Leon Pompa, ed. and trans. [Cambridge: Cambridge University Press, 2002], 151).

25. On the problem of "embodied subjectivity" or "psychical corporeality," see Elizabeth Grosz, *Volatile Bodies: Toward a Corporeal Feminism* (Bloomington: Indiana University Press, 1994), 22.

26. Quoted in Ayers, *Locke*, 2:255.

27. Zachary Mayne, "Essay on Consciousness," *Two Dissertations Concerning Sense, and the Imagination* (1728; rpt. edn., New York: Garland, 1976), 149.

28. Theodor Adorno and Max Horkheimer, *The Dialectic of Enlightenment,* John Cumming, trans. (New York: Continuum, 1972), 10.

29. Donald F. Bond, ed., *The Spectator,* 5 vols. (Oxford: Clarendon, 1965), 4: 575.

30. Bond, *Spectator,* 4:576–77.

31. Charles Kerby-Miller, ed., *The Memoirs of Martinus Scriblerus* (New York: Oxford University Press, 1988), 140.

32. Bond, *Spectator*, 4:576.

33. Taylor, *Sources,* 171.

34. Bond, *Spectator*, 4:579.

35. Bond, *Spectator*, 4:577.

36. Matthew Prior, *Dialogues of the Dead and Other Works,* A. R. Waller, ed. (Cambridge: Cambridge University Press, 1907), 223.

37. John Marshall, *John Locke: Resistance, Religion and Responsibility* (Cambridge: Cambridge University Press, 1994), 169.

38. Prior, *Dialogues*, 240.

39. Prior, *Dialogues*, 239–40. Perhaps echoing Prior, Laurence Sterne uses Locke's theory of property to explain Walter Shandy's appropriation of others' opinions; he later portrays Walter as spinning "every thread" of the Tristra-pœdia "out of his own brain" (Melvyn and Joan New, eds., *The Life and Opinions of Tristram Shandy, Gentleman*, vols. 1-3 of The Florida Edition of the Works of Laurence Sterne [Gainesville: University Presses of Florida, 1978-84], 1:262-63, 3.34; 1:445, 5.16.

40. Prior, *Dialogues*, 240–41.

41. Locke, *Essay*, 341, 2.27.17.

42. Review of *The Adventures of a Bank Note*, *London Journal* 39 (1770).

43. Charles Johnstone, *Chrysal, or The Adventures of a Guinea,* Malcolm Bosse, ed., 4 vols. (1761–65; rpt. edn., New York: Garland, 1979), 1:5.

44. Johnstone, *Chrysal*, 1:10.

45. Johnstone, *Chrysal*, 1:7.

46. Johnstone, *Chrysal*, 1:8–9.

47. Johnstone, *Chrysal*, 1:x.

48. Jonathan Swift, *The Poems of Jonathan Swift,* Harold Williams, ed., 2nd ed., 3 vols. (Oxford: Clarendon Press, 1958), 1:138, ll. 39–40.

49. Swift, *Poems,* 1:139, ll. 55–56.

50. Johnstone, *Chrysal,* 1:ix–x.

51. On the transplantation of human teeth as both a fashionable medical procedure and a telling period example of the fuzzy boundaries between things and persons, see my "'Extraneous Bodies': The Contagion of Live-Tooth Transplantation in Late-Eighteenth-Century England," *Eighteenth-Century Life* 28.1 (Winter 2004): 21–68.

52. Helenus Scott, *Adventures of a Rupee* (London: J. Murray, 1782), 145.

53. On eighteenth-century automata, see for instance Jessica Riskin, "The Defecating Duck, or, the Ambiguous Origins of Artificial Life," *Things*, Bill Brown, ed. (Chicago: University of Chicago Press, 2004), 99–133. On thinking matter in Locke, see Ayers, *Locke*, 2:142–53, 169–83. On the emergence of a consumer society in late eighteenth-century England, see for example Neil McKendrick, John Brewer, and J. H. Plumb, eds., *The Birth of a Consumer Society: The Commercialization of Eighteenth-Century England* (Bloomington: Indiana University Press, 1982).

54. Locke, *Essay*, 346, 2.27.26.

55. See Deidre Lynch, *The Economy of Character: Novels, Market Culture, and the Business of Inner Meaning* (Chicago: University of Chicago Press, 1998).

Covering Sexual Disguise: Passing Women and Generic Constraint

FRASER EASTON

> *Corke, July* 29. Last Sunday Morning a lusty young Heroine, dress'd in a Sailor's Jacket and Check Shirt, waited on Lieutenant Beamish, at his Rendezvous in Brown-Street, to enlist in his Majesty's Service as an able Landman [*sic*]; and carried on the Deception so well as to be received, was immediately new rigg'd, paid the Bounty, and sent on board a Tender at Cove: But her Sex being soon discovered, she was sent back, and to her great Mortification, made but little Profit of the Expedition. Whether her Motive was to serve the King, to play a Trick on the Officer, or to get off with a Sweetheart, is uncertain; perhaps her Apology was genuine in confessing the latter.
>
> *The Daily Advertiser* (10 August 1762)

This report of "a lusty young Heroine" is one of many accounts in *The Daily Advertiser* of that well-known eighteenth-century figure, the female soldier or sailor who, disguised in male garb, served in the military, often for many years, although not in this instance. The pension records of Christian Davies, Hannah Snell, and Mary Lacy confirm that some woman warriors were officially rewarded for their bravery and effectiveness at war.[1] The widely-disseminated memoirs of these three women, along with the extensive media coverage of the exploits of the Chevalier D'Eon (who, although actually a man, was thought to be a woman), brought the figure of the female soldier great cultural recognition over the course of the eighteenth century, as did the tradition of female warrior ballads that Dianne Dugaw has recovered and analysed.[2] What is striking in the present report is the way in which this woman's explanation of her behaviour is described as an "Apology." As a formal justification of one's actions, the apology is a spoken and written mode of long provenance; to see this young woman's self-defence in such terms, however loosely, is to link the confession of "her Motive" to an explicitly rhetorical framework. Whether or not she actually set out "to serve the King, to play a Trick on the Officer, or to get off with a Sweetheart," each stock motive entails a distinct variant of apology influenced by patriotic, criminal, or romantic elements. As the reporter knows, these inflections were themselves cultural commonplaces: this young woman might indeed be "genuine in confessing" that she enlisted to follow a lover to sea, like the romantic heroine of a female warrior ballad, but with only her word to rely on, the truth of whether or not this really was her motivation must necessarily remain "uncertain." Indeed, the report's notice of her "great Mortification" on being discovered, and its assertion that she "made but little Profit of the Expedition," seem designed to hint that she had other, perhaps more dubious, purposes.

The present article is part of a larger investigation of the role of generic constraint on the representation of eighteenth-century labouring-class women who passed as men. The figure of the passing woman is found across a wide range of eighteenth-century print forms, including trial records, newspapers, journals, ballads, chapbooks, memoirs, novels, and comedies. Within each of these forms, particular genres create specific mediations of the figure of the passing woman in terms of class, gender, and sexuality, on the one hand, and normalcy, transgression, and out-and-out fantasy, on the other. As a consequence, the print forms and associated genres selected by critics and scholars in their study of passing women have had a significant bearing upon the scope and nature of their analyses and conclusions. For example, cultural critics of early modern gender identities and sexualities, Terry Castle perhaps most influentially, have examined cases of cross-dressing women from print forms, such as sensationalizing chapbooks, theatrical autobiographies, and medical literature, which accentuate the transgressive sexuality of gender-bending women.[3] In contrast, a debunking historian like David Cressy has focused on cases from MS and print forms, such as Renaissance plays and the records of trials in church courts, which emphasize the regulation of plebeian disorder.[4] At stake in the choice of MS and print forms, then, is a related consideration, the status of claims of exemplarity: which examples are, in the end, typical of a culture, a class, or a social formation, and on what basis can a claim of cultural typicality be sustained? This is a general problem for cultural studies (whether literary or historical), of course, as well as for ideas of representation more broadly conceived. For literary studies the methodological challenge lies in part in being able to define the form of a discourse without basing it on a prematurely generalized set of instances, such as a few anecdotes. Looking at the role of generic mediation in a systematic sample of newspaper and other periodical reports is a particularly promising way in which to approach the presentation of popular figures, since unlike other forms of cheap print, individual periodical titles offer both a clear standard of completeness and a systematic chronological range. Finally, since newspapers in particular are a relatively open form, a look at reports of passing women in selected periodicals including newspapers is one way in which to explore the overall scope of presentations of the figure.

In what follows, I will examine press reports of passing women across long runs of three important serial publications: *The Daily Advertiser* (from 1731 to 1796), *The Gentleman's Magazine* (from 1731 to 1830), and *The Annual Register* (from 1761 to 1830). I have chosen these three periodicals for examination because they were all culturally influential and widely read, because of the completeness with which their long runs have been preserved, and because they allow for a comparison of the effects of different periodicities on news reporting.

The Annual Register was in essence a work of popular scholarship that covered a year's events in two substantial volumes and was noted above all for its long, original essay on "The History of Europe," a piece which treated, over several hundred pages, both British Parliamentary affairs and foreign political history for the relevant year.[5] Significant events that did not fit under the rubric of the historical essay were gathered from monthly magazines and other sources in a "Chronicle" of odd and remarkable occurrences. Although the "Chronicle" section was a relatively accessible feature, both the cost and the heavily retrospective nature of *The Annual Register* (it often appeared several years after the year it covered) meant that it was addressed to readers with money and a particular interest in past political affairs. *The Gentleman's Magazine*, in contrast, was a general interest publication with a wide following among educated and leisured readers (it had a circulation of about 3,000 copies per month in 1746, and 4,500 per month in 1797).[6] The availability of *The Gentleman's Magazine* in public venues such as London coffee-houses underscores its wide distribution, at least among well-to-do men.[7] Its miscellaneous contents included essays and letters on social, historical, and scientific topics, original poetry, and short news sections devoted to foreign and domestic events of note. The news was reprinted from the daily press, but significantly *The Gentleman's Magazine* was, like *The Annual Register*, "looked on as a work of reference," one based on the inclusion of "representative material."[8] Items in the "Historical Chronicle" (the news section) were cross-referenced and indexed just like the other features of *The Gentleman's Magazine*, a fact strongly suggesting that its news reports were selected as much for their presumed representativeness as for any other factor.

Finally, *The Daily Advertiser*, a London-based general-interest newspaper with a circulation estimated at over 2,500 copies per day in 1746, and 5,000 per day in 1779, was likely to have been the most widely disseminated of the three periodicals, both in London and in the country, particularly across economic classes.[9] Compared with *The Annual Register* and *The Gentleman's Magazine*, the greater social reach of *The Daily Advertiser* is evident from the way in which it is addressed to servants and labourers as well as to elite consumers and London tradesmen (for example, in its advertisements). Since newspapers generally were made available at inns and taverns, and not only in the largely masculine and elite milieu of the coffee-houses, readers of *The Daily Advertiser* would also have included significant numbers of artisanal and labouring-class individuals (as well as some women).[10] Other practices in the consumption of newspapers further supported a wide and socially diverse readership: papers could be shared, rented, and, in taverns and ale-houses for example, read aloud, and perhaps discussed, item by item.[11] Indeed, estimates suggest that each copy of a daily paper had as many as ten readers or auditors, so that on any given day a London title like *The Daily Advertiser* would have reached the equivalent of up to 10% of the metropolis's population.

In line with recent studies of other popular-print forms, I will argue in this essay that eighteenth-century periodical records of passing women are shaped by sophisticated rhetorical conventions. These press reports draw on a variety of generic modes, including romance, melodrama, rogue narrative, jestbook anecdote, the picaresque, and patriotic adventure, and these modes, as much as any information that is relayed, helped to give definition to the events being recounted. Significantly, the vast majority of reports of passing women treat individuals from the labouring and servant classes; that is, these reports are directly tied to the representation of plebeian identity.[12] Indeed, the chronological scope of passing-women periodical reports shows that such accounts were one of the key channels through which labouring-class identity and its engenderment reached cultural consciousness. As we will see, however, eighteenth-century editorial decisions about the representativeness and appropriateness of specific genres of reportage, or of reports on particular types of passing women, were tied in part to specific publication factors: what was too gauche, outré, or risqué for *The Annual Register*, for example, might be suitably amusing, newsworthy, or popular for *The Daily Advertiser*. In consequence, the editorial decisions of easily-consulted, reference-oriented periodicals such as *The Annual Register* and *The Gentleman's Magazine* have had a disproportionate effect on how eighteenth-century passing women have been represented and memorialized, and therefore on the approaches that some present-day scholars have taken in seeking to recover and understand this figure.

I will also argue that in addition to the constitutive role of rhetorical factors in the representation of passing women in periodical reports, it is critical to look at the frequency and distribution of different genres of reports of passing women both over time (something made possible by the preservation of long runs of particular periodical titles) and across different periodical titles. In *The Gentleman's Magazine*, for example, the frequency of all news reports of passing women is roughly constant from 1731 to 1830 (see Table 1.2 below). This is a startling outcome, especially given the current scholarly consensus, based on the works of Dugaw, Rudolf Dekker and Lotte van de Pol, and others, that there was a late eighteenth-century decline in reports of passing women (and in their representation) across a range of print and manuscript forms, and it is an outcome with important implications for how we understand the development of gender identity in Britain in this period.[13] Critics such as Susan Lanser, for example, have tied changes in the respresentation of sapphic identity to a rising transgressiveness in the representation of the cross-dressing woman over the eighteenth century.[14] It is therefore of the greatest significance that although the distribution of press reports shaped by particular genres is relatively constant in particular periodical publications over time, it is *not* constant across different publications but rather varies according to the publication frequency of the periodical in which the reports appear. In effect, the daily press embodied the widest generic range, the monthly press somewhat less so, and the annual memorialization or "first draft of history" the least of all. Instead, in *The Annual Register*'s yearly volumes, reports rooted in sensational sexual criminality gain greater prominence in relation to reports of women warriors or of passing women criminals (see Tables 3 and 4 below). This memorialization has the effect of recoding a mainly class-based representation of the passing woman as a good or bad servant into an increasingly sex-based one of the passing woman as an individual with a good or bad sexuality.[15]

A few examples from *The Daily Advertiser* will give us a preliminary sense of the range of genres at work in press reports of passing women:

> The noted Mary Harvey, alias Mackeig, who was confin'd in New-Prison upon her Escape from the Constables, after having receiv'd Sentence at Westminster-Hall for keeping a disorderly House, did, on Monday Night last, find Means to make her Escape out of the said Gaol in Man's Apparel. (26 May 1731)
>
> *Dublin, Sept*. 22. A very odd Circumstance happen'd lately in Liffy-Street, viz. two Servants liv'd with a Gentleman, the one as Man Cook, the other as House-keeper, for about 18 Years, and were married 16: Some Difference happening between them, the House-keeper declar'd the Cook was no Man, but a Woman, and had

> Reasons to believe that her said pretended Husband was with Child; which we hear upon Examination prov'd so. We are likewise inform'd, that the House-keeper is since marry'd to a young Lad of Eighteen. (27 September 1735)
> On Saturday a young Girl, inspir'd with the Love of her Country, equipp'd herself in a Jacket, Trowsers, &c. and enter'd herself on Board a Man of War. (24 February 1741)

These three reports, respectively, show the traces of criminal biography, jestbook anecdote, and martial panegyric. The third report, although very brief, telegraphs the patriotic heroism of this would-be female sailor by noting her careful preparation for sea: she only "enter'd herself on Board a Man of War" after having first "equipp'd herself" in the proper garb of a tar. As Suzanne Stark has noted, eighteenth-century warships often included women passengers, even among the enlisted ranks, so it was possible for plebeian women to sail to war in female garb.[16] But even if a woman in female garb were to accompany her spouse or lover on board as his companion, it was only while in male disguise that a woman could enter military service. The author of this account relies on the reader's knowledge of such facts, as well as of the general patterns of similar incidents; for example, in this case, the reader must assume that the woman's disguise has been discovered. In contrast to the brevity of this report, the account of Mary Harvey is more expansive. It starts by defining her as a repeat offender—she is a "noted" individual, notorious for earlier crimes, perhaps, or for her role as a brothel keeper—and, fittingly, she has at least one alias. She is shown to be proficient in crime, too, when she has to be locked up more securely after escaping from her confinement by the constables. It is only at the end of this account, after its elaboration of an implied background narrative of successful roguery, that the reader is informed of the event that makes the report newsworthy: Harvey has once again escaped, this time from New Prison in male disguise. Even more particularized is the report of a "Man Cook." The author of this paragraph on a female husband and her wife has turned to the canons of plebeian humour, and specifically to jestbooks, for inspiration in shaping the material, rather than to the rhetorics of sexual outrage or of criminal fraud.[17] The information that defines the situation as "odd," and therefore as newsworthy, is the remarkable length of time during which the two women remained married (sixteen years) and the cook's employment in male disguise undiscovered (eighteen years). The account is amusing, however, because of its presentation of the discovery in ribald comic terms: the stock world-upside-down inversion of the marriage of the old bride and young bridegroom, on the one hand, and the declaration of the wife that she "had Reasons to believe that her said pretended Husband was with Child," on the other, both depend on notions of the shameful and absurd excesses of unbridled female lust. The use of free indirect discourse further adds to the comic incongruity of the wife's words.

Although the level of accuracy in many eighteenth-century serials has been called into question, there is no doubt that the daily press sought to give the impression, at least, of care in newsgathering: *The Daily Advertiser*, for example, sometimes published corrections to its news items.[18] But to imagine that these short paragraphs are primarily determined by the information, accurate or not, that they purport to relay would be to overlook a large and growing body of scholarship that has shown how the rhetorical construction of documentary material is essential to its historical, as well as discursive, significance.[19] In the case of passing plebeian women, if we look at the variance in press reports of similar cases, of the same case in different publications, or even of the same case in the same publication, the fundamental importance of generic influences on their formulation is clear.

Consider, for example, the following accounts of three different female warriors from *The Daily Advertiser*:

> *Breda, May* 21. An extraordinary Affair is lately discover'd here: A Grenadier of the Regiment of Lintman, who had been three Years married to a young Person of this Town, having been discover'd to be of the same Sex with the Wife, and the Council of War having been informed thereof, they have been both arrested and committed to Prison. On their Examination since Confinement, it appears manifest, that the Girl before Marriage perfectly knew the Sex of her pretended Husband. (20 May 1751)
>
> *Edinburgh, June* 2. A Soldier under Cure in the Royal Infirmary, was discovered some Days ago to be a Woman. She has been three Years in the Service, without the smallest Suspicion of her Sex; and managed Matters so dexterously, that tho' she lately married a Wife, she had the Address to keep her Story still a Secret from the Regiment. When the late Draughts were made for Germany, she expressed a great Inclination to be one of them, from an ardent Desire to serve under a Prussian General. She was extremely alert in all the manual Exercise of a Soldier, was sober, and attentive to her Duty: In short, till the Discovery was made, she was always looked upon as one of the best Men in the Corps. (9 June 1759)
>
> *Marseilles, Jan.* 23. Capt. Faure, of Ciotat, Commander of the Rolland, is arrived here from Alexandria in Egypt; on board which Ship the Surgeon discovered (when the Vessel was disarming) a Girl between 16 and 17 Years of Age, in Disguise, among the Cabin-Boys, of which he informed the Captain; who, on questioning the Girl, found that Debauchery had no Share in this Adventure, but

> that the Desire of supporting her Mother, who was in great Distress, had induced her to put on Boy's Apparel, and enter for a Cabbin-Boy [*sic*]. This Girl, who is a Native of Sisteron in Provence, performed, during the Voyage, all the Duties of the Station, such as going aloft to furl the Sails, &c. with much Judgment and Spirit. The Proprietors of the Ship have thought proper to double her Pay; which she has accordingly received. (14 February 1765)

These reports each filter the story of a woman warrior in a drastically different way. In the first account the focus is entirely on the sexual impropriety of the grenadier's marriage to another woman; what is especially shocking in this "extraordinary Affair," we are told, is that "the Girl before Marriage perfectly knew the Sex of her pretended Husband."[20] The report takes its cue from the criminalization of the marriage by the military authorities, of course, and in that context the seeming consent of the wife to the relationship is significant (also significant, but not explicit, is the role of national legal jurisdiction). But positive responses to women warriors who married other women were also possible, as the next report confirms. In that report the "Address" by which the soldier keeps her comrades in the dark about her sex, even after her marriage to another woman, is assimilated not to a sexual crime (or indeed to any form of disreputable behaviour) but to a duty-oriented evasion of any "Suspicion of her Sex." What matters is her industriousness: as a soldier she is "alert," "sober, and attentive to her Duty." Indeed, soldiering is so much her vocation that she has "an ardent Desire" to promote her professional development by serving under a Prussian general. In contrast, the last report takes the narrative of military duty in a sentimental direction. Like the Edinburgh soldier, this female cabin-boy performs "all the Duties of the Station" to which she is assigned, "such as going aloft to furl the Sails, &c. with much Judgment and Spirit," and despite her discovery (or perhaps because of it) she is rewarded with "double her Pay." But rather than a story of professional exuberance, the report fashions her experiences as a sentimental tale of virtue rewarded. The assertion that "Debauchery had no Share in this Adventure," as we are told, is a significant one: the figure of a woman disguised as a cabin-boy was one of the few examples of a ballad topos in which a woman passing as a man for military purposes routinely received a bawdy presentation.[21] But it is also significant that this report does not describe a case of female self-determination: unlike the woman warrior in the Royal Infirmary, this woman exhibits no independent vocational aspirations; rather, it was "the Desire of supporting her Mother, who was in great Distress, [that] induced her to put on Boy's Apparel, and enter for a Cabbin-Boy."

In the Dutch trial records surrounding her legal travails, Maria von Antwerpen (the grenadier of the first report above) explained her decision to dress as a man and to marry another woman as due, in part, to a change in her sex that occurred when she was an adolescent and one day perceived that "something like a shaft shot out of her body whenever nature demanded the discharge of seed."[22] In an important sense, eighteenth-century descriptions of passing women typified the sexual mutability of these individuals according to a scheme of sexual difference in which this mutability could be fixed (both stabilized and normalized) by removing the external signs of disguise to reveal one of two anatomical types, male or female. Susan Lanser, in particular, has argued that, as explanations of sapphic identity keyed to tribadic anatomy declined over the eighteenth century, increased pressure was placed on sexual disguise, even as it guaranteed a bipolar notion of sexual difference, to function as one of a number of external masculine markers of a sapphic orientation in sexual desire.[23]

In line with Lanser's argument, newspaper reports that make use of sexual disguise to regularize sexual mutability appear throughout the period, beginning early in the century. Consider, for example, a pair of reports in *The Daily Advertiser* on a Parisian attorney's daughter: in the first report we learn that this woman, although her

> [S]ex was never question'd to the Age of 16, has since chang'd her Sex; and having thereupon made Application to the Parliament to be confirm'd in the Privileges of Manhood. The Courts, after due Examination, [ordered] that she shall take Place in the Inheritance of her Father's Estates accordingly. But to this last Article of the Sentence her *Younger* Brother has enter'd an Appeal, alledging [*sic*], that he is still the *Elder* Son. (24 August 1734)

This report structures its account both as the description of an extraordinary event and as an opportunity for a jest. The second report of the case shifts gears, however, when it reveals that "The Metamorphosis of a young Lady into a Man . . . has been found to be a Cheat." A suspicious uncle arranges, after the woman refuses to undergo a second examination, for

> several Men to hold her, [whereupon] they found she was still of the same Sex she was born, and had made use of certain surprising Artifices to appear otherwise. (9 September 1734)

The second report, by shifting from a jesting narrative of involuntary sexual change to a censorious narrative of deceitful sexual disguise, effectively criminalizes the woman's behaviour and imposes on her a binary typology of sexual anatomy. Although there is no overt reference to same-sex desire in either account, the second report succeeds in containing the sexual mutability of the attorney's daughter in part by evoking the anatomical ruses of the female husband.

Yet, contra Lanser, press reports of sexual disguise could also, depending on how they were plotted, undermine the sexual typologies they implicitly asserted. In the case of women who married other women, for example, it was the use of some sort of sexual "artifice" (such as a dildo), in addition to male garb, that was increasingly invoked, after mid-century, as crucial to a successful marital liaison. Consider the following report from *The Daily Advertiser* of a cross-dressing French woman who was "whipped, branded and banished" for marrying another woman:

> The Marriage of these two Girls has subsisted three Years. The Fear of Ridicule, it seems, made the deceived one keep a profound Silence. How it came to be discovered at last, is not known. (31 December 1764)

Although there is no direct reference to the use of a dildo in this report, the notion that the wife was "deceived" serves to define the liaison as one based, at least initially, on some sort of roguish sexual impersonation beyond that of cross-dressing alone. But in this instance it is the understanding of sexual mutability as impersonation, rather than transformation or intersexuality, that is overturned in a follow-up report:

> *Paris, Dec.* 16. The Girl who married another at Lyons last Year, and of whom we spoke on a former Occasion, is an Hermaphrodite. She would not have determined, it is said, to have taken upon her the Character of a Man, but that her Confessor had assured her, that of a Woman would not suit her so well. (28 January 1765)

Rather than having been deceived on purpose by a male impersonator, the "Girl" turns out to have married a hermaphrodite; that is, an intersexual individual. Taken together these two reports serve to remind us that the interpretation of sexual mutability as anatomical intersexuality remained a viable understanding in popular-print forms well after mid-century.

One of the reasons, I think, that stories of sexual mutability remained current, even after mid-century, is that throughout the period sexual impersonation was assumed to be able to go beyond the representation of sexual "character" alone to affect the sexual "person" as well, even when out-

and-out sex changes did not occur. As a pamphlet account of a passing woman who married another woman in 1699 puts it:

> nothing being wanting [for her] to immitate [*sic*] her contrary Sex but the Night-Performances, [she] behav[ed] herself in all Points, (except that) as like a Natural Man, as could possibly be imagined . . . .[24]

As I have argued elsewhere, the idea that the male sexed body could be successfully impersonated (not merely covered up) was a constant theme in accounts of so-called sexual disguise.[25] The decline of the tribade that so many historians of sexuality have identified over the eighteenth century did not therefore coincide with an end to appeals to intersexuality *tout court*. Indeed, sexual mutability continued to be explained by reference to intersexuality well into the early nineteenth century.[26] Rather, it was one feature of sexual embodiment in particular, the imitation of the male sexual body, that increasingly became the locus of ridicule, fear, and fascination.

Returning to the role of generic mediations in press accounts of passing women, we have another window on their functioning when the same incident is reported differently in different publications. For example, in its report of a woman who attempted to murder her lover's wife with a cleaver while dressed in his clothes, *The Gentleman's Magazine* emphasizes the debauchery of the victim's husband:

> he was charged upon oath by another woman with having enticed the prisoner [the disguised assailant] to commit the fact, and dressing her in his own clothes for that purpose. It appeared also that he had a child by the prisoner, and had lived in criminal conversation with her two years.[27]

The Daily Advertiser, which makes no mention of the husband's adultery or extra-marital child, turns this squalid crime into an occasion for high melodrama:

> When the Justice ordered the Husband to be removed to Newgate, the Wife, who was so far recovered of her Wounds as to be able to attend, fell on her Knees, and begged that he might be dealt more gently with, and declared if he was sent to Newgate it would occasion her Death: She likewise expressed a Readiness to forgive them both, but especially her Husband. (13 July 1752)

The differing selection of facts in these two accounts turns one into a sordid tale of criminal love and the other into a sentimental story of wifely forbearance. But there is no need to see the two reports as based on irreconcilable, or even differing, sources of information. The primary difference lies in the generic shaping of that information.

Even when there is no direct revelation or retraction of the use of sexual disguise (as in the reports of sexual mutability discussed above), the generic influences on press reports of passing women can be seen with special clarity when an incident is covered on more than one occasion in the same newspaper. Consider the following excerpt from the account of the discovery of Hannah Snell in *The Daily Advertiser*:

> It seems her Sweetheart being impressed into the Marine Service, she put on Men's Cloaths, and entered in the same Regiment, went to the East-Indies in the same Ship with him, and was his Mesmate [*sic*] while he lived (he dying in the Voyage) and was as Servant to one of the Lieutenants. (25 June 1750)[28]

In this instance, Snell is presented as both a self-motivated romantic heroine and as an individual seemingly under male protection, in line with the female warrior ballads' topos of romantic fidelity. Here we seem to have an example of how newspaper reports could serve as a popular-print conduit for elements from (largely) oral forms.[29] Furthermore, the dominant ballad stereotype of the woman warrior as a devoted wife or lover allowed plebeian passing women to represent themselves, or to be represented by others, within acceptable paternalistic codes of feminine devotion and deference.

Intriguingly, however, three days after its first report, *The Daily Advertiser* changed tack in its coverage of Snell, jettisoning romantic myth for a rather different understanding of her newsworthiness:

> What is remarkable in this Heroine, is, that at the Battle of Pondicherry she received twelve Wounds, six in her Right Leg, five in her Left, and the other in her Groin, from the last of which she extracted the Ball, and herself performed the Cure, in order to prevent her Sex being discovered. (28 June 1750)

In this report it is Snell's extraordinary service, not love, that is deemed "remarkable," as well as her determination and physical courage in sustaining her disguise. Snell's Chelsea Hospital outpension entry verifies this dedication by recording that she was indeed "wounded at Pondicherry in the thigh & both Leggs."[30] In this instance the press report serves as a vehicle for the circulation of information from Snell's pension claim, and it is her character as an

Amazon, or at least as an industrious subordinate, that is played up, so that her service at war can be justified, once again within acceptable codes, as the proper behaviour of a plebeian subordinate.

Based on the reports that I have analysed above, we can make a few observations. First, newspaper accounts of passing women, whether or not they made use of accurate information, routinely assimilated the details of events to stereotyped generic schemes and topoi. Even when a broadly sensational or novel event is being recounted, its precise force and meaning depends to a large degree on the rhetorical decisions of the reporter. A passing woman who marries another woman is always sensational, but the emphasis of specific reports may fall on such disparate topoi as the comedic, the criminal, and the dutiful. For example, although press reports of the female husband Mary Hamilton accurately allude to her use of a dildo to deceive her wife, they also give her a plethora of wives (for which there is no independent evidence), thereby falling back on the rhetoric of the "counterfeit bridegroom" as a confidence artist.[31] In contrast, women warriors, as we have seen, are nearly always presented in laudable terms, but reporters still had to decide if their meritorious service was romantic, industrious, or heroic at root.

Secondly, if press reports of passing women are subject to a variety of generic influences, this flexibility underscores not only the shaping power of such accounts in the presentation of events, but the diversity of the schemes, topoi, and tropes that editors and newsgatherers were able to draw upon. Taken as a whole over many years, we may view a newspaper like *The Daily Advertiser* as functioning as an open form, much like the novel: a form that welcomes the rhetorical possibilities of a range of genres, modes, and styles embodied in a variety of print, manuscript, and oral media. This openness to a variety of genres clearly served the commercial necessities of the newspaper form, allowing for the maximum generation of copy, on the one hand, and the largest embrace of readerly tastes, on the other.[32]

Lastly, if the newspaper as a form is open to a range of rhetorical influences in its coverage of recurring categories of events, we might expect to find specific genres becoming attached with some frequency to specific types of actions (recognizing, too, that a genre regularly attached to an action in some degree functions to create that action's "type"). And indeed, as we have seen, criminal and indecorous uses of disguise tend to be treated in ways that borrow presentational and thematic elements from such indecorous genres as criminal biography, trial reportage, jestbooks, and the picaresque, whereas virtuous and industrious uses of disguise are treated in ways that draw on such relatively respectable genres as ballad romances, sentimental fiction, and moral tales.

In contrast to the eighteenth-century serials that are my primary object here, the oral, MS, and print forms that have already been systematically examined by scholars for their treatment of passing women are comparatively uniform or closed ones. Dianne Dugaw's work on the motif of the female warrior in the Anglo-American popular ballad between 1650 and 1850, the most important contribution so far to the study of the discursive parameters of the passing woman, is emblematic in this regard. Dugaw traces the rise, popularity, and decline of the woman warrior across hundreds of ballads, and concludes that the motif of the passing woman who follows her lover to war displays a cultural "model" of heroic femininity that calls stable gender oppositions into question.[33] According to Dugaw, the female warrior ballads construct this model in part through "their use of traditional epic and romance structures" (8), especially the sort of "recognition scenes and devices that we find in narratives of male heroes who return from the wars in disguise" (9). If the female warrior ballad draws on a "disguised-returned-lover pattern" from the epic, Dugaw, however, argues that the female warrior ballad is more than a variant of this pattern because the need of the ballad heroine to disguise her sex means that "issues of identity and of gender permeate the narrative from start to finish. This is not so in the *Odyssey*, the romance of *King Horn*, or the ballad of *Willie and Mary*" (9). The result is the crystallization of "a predictable shape," based on an "underlying story pattern" (91) encompassing a set sequence of narrative topoi.[34]

Dugaw's systematic analysis of the female warrior motif has an interesting historical implication since it allows her to trace a decline in the prevalence of the pattern, and of its ideological commitment to gender flexibility, towards the end of the eighteenth century. Dugaw ascribes this decline to the pressure of new definitions of masculinity and femininity, and several important studies that treat passing women in specific genres or documentary contexts, with varying degrees of systematicity, have lent support to Dugaw's argument, including Julie Wheelwright's reception-study of the memoirs of the female warrior Christian Davies, Rudolf Dekker and Lotte van de Pol's examination of passing women in the records of the Dutch East India company, and Dror Wahrman's treatment of eighteenth-century prologues and epilogues.[35] The argument of Dekker and Pol is perhaps the most crucial, since they make the influential claim that after 1800 the social phenomenon of the passing woman goes into a rapid decline, and is eventually extinguished by a combination of new sexual practices, military physicals, and other factors. Dekker and Pol's historical conclusions, based on a Dutch archive, have been transferred to eighteenth-century British society by both historians of sexuality (e.g., Tim Hitchcock) and by queer theorists (e.g., Susan Lanser).[36] So, too, has Dekker and Pol's larger assertion about the passing woman as a cultural phenomenon, where they make the suggestion that, as a social practice, "The disappearance of female cross-dressing [from the documentary record] ran in parallel with its disappearance from cultural expressions."[37] In sum, then, for the passing woman as a social actor, as well as for her cultural representation, existing systematic studies have broadly concluded that a gender- and sexuality-transgressive eighteenth century was succeeded by a gender- and sexuality-conforming nineteenth century.

We should keep in mind, of course, that Dugaw never aimed to do more than to trace a single motif out of many in the popular genre of the ballad. It would be interesting to know, for example, how further work on ballad treatments of other types of passing women, such as female husbands, disguised women workers, and cross-dressing practical jokers, would affect the historical dimensions of her argument. Yet it is also the case that there is no simple measure of completeness to apply to the recovery of ballad records, a fact which leaves some methodological questions regarding the possible systematicity of any study of ballads, no matter how extensive the recovery effort upon which it were to be based. In contrast, individual newspaper and periodical titles offer a straightforward measure for their completeness. As for the work of Dekker and Pol, the direct application of their conclusions to British contexts raises numerous questions regarding the relevance of their ideas outside of Holland. For example, unsystematic historical studies by Anna Clark and others have turned up numerous passing women in nineteenth-century Britain, and a recent study of passing women in the American civil war by DeAnne Blanton and Lauren Cook provides extensive evidence of how hundreds of women were able to circumvent the required medical examinations (doctors were persuaded or bribed to keep their secret) or simply did not have to undergo one because, in the urgent search for recruits under difficult wartime conditions, the policy was not always upheld.[38] As we will see, however, when tested against the open form of the press report, the now commonplace historical and critical assertion that the passing woman and her cultural representation is in decline in early nineteenth-century Britain cannot be sustained.

A systematic study of the historical chronicle and death notices and their successor sections in *The Gentleman's Magazine* for the one hundred years from the magazine's inception in 1731 until 1830 reveals records of 54 different cross-dressing individuals (counting the Chevalier D'Eon twice, as a woman in the 1770s and a man in the 1810s), including 20 male and 34 female. All but three or four have plebeian origins or status.[39] Of the female reports, nine are crime-related, nine are women warriors, six are female husbands, one each involves a practical joke, resisting a press gang, a pretended sex change, a political escape, and a crime victim, and five are primarily work-related, although occupational information appears in many of the other reports; indeed, entering military service was essentially an occupation for many passing women. The distribution of female reports is relatively uniform, apart from a peak in the 1770s: there are reports of three passing women per decade except for the 1740s (four), 1770s (six), 1780s (four), and 1810s (two). (See Table 1.2.) A similar pattern is evident in combined male and female reports, which run at four or five a decade, except for the 1740s (six) and the 1770s (12 individuals). Indeed, *The Gentleman's Magazine* records show absolutely no marked decline after either 1780 or 1800: there are 30 individuals (19 women) reported between 1731 and 1780, and 24 (15 women) between 1781 and 1830 (this contrasts starkly with Dekker and Pol's Dutch evidence, which lists 33 women between 1731 and 1780 and 10 women between 1781 and 1830).[40] Continuity, rather than discontinuity, is what these records reveal.

Undergirding the continuity of reports of passing women in *The Gentleman's Magazine* is its emphasis on class relations (and on class formations of gender and sexuality), rather than on gender or sexuality abstracted from class relations. Given that theft, like prostitution, was a common recourse for the destitute poor, and that many formerly customary, labour-related practices were criminalized over the eighteenth century, the distribution of reports in *The Gentleman's Magazine* reveals a clear work- and subsistence-based pattern of plebeian cross-dressing, rather than a leisure- and performance-based one. There is, moreover, a striking dialectic posited in these materials between reputable and disreputable activities: if we set aside the five idiosyncratic cases detailed above, of the 29 remaining cross-dressing women recorded over the 100 years, nine reports involve criminal disguise and six disreputable/criminal female husbands (a total of 15), compared with nine women warriors and five passing women workers (a total of 14).

Thus although accounts of passing women in *The Gentleman's Magazine* do highlight reports of successful gender impersonation, and some of its sexually transgressive qualities, when examined systematically we see that these accounts also stress paternalistic social expectations for plebeian and middling-rank individuals. When "*George Smith*" sailed out for colonial service in Virginia in 1744 and was discovered to be a girl, for example, *The Gentleman's Magazine* printed the letter of a fellow passenger who was quick to see her career through the lens, not of criminality, but of a meritorious and industrious subordination. This letter-writer records how Smith told a tale of being orphaned at age twelve and abandoned by the trustees of her father's estate:

Table 1.1

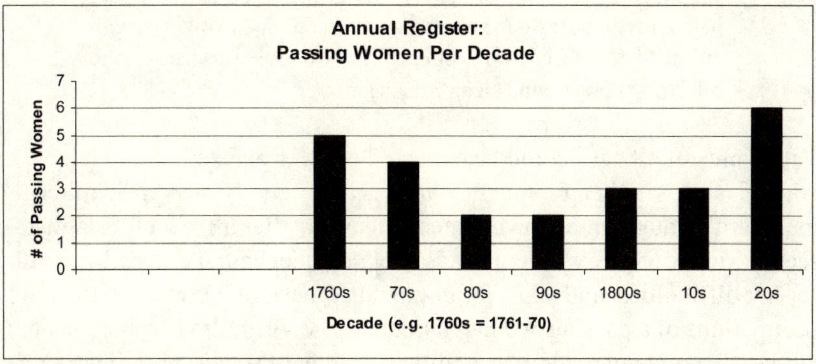

Table 1.2

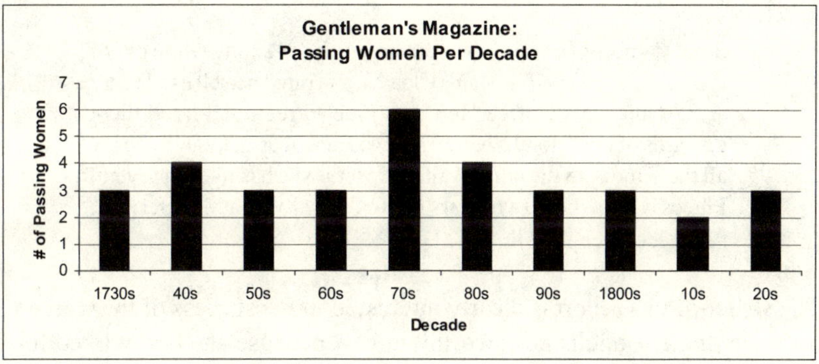

Table 1.3

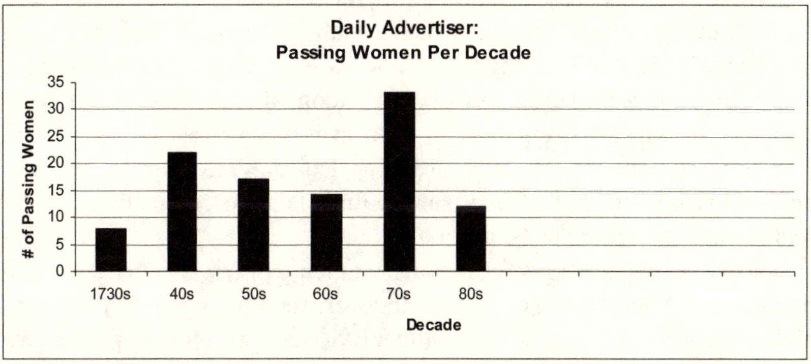

> Being friendless, and not getting Service, she soon spent all, and was forc'd to sell her Ear-Rings to buy Cloaths; which she chose should be Boys: Thus habited she liv'd three Quarters of a Year with a Taylor near *Bath*, and afterwards in *London* two Years, with one that lets out Coaches to hire, where her whole Business was to rub Horses Heels, and clean Coaches.[41]

Vagabonds of all ages could be expected to offer plausible fabrications, of course, and whether or not "*George Smith*" really was a disinherited merchant's daughter, as she claimed (this was, after all, a well-established scenario in the female warrior ballads), her defender here shows real sympathy for her difficulties, and takes for granted the merit of her work in the lowly occupations of a passing-woman labourer. The virtue at issue here, then, is neither that of gender nor of sexuality but rather of social subordination.[42]

Proper social subordination is the dominant idea through which many press reports of passing women were filtered. Consider the following account from *The Daily Advertiser*:

> Some Time ago a young Woman having been a long while out of Place, dress'd herself in Man's Cloaths, and hired herself as a Waiter at St. Dunstan's Coffee-House in Fleet-Street, and lived there upwards of two Months before she was discover'd, though she lay all the Time with the other Waiter. It seems she has lived in several Places within these two Years in the Capacity of a Man Servant. (20 December 1753)

The writer of this report is clearly interested in the success of the woman's disguise: the episode is newsworthy in part because she has worked for a variety of employers and shared a bed with a fellow servant without being discovered. But that is only one aspect of the report, which implicitly accepts that cross-dressing is a viable and even appropriate way for a poor woman to overcome the obstacles to female employment: "a long while out of Place," the account emphasizes that this woman finally gets "hired" only by putting on a "Man's Cloaths." Going into service was commonly viewed as a last resort for poor women seeking work in London; another was prostitution.[43] By using her wit and daring to adopt male disguise when she failed to secure service as a woman, the female waiter of St. Dunstan's avoided the shame of becoming a prostitute: that is, she successfully defended, rather than lost, her reputation as a virtuous plebeian woman.

The social expectations for passing-women workers that are evident in press reports appear more explicitly, and were therefore amplified for some eighteenth-century readers, in a number of longer print forms, particularly the memoirs of women warriors. For example, we can see the ideological tension that is entailed by these social expectations in the autobiography of Mary Lacy, a woman who went to sea in the navy and later apprenticed as a shipwright. Lacy presents her life working in male disguise as both industrious and disorderly. Perhaps uniquely, Lacy's work, *The History of the Female Shipwright* (1773), complements the statistical and other information we can cull from newspaper reports with an extended first-person account of the motivations and state of mind, as well as adventures, of an eighteenth-century passing woman worker. Compared with many short-form accounts of passing women, even industrious women workers like Elizabeth Ogden, whose life provided the occasion for a chapbook called *The Female Porter of Shoreditch* (1756), *The Female Shipwright* relies more on spiritual-autobiographical and sentimental modes than the conventions of popular comedy. Lacy's narrative does treat the romantic, lesbian, and disguise-related elements also found in the memoirs of other passing-women warriors such as Hannah Snell and Christian Davies; and indeed all three narratives clearly exhibit features of the "sapphic picaresque" as Lanser has defined it.[44] Significantly, though, Lacy's focus is on rendering the quotidian aspects of her working life, both as a naval servant and as a shipwright: keeping her secret, working hard, dealing with unexpected challenges. Lacy, who was to become a master shipwright and receive a military pension for her industrious service in male disguise, initially adopts male dress to escape the control of her parents and of a neighbour who employed her as a servant, as well as to avoid the shame of a failed love affair. Once in disguise, however, she struggled with the paternalistic social expectations surrounding a properly subordinate daughter/servant: her letters home, for example, frame her independence as a form of disobedience. Addressing her parents, Lacy initially signs herself "*Your undutiful Daughter*" and elsewhere she laments leaving them.[45] In the same way, she writes of being "insensible of the good treatment [she] met with" as a servant and of failing to apply herself "with proper care and industry" (6) before choosing to run away in male disguise. In these contexts, Lacy presents her decision to pass as a man in starkly negative terms, associating it with insubordination both at home and at work.

I have explored Lacy's account in some detail because it allows us to see how the genres through which the passing woman's experience was constructed could both uphold and transgress the parameters of paternalist control and heterosexual expectation. Passing as a man allowed a woman freedoms that could be either industrious (military service) or disorderly (same-sex marriage). In male disguise a woman might secure work or she might commit a theft. Of course, the actual behaviour of many plebeian passing women did not fall into neat divisions of husband versus warrior or worker versus criminal over their life history. Instead, these categories form part of the representation of acceptable versus unacceptable behaviour among passing plebeian workers and, in being imposed on the everyday lives of passing women (for example, through criminal proceedings), they also formed part of the regulation of their behaviour.[46] In terms of the present study, this conclusion suggests that the generic mediations of press reports served, *de facto*, an important regulatory role. Decisions had to be taken, from the point of view of social order, to categorize passing women, and cross-genre borrowings were one way in which to organize the raw information from which these reports were composed in a fashion that would be consistent with such decisions. It is doubly inadequate, then, to assume that the passing woman is necessarily transgressive: both as a social actor, and in terms of the categories of her representation, the passing-woman worker was as often an upholder of appropriate heterosexual gender behaviours for plebeian women as she was their underminer. Significantly, if counter-intuitively, this is also true of passing-women workers who married or cohabited with other women.

Of course, the category of the sapphic homo-adventurer, as characterized by Lanser, is a powerful rubric through which to understand the rhetorical underpinnings of the reports of some passing women: it reveals much about the press coverage of Mary Hamilton and of some of the counterfeit bridegrooms, for example, and it directs our attention as well to the hidden dimensions of other accounts, such as the sapphic exuberance entailed by the numerous courtships of other women in the memoirs of female warriors like Lacy. Yet it is also the case that many reports, even of female husbands, contain no such dimension, as we have seen with the report of the man cook. Indeed, in plebeian milieux in which male disguise was above all an approved avenue for labouring-class women to escape respectably from certain aspects of social paternalism, disguise could function to normalize both gender and sexual deviance. Thus James How, after the death of her wife, was able to establish her virtue as an industrious and chaste plebeian woman in part *because* of her use of sexual disguise, despite initially hostile actions from her dead wife's relations and the threat of blackmail from another party.[47]

In its broad outlines, the same dialectic of repute and disrepute that is evident in *The Gentleman's Magazine* (and is elaborated in Lacy's narrative) also appears in the records of passing women in *The Daily Advertiser*. For the sixty-six years from the inception of this newspaper in 1731 until its dissolution in 1796, I have been able to gather reports on 176 individuals (64 men and 112 women), compared with 39 individuals (13 men and 26 women) for the same period in *The Gentlemen's Magazine*. Of the female reports in *The Daily Advertiser*, 41 are crime related, 35 are women warriors, nine are female husbands, nine are miscellaneous, and 18 are primarily work-related, for a total (after setting aside the miscellaneous cases) of 50 disreputable to 53 reputable passing women (compared to 13 disreputable to 10 reputable passing women, excluding three miscellaneous cases, in *The Gentleman's Magazine* for this period). (See Table 2.) Once again, too, the distribution of female reports is relatively uniform apart from a peak in the 1770s: there are roughly 10 to 20 reports of passing women per decade (ranging from a low of eight to a high of 22) except for the 1770s when there are reports on 33 individual passing women (see Table 1.3). A similar pattern is evident in combined male and female reports, which run at between roughly 20 to 30 per decade (ranging from a low of 18 to a high of 30), again apart from the 1770s, when there are a total of 41 reports. Once again, it is continuity, rather than discontinuity, that these records reveal.

Table 2

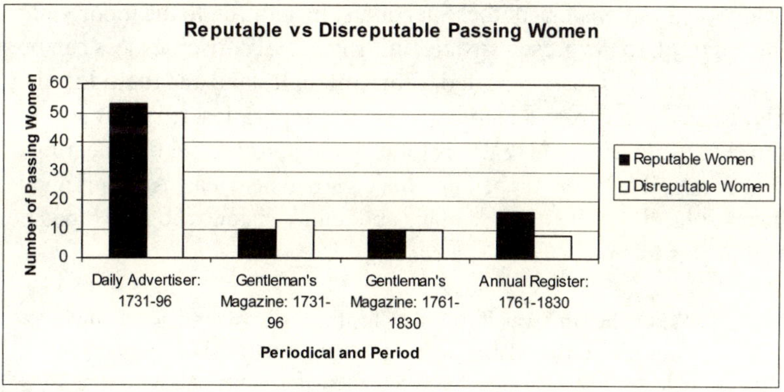

As a daily paper addressed in part to plebeian and urban commercial audiences, it is easy to see why *The Daily Advertiser* presents a significantly larger number of reports on individuals and somewhat more coverage of criminal activity than *The Gentleman's Magazine*. A general emphasis on property crime, incidentally, seems to be the reason for the slightly larger proportion of male cross-dressers reported here; there are only a few reports of the cross-dressing male homosexuals sometimes known as mollies.[48] Yet if reports in *The Daily Advertiser* often embody paternalistic codes, they also sometimes reveal a popular, less magistrate-derived, sensibility, as with the report on the married man cook and housekeeper, first examined above, which evokes the sexual humour of the jestbook or chapbook:

> Some Difference happening between them, the House-keeper declar'd the Cook was no Man, but a Woman, and had Reasons to believe that her said pretended Husband was with Child. . . . We are likewise inform'd, that the House-keeper is since marry'd to a young Lad of Eighteen. (27 September 1735)

I have elsewhere examined the development of the representation of cross-dressing working-class women who married other women, which shifted over the course of the eighteenth century from the figure of a counterfeit bridegroom to a female husband; that is, from the figure of an economic to a sexual criminal.[49] But in this story of a cook and a housekeeper there is no crime, whether sexual or economic, only the comic incongruities of a pregnant husband and an aged bride.

It is in *The Daily Advertiser* that we also see, due perhaps to the volume of reports of passing men and women, some overt reflection on the generic and categorical dimensions of these accounts. In addition to the report quoted as the epigraph to the present article, this rhetorical consciousness can be seen in another curious case reported from Cork in Ireland and reproduced in *The Daily Advertiser* from a Dublin paper. The report describes a man's plan to run away with a woman that was foiled by her brother, who on hearing of the plot arranged to be kidnapped in female garb in her stead. After his abduction he was placed for the night with his abductor's sister, whom he raped before making his escape:

> When the Bird was flown the Cheat was discovered, to the great Mortification and Disappointment of the intended Bridegroom, on whose Sister Marks of Pregnancy soon after appeared. Whereupon Bills of Indictments for a Rape were found against the Hero of the Farce, for which he stood his Trial, and was honourably acquitted. (13 April 1769)

After these direct references to farce and the mock-heroic, the report concludes with the following parenthetical statement:

> The above Extract is taken from the Dublin Gazette, and is inserted as a Specimen of the absurd Stories which have frequently of late been intruded on the Publick.

Of course, *The Daily Advertiser* effectively continued the intrusion by reproducing the paragraph, which in any event is fetched only a little further than many other reports in this newspaper.[50] But by calling attention to its putative absurdity as a story, the author of this comment reveals a sense of the limits, as well as uses, of cross-genre borrowings in reports of sexual disguise.

In contrast to the rhetorical diversity and self-consciousness exhibited in *The Daily Advertiser*, reports in the "Chronicle" section of *The Annual Register* (founded in 1758) indicate something of a reification of passing-women typologies, emphasizing both sexual criminality and military heroism. This reification certainly makes sense, given the emphasis in *The Annual Register* on historical representativeness. Even so, the dialectic of repute and disrepute that I have been delineating also structures the records of passing women in this annual publication. In the seventy years from 1761 to 1830, I have been able to gather reports on 35 individuals (10 men and 25 women) in *The Annual Register*, compared with 40 individuals (16 men and 24 women) for the same period in *The Gentlemen's Magazine*. Of the female reports in *The Annual Register*, apart from one miscellaneous case, four are crime-related, 10 are women warriors, four are female husbands, and six are primarily work-related, for a total of eight disreputable to 16 reputable passing women (compared to 10 disreputable to 10 reputable, exclusive of four idiosyncratic cases, in *The Gentleman's Magazine* for this period). (See Table 2.) Once again, the distribution of female reports is relatively uniform apart from a couple of moderate peaks: there are two to four reports of passing women per decade except for the 1760s (five) and the 1820s (six). (See Table 1.1.) A similar pattern is evident in combined male and female reports, which run at between five and seven per decade, except for a low of two per decade in the 1790s and the 1800s.

There are some distinctive trends for these years in *The Annual Register*, however, such as a reduction in the coverage of quotidian passing-women criminals (for example, *The Gentleman's Magazine* reports on six criminals, as well as four miscellaneous cases, for this period).[51] Much more significant, perhaps, is that the dialectic between reputable and disreputable passing women becomes increasingly polarized as we move up from daily through monthly to yearly coverage. By the time we reach *The Annual Register*, what gains greater prominence, and therefore becomes increasingly memorable and "typical" about passing women, is their exemplification of outrageous sexuality. For the sixty-six years of *The Daily Advertiser* between 1731 and 1796, the proportion of female husbands to other passing-women criminals is nine to 41, or roughly one to four, whereas the ratio is five to eight for *The Gentleman's Magazine* for the same period. Now, significantly, this ratio changes little in *The Gentleman's Magazine* from the period between 1731 and 1796 to the period between 1761 and 1830. In the latter period, it is four to six, or exactly two female husbands to three passing-women criminals. But for the period between 1761 and 1830 in *The Annual Register*, the ratio is four female husbands to four passing-women criminals. In short, in moving from a daily to a yearly periodical, we go from about one report of a female husband for every four passing-women criminal reports, to one report of a female husband for each passing-woman criminal report. (See Table 3.) To put it another way, out of a total of 112 passing women in *The Daily Advertiser* over a period of nearly 70 years, nine are female husbands; whereas out of a total of 25 passing women in *The Annual Register* over 70 years, four are female husbands. We shift, then, from 8% female husbands in the daily paper to over 16% female husbands in the yearly periodical (see Table 4.1). Non-sexual criminals, for example, hardly disappear from the annual records, but they are pushed firmly towards the margins. The polarization revealed by this quantitative data indicates a movement from the representation of passing-women workers in the context of paternalistic regulation to their representation in a more narrowly gender-based, and gender-bending, framework. In short, it is due to discursive differences tied to the periodicity of different press forms, rather than any historical change, that the representation of plebeian women's cross-dressing becomes increasingly seen to be about challenging the norms of sexuality and gender, and consequently viewed as transgressive.

Table 3

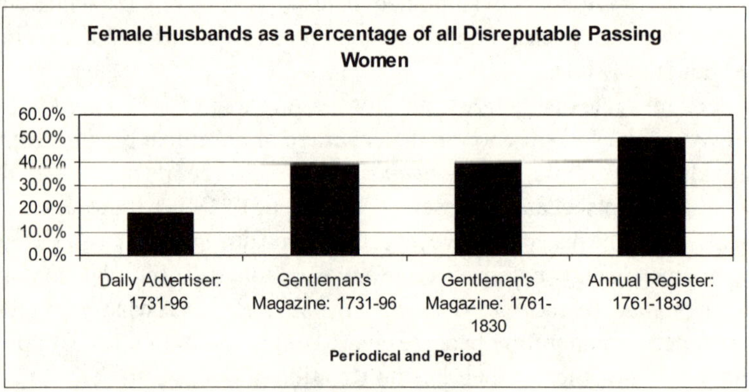

It is here, in this polarization, that we can identify the original rationale for emphasizing the passing woman *tout court* as an exceptional figure, whether heroic or transgressive, in the eighteenth century (see Table 4.2). When Mary Wollstonecraft lists examples of exceptional women in *A Vindication of the Rights of Woman*, she includes the Chevalier D'Eon (who was thought to be a woman).[52] The figure of female husbands like Mary Hamilton gained a permanent station in the medical and legal literature of the eighteenth century. But the use of male disguise simply to work, or to enlist to go to war for unromantic or unheroic reasons, tends to drop out of the record. Thus in sixty-six years of *The Daily Advertiser* there are reports of 35 women warriors; whereas in seventy years of *The Annual Register* there are 10 reports. As the present systematic study of patterns in the periodical coverage of passing women shows, the emphasis placed by present-day scholars on the exceptional bravery or disreputable sexuality of these women is not so much anachronistic as it is partial, derived from specific print forms, on the one hand, and tied to the publication frequency of different periodicals, on the other. As a result, a variation in the memorialization of passing women was created by those publications that saw themselves as representative reference works (rather than complete inventories) for public events. For scholarly recuperations of passing women it is especially significant that this representative pattern of memorialization spread beyond press publications to other historically-oriented forms, so that, for example, the collections of odd information that appear in the early nineteenth century ended up following a similar tack to *The Annual Register* in their coverage of passing women.[53]

Table 4.1

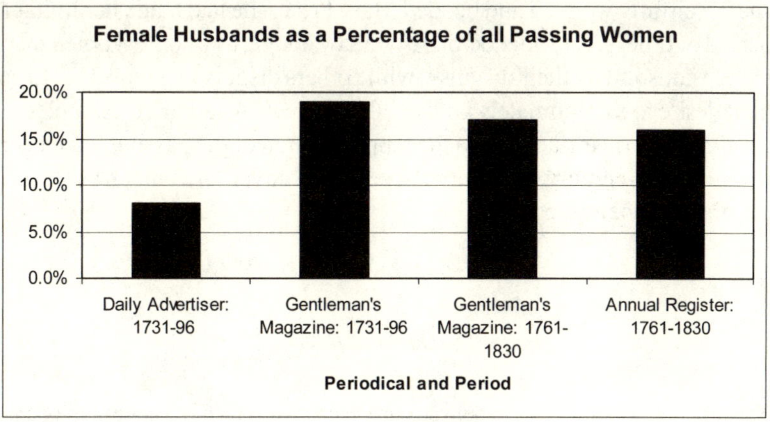

Table 4.2

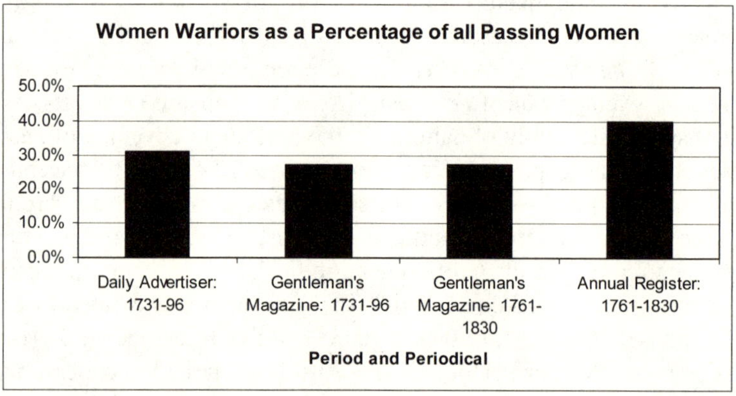

As we have seen, there is implicit evidence in press reports that passing women's lives were far more fluid than my reliance here, following eighteenth-century perspectives, on specific types of passing women (such as husbands, warriors, criminals, and workers) suggests. Numerous examples can be found of female husbands who served in the military, women warriors who committed crimes in disguise, passing workers who enlisted or married, and criminals who served bravely. The transcripts of Mary Hamilton's trial show that, before she deceitfully wedded and bedded Mary Price, she had made her living for a period of time as a quack doctor. As we saw above, too, some women married to help consolidate their disguise, while others disguised themselves to cover their desire to live intimately with another woman. As all these examples make explicit, generic influences on the representation of the passing woman, even in eighteenth-century press reports, served to cover up as much as to provide coverage of their lives.

NOTES

This article expands on a paper delivered in October 2003 to the meeting of the Canadian Society for Eighteenth-Century Studies in Vancouver. I would like to thank the participants in the session in which I spoke and the organizers of the conference, especially Nicholas Hudson and Miranda Burgess. Research for this study was made possible in part by the SSHRC Institutional Grant at the University of Waterloo and, more recently, a SSHRC Standard Research Grant. I would also like to thank the graduate student assistants who have helped me to read through the periodicals that I analyse here, especially Shannon Hartling, Bridget Hinnegan, Julia Mamolo, and Y-Dang Troeung.

1. For an examination of these records, see Fraser Easton, "Gender's Two Bodies: Women Warriors, Female Husbands, and Plebeian Life," *Past and Present* 180 (August 2003): 144–45.

2. Anon., *The Life and Adventures of Mrs. Christian Davies, the British Amazon, Commonly Called Mother Ross*, 2nd ed., 2 parts and appendix (London, 1741); Anon., *The Female Soldier; or, The Surprising Life and Adventures of Hannah Snell* (London, 1750); and Mary [Lacy] Slade, *The History of the Female Shipwright* (London, 1773). On D'Eon, see Gary Kates, *Monsieur D'Eon is a Woman: A Tale of Political Intrigue and Sexual Masquerade* (New York: Basic Books, 1995); on the ballads, see Dianne Dugaw, *Warrior Women and Popular Balladry, 1650–1850* (Cambridge: Cambridge University Press, 1989).

3. Terry Castle, "Matters Not Fit to be Mentioned: Fielding's *The Female Husband*," *ELH* 49 (1982): 602–22. See also, for example, Kristina Straub, *Sexual Suspects: Eighteenth-Century Players and Sexual Ideology* (Princeton: Princeton University Press, 1992), Judith Halberstam, *Female Masculinity* (Durham: Duke University Press, 1998), and Susan S. Lanser, "Sapphic Picaresque, Sexual Difference, and the Challenges of Homo-Adventuring," *Textual Practice* 15 (2001): 251–68.

4. David Cressy, "Cross-Dressing in the Birth Room: Gender Trouble and Cultural Boundaries," ch. 7 of *Travesties and Transgressions in Tudor and Stuart England: Tales of Discord and Dissension* (Oxford: Oxford University Press, 2000).

5. T. O. McLaughlin, "The *Annual Register* 1785–93: New Evidence," *The Library* 12 (1990): 223.

6. Morris Golden, "Introduction," in Alvin Sullivan, ed., *British Literary Magazines: The Augustan Age and the Age of Johnson, 1698–1788* (Westport, CN: Greenwood, 1983), xvii.

7. Cornelius P. Darcy, "The Gentleman's Magazine," in Sullivan, ed., *British Literary Magazines*, 138. For the extensive provincial distribution network organized by Edward Cave, the first editor and publisher of *The Gentleman's Magazine*, see C. Lennart Carlson, *The First Magazine: A History of The Gentleman's Magazine* (Providence, RI: Brown University Press, 1938), 60.

8. Carlson, *The First Magazine*, 57. A letter published in *The Gentleman's Magazine* for April 1732 records how "It serves me, and to my knowledge several others, for what your title truly expresses it, that is, a Magazine or Repository of everything worth remarking, and for that Reason will be many Years hence an authentick Collection for Historians to refer to . . . ." (cited in Carlson, *The First Magazine*, 59).

9. Michael Harris, *London Newspapers in the Age of Walpole: A Study of the Origins of the Modern English Press* (London and Toronto: Associated University Presses, 1987), 190; Hannah Barker, *Newspapers, Politics, and English Society, 1695–1855* (Harlow, England: Longman, 2000), 32.

10. This is in addition to the male and female servants of merchant and gentry families who might have had access to other kinds of serial publications, including *The Annual Register* and *The Gentleman's Magazine*.

11. Barker, *Newspapers, Politics, and English Society*, 46–53. Significantly, not all shared reading entailed access for individuals of modest means. Harris documents how the well-to-do merchant Stephen Monteage routinely read *The Daily Advertiser* but was not a regular buyer of it (*London Newspapers in the Age of Walpole*, 191).

12. It is probable that most passing women were indeed drawn from plebeian ranks; but it should be noted that there were limits on the nature and extent of the coverage that eighteenth-century newspapers could give to the foibles of the well-to-do, and, as a result, domestic news often focused on plebeian activities: see G. A. Cranfield, *The Development of the Provincial Newspaper, 1700–1760* (Oxford: Clarendon Press, 1962), 69–71.

13. Rudolf M. Dekker and Lotte C. van de Pol, *The Tradition of Female Transvestism in Early Modern Europe*, trans. Judy Marcure and Lotte C. van de Pol (London: Macmillan, 1989).

14. Susan S. Lanser, "'Queer to Queer': The Sapphic Body as Transgressive Text," in Katharine Kittredge, ed., *Lewd and Notorious: Female Transgression in the Eighteenth Century* (Ann Arbor: University of Michigan Press, 2003), 33–4.

15. It must be stressed that, in press forms, this phenomenon is more or less confined to yearly memorializations, even in the early nineteenth century. The daily and monthly periodicals that I have examined continue to focus much more on passing women as either good or bad subordinates.

16. Suzanne J. Stark, *Female Tars: Women Aboard Ship in the Age of Sail* (Annapolis: Naval Institute Press, 1996), 101.

17. See Simon Dickie, "Hilarity and Pitilessness in the Mid-Eighteenth Century: English Jestbook Humor," *Eighteenth-Century Studies* 37 (2003–04): 1–22.

18. Most often, of course, these corrections involved the coverage of the well-to-do: when it was reported in *The Daily Advertiser*, for example, that Admiral Byng dressed in women's clothes to escape from confinement, the account was quickly corrected (1 and 3 September 1756). Even reports of ordinary passing women might, however, be revised in light of what were understood to be new facts: see, for example, *The Daily Advertiser* for 2 and 9 December 1735.

19. The work of Michel Foucault is perhaps foundational in this respect, but for more recent examples see Natalie Zemon Davis, *Fiction in the Archives: Pardon Tales and Their Tellers in Sixteenth-Century France* (Princeton: Princeton University Press, 1987) and Garthine Walker, *Crime, Gender, and Social Order in Early Modern England* (Cambridge: Cambridge University Press, 2003).

20. The "pretended Husband" is Maria van Antwerpen; see Dekker and van de Pol, *The Tradition of Female Transvestism in Early Modern Europe*, 24 and *passim*.

21. See, for example, Anon., "'The Female Cabin-Boy' (c.1730)," in Terry Castle, ed., *The Literature of Lesbianism* (New York: Columbia University Press, 2003), 248–49.

22. Cited in Dekker and van de Pol, *The Tradition of Female Transvestism in Early Modern Europe*, 67.

23. Lanser, "'Queer to Queer,'" 34.

24. *The Uufortunate* [*sic*] *Maid Cheated* (London, 1699), 4.

25. I provide evidence for an eighteenth-century distinction between a sexed and a sexual body in "Gender's Two Bodies," 135 and *passim*.

26. Thus James Allen's fellow workmen thought him to be "of that rare and peculiar class of human beings who have no positive claim to either sex," and when, after Allen suffers a fainting fit that exposes his chest, a neighbour comments on "'what a beautiful bosom your husband has,'" Allen's wife "did not think much about it, having long considered her husband of the doubtful class before alluded to . . . ." (Anon, *An Authentic Narrative of the Extraordinary Career of James Allen, the Female Husband* [London, 1829], 20, 26).

27. *The Gentleman's Magazine* (1752): 286.

28. Of course, some women may have really followed a lover or husband; when Ann Holt's disguise "was discovered by the young man her favourite," "the commanding officer, ordered them to be married" (*The London Chronicle*, 21–3 July 1763, 79). Dekker and van de Pol provide some Dutch examples in *The Tradition of Female Transvestism*, 27–30. As already noted, however, Stark casts doubt on the prevalence of this motive in the British context, since "a woman could usually go to sea with her lover in her own right," *Female Tars*, 101.

29. On print-oral interfaces in popular culture, see, for example, Cathy Lynn Preston and Michael J. Preston, eds., *The Other Print Tradition: Essays on Chapbooks, Broadsides, and Related Ephemera* (New York: Garland, 1995).

30. Entry for 21 November 1750 in "Chelsea Hospital Admission Book": PRO, WO 116/4, fo. 93.

31. See the account of Hamilton in *The Daily Advertiser* for 7 November 1746, which accurately reports the gist of Mary Price's deposition by describing Price's claim that she "thought the Prisoner a Man, owing to the prisoner's using certain vile and deceitful Practices, not fit to be mention'd," but which also relays the fanciful assertion that Price was Hamilton's fourteenth wife. For the trial transcripts, see Sheridan Baker, "Henry Fielding's *The Female Husband*: Fact and Fiction," *PMLA* 74 (1959): 219–20.

32. For information on the general contents of eighteenth-century newspapers, and their emphasis in domestic news on violence and sex, see Cranfield, *The Development of the Provincial Newspaper*, ch. 4.

33. Dugaw, *Warrior Women and Popular Balladry*, 41. Further references to this work will be given parenthetically in the text.

34. These topoi are: courtship and separation; proposal of disguise; trials of the disguised woman; trials of the lover and parents; and resolution (usually happy). See Dugaw, *Warrior Women and Popular Balladry*, 92–93.

35. See Julie Wheelwright, "'Amazons and Military Maids:' An Examination of Female Military Heroines in British Literature and the Changing Construction of Gender," *Women's Studies International Forum* 10 (1987): 489–502; Dekker and van de Pol, *The Tradition of Female Transvestism*; and Dror Wahrman, "*Percy*'s Prologue: From Gender Play to Gender Panic in Eighteenth-Century England," *Past and Present* 159 (1998): 113–60.

36. Tim Hitchcock, "Redefining Sex in Eighteenth-Century England," in Kim M. Phillips and Barry Reay, eds., *Sexualities in History* (New York: Routledge, 2002), 196; and Lanser, "'Queer to Queer,'" 40–41.

37. Dekker and van de Pol, *The Tradition of Female Transvestism*, 103.

38. Deanne Blanton and Lauren M. Cook, *They Fought Like Demons: Women Soldiers in the Civil War* (New York: Vintage, 2003), 27–29. For nineteenth-century British passing women, see for example Anna Kirsten Clark, "Womanhood and Manhood in the Transition from Plebeian to Working-Class Culture: London, 1780–1845" (Rutgers University Ph.D. thesis, 1987) and Camilla Townsend, "'I am the Woman for Spirit': A Working Woman's Gender Transgression in Victorian London," *Victorian Studies* 36 (1992–3): 293–314.

39. I start with *The Gentleman's Magazine* because of its cultural centrality in the eighteenth century and because of its publication span, which takes in both the middle and later eighteenth century and the early nineteenth century. I will consider *The Daily Advertiser* and *The Annual Register* below.

40. Dekker and van de Pol, *The Tradition of Female Transvestism*, 109–11.

41. *The Gentleman's Magazine* (1744): 336.

42. We see the same thing at the other end of the period as well: when she died in 1823, for example, Mary Wells, who dressed partly in men's clothes for her work, was described as "very industrious" (*The Gentleman's Magazine* (1823) 2: 572).

43. Deborah Valenze, *The First Industrial Woman* (New York: Oxford University Press, 1995), 24. Service was a last resort because the majority of women's positions were dirty, laborious, and lacked the prestige of upper service (only the housekeeper, lady's maid, and perhaps cook were upper servants); also, male servants were better paid (Valenze, 161–62).

44. See Lanser, "Sapphic Picaresque," 255–58.

45. Mary Lacy, *The Female Shipwright*, 34. Subsequent references to this work will appear parenthetically in the text.

46. As I have argued elsewhere: see Easton, "Gender's Two Bodies," 151.

47. See the reports on James How/Mary East in *The Gentleman's Magazine* (1766): 359–60; *The London Evening-Post* (12–15 July 1766); and *The Public Advertiser* (18 July 1766).

48. See, for example, Randolph Trumbach, "Sodomitical Subcultures, Sodomitical Roles, and the Gender Revolution in the Eighteenth Century: The Recent Historiography," *Eighteenth-Century Life* 9 (n.s.) no. 3 (May 1985):109–21, Rictor Norton, *Mother Clap's Molly House:The Gay Subculture in England, 1700–1830* (London: GMP Publishers, 1992), and Fraser Easton, "Christopher Smart's Cross-Dressing: Mimicry, Depropriation, and *Jubilate Agno*" *Genre* 31 (1998), esp. 213–22.

49. Easton, "Gender's Two Bodies," 149–57.

50. For example, *The Daily Advertiser* for 25 January 1783 reprints an item from an American newspaper claiming that "Our great and excellent General Washington is actually discovered to be of the Female Sex." This startling revelation supposedly derives from the death-bed confession of Martha, his/her wife: "What is extraordinary, the Lady knew this Circumstance previous to the Ceremony of Marriage, and both agreed to live together from Motives of the most refined Friendship."

51. Excluding one miscellaneous case, there are 10 instances of quotidian passing women (= criminals + workers) to 14 instances of exceptional passing women (= warriors + husbands) in *The Annual Register* from 1761 to 1830, compared with 59 quotidian

to 44 exceptional instances in *The Daily Advertiser* from 1731 to 1790 (excluding nine miscellaneous cases), and 14 quotidian to 15 exceptional instances in *The Gentleman's Magazine* from 1731–1830 (excluding five miscellaneous cases).

52. Mary Wollstonecraft, *Political Writings*, ed. Janet Todd (Oxford: Oxford University Press, 1994), 149.

53. For example, across six volumes R. S. Kirby presents one female husband, one female coffee-house habituee, and five female soldiers (four of whom are outstanding heroes). See R. S. Kirby, *Kirby's Wonderful and Scientific* [later, *Eccentric*] *Museum*, 6 vols. (London, 1803–20).

Sapphic Self-Fashioning in the Baroque Era: Women's Petrarchan Parody in English and Spanish

DIANNE DUGAW AND AMANDA POWELL

Poems by women who lovingly address other women in erotic terms constituted a fashion in the court-oriented lyric of early modern Europe.[1] Such poems are found in the literatures of Britain, Spain, New Spain, France, the Netherlands, the Spanish Netherlands, and Italy.[2] Remarkably similar in import despite distinct features of language and cultural expression, these poems constitute a shared idiom, a literary fashion in the sense found in one dictionary as "a prevailing style or custom, as in dress or behavior"; something in "the current mode" or "the style characteristic of the social elite."[3] When early modern women wrote poetry to and about other women, they typically cast it in a sapphic reworking of the petrarchan tradition, an inheritance that offered poets entwined topoi ready to be reimagined, from the charm of the enraptured gaze to the cold thud of deception.[4] Just as formulaic vestimentary codes enabled some women to act transgressively as men, both in life and in literature, so the framework of petrarchan address allowed women poets to articulate a sapphic eroticism that functioned in a paradoxical combination of conservative and liberatory ways.[5] Women poets linked the conventionalized petrarchan stance, in which the poet contemplates a beloved, to the context of aristocratic court culture in texts that foreground female homoerotic passion and sexuality, satirize the silencing of women, and often advocate for their equality with men.[6]

A deliberate gender-play, a move that subverts gendered relations of power, hierarchy, and desire, repositions the woman author and addressee as mutual subjects in this love poetry of one woman for another. Rather than voicing conventionalized desires of the eager male poet who enjoins his 'coy mistress,' his 'new-found land,' to unlace and lie down, these poems rewrite the voiceless passivity of the sexualized mistress-as-object. The sexual and sexualizing poet constructs a reciprocal relationship of desiring equals with *her mistress*.[7] These lyrics valorize the woman addressed *and* the woman writing, creating within familiar lyric structures a dynamic space that employs convention in order to question, subvert, and recreate it. The texts voice a cheeky cognizance of this supplanting move, a wink not only to the addressee, but to the reader or listener as well, that attests both to the defining role of sexualities in modern subjectivity, and to the capacity of self-awareness about gender and restrictions of sexual desire to undo the hierarchies of a masculinist tradition. To quote Katherine Philips to her woman addressee: "... all our titles shuffl'd so,/ Both Princes, and both Subjects too."[8]

Seventeenth-century sapphic lyric presents a woman-centered vision that finds strength in cultural sites that modern feminism has eschewed as retrogressive, irrational, or unscientific. With its emphasis on a courtly frame of reference and occasional evocation of a 'third sex' or hermaphroditism, this sapphic discourse has been hard for latter-day critics to read. Poets writing in this vein call upon aristocratic networks of friendship and patronage not only to cement particular, personal advantages but, more generally, to claim a place for women in the public sphere against the encroaching bourgeois mandate of domesticity for women. Laudatory address to a woman beloved harks back to the powers and privileges of the nobility.[9] Furthermore, the classical allusions that underscore this highly cultivated cultural site of the courtly petrarchan lyric serve another purpose as well: they offer an alternative to strictly binary sex-gender positions. Especially in the poems discussed below by Aphra Behn and Juana Inés de la Cruz, a neo-platonic view of the 'neutrality' of non-gendered souls brings into play possibilities outside physical, and thus socially mandated, masculinity or femininity. Indeed, the classical figure of the hermaphrodite was, in the early modern period, being excised from medical literature precisely because of a perceived threat of (what our age calls) lesbianism.[10]

The following elements distinguish what we identify as sapphic poetry by women lyricists of the period: (1) loving address by a woman to a woman, often framed as wooer-to-beloved; (2) foregrounding of an interlocutor's high social status, which emphasizes the courtly flourish and context; (3) erotically charged, not just affectionate, language, that often acknowledges and plays with the reader's possible discomfort at such woman-to-woman ardor; (4) stock vocabulary, imagery and modes of address from the petrarchan tradition; (5) humorous elements that put a parodic turn on standard (male-authored) petrarchan lyric; (6) obvious play with gender roles, to mock assumptions of male superiority and insist on female agency; (7) construction of interpersonal intimacy between addressee and speaker, with an (implied or explicit) equality of subject and object that contrasts to the speaking-male-to-silent-female tradition of petrarchan address.

The poets we consider here published their verse to acclaim in the latter seventeenth century in the Spanish- and English-speaking worlds: Sor Violante del Cielo of Portugal (1601–1693), the British writers Katherine Philips (1631/2–64) and Aphra Behn (1640?–89), and Sor Juana Inés de la Cruz of New Spain, now Mexico (1648/51?–1695). In writing erotically charged poems to women, Philips and Behn join the company of other British women poets of their era, including "Ephelia," Anne Killigrew, Mary Chudleigh, and Elizabeth Singer Rowe; while Sor Violante and Sor Juana share their context with such poets as Marcia Belisarda (Sor Isabel de Jesús) and Catalina Clara Ramírez de Guzmán.[11]

We bring together British and Iberian/New Spanish women to demonstrate the international character of this mode, across northern and southern European traditions, and building on English and Spanish literatures' shared tracing of Italian Renaissance models. Examining these writers together cuts across the biases of a modern scholarly practice, based on the boundaries of nation states, that rarely acknowledges the cultural connections linking baroque, pre-Enlightenment England and Spain. In particular, seventeenth-century literary culture in Britain is consistently read in a distorting isolation.

European court culture in the baroque era was an international context that saw aristocratic and bourgeois women making inroads in the arts, humanities, and sciences as poets, dramatists, painters, composers, actresses, essayists, and philosophers. By the middle of the eighteenth century, these opportunities waned, and women of letters were largely relegated to a reductively 'female' genre, the domestic novel. The pan-European context we propose sheds new light especially on often-discussed English writers such as Philips and Behn, whose literary forms and modes, Tory politics, aristocratic affiliations, and high-church or Catholic leanings routinely perplex critics. (Such scholarly perplexity also meets other English writers whose sensibility similarly reflects European baroque court culture; these include William D'Avenant, Margaret Cavendish, and even, to some degree, John Dryden.)[12] As with the poems we consider here, apparent idiosyncrasies fade when such work is placed within the larger context of baroque court culture and art. Similarly, the sapphic poetry originating in convents and courtly circles in Iberia and colonial Spanish America is brought from the margins (to Anglo-centric eyes), to show its connections to a wider literary context that more accurately reflects the sensibilities of these women authors, all of whom read and wrote in multiple languages. We hope our approach will prompt further study of the poets we note here from French, Dutch, Flemish, and Italian literatures and will encourage recovery of women writing in the baroque sapphic mode in other traditions.

The Study of this Poetry

To date, in considering early modern love poems by women addressed to women, critical approaches miss the import of this poetry as a conventional expressive category across European languages. Often critics hew to a binary consideration of genre and to *either/or* definitions of sexuality that locate the poems within the discourse *either* of friendship *or* of passionate love, tending to emphasize the former and to back away from the latter. The poems are taken to represent de-sexualized "romantic friendships," although the texts themselves deliberately introduce the courtship trope familiar from male love poems to women. The *either/or* conceptual formulation of critics falls short of the poems' playful, often paradoxical collapsing or synthesizing of the two categories.

The love poems that we discuss indeed participate in a poetic rhetoric of friendship, wherein male writers enlist friendship as a mark of courtly (and increasingly, bourgeois) self-fashioning.[13] As women writers stepped into male-dominated lyric discourse, they used as one point of departure these homosocial friendship tropes to show their command of valorized discursive practices.[14] However, this rhetoric of women's friendship in the work of some female poets emphatically abuts and shades into the eroticism of seduction and consummation.[15] Such poems frequently stress ambiguities and shifting boundaries between friendship and erotic relations, accentuating and reworking inequities of gender on the one hand and forwarding expressions of homosexual desire on the other.[16] In conflating love and friendship, the poets discussed below pique their readers' interest by evoking and then undoing assumptions about female decorum and docility. Meanwhile, their addressees are the more honored, when praised in culturally prestigious terms provided by the conventions of centuries of male-to-female verse. Because these conventions are used by women to women, they evoke a heroic hermaphroditic ideal of baroque neo-platonism.

Another analytical stance elides discussions of sexy strategies and content by relegating meaning to the "purely literary." Critics of one of the poets discussed here have said:

> It would be an anachronism to limit our interpretation of these poems to an expression of lesbian love.... [T]his feminine union can be perceived in terms purely literary, as an attempt of liberation from masculine literary authority. In these poems, Sor Violante, like Sappho, conceives poetic creation as a literature written by women for women. And in this poetic world, man is cast to the periphery, if not relegated to the role of intruder.[17]

But what is a concept that is "purely literary"? A woman poet who writes to another woman and enlists the conventions of erotic discourse explicitly calls up the physical enactments of desire and the centuries-long discursive representations of sexual expression. Scholars do not explain away eroticism in the poetry of Garcilaso or Góngora, Sidney or Shakespeare (except in study of the latter's sonnets, where critics have leaned hard on the "dark lady" to explain away the "young man"). Nor when a male poet addresses a woman do commentators reassure readers that "He didn't mean this 'heterosexually,' not as we use the concept 'heterosexual' today." Fear of anachronism arises especially with the possibility of queer (especially sapphic or lesbian) readings. The poems we consider not only invite, but themselves insist, on such readings, as their parodic reworkings of convention forward a mutual empowerment of speaker and addressee in erotic terms.

Another critical approach reads in the early modern texts a lesbian identity and biographical experience of the modern or postmodern sort, looking for genital expression of a sexual lesbianism 'between the sheets,' so to speak. Rarely does evidence support a modern-seeming lesbian identity enacted in the lives of these poets, though bits of fact suggest physically expressed intimacies in particular cases.[18] But poetry in itself does not constitute such evidence (a fact equally true for the expressions of heterosexual desire in lyric). As we show, it does however evince a markedly erotic sapphic sensibility across the culture of baroque Europe, in the prevalence of this lyric fashion.[19]

Early modern women, especially before the latter half of the eighteenth century, seem to have relished forms of behavior and representation that displayed same-sex attraction, sexuality, and love.[20] A curtailed yet rich array of textual evidence shows that people spoke of and enacted same-sex eroticism, as they did other phenomena, in terms of role-playing and the figurative tropes and traditions of literary expression. Their ongoing manipulation of petrarchan courtship conventions fits with this literariness in its figurative quality, its conceptual models, and the ironic disjunctions within the borders of its representations, which are behavioral as well as artistic.[21] The evincing of sapphic desire within the frame of conventionalized courtship language constitutes a good part of the meaning of the works, arguably their *raison d'être*. Encountering the homoerotic display and innuendo in the poems, one cannot avoid imagining women romancing women, and it is perverse to pretend that one can.

Sor Violante del Cielo/do Ceu (1607–1693)

Sor Violante del Cielo (her full religious name in Spanish; *do Ceu* [of Heaven] in Portuguese) wrote in both Spanish and Portuguese from a Dominican convent in Lisbon. Her extensively (though not exclusively) woman-centered verse is richly erotic and evokes a devout Catholic setting and powerful courtly connections. In the convent, Sor Violante continued to receive visitors and to study as she had before her entrance at age 29.[22] Her poetry, in which women receive elaborate textual focus, displays the elements outlined above as distinguishing early modern sapphic verse, including aristocratic addresses, petrarchan imagery, and parodic humor that mocks or overturns gendered hierarchies.

In 1646, the *Rimas varias de la Madre Soror Violante del Cielo, religiosa en el monasterio de la Rosa de Lisboa* was published in Rouen, France.[23] The opening sonnet-sequence leaves no doubt that author, patron, and publisher granted the sapphic mode pride of place. The volume begins with witty displays of fervent dedication to various female objects of love and admiration (poems number 1–4 and 6–8 fit this description, while 9 is a sonnet on female friendship). Some addressees' identities are masked, or fabricated, by courtly names from the pastoral tradition: Elisa [1], Nise [4], Belisa [9]. Other addressees are identified by aristocratic titles: Duchess of Aveiro [7], Countess of Penaguião [8]. The opening series brings to the fore the loving address and the courtly, homosocial context of this poetry.

Throughout, a familiar imaginary prevails as standard themes, metaphors, and antitheses place the initial poems in the petrarchan patrimony. The *Canzoniere*-like series highlights this lineage. Thematically, the first, elegaic lament to "Elisa" evokes the traditional suffering of (male) poets immortalizing (female) beloved objects: "*¡Ay decreto cruel del bien que adoro,/ que poseyendo tú, me des la muerte, / y que escribiendo yo, te dé la vida!*"[24] Both grieving speaker and deceased addressee are women, but the poem is freighted with the paradigmatic desire and loss of Petrarch's mourning for Laura. *Rimas* 2 complains that while the commonplace that "*la ausencia es* *homicida*"[25] is harsh enough, the crueler truth is that life-in-love itself causes the lover to die: "*que si la dura ausencia diera muerte, / no me matara a mí la propia vida.*"[26] Soon after (in nos. 4 and 5), an admired Nise is described as a "*Sol*" [sun] whose splendor cannot be dimmed by "*pardas nubes*" [dark clouds], underscoring the petrarchan mode with standard epithet and antithesis. These elements summon a grammar and a vocabulary of lyric love that is by tradition both idealized and erotic.

Nor does the poet shy from an erotic language that brings to the fore the petrarchan idea of a feverishly swooning courtship. In *Rimas* 8 (see appendix) the admired woman is addressed, vocatively, as "*o rara suspensión del pensamiento*" (l.5)[27] that leads to "*el exceso feliz con que deliro*" (l.7).[28] In the speaking, this knee-buckling admiration deftly manages its loss of control, at the end calling explicitly on the baroque "*ingenio*" [wit] that makes possible its conceits. In its over-the-top exaggerations, *Rimas* 8 introduces the humor, self-parody and gender play that become more explicit in the remarkable poems on three-way female love triangles later in the volume.

Sor Violante's *Rimas* 8 employs the means (strangeness, astonishment, admiration, suspension) by which literary and other artists of the baroque achieve an intensity capable of effecting new receptivities in readers and audience.[29] Terms of esteem, admiration and marvel weave through the poem (*admiro, admiración*, ll.1, 4, 7, and 10). The imagery draws on the then recent, presumably astonishing concept of financial credit:

> *Si como admiro en vos, lo que en vos miro,*
> *explicara de mi lo que en mi siento,*
> *no hallara en el abono detrimento*
> *lo que en mi siento, y lo que en vos admiro.* (ll.1–4)[30]

Along with its worldly images of value and loss (*abono* and *detrimento*), the sonnet evokes the religious mysticism of such writers as Teresa de Avila and Pedro de Osuna, when Sor Violante's speaker compares the awe of gazing on the object of desire—and "*tal objeto*" [what a remarkable object; l.9]—to that of one lost at sea. As in the mystics, verbal expression is caught up in silence, and arrival is assured by lost wandering: *como en inmenso mar se va perdiendo / callando significa, acierta errando*" (ll.10–11).[31] Sanity cannot capture such beauty or make sense of such feeling; only wit suffices to command the paradox and to yoke the extremes that, as we shall see, also characterize the poetry of Philips, Behn, and Sor Juana. In this blinding light where good sense goes delirious, the reasoned esteem of "friendship" and the passion of "love" are indistinguishable. The addressee is elevated by the poet's terms for her, and the poet by her displayed command of prized discursive modes imitative of Garcilaso and Quevedo.

Moving from the allusion of the previous poem to more outright parody, Sor Violante's *romance*, *"Amada prenda del alma"* (*Rimas*, 114–17) presents an all-female love-triangle that implicitly pokes fun at the inevitability of heterosexual possessiveness. In contrast to standard lyric treatments of jealousy (which present threats to male honor as lodged in the female body), this speaker appears well-pleased with both the other points of the triangle. "Nise," herself an admired female, previously possessed the unnamed beloved. The latter is the "*amada prenda del alma*",[32] "*zona del cielo*",[33] and "*premio.*"[34] But Nise has cast her off and handed her over to the speaker:

> *premio que otorgarme quiso*
> *la más rara discreción, ...*
> *¡oh, qué diversas estamos,*
> *dulce prenda, vos y yo!:*
> *vos infelice conmigo,*
> *y yo dichosa con vos.*
> *¡Qué diferentes extremos*
> *Nise en las dos igualó!,*
> *pues para vos fue castigo*
> *lo que para mí favor.* (ll. 13–14, 17–24)[35]

Woman, the desired object of exchange, moves not between men, but from woman speaker to woman addressee.

Sor Violante gives burlesque treatment to the usually hallowed (or harrowing) theme of jealousy. The conventional "rival" is here a benefactor ("*pues si Nise no os largara, / no os consiguiera mi amor*" (ll. 31–32).[36] In this gynocentric configuration, the extremes are not of hierarchical gender positions, but of feeling. Irony abounds in energetic lines that undercut the typically mournful or choleric expressions of jealousy in male-authored, heterosexual verse. The beloved languishes (in parodically archaized diction) "*infelice conmigo,*"[37] while the speaker, "*dichosa con vos,*"[38] is cozily contented with her relation to the other. The poet casts before us the egocentrism of male possession of women, here rendered outdated and ridiculous. At the same time, she posits a compelling, erotically cast intimacy between women. Such a relationship, with its poetic expressions of triumph, tenderness, and tension (indeed, all the ranges of elevated and humorous address to women in the *Rimas* referred to here) is not idiosyncratic or confined to Sor Violante.

Katherine Philips (1631/2–1664)

Sapphic poetry in English from the same era cannot be contextualized without considering, at the socio-political level, baroque court culture and, at the discursive, formal and aesthetic level, the same petrarchan tradition enlisted by Sor Violante.[39] As Jane Spencer and others note, Katherine Philips and Aphra Behn are pivotal figures in English literary history.[40] Both were translators, keenly aware of and influenced by the continental literature that enriched their allusive range and shaped their strategies. From their own era onwards, readers and critics have contrasted and related the two as models. The 'chaste' Philips, hailed as "Matchless Orinda," serves as a 'good mother' for subsequent women writers. The rambunctious, commercial, and self-promoting Behn is a cautionary 'bad mother' from whom subsequent women are pressured to distance themselves. We suggest seeing Philips and Behn within a pan-European baroque culture that included this mode of sapphic verse. *Both* authors, the 'good' and the 'bad' mother-to-be, write themselves as sapphists whose parodic recastings of petrarchan poesy are markedly aware of the politics of gender, culture, and the self. Many recent readings of Philips and Behn bring to view the homosexual character of the verse, notably those by Harriette Andreadis, Carol Barash, and Elizabeth Wahl.[41] However, the parodic character of the poetry, especially *vis-à-vis* the petrarchan framework, and the relationship of this mode and its sapphic sensibility to the pan-European context of baroque court culture call for the placement of these poets in the context of other European writers such as those discussed here.

Katherine Philips (1631/2–64), the greater part of whose short life was lived with her much older husband in the southwest corner of Wales, wrote poetry that circulated in manuscript among a courtly group of friends in the 1650s and early 1660s. In 1664 an unauthorized volume of her poetry was published in London, the year after a production in Dublin of her translation of Corneille's *Pompey*.[42] As with Sor Violante, circumstances limited Philips's reach but did not prevent her achievement (respectively, the former's relative isolation in the convent and the latter's in provincial Wales). Talented and ambitious, Philips was poised to move into the literary circles of Restoration London at the time of her death. Her poetry, celebrated for two generations, draws on and reshapes the metaphysical intellectuality of Donne and the *précieux* neo-platonism of the 1640s court of Charles I and Henrietta Maria.[43]

Among her works are many amorous addresses to and poems about women that express intense intimacy. "Mutual affection between Orinda and Lucatia" is a song set to music by Henry Lawes, the former Stuart court composer and Philips's childhood teacher. Like most songs, this work is misrepresented if considered only as a text stripped of its musical setting. "Lucatia" (or "Lucasia") was the pastoral name that identified Philips's friend, Anne Owens. The song text (see appendix) sets before us a playfully parodic recasting of verities of religion, politics, and alchemy in the style of Donne, in order to voice the "subjectivity" of equal "selves." Like Sor Violante, Philips recasts petrarchan love address to thread the courtship trope through paradoxical juxtapositions of disparate cultural realms, especially weaving together the secular and the religious in surprising ways. The playfully naïve yet pointed irreverence barely belies the speaker's "shuffling" of realms and "titles." In the 1650s, after the recent civil war and killing of a king, such reversals reverberated with a dark irony; more so, one supposes, than such imagery would have borne in Donne's pre-Cromwellian Britain.

Philips employs a two-pronged strategy of figuration, by metaphor and allusion, through the series of images and references. A figurative playfulness, metaphysical in mode but unsettling for its seeming flippancy, laces its way through grave political, religious, and historical fields that crackle with then-recent events and issues. The yoking of somber political and especially religious reference with such impudent images as appetitive "Angels" who, with "greedy choice," are "determin'd to their joyes" creates an irony reminiscent of the "*exceso feliz*" [felicitous excess] in Sor Violante's playfully ardent expressions of love.

Through its six stanzas, the poem steps from one antithetical point of institutional reference to another with hybrid yokings that unsettle convention and ultimately elevate the speaker and her beloved. The bitter religious contention of Philips's Britain first arises in the poem's notably Catholic-referenced "miracles" in stanza 1, where "Religion" is transposed onto woman-for-woman "Love": miraculous "wonder" and "prodigie" will constitute a proof of their parodically heightened 'devotion.' Throughout the poem, such allusive and figurative conflations of the institutional and the personal recast the solemn paradoxes conventional to theological and philosophical argument with irreverent and implicitly feminist ends. Nonetheless, the somber reference fields, parodically enlisted, evoke the ominous tenor of troubled times. Thus, the figures for this "Love" move from the "miracles" of stanza 1 to a declaration of its "liberty" and "Election" (Puritan catch-words) in stanza 2, then to the images of "banishment" and the "captivity" of "Thrones" in stanza 3, a trajectory that brings to mind the national drama of the recently beheaded king. Such love thus becomes a redemptive alternative in this troubled terrain. Against the backdrop of usually solemnly invoked images of spiritual and national strife, the speaker makes her pivotal parodic move in stanza 4. The observation that "We are our selves but by rebound" allows a mirroring self-fashioning by which she declares the equivalent reciprocity of the devoted couple. Their love "shuffles titles" so as to make them "both Princes, and both Subjects too." This line emphatically reformulates the masculinist hierarchy of Donne's imperial "She is all States, and All Princes I."[44] Like Sor Violante's reworking of the love triangle, Philips echoes the earlier text in a pointedly parodic "imitation with a difference" (in Linda Hutcheon's formulation).[45]

Not only the words are buoyant in their parody. Henry Lawes's musical setting underscores the complicated ironies that layer the text. The composition fits the stylistic designation of a "tuneful song," which musicologist Pamela Willetts characterizes as a piece "often composed in triple time, with no pretension to depth of feeling and no particular attention to the word-setting. A light catchy tune repeated for each stanza is the aim."[46] Discussing the music, one commentator accuses Lawes of treating Philips's lyric (and its sapphism) with disrespect, castigating him for composing for the text in strophes rather than in a through-composed declamatory setting in the style, say, of Monteverdi.[47] However, recognizing the ironic play typical of women's baroque sapphic verse, we see Lawes's music as composed in a style that matches, intentionally and perhaps even with Philips's collaboration, the irreverence and parodic self-awareness of the text. The musical setting accentuates the moments of paradox and surprise in the text's profound, if playful, reworking of petrarchan forms and the gendered, heterosexual world order that they assume, and which Philips undoes.

In fact, this setting aptly carries the poem's urgently situated paradoxes, as the music enacts a solemn-humorous hybridity parallel to that of the text, to suggest a celebration facetiously parodic, yet fervent. Stepping forward in its triple meter, the music proposes itself as a gaity, so to speak, *with a difference*. Text and tune together enact what we postmoderns have come to call 'queering' strategies that signal difference through moves of parodic self-awareness. Initially Lawes moves ahead in the first phrase with the regularity and forward-moving harmonic changes of Anglican church music. The tune finds its first and accentuated cadence with the hymnlike harmonic movement from the II chord (A major) to the V chord (D major) in measures 7–8 (fig. 1; A): "since we see that miracles mens *faith do move*." Indeed, by way of this harmonic allusion, the setting echoes hymnody's efforts to "move mens faith."[48] The music then enacts the text's "wonders" and "prodigies" in the quickening quarter-note rhythms of measures 9–11 (fig. 1; B) and the harmonic surprise of the flattened seventh at the melody's apex at the beginning of the word "prodigies."

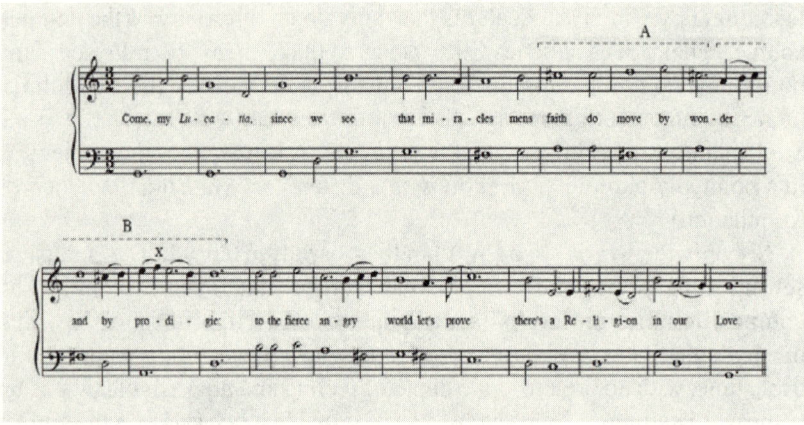

Figure 1. Musical setting by Henry Lawes of "Mutual affection..." by Katherine Philips, suggesting parodic emphases.

The weirdly "wondrous" musical cast of these measures, which first establish an orderly hymn-based point of departure (meas.7–8) and then stretch to a startlingly dissonant asymmetry (meas. 9–10), emphasizes the antitheses of each stanza: stanza 2's statement that "design'd t'agree,/ that Fate no liberty destroys," we "Elect" to follow "Angels…with greedy choice"; stanza 3's "Election" that moves to a "captivity" "more great and innocent" than "Thrones" so that "'Twere banishment to be set free"; stanza 4's miracle of "mixture" to "addition" so that "both difuse, and both ingross"; stanza 5's concluding paradox of the easing of "griefs" by a union that imagines "our selves but by rebound"; and stanza 6's "hearts" that become George Herbert-like "Altars, Priests, and Offrings" finally made "deathlesse by the sacrifice." Lawes, far from undermining the text, underscores its parodic voice by enacting the poem's unsettling journey through paradoxical allusions redolent of the social conflict of the time. Like Sor Violante and probably in collaboration with her composer, Philips enlists topical and traditional elements to reinvent the petrarchan paradigm with an unsettling wit and self-awareness.

This strategy of parody typifies many of Philips's sapphic poems. Thus, "Friendship in emblem, or the Seale, to my dearest Lucasia" reworks the compass image of Donne's "A Valediction Forbidding Mourning" to a purpose similar to the reformulation in "Mutual affection": to identify in the two female lovers an equal agency that contrasts to the masculinist dominance of the "mistress" by the man in Donne.[49] Lavish homeric similes often begin women's poems to women and set up a mirroring of heroic verse that ennobles poet and addressee, while the two implicitly share a smile at the masculinist fanfare of epic convention. Philips begins "To Mrs M. Karne, when J. Jeffreys Espre courted her" with such a simile that continues for thirteen lines: "As some great Conquerour, who knows no bounds,/ But hunting honour in a thousand wounds…&c." Such homeric framings often indulge a facetious overstatement of their model that deflates the simile with the arrival of the tenor. This simile resolves when its "Conquerour… retreats, and spending hate no more,/ Thinks mercy now what courage was before" (ll.9–10), similar to the heroic addressee ("Madam," l.13) who grants "clemency" in consideration of the "power of [her] eyes"(ll.18–19).[50] Another of Philips's poems, "To the truly noble, and obleiging Mrs. Anne Owen (on my first approaches)," opens in the same manner ("As in a triumph conquerours admit/ Their meanest captives to attend on it…&c."), only for the speaker to take on the captive's identity and confess a "plot" that is the poem itself: "But I have plots in't: for the way to be/ Secure of fame to all posterity,/ Is to obtain the honour I pursue,/ To tell the world I was subdu'd by you" (ll.13–16).[51] Another text in which Philips plays with the conventional 'tyranny' of love is "To the Lady E. Boyl," "so full of charms,/ That neither Sex can from them flie,/ Nor take against them arms" (ll. 2–3).[52] "Dear Tyrant, why will you subdue/ *Orinda's* trivial heart?" Philips queries. Such flirtatious discourse, conventionalized across sapphic lyric, builds on its petrarchan models to express and enact a pointedly courting passion, while simultaneously undermining the models to ally the women in shared understandings.

Aphra Behn (1640?–1689)

Aphra Behn, well-known playwright, poet, novelist, and translator of the Restoration era, moved in London literary and theater circles until her death. The second-most-produced playwright of her generation, Behn was significant in her own time and popular and influential through the first half of the eighteenth century. While her presence in the ranks of professional writers drew startled and sometimes vicious criticism throughout her career, her importance to English literary history can hardly be overstated. The eclipsing of her importance in the historiography of English letters demonstrates both gender-bias and a nineteenth-century legacy of scholarly prudishness. At the same time, Behn represents a pre-Enlightenment and pan-European baroque sensibility whose values and modes have remained beyond our easy comprehension, especially as they appear in English writers.

A mode of irreverence and of figurative suggestiveness and simultaneous evasion similar to that in Sor Violante and Philips characterizes Behn's "To the fair Clarinda, who made Love to me, imagin'd more than Woman," perhaps her most anthologized poem (see appendix).[53] The erotic title gives a startling, ambisexual recasting to the conventional apostrophe to the alluring but aloof petrarchan mistress. The address frames the familiar courtliness in a bi-gendered way: "Fair lovely Maid" ... "Lovely Charming Youth." Between these self-proclaimingly contradictory "Titles," the speaker's careful terms ("Title," "Nobler," and "Permit") suggest, or parody, obeisance to a social superior, as do halting repetitions ("Too weak, too Feminine"), and tentative comparatives ("Nobler," "more Approaches"). All are reminiscent of the titular addresses employed in other sapphic works. Like Philips and Sor Violante, Behn sets up her eroticized appeal as a parodic transgression. The conventions of loving address on the part of the female speaker boldly yet mischievously echo familiar petrarchan stances of courtship and sexual desire. Yet the poem works changes on the well-worn enterprise of symbolic seduction. Directing our focus to cultural as well as physical gendering, the speaker bemoans the "deluding" bi-gendered form of the "beauteous Woman...in view" who seduces as a (seemingly male) "Youth."

The either dual- or ambiguously-gendered "Clarinda" becomes a stock figure (with a difference) from literary pastoral as the desiring speaker bemoans: "Against thy Charms we struggle but in vain/ With thy deluding Form thou giv'st us pain,/ While the bright Nymph betrays us to the Swain." The extension of the rhyme beyond the couplet into a tercet here (l.11) sharpens this "struggle" and "pain" even as the pastoral allusion draws attention to the cliché of such a "betrayal" and alerts us to the parodic refashionings of well-worn elements. Meanwhile, the tercet itself enacts the opening up of space for a 'third sex' and loving of "a different kind" as the rhyme pushes past the couplet. The concluding sestet will propose this space as a liberatingly transgressive possibility.

At midpoint, "To the Fair Clarinda" summons the unequal gendering of courtship conventions. The speaker identifies herself as a member, with "fair Clarinda," of "our sex" (l.12), and proposes "That we might Love, and yet be Innocent." Such love liberates its lovers from the weight of custom's condemnation of sex as a "Crime," especially for women. A startling couplet quickly follows: "For who, that gathers fairest Flowers believes/ A Snake lies hid beneath the Fragrant Leaves." The serpentine image not only carries phallic resonance, but conjures as well the Edenic Fall as the literary pastoral mutates into its religious counterpart. Here the poem's invocation of "Crimes" aligns with the biblical heritage, certainly for Behn's Restoration generation with overtones of the self-assured 'reforms' of Puritan discourse and policy. As we have seen, such mock-solemn invocations of religious tenets and traditions, as in Philips and Sor Violante, characterize the parodic reimagining of love lyric in sapphic poems.

The final sestet leaves behind anxieties regarding "Crimes" and "hidden Snakes," even as it shifts from abstract pronominative addresses (the "thou's" and "thee's" used earlier) to a paradoxical nominative pairing. Releasing pastoral and Biblical tensions into a flight of classical allusion and homosexual valence, the poem double-names Clarinda as "Soft *Cloris* with dear *Alexis* join'd." Both names carry transgressive and homoerotic implications from antiquity: "Chloris" signifies a prostitute as well as the goddess of flowers; "Alexis" is the youth beloved by the shepherd of Virgil's unabashedly homoerotic second eclogue.[54] "We" are called at the poem's end to "extend" our "noblest Passions" in a final chiasmic allusion to the ancient classical world: "The Love to *Hermes, Aphrodite* the Friend." Within the passionate clasp of our "love" and "Friendship" stands the "wondrous" and "hermaphroditic" Clarinda. We cannot read or hear this and settle *only* on love OR *only* on friendship. As does Sor Violante, Behn accentuates the collapse of a distinction between friendship and sexual love. In its reworking of petrarchan address, "To the Fair Clarinda" evokes in "this beauteous Wonder" the sexual, the intimate, and the paradoxical in a baroque moment of mystified astonishment.

Other poems by Behn call for consideration in connection with parodic sapphism. "To my Lady Morland at Tunbri[d]ge" opens with an exaggerated epic simile ("As when a Conqu'rour does in triumph come…&c.") that, after thirteen lines, tumbles into the female speaker's admission that she herself "much a Lover grew" of the victorious "lady," despite the conquest of her own "Faithless Swain" by her admired addressee.[55] Pastoral tropes and petrarchan clichés are likewise vigorously reworked in "Verses design'd by Mrs. A. Behn, to be sent to a fair Lady" and "A Translation" ("Lydia, Lovely Maid, more fair").[56] Like other sapphist poets, Behn steers directly and parodically into inherited cultural and poetic traditions: the culturally charged and privileged petrarchan address to the mistress, related pastoral *topoi*, biblical and religious allusion, the often homoerotically inclined realm of classical mythology.[57] At the same time, she voices the poet as a woman, a NOT silent mistress, stepping out of the conventional female silence and lack of agency pervading these traditions. Indeed, in "To the Fair Clarinda," we ultimately cannot assign solely feminine *or* masculine gender even to the speaker, who shares with the richly ambiguous addressee, membership in "our sex," which, as a result of the poem, now includes the "third." Behn's move, in its playfulness, brings into the shifts of difference and self-consciousness a desire that advocates an ambiguously shapeshifting love "of a different kind."

Sor Juana Inés de la Cruz in New Spain (1648?/51?–1695)

Critics acknowledge the seventeenth-century colonial Mexican poet, dramatist and intellectual Sor Juana Inés de la Cruz as the last great figure of the literary baroque of Spain and its colonies. She also holds a crucial place in the history of women's writing and feminist consciousness. Her writing life unfolded between two force fields: scrutiny by powerful religious superiors on the one hand, and support from viceregal couples with political power on the other.[58] Sor Juana wrote love-and-tribute poems to three vicereines to express affection, render homage, and enhance the security of her own precarious position. These poems emphasize the sapphic motifs examined here. Sor Juana's humor overturns poetic and social conventions not only to undo petrarchan paradigms that objectify, silence and separate women, but also to point beyond the heterosexual grounding of these paradigms. She addressed more than forty love poems to women.[59] The pastoral *"Laura," "Lysi/Filis,"* and *"Elvira"* serve as poetic names for the vicereines Leonor, María Luisa, and Elvira de Toledo. Information in the initial publications makes clear Sor Juana's real-life, political-amicable relationship to each celebrated woman. (By contrast, while she wrote love poems with male addressees, none is directed to a stated, extra-literary beloved. Nonetheless, earlier criticism of Sor Juana rarely hesitated to *chercher l'homme*, while going to lengths to *éviter la femme*.)

As critics have observed, Sor Juana reverses the maneuvers of the petrarchan paradigm: while she evokes women's bodies and beauties in conventionally superlative fragments such as hair, eyes, forehead, nose, cheeks, mouth, and hands, the women are portrayed as unusually intact subjects. The combination of lavish tribute and knowing humor renders a woman beloved with an autonomous life, full of detail; hers is notably *not* an existence reduced to a screen for the poet's projections.[60] The friends' bodies are cherished not in the abstract but in relation to their minds and life-circumstances, similar to Philips's celebration of "mutual affection" with "Lucatia" or Sor Violante's cheerful depiction of the love-triangle of speaker, rival, and beloved. Sor Juana's poems demonstrate a different emotional economy than that in, say, Garcilaso de la Vega or Luis de Góngora, by evoking a confidently reciprocal exchange; her lyric speaker is both more empowered and less arrogant. As in Philips's lines, friendship is confidently assumed and, especially with María Luisa, surpassed.

In several poems, Sor Juana enlists an erotic rhetoric from female speaker to female recipient. Typically, Maria Luisa's "blazing" beauty hyperbolically and parodically overwhelms the poet. This over-the-top display lets Sor Juana exercise full poetic powers, as in the complex *romance decasílabo 61*, which touts her prowess by beginning each line with a word accented on the antepenultimate syllable: "*Cárceles tu madeja fabrica* …,"[61] "*Lágrimas del Aurora congela, / búcaro de fragancias, tu boca,*"[62] and "*Tránsito a los jardines de Venus, / órgano de marfil, en canora / música, tu garganta, que en dulces / éxtasis aun al viento aprisiona.*"[63] As in Philips's expansive theological allusions, the hyperbole of such tributes frequently tips to humor, accentuating Sor Juana's homoerotic avowals that profess enslavement to the other's charms.

Many poems exploit a seductive and sexually ambiguous voice for the petrarchan supplicant that accentuates the speaker's female identity and highlights the sapphic character of the relation. This boldness alarmed an early editor, who warned readers *not* to read the poems as what they appear to be: passionate declarations of love by one woman to another. Rather, they are "pure."[64] But Sor Juana calls up the "pure" neo-platonic "sexlessness" of the soul, only to undo it in a move reminiscent of the ironic masking of the erotic in Philips. Such parody emphasizes the slippery, transgressive nature of a love that makes use of all, yet evades aligning with any conventional statements.

In *romance* 19 Sor Juana flirtatiously asks permission for a daring incursion ("*permite escale tu Alcázar / mi gigante atrevimiento*")[65] as she sets out to write a jocular homage. In the erotics of the petrarchan schema, the poet lover is suppliant before the mighty beloved; Sor Juana thoroughly occupies her role as wooer. Entwined concepts of temerity and attainment evoke, yet parody, a taking of the beloved's 'stronghold' by erotic assault:

> *Logros de errar por tu causa*
> *fue de mi ambición el cebo;*
> *donde es el riesgo apreciable*
> *¿qué tanto valdrá el acierto?*
> *Permite, pues, a mi pluma*
> *segundo arriesgado vuelo,*
> *pues no es el primer delito*
> *que le disculpa el ejemplo.*
> (ll. 5–12)[66]

The poem's evocation of "dangers" and the manipulation of the traditional framework of risky erotic enterprise (the "hazardous undertaking" as the quill-pen's "flight") recall Behn's "To the Fair Clarinda" in its foregrounding of threat (Sor Juana evokes Icarus; Behn, the serpent) to create a new space for a "different kind" of love.

The rest of the poem draws attention to the sapphic stance. The reader *must* here consider female homoeroticism: can a woman properly write in this way to and of another woman? Sor Juana gives natural, aesthetic, and courtly justifications for this enthusiasm: "*Pues siendo tú el más hermoso,/ grande, soberano exceso / que ha visto en círculos tantos / el verde torno del Tiempo*" (ll. 174–77).[67] Her hyperbole introduces humor; its excess, while parodying laudatory petrarchan discourse, marks the assured intimacy of the poet's address, which makes clear the degree of understanding between the two women. The addressee, feeling praised, will at the same time know that the conventions of praise are themselves mocked, as woman woos woman. With the satirizing poet, the knowing addressee has insider status and will see through the deceptive masculinist conventions that, while seeming to praise, work to misogynist effect. This delineation of fresh terms for intimacy draws attention to the limits of women's positioning, making possible her re-positioning of both lesbian lover and beloved as empowered equals. Such 'conquests' between equals characterize seventeenth-century sapphic verse, as in Philips's evocation of "angels with greedy choice" who become "both Princes and both Subjects too."

We reread as parodic the protestations of "pure" love, as the poem itself provides a context that undoes them with insistence on an embodiment that our age calls 'sexiness.' Early on, the poem seems to eschew any physical cult of admiration for the divinized beloved, upon whose "altars" "*ni sudor arde Sabeo, / ni sangre se efunde humana, / ni bruto se corta cuello*" (ll. 45–48).[68] The poem contrasts disembodied love to the bodily, combative desires of the physical heart, which are "*holocausto poluto / ... materiales afectos*" (ll. 52–53).[69] What should prevail at these "altars" is the soul's "*sacrificio puro / de adoración y silencio*" (ll. 55–56).[70] The assertion of silence does not however hush this notably talkative poem. At its climactic moment, the text veers back from the disembodied and with a rush enters the *purely* physical with an image of the early modern physics of irresistible attraction:

> *como a lo cóncavo el aire,*
> *como a la materia el fuego,*
> *como a su centro las peñas,*
> *como a su fin los intentos; ...*
> (ll. 97–100)[71]

Air, fire, and earth inexorably rush where they must; only water (which might douse ardor) is missing, as the poem reveals its seductive intent: "*¿para qué es cansarse?/ como a ti, Filis, te quiero*" (ll. 105–106).[72]

Near the close of this *romance* Sor Juana summons neo-platonism not to dismiss physical love between women but to challenge the culture that renders such love indecent. When we reach the best-known lines, "s*exo*/sex" means male/female, the seemingly unyielding binary:

> *Ser mujer, ni estar ausente,*
> *no es de amarte impedimento;*
> *pues sabes tú, que las almas*
> *distancia ignoran y sexo.*
>
> (ll. 109–12)[73]

Critics often cite this passage as proof of a 'safe,' neo-platonic love. However, the language at this point itself voices uneasiness at the sapphism the poem is provoking. A curious illogic thus underlies the solemn assertion of the "sexless" human soul. A love of abstract "souls," limited neither by "sex" (the supposed obstacle of both being female) nor "distance" (including, presumably, the obstacles of physical separation as well as difference in social standing), has been shown by the poem to inhere in a spiritual plane of the "pure sacrifice" of "silence" mentioned earlier. But this is a silence the poem refuses, continuing prolifically for another 132 verses rather than ending at line 56 with the encomium to silence as the only fit expression for this love. We are not meant to believe in either the unspokenness or the nonphysicality of this love. Rather, we are drawn inescapably to fill the vacuum with presence, to speak into the silence our knowledge of the love professed. But here, as elsewhere, Sor Juana's lyric seductions eschew the trope of possessing the other.[74] Her gaze and address are not leveling but humanizing, for she does not diminish or possess, as the petrarchan poet does. Instead she affirms an empowering and erotic intimacy between women in a sapphic mode shared by all the poems discussed here.

The rambunctious early modern era provokes our perplexity. Both popular and polite culture in Western Europe in the seventeenth and eighteenth centuries appear sufficiently familiar for us to recognize ourselves in our forebears. At the same time, we encounter more than enough of the seemingly inexplicable to feel chagrined and bemused, especially about sex. In this pre-Enlightenment, pre-Darwinian, pre-Freudian world, we meet sexualities that are conceptually 'other' for us, though we see modern configurations coming into being. We pilot perilously between a Scylla of distorting anachronism in applying our own categories where they do not fit, and a Charybdis of erasing or denying kindred friends and lovers whom we need and want to know: for example, women before us who valued women in myriad ways. In the baroque period's profoundly rhetorical conceptualizing of reality, meaning resides in the dynamically signifying play between the metaphorical vehicle and its tenor, in the distance rather than approximation between signifier and signified. Our approach emphasizes the literariness and epistemological grounding of this parodic discourse of homoeroticism and its courtly context.

The sapphic poems of Sor Violante, Katherine Philips, Aphra Behn, and Sor Juana Inés de la Cruz neatly counter prohibitions and erasures of same-sex desire. Valerie Traub points out that the (con)fusion in our time of the categories 'gender' and 'sexuality' melds the two categories so as to erase sexualities other than hetero-. "What is it that allows (requires?) the elision of erotic difference at the same time one reasserts gender difference?" she asks.[75] The reworked petrarchan discourse of this amatory verse establishes women's authorial and affectional legitimacy as the poems echo prized classical and Renaissance models of courtship and trump them in parody. As they do so, these sapphic lyrics deliberately call into question not only the commonplaces of male agency and female passivity, but also the hegemony of desire known to us as heterosexuality.

APPENDIX: Sample Texts

Katherine Philips, "Mutuall Affection betweene *Orinda* and *Lucatia*"

Come, my *Lucatia*, since we see
    That miracles mens faith do move
By wonder and by Prodigy,
    To the dull, angry world let's prove
    There's a religion in our Love.

For though we were design't t'agree
    That fate no liberty destroys,
But our election is as free
    As Angells, who with greedy choice
    Are yet determin'd to their Joys.

Our hearts are doubled by their loss,
    Here mixture is addition grown;
We both diffuse, and both engrosse,
    And we, whose minds are so much one,
    Never, yet ever, are alone.

We court our own captivity,
    Then Thrones more great and innocent:
'Twere banishment to be set free,

Since we weare fetters whose intent
Not bondage is, but Ornament.

Divided Joys are tedious found,
And griefs united easyer grow:
We are our selves by rebound,
And all our titles shuffled so,
Both Princes, and both subjects too.

Our hearts are mutuall victims lay'd,
While they (such power in friendship ly's)
Are Altars, Priests, and offerings made,
And each heart which thus kindly dy's,
Grows deathless by the sacrifice.[76]

Sor Violante del Cielo, A la Señora Condesa de Penaguião

Si como admiro en vos, lo que en vos miro,
explicara de mi lo que en mi siento,
no hallara en el abono detrimento
lo que en mi siento, y lo que en vos admiro.
Mas ay que a tanto bien en vano aspiro,
o rara suspensión del pensamiento,
explique admiración, y sentimiento,
el exceso feliz con que deliro.
Que quien en tal objeto contemplando
como en inmenso mar se va perdiendo
callando significa, acierta errando:
Pues admirando al paso que sintiendo
si ofende la cordura delirando,
acredita el ingenio conociendo.[77]

"To the Lady Countess of Penaguião"

If as I admire in you what in you I see,
I could explain for myself what in me I feel,
Then what in myself I feel and admire in you
Would in no way diminish its guarantee.
But since with such treasure I vainly seek success—
With you, astounding halt to thought and reason—
Let this explain my astonishment and feeling,
And my mad dream of felicitous excess.
To contemplate profoundly such an object

Is to be lost upon the boundless sea
Where silence speaks; where straying, one is found:
          For the more I feel, feeling the more astonished,
If I offend good sense with my mad dream,
May wit restore the balance by what I've learned.

Aphra Behn, "To the fair Clarinda, who made Love to me, imagin'd more than Woman"

Fair lovely Maid, or if that Title be
Too weak, too feminine for Nobler thee,
Permit a Name that more Approaches Truth:
And let me call thee, Lovely Charming Youth.
This last will justifie my soft complaint,
While that may serve to lessen my constraint;
And without Blushes I the Youth persue,
When so much beauteous Woman is in view,
Against thy Charms we struggle but in vain
With thy deluding Form thou giv'st us pain,
While the bright Nymph betrays us to the Swain.
In pity to our Sex sure thou wer't sent,
That we might Love, and yet be Innocent:
For sure no Crime with thee we can commit;
Of if we shou'd—thy Form excuses it.
For who, that gathers fairest Flowers believes
A Snake lies hid beneath the Fragrant Leaves.

Thou beauteous Wonder of a different kind,
Soft *Cloris* with the dear *Alexis* join'd;
When e'r the Manly part of thee, wou'd plead
Thou tempts us with the Image of the Maid,
While we the noblest Passions do extend
The Love to *Hermes*, *Aphrodite* the Friend.[78]

Sor Juana Inés de la Cruz, Romance Decasílabo

[Pinta la proporción Hermosa de la Excelentísima Señora Condesa de Paredes, con otra de cuidados, elegantes Esdrújulos, que aún le remite desde Méjico a su Excelencia.]

Lámina sirva el cielo al retrato,
Lísida, de tu angélica forma:
cálamos forme el Sol de sus luces;
sílabas las estrellas compongan.

Cárceles tu madeja fabrica:
Dédalo que sutilmente forma
vínculos de dorados Ofires,
Tíbares de prisiones gustosas.

Hécate, no triforme, mas llena,
pródiga de candores asoma;
trémula no en tu frente se oculta,
fúlgida su esplendor desemboza.

Círculo dividido en dos arcos,
Pérsica forman lid belicosa;
áspides que por flechas disparan,
víboras de halgueña ponzoña.

Lámparas, tus dos ojos, Febeas
súbitos resplandores arrojan:
pólvora que, a las almas que llega,
Tórridas, abrasadas transforma.

Límite de una y otra luz pura,
último, tu nariz judiciosa,
árbitro es entre dos confinantes,
máquina que divide una y otra.

Cátedras de Abril, tus mejillas,
clásicas dan a Mayo, estudiosas:
métodos a jasmines nevados
fórmula rubicunda a las rosas.

Lágrimas del Aurora congela,
búcaro de fragancias, tu boca:
rúbrica con carmines escrita,
cláusula de coral y aljófar.

Cóncavo es, breve pira, en la barba,
pórfido en que las almas reposan:
túmulo les eriges de luces,
bóveda de luceros las honra.

Tránsito a los jardines de Venus,
órgano es de marfil, en canora
música, tu garganta, que en dulces
éxtasis aun al viento aprisiona.

Pámpanos de cristal y de nieve,
cándidos tus dos brazos, provocan
Tántalos, los deseos ayunos:
míseros, sienten frutas y ondas.

Dátiles de alabastro tus dedos,
fértiles de tus dos palmas brotan,
frígidos si los ojos los miran,
cálidas si las almas los tocan.

Bósforo de estrechez tu cintura,
cíngulo ciñe breve por zona;
rígida, si de seda, clausura,
músculos nos oculta ambiciosa.

Cúmulo de primores tu talle,
dóricas esculturas asombra:
jónicos lineamientos desprecia,
émula su labor de sí propia.

Móviles pequeñeces tus plantas,
sólidos pavamentos ignoran;
mágicos que, a los vientos que pisan,
tósigos de beldad inficionan.

Plátano tu gentil estatura,
flámula es, que a los aires tremola:
ágiles movimientos, que esparcen
bálsamo de fragantes aromas.

Índices de tu rara hermosura,
rústicas estas líneas son cortas;
cítara solamente de Apolo,
méritos cante tuyos, sonora.[79]

Ballad, each line beginning with a dactyl

[She describes the lovely proportions of the Countess of Paredes, with this poem in which each line begins accented on the antepenultimate syllable, sent from Mexico to her Excellency in Madrid.]

Heavenly should be the canvas to bear the portrait,
Lysida, of your angelic figure and face;
paintbrushes I now summon in beams of the sun,
syllables among the stars be set in array.

Prisonhouse fetters are fashioned by your tresses,
Daedalus-like, that with intricate subtlety make
bondage-chains smelted from deep gold caverns of Ofir,
Tibar-lands hammered into delightful jails.

Hecate, never a crescent, nor half, but full,
prodigy of smooth brightness who shines out
tremulous never, never diminished or hiding,
brilliantly shedding her moon-glow from your brow.

Circular once, then divided in two perfect arches,
bellicose, each eyebrow serves as a Persian bow,
arrowheads there unleashed may be fatal as adders,
viperous poison on darts that bring sweet woe.

Luminous, your two dazzling eyes their sudden
Phoebus-like radiance toss down briskly before us;
gunpowder that as it touches our souls, into
kindling in the torrid zones transforms us.

Boundary setting the one pure light off from the other,
separate ever, thanks to your sensible nose –
arbiter as it must be between two seclusions,
instrument holding distinct bright orb from bright orb.

Scholarly cheeks have mastered the lessons of April, and
studious, serve as classic instruction to May:
disciplined methods set down for the snowy jasmine;
rubicund formulas taught to the rose on the spray.

Lachrymal droplets of Dawn, condensed within a
sweet-scented vessel – your mouth, with its perfumes:
signature-flourish in finest inks of crimson,
codicil written with coral and pearls of dew.

Conical dimple, a tiny pyre of purest
porphyry captures the souls that rest in your glory:
catafalque that your brilliance constructs around them,
cupola filled with stars that you raise up for them.

Transiting to the sumptuous gardens of Venus,
musical organ of marble, your sculpted throat
captivates even the air, in its bewitching
ecstasies of a melody long and low.

Filaments, tendrils fashioned from crystal and snow,
lily-white, your two arms frankly incite
Tantalus in your observers' unmet hungers,
envious of fruits and fountains in their sight.

Fertilely, dates of alabaster spring forth
silvery from your two palms to become your fingers –
glaciar-cool should mere eyes gaze at them,
tropical to the souls that embracing, linger.

Slenderness, straits of the Bosphorous, this is your waist
circumscribed by a sash with map-maker's precision:
rigidly cloistered, though only by the silk cord
eagerly hiding abdominals from our vision.

Consummate gathering of excellence, your figure
stupefies antique Doric statuary;
classical columns of Ionian lines it disdains, this
spectacle equalled only by its own graces.

Delicate quickenings, as your little feet
heedlessly overlook solid floors and pavement,
magically they go tripping down the breezes
scattering under them lovely but fatal venom.

Tremulous, airy as the swaying banana-plant,
billowing like a light streamer, your form on high
agilely carries out elegant motions, releasing
redolent healing fragrances far and wide.

Inquiry into your matchless beauty produces
shortcomings only, in my ungainly verse;
zither-strings in the hands of the poet Apollo
qualify solely your eminence to rehearse.

NOTES

We thank the University of Oregon Center for the Study of Women in Society and the Oregon Humanities Center for support for this project. Portions of this essay were presented at the 2004 meeting of the Northwest Society for Eighteenth-Century Studies and Canadian Society for Eighteenth-Century Studies, and at the 2004 meeting of AEEA (Medieval and Early Modern Women Writers of Spain and Colonial Latin America).

1. Scholars who have observed this fashion within and to some degree across the literatures include Harriette Andreadis in *Sappho in Early Modern England: Female Same-Sex Literary Erotics, 1550–1714* (Chicago: University of Chicago Press, 2001); Emma Donoghue in *Passions between Women: British Lesbian Culture 1668–1801* (NY: Harper Collins, 1993); Susan Lanser in "Befriending the Body: Female Intimacies as Class Acts, " *Eighteenth-Century Studies*, 32 (1998–99): 179–98 and " *'Au sein de vos pareilles'*: Sapphic Separatism in Late Eighteenth-Century France," *Journal of Homosexuality*, 41 (2001): 105–16; Adrienne Martin in "The Rhetoric of Female Friendship in the Lyric of Sor Violante del Cielo," *Calíope*, 3 (1997): 57–71 and "The Mediation of Lesbian Eros in Golden Age Verse" in Alain Saint-Saëns and María José Delgado, *Lesbianism and Homosexuality in Early Modern Spain: Literature and Theater in Context* (New Orleans: University Press of the South, 2000), 343–62; and Elizabeth Wahl, *Invisible Relations: Representations of Female Intimacy in the Age of Enlightenment* (Stanford: Stanford University Press, 1999).

2. Our cursory survey reveals the following writers of such poems in European literatures other than Spanish and English: in Italian, Isabella di Morra (1515/20–1548?), Laura Terracina (1519–1577?), Isotta Brembate (1530?–1586), and Tarquinia Molza (1542–1617); see Irma Jaffe with Gernando Colombardo, *Shining Eyes, Cruel Fortune: The Lives and Loves of Italian Renaissance Women Poets* (New York: Fordham University Press, 2002), 144, 163, 280, and 320; in French, Anne de Rohan (1584), Mme. de C*** (n.d.), and Pauline de Simiane (1676–1737); see Domna Stanton, ed., *The Defiant Muse: French Feminist Poems from the Middle Ages to the Present* (NY: Feminist Press, 1986), 71 and 96–9; and in Flemish and Dutch, Katharina Questiers (1631–69), Cornelia Van Der Veer (1639–1702?), Katharina Lescailje (1649–1711), Titia Brongersma (late seventeenth century); see Maaike Meijer, ed., *The Defiant Muse: Dutch and Flemish Feminist Poems from the Middle Ages to the Present* (New York: Feminist Press, 1998), 59–61; and Lia van Gemert, "Hiding Behind Words? Lesbianism in Seventeenth-Century Dutch Poetry," *Thamyris*, 2 (1995): 11–44. Van Gemert's study of Dutch poets shows the characteristics that we discuss here and suggests to us that this sapphic mode is to be found across baroque literary traditions in a range of languages.

3. *American Heritage Dictionary*, Fourth Edition (Boston: Houghton Mifflin Co., 2000).

4. We use the term "sapphic" for this poetry, not because it is one the poets themselves used, but because the term conveys the presence of a classical past associated

with a valorized homoeroticism. On the conventionality of petrarchan tropes, see Leonard Forster, *Icy Fire: Five Studies in European Petrarchism* (Cambridge: Cambridge University Press, 1969).

5. For consideration of the feminist implications of this poetry in connection with the homoerotic heritage of neo-platonism, see Dianne Dugaw and Amanda Powell, "Baroque Sapphic Poetry: A Feminist Road Not Taken" in David Castillo and Massimo Lollini, eds., *Reason and Its Others in Early Modernity: Spain/Italy 1500s–1700s* (Nashville: Vanderbilt University Press, Hispanic Issues Series, forthcoming). For studies of transvestism as a mode for women in Iberian and Spanish-American culture, see Rima Vallbona, *Historia de la Monja Alférez: Autobiografía atribuída a doña Catalina de Erauso* (Tempe, Arizona: ASU Center for Latin American Studies, 1992). For Anglo-American culture, see Dianne Dugaw, *Warrior Women and Popular Balladry, 1650–1850* (Cambridge: Cambridge University Press, 1989; pbk. ed., Chicago: University of Chicago Press, 1996). Van Gemert makes a similar link *vis-à-vis* the Dutch poet Lescailje in "Hiding Behind Words?" 25.

6. Taking as a point of departure Michel Foucault's *The History of Sexuality*, literary scholarship of the last twenty years has wrestled with how to think about same-sex eroticism before the formation of modern sexual identities. At present, conceptualizations of erotic love between women in pre-modern texts include such terms as "same-sex love and desire between women" (Francesca Canadé Sautman and Pamela Sheingorn, "Introduction" in Sautman and Sheingorn, eds., *Same-Sex Love and Desire Among Women in the Middle Ages* [New York: Palgrave, 2001], 1–47); the "silent sin" (Alain Saint-Saëns, "Homoerotic Suffering, Pleasure and Desire in Early Modern Europe, 1450–1750" in Alain Saint-Saëns and María José Delgado, eds., *Lesbianism and Homosexuality in Early Modern Spain: Literature and Theater in Context* [New Orleans: University Press of the South, 2000], 1–86); "female homoeroticism" (Bernadette Brooten, *Love Between Women: Early Christian Responses to Female Homoeroticism* [Chicago: University of Chicago Press, 1996]); "lesbian-like" presence (Judith Bennett, "'Lesbian-like' and the Social History of Lesbians," *Journal of the History of Sexuality*, 9 [2000]: 1–24); "queer desire" (Valerie Traub, "Desire and the Differences It Makes" in Valerie Wayne, ed., *The Matter of Difference: Materialist Feminist Criticism of Shakespeare* [Ithaca: Cornell University Press, 1991], 81–114); "female intimacy" (Elizabeth Wahl, *Invisible Relations*); and "sapphism" (Susan Lanser, "Befriending the Body"). As noted, because of the literariness of our interest and that of the writers we consider here, we follow Lanser's use of the term "sapphic" for expressions of erotic love between women. See also Marie-Jo Bonnet, "Sappho, or the Importance of Culture in the Language of Love: Tribade, Lesbienne, Homosexuelle" in *Queerly Phrased: Language, Gender and Sexuality*, ed. Anna Livia and Kira Hall (Oxford: Oxford University Press, 1997), 147–66.

7. See Emilie Bergmann and Leah Middlebrook, "*La mujer petrarquista: 'Hollines y peces'. Poética renacentista de la óptica de sor Juana*" in Iris M. Zavala, ed., *Breve historia feminista de la literatura española (en lengua castellana)*, Vol. II: *La mujer en la literatura española: Modos de representación desde la Edad Media hasta el siglo XVII* (Barcelona: Editorial Anthropos, 1995): 145–58.

8. From "Friendship's Mysterys, to my dearest Lucasia," ll.24–25 in *The Collected Works of Katherine Philips, the Matchless Orinda*, Vol. I, *The Poems*, ed. Patrick Thomas (Stump Cross: Stump Cross Books, 1990), 91.

9. Amidst systemic changes in both the Spanish and English courtly context, women of the courtier class and the upcoming bourgeoisie moved into new cultural spaces contingently open to them. A shift occurred that later disappeared in the incipiently modern and capitalist patriarchal system. See Giulia Calvi, "Introducción," in Calvi, ed., *La mujer barroca,* trans. José Luis Gil Aristu (Madrid: Alianza Editorial, 1995),1–27 (orig. *Barroco al femminile* [Rome-Bari: Gius. Laterza & Figli Spa, 1992]); Joan Kelly, "Did Women Have a Renaissance?" in *Women, History, and Theory* (Chicago: University of Chicago Press, 1984),19–50; Lanser, "Befriending the Body"; and Clarissa Campbell Orr, ed., *Queenship in Britain, 1660–837* (Manchester and New York: Manchester University Press, 2002), 1–36.

10. Katharine Park, "The Rediscovery of the Clitoris: French Medicine and the Tribade, 1570–1620" in *The Body in Parts: Fantasies of Corporeality in Early Modern Europe*, David Hillman and Carla Mazzio, eds. (New York: Routledge, 1997) and "The Hermaphrodite and the Order of Nature: Sexual Ambiguity in Early Modern France," *GLQ: A Journal of Lesbian and Gay Studies*, 1 (1995): 419–38.

11. For other women who wrote sapphic lyric in English, see Maureen Mulvihill, ed., *Poems by Ephelia* (Delmar, NY: Scholars' Facsimiles and Reprints, 1992), 87–90 and 107–12; Hilda Smith, *Reason's Disciples* (Urbana, Chicago, and London: University of Illinois Press, 1982), 163 and 175; Marilyn Williamson, *Raising Their Voices: British Women Writers, 1650–1750* (Detroit: Wayne State University Press, 1990), 19, 111–12 and 151–52; and Kathryn King, *Jane Barker, Exile: A Literary Career, 1675–1725* (Oxford: Clarendon Press, 2000), 55; for women who wrote in Spanish, see Julián Olivares and Elizabeth Boyce, eds., *Tras el espejo la musa escribe: Lírica femenina de los siglos de oro* (Madrid: Siglo XXII, 1993); and Julián Olivares and Elizabeth Boyce, eds., *En desagravio de las damas: Women's Poetry of the Golden Age* (Asheville, N.C.: Pegasus Press, 2005).

12. For consideration of Dryden with regard to this idea of a baroque style with continental affiliations, see Dianne Dugaw, "'The ~~Rationall~~ Spirituall Part': Dryden and Purcell's Baroque *King Arthur*" in Jayne Lewis and Maximillian Novak, eds., *Enchanted Ground: Reimagining John Dryden* (Toronto and London: University of Toronto Press, 2004), 273–89.

13. See Paul Hammond, *Figuring Sex between Men from Shakespeare to Rochester* (Oxford: Clarendon Press, 2002), 2 and 6–9. See also Gordon Braden, *Petrarchan Love and the Continental Renaissance* (New Haven: Yale University Press, 1999), 129–61.

14. Early modern lyric discourse draws on centuries of courtly love tradition in which the language of friendship opens onto sexual as well as affectional connotations from troubadour verse across languages. On male troubadours' address to the 'lady' (*domna)* as 'my lord' (*mi dons*) which female poets imitate, see Angelica Rieger, "Was Bieiris de Romans Lesbian?: Women's Relations with Each Other in the World of the Troubadors" in William Paden, ed., *The Voice of the Trobairitz: Perspectives on the Women Troubadours* (Philadelphia: University of Pennsylvania Press, 1989), 74–5,

and Sautman and Sheingorn's critique of Rieger in *Same-Sex Love and Desire*, 30–31. For a consideration of this address to the woman beloved as *dueño* and *señor*, see also Amanda Powell, " '*¡O qué diversas estamos,/ dulce prenda, vos y yo!*': Multiple Voicings in Love Poems to Women by Marcia Belisarda, Catalina Clara Ramírez de Guzmán, and Sor Violante del Cielo" in *En desagravio de las damas: Studies on Women's Poetry of the Golden Age*, ed. Julián Olivares (Asheville, NC: Pegasus Press, 2005).

15. On other strategies used by women writers, see Ann Rosalind Jones, *The Currency of Eros: Women's Love Lyric in Europe, 1540–1620* (Bloomington: Indiana University Press, 1991), 1–35. Jones shows how women's love poems to men in the earlier period carry the ideological charge of breaking expectations by having the conventionally silent woman speak her desire. See also Ester Gimbernat de González, "Speaking through the Voices of Love: Interpretation as Emancipation" in Stephanie Merrim, ed., *Feminist Perspectives on Sor Juana Inés de la Cruz* (Detroit: Wayne State University Press, 1999), 162–76. Neither critic discusses sapphic lyric.

16. Arlene Stiebel's observation of the conscious and ironic "mask" in Katherine Philips's poems to Lucatia, at once drawing attention to and undermining the neoplatonic "innocence" of this love, applies as well to poems by the other three authors studied here. See Arlene Stiebel, "Subversive Sexuality: Masking the Erotic in Poems by Katherine Philips and Aphra Behn" in Claude J. Summers and Ted-Larry Pebworth, eds., *Renaissance Discourses of Desire* (Columbia and London: University of Missouri Press, 1993), 223–36.

17. Julián Olivares and Elizabeth Boyce, "Sor Violante del Cielo (y de la Tierra): The Subversion of Amorous Lyrical Discourse," in Adelaida López de Martínez, ed., *A Ricardo Gullón: Sus Discípulos* (Erie, Pennsylvania: ALDEEU, 1995), 196.

18. For example, in the case of the English Aphra Behn and the Dutch Katharina Questiers. See Janet Todd, *The Secret Life of Aphra Behn* (London: André Deutsch, 1996), 125, 176, 190–91, 382–83, and 393, and Meijer, ed., *Defiant Muse*, 59–61.

19. In considering the character of the love expressed in women's petrarchan poems addressed to women, we appreciate Martha Vicinus's caveat that the recognition of what our age terms lesbian love should not be held to a higher evidentiary standard than our recognitions of heterosexual love in texts. See her "Lesbian History: All Theory and No Facts or All Facts and No Theory?" *Radical History Review*, 60 (1994): 57–75, especially 59. Usefully, Sautman and Sheingorn (*Same-Sex Love and Desire*) articulate for the medieval period their interest in "the powerful consequences of same-sex affectivity, especially when strong erotic tension is present, with the understanding that not all such relations need develop into full-fledged intercourse to warrant our attention. In particular… those relationships between women that make all others in their lives secondary" (4).

20. See for example, on women in Britain, Emma Donoghue, *Passions Between Women* and Andreadis, *Sappho in Early Modern England*; on women in the Hispanic world, Adrienne L. Martin, "Mediation of Lesbian Eros."

21. On role-playing and deceptive masking as an idea permeating thought and behavior in the long eighteenth century, see Gordon S. Wood, "Conspiracy and the Paranoid Style: Causality and Deceit in the Eighteenth Century," *The William and Mary*

Quarterly, 3rd Series, 39 (1982): 425. Among literary studies that explore the idea are Terry Castle, *Masquerade and Civilization: The Carnivalesque in Eighteenth-Century Culture and Fiction* (Stanford: Stanford University Press, 1986) and Dugaw, *Warrior Women and Popular Balladry.*

22. Manuel Serrano y Sanz, *Apuntes para una biblioteca de escritoras españolas*, I (Madrid: Tipografía de la "Revista de Archivos, Bibliotecas y Museos," 1905), 264–5.

23. Sor Violante del Cielo/Violante do Ceu, *Rimas varias* (Rouen [Ruán], France: Maurry, 1646). The book was dedicated to her sponsor, Vasco Luis de Gama, Count of Vidigueira, Portuguese ambassador in Paris, who had ties to the Portuguese-Jewish community of Rouen. See Andrés José Pociña, *Sóror Violante do Céu* (Madrid: Ediciones del Orto, 1998), 40–42. For a modern edition that corrects the 1601 birthdate appearing elsewhere, see Margarida Vieira Mendes, ed., *Rimas várias* (Lisboa: Editorial Presença, 1993); substantial selections appear in Olivares and Boyce, eds., *Tras el espejo* and *En desagravio de las damas: Women's Poetry.*

24. "Oh cruel decree of the treasure I adore, / that while you possess me, you bring me death, / and while I write of you, I give you life!" [Translations are by the authors of this essay.]

25. "absence is murderous."

26. "if harsh absence could cause my death / my own life would not slay me."

27. "rare/precious/strange suspension of thought."

28. "the felicitous excess of my delirium."

29. See José António Maravall, *Culture of the Baroque: Analysis of a Historical Structure*, trans. Terry Cochran (Minneapolis: University of Minnesota Press, 1986), especially 207–24.

30. If as I admire in you what in you I see,
I were able to explain about me what in me I feel,
then what I feel in me and admire in you
would in no way detract from its guarantee.

31. "as on a vast sea, becoming lost/one gives meaning by keeping silence, erring hits the mark."

32. "beloved treasure of my soul."

33. "region of heaven."

34. "prize"

35. . . . a prize that the finest intelligence
was pleased to bestow on me. . .
oh what different states we hold,
sweet treasure, you and I!
For you are doleful with me,
I a lucky woman with you.
And what opposite extremes
Nise leveled in us two,
for what to you was punishment
was a kindness to me.

36. "if Nise hadn't sent you packing / I would never have made you mine."

37. "unhappy with me."

38. "fortunate with you."

39. On English links to continental court culture, see Orr's "Introduction" in *Queenship in Britain*, 1–52, especially 1–13 and 29–36. See also R. Malcolm Smuts, *Court Culture and the Origins of a Royalist Tradition in Early Stuart England* (Philadelphia: University of Pennsylvania Press, 1987); (ed.), *The Stuart Court and Europe* (Cambridge: Cambridge University Press, 1996); and Joseph Levine, *Between the Ancients and the Moderns: Baroque Culture in Restoration England* (New Haven: Yale University Press, 1999).

40. Jane Spencer, *Aphra Behn's Afterlife* (Oxford: Oxford University Press, 2000), 6–12.

41. See Andreadis, *Sappho in Early Modern England*; Carol Barash, *English Women's Poetry, 1649–1714* (Oxford: Clarendon Press, 1996) and "The Political Possibilities of Desire: Teaching the Erotic Poems of Behn," in *Teaching Eighteenth-Century Poetry*, Christopher Fox, ed. (New York: AMS Press, 1990), 159–6; and Wahl, *Invisible Relations*, 130–70.

42. Thomas, "Biographical Note" in *Collected Works of Katherine Philips*, 17–20. See also, Philip Souers, *The Matchless Orinda* (Cambridge, MA: Harvard University Press, 1931), 149–248.

43. Erica Veevers, *Images of Love and Religion: Queen Henrietta Maria and Court Entertainments* (Cambridge: Cambridge University Press, 1989).

44. "The Sunne Rising," l.21.

45. Throughout our discussion, we rely on Linda Hutcheon's analysis of the workings and import of parody as imitation with critically salient difference. See her *A Theory of Parody* (New York: Methuen, 1985).

46. Pamela Willetts, *The Henry Lawes Manuscript* (London: Trustees of the British Museum, 1969), 4, quoted in Lydia Hamessley, "Henry Lawes's Setting of Katherine Philips's Friendship Poetry in his *Second Book of Ayres and Dialogues*, 1655: A Musical Misreading?" in Philip Brett, Elizabeth Wood, and Gary Thomas, eds., *Queering the Pitch* (New York and London: Routledge, 1994), 136.

47. Lydia Hamessley, "Henry Lawes's Setting."

48. Religious tunes in triple meter in Philips's time were certainly rare, but not unheard of. See, for example, Thomas Ravenscroft's setting for "Psalm 104" in *The Whole Booke of Psalmes: with The Hymnes Evangelicall, and Songs Spirituall* (London: Thomas Harper, 1633), 180–82. Of course, the hybridity and parodic character of the setting's witty and surprising hymn reminiscences are accentuated when they are rendered in an unexpected meter.

49. Philips, *Collected Works*, 106–8. For discussion of this poem, see Dugaw and Powell, "Baroque Sapphic Poetry."

50. Philips, *Collected Works*, 99–100.

51. Philips, *Collected Works*, 102–3.

52. Philips, *Collected Works*, 222–3.

53. Aphra Behn, *The Works of Aphra Behn*, Vols. 1–7, ed. by Janet Todd (Columbus: Ohio State University Press, 1992–96), Vol. 1, 288.

54. *Lempriere's Classical Dictionary* (London: Bracken Books, 1984), 162 and 39.

55. Behn, *Works*, Vol.1, 61–2.

56. Behn, *Works*, Vol.1, 356 and 99–100.

57. Hammond, *Figuring Sex*, 44–61.

58. One of these, the aristocratic María Luisa Gonzaga y Manrique de Lara, Countess of Paredes, Marquise of la Laguna, especially supported Sor Juana and arranged the publication of her works in Spain. Critical readings of the love poems to María Luisa tend to see them as expressions of gratitude, downplaying their intimacy and eroticism. See Octavio Paz, *Sor Juana Inés de la Cruz*, trans. Margaret Sayers Peden (Cambridge, MA: Harvard University Press, 1988), and Nina Scott, "*Ser mujer, ni estar distante/no es de amarte impedimento*" in Sara Poot Herrera, ed., *Y diversa de mi misma/entre vuestras plumas ando* (Mexico, D.F.: Colegio de México, 1993), 159–69.

59. In Juana Inés de la Cruz, *Obras Completas*, Vol. I, Alfonso Méndez Plancarte, ed. (Mexico, D.F.: Fondo de Cultura Económica, [1951] 1994). Poems are cited by their numbers in this edition.

60. See Bergmann and Middlebrook, "*Mujer petrarquista*," 154–6.

61. "Prisonhouse fetters are fashioned by your tresses."

62. "Lachrymal droplets of dawn, condensed within a / sweet-scented vessel—your mouth, with its perfumes."

63. "Transiting to the sumptuous gardens of Venus, / musical organ of marble, your sculpted throat, / captivates even the air, in its bewitching / ecstasies of a melody long and low."

64. A preface before *romance* 16, not written by the poet herself, says, " *Advertencia. O el agradecimiento de favorecida y celebrada, o el conocimiento que tenía de las relevantes prendas que a la Señora Virreina dió el Cielo, o aquel secreto influjo (hasta hoy nadie lo ha podido apurar) de los humores o los Astros, que llaman simpatía, o todo junto, causó en la Poetisa un amor a Su Excelencia con ardor tan puro, como en el contexto de todo el libro irá viendo el lector*." [Warning/ Notice: Either her gratitude at being favored and celebrated, or her knowledge of the outstanding gifts that Heaven bestowed on the Lady Vicereine, or that secret influence (which to this day no one has been able to verify) of the humors or of the Stars, that is known as sympathy, or all these things together, caused the Poet to bear a love for Her Excellency with such a pure ardor as the reader shall see throughout this entire book.] (Sor Juana, *Obras*, 48). On the anonymous authorship of the epigraphs preceding Sor Juana's poems, see Frederick Luciani, "*Sor Juana Inés de la Cruz: Epígrafe, epíteto, epígono*," *Revista Iberoamericana*, 51 (1985): 777–83.

65. "permit my giant audacity / to scale your towering fortress."

66. The chance that my errors might do you honor
is a bait to draw my ambition on;
when a great risk looms so substantial,
what value falls a mere good shot?
Then permit the hazardous undertaking
to a wingéd quill that longs to fly;

if this crime can find excuse
in precedent, it will not be the first time.

67. "Since you are the most beautiful,/ grandest, most sovereign excess/ the green orbit of Time ever looked upon/ in all its revolutions."

68. "no Sheban fragrances arise / no human blood is ever spilled/ nor beast's neck comes beneath the knife."

69. "impure burnt offerings . . . lowly matter."

70. "pure sacrifice / of adoration and silence."

71. . . . like air drawn to what is hollow,
like fire, to feed on matter,
like boulders tumbling to the earth
and intentions, to their goal . . .

72. "but why should one wear oneself out?/ just so, Phyllis, do I love you."

73. Your being a woman, your being gone
cannot pose the slightest hindrance
to my love, for you know that our souls
have no gender and know no distance.

74. For example, the humorous *ovillejo* discussed by Bergmann and Middlebrook in "*La mujer petrarquista*."

75. Traub, "Desire and the Difference It Makes," 82.

76. Henry Lawes, *The Second Book of Ayres, and Dialogues, For One, Two, and Three Voyces* (London: John Playford, 1655), 46. The text is in Philips, *Collected Works*, Vol. 1, 90–1.

77. Violante del Cielo, *Rimas varias* (Rouen: [Ruán], France: Maurry, 1646), 8.

78. Behn, *Works*, Vol. 1, 288.

79. Juana Inés de la Cruz, *Obras completas*, I, no. 61, 171–173.

"Why, you . . . I oughta' . . .": Aposiopesis and the Natural Language of the Passions, 1670–1770

ROBERT G. DIMIT

"Why, you . . . I oughta' . . .": this formulaic expression of anger is probably most familiar to readers today either from "Three Stooges" shorts and Warner Brothers cartoons, or from David Letterman's facetious asides on late-night television. The device has a much longer and more serious history than these particular examples suggest, however, one that reveals much about eighteenth-century ideas concerning language and the display of the passions. In this article I consider the use of this device in imaginative writing between the 1670s and 1770s as a sort of test case for the claim, widespread then, if counterintuitive for many of us now, that rhetorical figures constitute the "natural Language of the Passions."[1] I trace the changes in theoretical discourse on passional language during this period, and show how the primary argument supporting the naturalness of rhetorical figures was co-opted by those who rejected rhetoric for its lack of naturalness.

The device used in the phrase, "Why, you . . . I oughta' . . . ," is the figure known in classical rhetoric by such names as "aposiopesis," "reticentia," "obticentia," "interruptio," and "praecisio."[2] Heinrich Lausberg describes this figure as "the omission of the expression of an idea, made known by breaking off a sentence already begun, sometimes also explicitly confirmed afterwards."[3] Thus, when we hear, "Why, you… I oughta'…," we understand, "Why, you little rat. I oughta' punch your lights out," or something similar.

There is more to aposiopesis, however, than the simple truncation of a grammatical structure. Aposiopesis implicitly communicates the sense of the unspoken parts of the statement, but it also communicates the intensity of the speaker's passions. Quintilian observed that "aposiopesis . . . itself displays the passions: either anger . . . or anxiety and, as it were, scruple . . . ," and illustrated the use of this figure with a passage from the *Aeneid*: "Whom I—but better first to calm the waves."[4] At this point in Virgil's epic, Juno has enlisted the help of the winds to stir up a storm that will drive Aeneas's fleet back from the shores of Italy. The aposiopesis occurs when Neptune, roused by the violence of the storm, summons the winds and angrily rebukes them. Here is the full speech as it is given in John Dryden's 1697 translation:

> Audacious Winds! from whence
> This bold Attempt, this Rebel Insolence?
> Is it for you to ravage Seas and Land,
> Unauthoriz'd by my supream Command?
> To raise such Mountains on the troubl'd Main?
> Whom I——But first 'tis fit the Billows to restrain,
> And then you shall be taught obedience to my Reign."[5]

"Quos ego . . ." or "Whom I . . . ," then, communicates anger and an implied threat of physical violence, just as "I oughta' . . ." does.

While it may be unlikely that David Letterman's writers have ever borrowed directly from Quintilian or Virgil, early modern rhetoricians did so regularly. The "quos ego" passage was the standard example of aposiopesis in European rhetorical manuals published during the sixteenth and seventeenth centuries. Many such works included this example in their discussions of aposiopesis; some also repeated Quintilian's claim that this figure is particularly suited for the display of certain passions.[6]

The broadest claims for the passional expressivity of aposiopesis and other figures were made by Bernard Lamy, in his *De l'art de parler*. Published anonymously in 1675 and translated into English the following year as *The Art of Speaking*, this text established the terms for Western European discourse on the "natural language of the passions" during the century that followed.[7] It is true that classical writers had sometimes linked certain figures to the display of specific passions, as Quintilian had done with aposiopesis, and that early modern rhetoricians before Lamy sometimes followed their ancient models in this as in other matters. But Lamy went beyond them by treating the display of the passions as an essential rather than a merely accidental attribute of rhetorical figures, by attributing this passional function to all figures rather than a selected few, and by explaining this function in terms of Cartesian passional theory.

Since typologies of rhetorical devices vary, and since "figural" or "figurative" language is now commonly understood to mean metaphorical language, let me clarify the sense in which I use the term "figure." Like Lamy and others in his day, I understand figures to be instances of language employed in unusual, vivid, or otherwise striking ways, but in which individual words retain their usual meanings. I thus distinguish figures from tropes (i.e., metaphor, metonymy, etc.), in which words bear meanings they do not ordinarily have. This distinction is important because some writers in the period under consideration viewed an abundance of tropes as the very antithesis of natural, passional speech, a view that many readers today are likely to share.

Lamy writes that, "les passions ont des caractères particuliers avec lesquels elles se peignent elles-mêmes dans le discours." By "caractères," he means something like "distinctive markings" or "characteristic traits." He continues, "Ces tours, qui sont les caractères que les passions tracent dans le discours, sont ces figures célèbres dont parlent les rhéteurs, et qu'ils définissent *des manières de parler éloignées de celles qui sont naturelles et ordinaires*: c'est-à-dire différentes de celles qu'on emploie quand on parle sans émotion."[8] As described by Lamy, then, the figures are symptoms or (in the terminology of late modern semiotic theory) indexical signs of the passions. The definition of the figures as ways of speaking that are different from natural and ordinary speech was traditional; Lamy's innovation lay in the added qualification that "naturelles et ordinaires" means "sans émotion." By this addition, Lamy resolved an apparent contradiction between the standard definition of the figures as departures from normal ways of speaking and the claim (advanced by him and others) that rhetoric merely codifies the ways people normally speak.[9]

Most often, Lamy describes the figures as though they were simply natural effects of the passions. In other passages, though, he treats the figures as devices of rhetorical art, as when he writes, "quand on fait parler une personne émue de quelque passion, si on veut faire une peinture exacte de cette passion, on doit donner à son discours toutes les figures propres, et les tourner en la manière qu'une personne, animée d'un mouvement semblable, figure et tourne son discours."[10] Lamy never explicitly reconciles these two notions of rhetorical figures, but it is clear that he sees them first as naturally occurring signs of the passions, and second as technical devices by which a writer or speaker may imitate those natural signs.

Lamy's explanation of the mechanisms by which the passions cause the figures is not as rigorous or orderly as we today might wish. Nonetheless, it is possible to show that he attributes most of the figures to one of a few passional processes. Some figures result from the force with which the passions fix the soul's attention on its object: the passions magnify the object, causing the soul to become entirely preoccupied with it. Such intense presence to the soul of a perceived, imagined, or remembered object may result in precise description, in repetitions of the same thought variously expressed, or in such complete preoccupation with the object as to render the speaker oblivious to his or her immediate surroundings.[11] Other figures result from the changeable nature of intense passions, which may cause interruptions in mid-sentence, abrupt leaps from one incompletely expressed thought to another, or even more radical deviations from proper syntax.[12] Those aspects of the figures that link them to the passions, then, are primarily logical or syntactic disruptions and intensity of visualization.

Lamy credits aposiopesis to the abrupt changes he says are typical of intense passions. "Aposiopèse est une espèce d'ellipse ou d'omission. Elle se fait lorsque, venant tout d'un coup à changer de passion, ou à la quitter entièrement, on coupe tellement son discours, qu'à peine ceux qui écoutent peuvent-ils deviner ce que l'on voulait dire. Cette figure est fort ordinaire dans les menaces. *Si je vous*, etc. *Mais*, etc."[13] Following Quintilian, and reflecting both ancient and late modern practice, Lamy links aposiopesis particularly with threatening speech. Of ellipsis more generally, Lamy writes, "Une passion violent ne permet jamais de dire tout ce que l'on voudrait dire. La langue est trop lente pour suivre la vitesse de ses mouvements . . . ."[14]

Underlying the explanations Lamy gives for the genesis of each figure is a Cartesian understanding of the passions. René Descartes is not mentioned by name, but the influence of his account of the interaction of body and soul in the passions is readily evident in Lamy's text, particularly in the paragraph on exclamation. The violent exhalation of breath that produces an exclamation, Lamy writes, is caused by the animal spirits that have been set in motion by a violent movement (or passion) of the soul.[15] While the echoes of Descartes's *Les passions de l'âme* are most obvious in this description of exclamation, Lamy sees all figures as arising from the effects on spoken language of passional alterations in the soul-body compound.

The idea of the figures as natural signs of the passions remained current through much of the eighteenth century, and was given explicit expression by numerous British writers. Dryden wrote, in 1677, that the figures "are principally to be us'd in passion; when we speak more warmly, and with more precipitation than at other times . . . . Aggravations are then in their proper places, Interrogations, Exclamations, Hyperbata, or a disorder'd connexion of discourse, are graceful there, because they are Natural." In 1704, John

Dennis called the figures "the natural Language of the Passions." Robert Lowth described the "language of passions" primarily in terms of rhetorical figures (1753); John Lawson wrote that "FIGURES are the Language of Passion" (1758); while for Henry Home, Lord Kames, the "Language of Passion" consists primarily of rhetorical figures, though the figures are not equally appropriate for every passion (1762). Hugh Blair, in lectures published in 1783, called the figures "that Language, which is prompted either by the imagination, or by the passions," and wrote of several individual figures as "the native language of passion."[16]

While it isn't clear that all of these writers were directly influenced by Lamy's account of the figures, such discussions as theirs of the "natural language of the passions" only began in English critical discourse after the publication of *De l'art de parler*. It is possible that Lamy was merely giving voice to ideas that were then "in the air," but, if so, he seems to have been the first to articulate them in print.

Whatever Lamy's role as inspiration or source may have been, British accounts of "the natural language of the passions" differ from his explanations in important respects. Lamy was oriented toward the classroom and the longstanding role of formal rhetoric as the foundation of all education. Dryden, Dennis, Kames and their countrymen were oriented instead toward polite society and new conceptions of taste and criticism as elements of the good life within that society. Given these differences in outlook and social context, it is unsurprising that British writers adopted much of Lamy's analysis but separated it from his discourse on rhetoric. Thus, in 1701, Dennis wrote, "Poetry is Poetry, because it is more Passionate and Sensual than Prose. A discourse that is writ in very good Numbers, if it wants Passion, can be but measur'd Prose. But a Discourse that is every where extremely pathetick and, consequently, every where bold and figurative, is certainly Poetry without Numbers. Passion then, is the Characteristical Mark of Poetry, and, consequently, must be every where."[17] Like Lamy, Dennis here assumes that "extremely pathetick" (i.e., extremely passionate) discourse will necessarily be "bold and figurative." But the real focus of his attention is the need for passion in poetry. For Lamy, the essential link was between passions and figures; for Dennis, it is between passions and poetry.

Lowth also posits an essential connection between the passions and poetic language in place of that between the passions and rhetorical figures. In his *Lectures on the Sacred Poetry of the Hebrews*, he writes that the "language of poetry" is "the effect of mental emotion."[18] But while Dennis seems merely uninterested in rhetoric, Lowth is explicitly hostile toward it. In this same work, Lowth uses language that might easily have been paraphrased from Lamy to describe the ways the passions naturally manifest themselves in speech. "For the passions . . . wonderfully magnify and exaggerate whatever dwells upon the mind, and labour to express it in animated, bold, and magnificent terms. This they commonly effect . . . partly by employing new and extraordinary forms of expression, which . . . in some degree imitate or represent the present habit and state of the soul. Hence those theories of Rhetoricians, which they have so pompously detailed, attributing that to art, which above all things is due to nature alone."[19] Lowth accepts Lamy's insight that all figures occur as natural signs of the passions, but dismisses efforts by rhetoricians to analyze or imitate those signs. In a similar manner, Blair, who describes rhetorical figures as "the native language of passion," writes that "those terms of expression, which we now distinguish by the learned names of Hyperbole, Prosopopoeia, Simile, &c. . . . are no other than the native original language of Poetry, among the most barbarous nations."[20]

In each of these comments, Lamy's conception of rhetorical figures as marks of the passions has been taken to conclusions he seems not to have considered. His account of the figures as the passions' natural effects on language was offered primarily as a basis for teaching how rhetorical devices might mimic those effects. The British critics who followed, however, took Lamy's insights as grounds for rejecting rhetoric. They chose to bypass the artful imitation of natural linguistic effects in favor of a poetry born directly from those effects themselves. One can't help but notice the similarities between this view of poetry and William Wordsworth's assertion that "good poetry is the spontaneous overflow of powerful feelings."[21] Indeed, M. H. Abrams and others long ago wrote about the eighteenth-century discourse on the "natural language of the passions" as part of a pre-Romantic conception of poetry, and John Morillo has recently argued that Wordsworth's poetic conceptions were particularly indebted to those of Dennis.[22]

Given their claims that rhetorical art is unnecessary, it is hardly surprising that eighteenth-century British writers pay much less attention than Lamy to the technical details of classical rhetoric, even in works that are ostensibly about rhetoric. In his *Lectures on Rhetoric and Belles Lettres*, for example, Blair discusses only a limited number of tropes and figures, and does so only after declining to follow the "scholastic writers on Rhetoric" whose "patient and frivolous industry" has produced nothing but an elaborate taxonomy of such devices, "as if the mere knowledge of the names and classes of all the Tropes that can be formed, could be of any advantage towards the proper, or graceful use of Language."[23] Lawson, in the *Lectures Concerning Oratory*, declines to treat individual figures, on the grounds that "they may be found in the Writings of every Rhetorician, deduced indeed usually with tiresome Exactness."[24]

As a consequence of this diminished attention to the technical details of rhetoric, discussion of aposiopesis is rare even in those eighteenth-century works that consider individual figures. Yet it is more accurate to say that uses of the technical term "aposiopesis" are rare: works on rhetoric often describe this and similar figures in relation to the passions, without naming them. John Walker, for example, writes that, "Anger, when violent, expresses itself . . . sometimes with interruption and hesitation, as if unable to utter itself with sufficient force"; while Joseph Priestley writes of forms that "are most natural in great agitation of mind, when the succession of ideas is uncommonly rapid, and when, consequently, it may be expected that some thoughts should interfere with others, and occasion frequent breaks in sentences, and interruptions in a chain of reasoning."[25] Echoes of Lamy's account of aposiopesis are evident in each of these passages, in the linguistic disruption described, the attribution of that disruption to the passions, and the process by which the passions are said to cause the disruption. That "aposiopesis" was sometimes translated as "interruption" (after the Latin "interruptio") further suggests that both of these authors were describing the figure without using the term. And, since Lamy's and other earlier rhetorical manuals continued to circulate throughout this period, detailed accounts of aposiopesis and other passional figures were certainly available. Laurence Sterne at least was familiar enough with aposiopesis to use its adjectival form in *Tristram Shandy*.[26]

This brief account of eighteenth-century discourse on "the natural language of the passions" shows why aposiopesis was then understood as a valid sign of strong passion. Lamy seems likely to have been the primary, if indirect, source for the British authors discussed here, but in their accounts they substantially altered his understanding of the relationship between passions and language. Dennis, Blair, and others variously shifted the focus from rhetorical theory to poetic practice, paid correspondingly less attention to rhetorical techniques and terminology, and rejected the imitation of natural passional signs in favor of a direct connection between those signs and a writer's experience of actual passions. These changes were uneven, however, and should not be taken to constitute a general linear progression (toward a Romantic view of affect's role in literary creation, for example). And, despite such changes, eighteenth-century British critics generally continued to see aposiopesis and other figures as marks of strong passion.

The theoretical writings considered here prompt two practical questions. First, were aposiopesis and the other passional figures actually used in the period's poetic or other literary writings? And, if so, were there changes in the use of these figures corresponding to eighteenth-century shifts in attitude toward technical rhetoric? The answer to the first question is that the figures were indeed used, particularly in dramatic dialogue of the late seventeenth and early eighteenth centuries. The answer to the second is that there were changes in the way the figures were used, but that those changes were no more consistent or linear than the changes in theoretical accounts.

Though the primary focus of this essay is on British works, the playwright from this period who made the most extensive and effective passional use of aposiopesis and other figures was Jean Racine. In this respect, as in others, Racine offered an important example to his colleagues across the Channel.

Athalie, Racine's last play, offers an example of aposiopesis that perfectly illustrates the usefulness of this figure in angry threats. The title character here confronts Joad, the high priest, in the temple, expecting him to turn over the last surviving heir to David's throne.

> Je devrais sur l'Autel, où ta main sacrifie,
> Te . . . Mais du prix qu'on m'offre il faut me contenter.[27]

Despite the disruption produced by the aposiopesis, Athalie's (incomplete) threat to sacrifice Joad on the temple altar is clear enough. The objective personal pronoun "te" with which the second line begins gives the construction a force that cannot be easily preserved in translation, given the ambiguity of the English "you." Otherwise, the menacing use here of aposiopesis closely resembles "quos ego . . ." and "I oughta' . . ." in the examples discussed above.

Dryden and Nathaniel Lee offer a similar threatening aposiopesis in *The Duke of Guise*. Before this passage, the popular and powerful Duke of Guise had been commanded by the King to stay away from the court.

> GRILL[ON]. My Lord, the *Guise* is come.
> KING. Is't possible! ha, *Grillon*, said'st thou, come?
> GRILL. Why droops the Royal Majesty? O Sir——
> KING. O Villain, Slave, wert thou my late born Heir,
> Giv'n me by Heav'n, ev'n when I lay a dying;——
> But peace, thou festring thought, and hide thy Wound;
> Where is he?[28]

The aposiopesis shows the intensity of the King's anger at being defied, while the figures in his initial reaction to the news (interrogation; exclamation) and Grillon's reply ("Why droops the Royal Majesty?") suggest that his anger is mixed with fear of the Duke's power. From the context we understand the

King's interrupted statement as a threat to have the Duke killed, a threat that will be carried out in the play's last act. What is unusual is that the threat here occurs within an apostrophe to the absent Duke. In terms of Lamy's analysis, the enunciation of the threatening aposiopesis within an apostrophe implies an even greater intensity of passion than would be the case if the Duke were actually present.

These two examples illustrate the usefulness of aposiopesis in displays of anger and show continuity with Quintilian's theory and Virgil's practice. But the figure's use was not limited to threats alone. Elsewhere in Racine's work, aposiopesis is used, most often in combination with other figures, to display a range of passions. His play *Andromaque* has only a few scenes that do not include abundant passional figures. In the work's central action, Pyrrhus has given Andromaque an impossible choice: agree to marry him, thereby dishonoring herself and her dead husband, Hector, or refuse and watch her son be killed. In the exchange that follows, Céphise has been urging Andromaque to consent to marry Pyrrhus.

> ANDROMAQUE
> Dis-lui que de mon fils l'amour est assez fort . . .
> Crois-tu que dans son cœur il ait juré sa mort?
> L'amour peut-il si loin pousser sa barbarie?
> CÉPHISE
> Madame, il va bientôt revenir en furie.
> ANDROMAQUE
> Hé bien! va l'assurer . . .
> CÉPHISE
> De quoi? de votre foi?[29]

We understand from the first aposiopesis that, though Andromaque seems ready to say she will marry Pyrrhus, the passions motivating her to refuse—love for Hector, horror at Pyrrhus, desire to maintain her honor—are too strong. This is evident as well from the two instances of interrogation that follow: her impassioned questions about the sincerity of Pyrrhus's threat to kill her son imply that she intends, or at least wishes, to refuse the offer of marriage. The second aposiopesis ("Va l'assurer . . .") shows again how the strength of her passions prevents her from voicing her assent.

In this passage and throughout his theatrical works Racine uses combinations of figures to simulate the effects of strong, conflicting passions on his characters' speech. Aposiopesis, interrogation, and exclamation all contribute to our sense of Andromaque's disordered thought. Though most of his plays were written before *De l'art de parler* appeared, Racine's passional dialogue perfectly exemplifies the theory of rhetorical figures developed in Lamy's treatise.

Among British plays, Dryden's *All for Love* comes closest to Racine's work in its extensive use of the passional figures recommended by Lamy. Despite Dryden's tactical denigration of Racine's "Monsieur Hippolite" in the "Preface" to *All for Love*, one can easily read this play as an experiment in Racinian tragedy adapted for the English stage.[30] Dryden gives Antony an aposiopesis in act four that, though it is driven in part by anger, does not carry an implied threat. Antony believes that Cleopatra and his dear friend Dollabella have betrayed him by becoming lovers. When he confronts them, and they deny his accusations, Antony responds with a tirade that reads in part,

> Heav'n should be ingenious
> In punishing such crimes. The rowling Stone,
> And gnawing Vulture, were slight pains, invented
> When *Jove* was young, and no examples known
> Of mighty ills; but you have ripen'd sin
> To such a monstrous growth, 'twill pose the Gods
> To find an equal Torture. Two, two such,
> Oh there's no farther name, two such——to me,
> To me, who lock'd my Soul within your breasts,
> Had no desires, no joys, no life, but you . . . .[31]

As in the speeches from *Andromaque* and *The Duke of Guise*, the simulation of passional intensity does not depend on a single figure, but on a series of figures. Antony twice begins his accusation ("Two, two such") but gives up because there is no word strong enough to describe the supposed lovers as his passions make them appear to him. He begins a third time, trying to say what sort of terrible people (traitors? monsters?) they are, but leaves the thought incomplete. The expression of a different thought follows this aposiopesis, though it is itself truncated by his passions. While the allusions to classical myth and the argument about appropriate punishment in this speech's early lines may seem too studied to be the results of actual passion, the figures in the last lines create an effective sense of Antony's disorder and passional intensity. Throughout *All for Love*, Dryden makes extensive use of similar figures to simulate the passions' effects on the speech of Antony and Cleopatra.

Other British playwrights of the Restoration and early eighteenth century made use of aposiopesis, though none as extensively or effectively as Dryden in *All for Love*, or Racine. In Joseph Addison's *Cato*, for example, Lucia says, "O Marcia, should thy brothers for my sake!— / I die away with horror at the thought" (her fear is that the "clash of swords" they have heard may be the brothers fighting over Lucia's love).[32] This passage is exceptional in *Cato*, however, since the play contains almost no other passional figures. While the passional effects achieved by Racine and Dryden at his best were seldom matched by later playwrights, passional figures continued to be used in dramatic dialogue well into the nineteenth century.[33]

The usefulness of the figures to a playwright was obvious, since contemporary critical writing attributed their passional significance primarily to occurrences in spoken language. What is perhaps more surprising than the use of passional figures in plays is the frequency of their use in epistolary novels. In the first 19 letters of Samuel Richardson's *Clarissa*, aposiopesis is used as a sign of passion no fewer than 10 times. Some of these figures occur in reported speech, as when Clarissa recounts her family's efforts at persuading her to marry the loathsome Mr. Solmes. Clarissa quotes her mother as saying, "Have I not conjured you, as you value my peace—What is it that *I* do not give up?"[34] The implied argument is that Clarissa must make dutiful sacrifices to her father's will, just as her mother has. We know from the context that the disruption in Lady Harlowe's discourse is a mark of her anger and indignation at her daughter's obstinate refusal of the match her family has proposed. Allowing for the obvious differences between the political struggles represented on the stage and the domestic conflicts in the novel, the passional functions of the aposiopesis in this passage and of those in the plays of Dryden and Racine are essentially the same. In other passages, however, Richardson's use of aposiopesis is quite different.

Concerning Lovelace, Clarissa writes, "But, hang the man, I had almost said—what is he to me? What *would* he be—were not this Mr. Sol—Oh, my dear, how I hate that man in the light he is proposed to me!" A few letters later, she writes, "*I* to have that Mr. Solmes!—No indeed!—I will sooner——But I will write first to other parts of your letter that are less concerning, that I may touch upon this part with more patience."[35] We easily understand both the referential sense of each passage, including to a certain extent the parts that remain unspoken, and the passional charge carried by each aposiopesis. The problem with these passional figures, however, is that they occur in a fictive letter rather than in fictive speech. Rhetorical figures were thought to constitute the natural language of the passions because they were taken for imitations of the passions' natural effects on speech. Lamy's explanations rested on his understanding of the ways that passions affected the body and soul together, thereby engendering the ways of speaking identified as figures. Passional figures are thus natural in spoken language, or in reports of spoken language. But, unless we imagine that Clarissa is engaged in something like automatic writing, the idea that her passions would cause her to write as she does in the last passage quoted is implausible. The intent and purposive actions necessary before one can even begin writing a letter, and the normal delay between thinking of what to write and actually doing so argue against the sort of spontaneous outburst represented in these lines. Also, since a letter may be put down at any point, and taken up again at a later time (as Clarissa does on more than one occasion), her explanation for breaking off in the second instance ("But I will write first to other parts of your letter that are less concerning . . .") seems specious.

In fact, such epistolary uses of this figure suggest that, for Richardson, the theory which originally justified spoken aposiopesis as a natural sign of the passions had fallen from view. In its place was an understanding of aposiopesis as a conventional sign of passion, which is to say as a literary convention, an understanding closer to our own than to Lamy's. Richardson appears to employ passional figures in his novel, not because he believes that is the way people naturally speak under the influence of strong passion, but because that is the way strong passions are indicated in other imaginative writing.

That aposiopesis and other figures were coming to be seen as purely conventional devices in the later eighteenth century is also suggested by the following passage from *Tristram Shandy*:

> Let me stop and give you a picture of the corporal's apparatus; and of the corporal himself. . . .
>
> The corporal——
>
> ——Tread lightly on his ashes, ye men of genius,——for he was your kinsman:
>
> Weed his grave clean, ye men of goodness, ——for he was your brother.——Oh corporal! had I thee, but now,——now, that I am able to give thee a dinner and protection,——how would I cherish thee! . . . But alas! alas! alas! now that I can do this, in spight of their reverences——the occasion is lost——for though art gone . . . .[36]

Here the question of plausibility raised by Richardson's use of passional figures in epistolary fiction seems irrelevant. Sterne's copious piling on of figures—aposiopesis, apostrophes, exclamations—is so exaggerated that we today have difficulty reading this passage as anything but a parody of their use (or inept use) to show the passions. Such parody is perhaps to be expected given the increasing dismissal of rhetoric as a discipline and the diminished interest in rhetoric's technical details in the later eighteenth century.[37]

And yet, it would be wrong to imagine that aposiopesis and other passional figures had fallen into disuse by the end of the eighteenth century, or that they could no longer be taken seriously. In Wordsworth's "Tintern Abbey," we read,

> If this
> Be but a vain belief, yet, oh! how oft,
> In darkness, and amid the many shapes
> Of joyless daylight . . . have I turned to thee,
> O, sylvan Wye![38]

Here, in one of the foundational texts of English Romanticism, we find Lamy's passional figures used with an earnestness equal to that with which the Restoration playwrights used them.[39] Just as the theoretical understanding of the passional charge carried by rhetorical figures survived the ostensible overthrow of formal rhetoric, so, too, did the use of such figures to display strong feeling in literary texts.

I have given here a brief sketch of aposiopesis as a mark of the passions in British literature and criticism between 1670 and 1770. The reasons why a critic or rhetorician at the end of the seventeenth century would believe that the figures constitute the "natural language of the passions" are clear enough. However foreign that belief may remain to our own experience, we should be able intellectually to recognize its reasonableness. I have also shown how Lamy's explanation of the use of rhetorical devices to make dramatic dialogue and other literary language more naturalistic was later incorporated into an argument about the artificiality of rhetorical language. Still, any attempt to trace a progression from Lamy's position to something like our late modern response to aposiopesis and similar figures is complicated by the non-linear changes in literary practice suggested by the passages from *Tristram Shandy* and "Tintern Abbey."

Whether we today find aposiopesis and other such figures believable signs of passion (or emotion) depends in part on how believable we find the plot situations and surrounding dialogue. The serious intentions and skill of the actor delivering the lines also make a difference. When David Letterman or Daffy Duck delivers an aposiopesis, we know we're supposed to laugh at it as a stereotypical expression of anger. But we are unlikely to laugh at the same figure when we encounter it in a well acted production of a David Mamet play.[40]

Few scholars today are truly interested in the details of rhetorical theory, however, and many would gladly join Lowth and his contemporaries in dismissing rhetoric altogether. Those scholars . . . whom I . . . but that issue is beyond the scope of this article.

NOTES

An earlier version of this paper was delivered at the 2004 Annual Meeting of the American Society for Eighteenth-Century Studies in Boston, MA.

1. The phrase is from John Dennis, as discussed below.

2. Heinrich Lausberg, *Handbook of Literary Rhetoric: A Foundation for Literary Study*, trans. Matthew T. Bliss et al., ed. David E. Orton and R. Dean Anderson (Leiden: Brill, 1998), 394–7. In an article on "reticentia," Lausberg cites classical authorities giving these other terms as synonyms. For the sake of clarity, I use "aposiopesis" throughout.

3. Lausberg, *Handbook of Literary Rhetoric*, 394.

4. Quintilian, *Institutio oratoria; The Orator's Education* 9.2.54, 5 vols., ed. and trans. Donald A. Russell (Cambridge, MA: Harvard University Press, 2001), 4:64–5. "[aposiopesis] . . . ipsa ostendit adfectus, vel irae, . . . vel sollicitudinis et quasi religionis . . ."; "quos ego—sed motos praestat componere fluctus." The translation has been slightly modified.

5. John Dryden, *Virgil's Aeneis* 1.188–94, in *The Works of John Dryden*, 20 vols., ed. Edward Niles Hooker et al. (Berkeley and Los Angeles: University of California Press, 1956–2000), 5:348.

6. See, among others, Omer Talon, *Rhetorica*, in *Dialecticae lib. duo. cum Rhetorica* (Frankfurt: Zacharias Palthenius, 1600), 82; Abraham Fraunce, *The Arcadian Rhetoric* (1588; reprint, Menston, England: Scolar, 1969), fol. F7r; Bartholomew Keckermann, *Systema rhetoricae* (Hanover: Guilielmus Antonius, 1608), 284; Thomas Farnaby, *Index rhetoricus* (1625; reprint, Menston, England: Scolar, 1970), 25; John Smith, *Mystery of Rhetoric Unveiled* (1657; reprint, Menston, England: Scolar, 1969), 148; Bernard Lamy, *La rhétorique ou l'art de parler*, critical ed., ed. Benoît Timmermans, (Paris: Presses Universitaires de France, 1998), 194.

7. *De l'art de parler* was gradually expanded in later editions and appeared as *La rhétorique ou l'art de parler*, with Lamy's name on the title page, beginning in 1688. Various editions, printings, and translations of this text circulated widely throughout the eighteenth century. For an account of this complex publishing history and of Lamy's progressive revisions, see Timmermans, "Annexe 1" and "Annexe 2," in Lamy, *La rhétorique ou l'art de parler*, 575–89.

8. Lamy, *La rhétorique ou l'art de parler*, 181, 184 ; italics in original.

9. Lamy, *La rhétorique ou l'art de parler*, 218–19.

10. Lamy, *La rhétorique ou l'art de parler*, 185.

11. Lamy, *La rhétorique ou l'art de parler*, 181, 196.

12. Lamy, *La rhétorique ou l'art de parler*, 182, 191–6.

13. Lamy, *La rhétorique ou l'art de parler*, 194. The "quos ego" line immediately follows this passage.

14. Lamy, *La rhétorique ou l'art de parler*, 193.

15. Lamy, *La rhétorique ou l'art de parler*, 191.

16. Dryden, "The Authors Apology for Heroique Poetry; and Poetique Licence," in *Works of John Dryden*, 12:93; John Dennis, *The Grounds of Criticism in Poetry*, in *The Critical Works of John Dennis*, 2 vols., ed. Edward Niles Hooker (Baltimore: Johns Hopkins University Press, 1939), 1:359; Robert Lowth, *Lectures on the Sacred Poetry of the Hebrews*, 2 vols., trans. G. Gregory (1787; reprint, Hildesheim: Georg Olms, 1969), 1:309–10; John Lawson, *Lectures Concerning Oratory* (1758; reprint, Menston, England: Scolar, 1969), 252; Henry Home, Lord Kames, *Elements of Criticism*, 6th. ed., 2 vols. (Edinburgh: John Bell and William Creech, 1785), 1:494–500, 2:228–63; Hugh Blair, *Lectures on Rhetoric and Belles Lettres*, 2 vols. (London: Strahan and Cadell, 1783) 1:275, 1:356, 2:54.

17. Dennis, *The Advancement and Reformation of Poetry*, in *Critical Works of John Dennis*, 1:215.

18. Lowth, *Lectures on the Sacred Poetry*, 1:365.

19. Lowth, *Lectures on the Sacred Poetry*, 1:309–10.

20. Blair, *Lectures on Rhetoric and Belles Lettres*, 2:315.

21. William Wordsworth, "Preface to *Lyrical Ballads*, 1800," in Lyrical Ballads, *and Other Poems, 1797–1800*, ed. James Butler and Karen Green (Ithaca and London: Cornell University Press, 1992), 744.

22. M. H. Abrams, *The Mirror and the Lamp: Romantic Theory and the Critical Tradition* (New York: Norton, 1953); P. W. K. Stone, *The Art of Poetry 1750–1820: Theories of Poetic Composition and Style in the Late Neo-Classic and Early Romantic Periods* (London: Routledge and Kegan Paul, 1967); John D. Morillo, *Uneasy Feelings: Literature, the Passions, and Class from Neoclassicism to Romanticism* (New York: AMS Press, 2001), 16–43.

23. Blair, *Lectures on Rhetoric and Belles Lettres*, 1:290–91.

24. Lawson, *Lectures Concerning Oratory*, 254.

25. John Walker, *Elements of Elocution*, 2 vols. (1781; reprint, Menston, England: Scolar, 1969), 2:318; Joseph Priestley, *A Course of Lectures on Oratory and Criticism* (1777; reprint, Menston, England: Scolar, 1968), 112.

26. Laurence Sterne, *The Life and Opinions of Tristram Shandy, Gentleman* 4.27, in *The Florida Edition of the Works of Laurence Sterne*, 6 vols., ed. Melvyn New et al. (Gainesville: University Press of Florida, 1978–2002), 1:383. Of course, Sterne's use of this particular term is not necessarily a sign that it had wide currency then.

27. Jean Racine, *Athalie* 5.5.1712–13, in *Œuvres Complètes*, 2 vols., ed. Georges Forestier (Paris: Gallimard, 1999) 1:1080.

28. Dryden and Nathaniel Lee, *The Duke of Guise* 3.2.5–10, in *Works of John Dryden*, 14:256.

29. Racine, *Andromaque* 3.8.1039–43, in *Œuvres Complètes*, 1:235.

30. Dryden, "Preface" to *All for Love or, the World Well Lost*, in *Works of John Dryden*, 13:12–13. On Dryden's debts to Racine and his efforts to conceal them, see Norman Suckling, "Dryden in Egypt: Reflections on *All for Love*," in *Twentieth Century Interpretations of All for Love: A Collection of Critical Essays*, ed. Bruce King (Englewood Cliffs, NJ: Prentice-Hall, 1968), 46–54; and David Bruce

Kramer, *The Imperial Dryden: The Poetics of Appropriation in Seventeenth-Century England* (Athens, GA: University of Georgia Press, 1994).

31. Dryden, *All for Love* 4.1.474–83, in *Works of John Dryden*, 13:88.

32. Joseph Addison, *Cato: A Tragedy* 4.3.4–5, in Cato: A Tragedy *and Selected Essays*, ed. Christine Dunn Henderson and Mark E. Yellin (Indianapolis: Liberty Fund, 2004), 75.

33. See, for example, the melodramas collected in Michael R. Booth, ed., *English Plays of the Nineteenth Century*, vol. 1, *Dramas 1800–1850* (Oxford: Oxford University Press, 1969).

34. Samuel Richardson, *Clarissa or the History of a Young Lady*, ed. Angus Ross (Harmondsworth: Penguin, 1985), 91.

35. Richardson, *Clarissa*, 84, 104.

36. Sterne, *Tristram Shandy* 6.25, 2:544–5.

37. In addition to the discussion above, see Brian Vickers, *In Defence of Rhetoric* (Oxford: Oxford University Press, 1988), 196–204.

38. Wordsworth, "Lines Written a Few Miles above Tintern Abbey, on Revisiting the Banks of the Wye During a Tour, July 13, 1798," lines 50-3, 56–7, in Lyrical Ballads, *and Other Poems, 1797–1800*, 117.

39. The figure in this passage is most correctly described as anacoluthon, but its structure and passional function are like those of aposiopesis.

40. See, among others, these lines: "To look in the goddamn . . . Forget it. Forget it. *Don't* let me see it" (David Mamet, *American Buffalo* [New York: Grove, 1977], 62); "What is the five grand? (*Pause.*) What is the, you said that we were going to *split* five . . ." (David Mamet, *Glengarry Glen Ross* [New York: Grove, 1984], 26).

From Geneva to Glasgow: Rousseau and Adam Smith on the Theater and Commercial Society

RYAN PATRICK HANLEY

The delivery of the two sets of lectures today known as the *Lectures on Rhetoric* and the *Lectures on Jurisprudence* was hardly the only university business that occupied Adam Smith in the winter of 1762–63. That term he served the University of Glasgow not only as Professor of Moral Philosophy but also as a member of a faculty committee organized by the university to thwart the construction of a theater in the city.[1] This detail will interest Smith's students for several reasons. Students of his biography will consider it incongruous given his well-documented enthusiasm for the drama.[2] Students of his political thought will be struck by it given his explicit recommendation of the social utility of dramatic representations in the *Wealth of Nations*.[3] Students of his moral philosophy will be surprised to find a hint of possible anti-theatrical ire from one who offers long comparisons of the merits and mechanics of comedy and tragedy, takes frequent recourse to examples drawn from the classical and the contemporary stage, and whose moral system is itself built on the eminently theatrical concepts of sympathy and spectatorship.[4] The centrality of the stage to Smith's thought is further suggested by his first biographer, who notes that his projected works included a treatise on the history of the theater and "the principles of dramatic composition."[5] How then to make sense of his anti-theater stance in 1762?

Several explanations suggest themselves. Perhaps the committee was an exercise in prudence and an attempt to preempt possible student and town riots.[6] More plausible, perhaps, is the suggestion that Smith and the Glasgow authorities sought to avoid another theological conflagration like that which had erupted in Edinburgh five years earlier after the initial performances of Reverend John Home's controversial *Douglas*.[7] Smith would not have missed the warning of his good friend Hume that support of the stage during that controversy gave further encouragement to those already seeking his excommunication.[8] But prudential considerations alone do not fully explain the anti-theatrical activity of one who otherwise seems such a steadfast supporter of the stage. Where then might the Professor of Moral Philosophy have found a philosophical justification for his position? One possibility is that he discovered his defense in the most renowned anti-theater polemic of his day: Rousseau's 1758 *Letter to d'Alembert*.

That Smith knew the *Letter* seems likely given the available evidence.[9] But here I focus less on this claim and instead suggest that Smith's treatments of the theater and its place in commercial society illuminate an overlooked side of a much broader, sustained engagement with Rousseau.[10] We might expect theirs to have been a relationship of opposition, with Smith, avowed champion of commerce, the theater, and the plays of Voltaire, out to correct the errors of Rousseau, sworn enemy of all three. Yet as their discussions of the theater reveal, the Rousseau of the *Letter* and the Smith of *The Theory of Moral Sentiments* share a common understanding of the nature of modern morality and also propose a similar remedy for modernity's corruptions of that morality. This remedy is distinguished by its moderation. Both Rousseau and Smith call for moralists to reform modern corruption from within the context and constraints of modernity itself.[11] Indeed for all their substantive political differences, their concrete proposals for countering commercial corruption are both grounded in this fundamental similarity. For both insist that solicitude for the opinions and esteem of others is the distinguishing quality of modern commercial society, and that any attempts to shape contemporary morals must begin with this first principle – a fact which animates their parallel discussions of the difference between theatrical duplicity and the genuine utility of a certain type of spectatorship in political life.

Attention to their shared conception of the role of theater and theatricality in modern society thus reveals important additional points of agreement between the two thinkers. These agreements further challenge received views of Rousseau as republican reactionary and Smith as champion of commercial modernity. Smith's treatment of the theater in fact reveals that he was deeply aware not only of the advantages of commercial society, but also, like

Rousseau, of its moral shortcomings. Even his defense of the theater in the *Wealth of Nations* (which on its face seems his most explicitly anti-Rousseauian position), is itself part of a larger, characteristically Rousseauian project to minimize these shortcomings, and particularly to moderate religious enthusiasm and factionalism. Thus the claim that I wish to defend is that both Smith's opposition to the theater in 1762–63 and his support of it in 1776 are defensible on Rousseau's standard as set forth in the *Letter*: that the theater is not simply bad for the good, but also good for the bad. Smith's development of Rousseau's critique is thus a domestication of that critique of enlightenment within the Enlightenment. His treatment of the theater reveals him to be neither a complacent champion nor a reactionary opponent of commercial society, but a friend who, in refusing to flatter it, sought a moderate means by which its characteristic vices might be put in the service of ameliorating the worst effects of those vices.

Rousseau presents the central moral problem of modern commercial society with admirable clarity in the *Second Discourse*, in a line Smith knew well: after the birth of commerce, "to be and to appear became two entirely different things" (SD, 170/OC III, 174).[12] This distinction between being and appearing is itself the central theme of the *Letter to d'Alembert*, in which it takes the form of a distinction between doing and imitating. This same distinction is also at the heart of *The Theory of Moral Sentiments*, in which the separation of the desire to appear from the desire to be takes the form of the separation of the love of praise from the love of praiseworthiness. In each case claiming and deserving are distinguished; the selfish desire to claim attention and recognition is separated from a nobler desire to act in such a manner as to be worthy of attention and recognition. This distinction is itself the foundation of their treatments of the place of the theater in commercial society. It is especially evident in their discussions of the theater's principal participants: authors, actors and spectators.

With regard to the first category, Smith and Rousseau agree that most authors are motivated by the desire for applause and that their obsessive solicitude for praise leads them to grow indifferent to the merit and consequences of their productions. Rousseau often claims that pride gives rise to philosophy and that authors seek honor and attention (FD, 19/OC III, 21; PN, 97–98/OC II, 965–66; PN, 105n/OC II, 974n). Smith likewise claims that philosophers and poets are driven by the love of praise and consider the public's admiration as almost the whole compensation for their efforts (WN I.x.b.24; LJ(A) vi.62; cf. LJ(B) 226). The dangers of this solicitude are noted by Rousseau, who explains that authors strive "to excite the curiosity of the public" through productions of wit which "have for their end only applause," and that once this end has been achieved "no other advantage is sought" (L, 27/OC V, 25). Such a monomaniacal focus on attention from others, he insists, leads authors to forget their real duties to them. His critique of Molière drives the point home: Molière may have been an essentially decent man but "he had to make the audience laugh," and "for the sake of multiplying his jokes, shakes the whole order of society" (L, 41/OC V, 38; L, 35/OC V, 32).

Rousseau and Smith thus agree that authors, caring only for praise, often grow indifferent to praiseworthiness. Actors suffer from the same vice, yet to the solicitude for recognition the actor adds dissimulation and deceit. In his struggle for praise, Rousseau claims, the actor learns to cultivate "the art of counterfeiting himself, of putting on another character than his own, of appearing different than he is" (L, 79/OC V, 72–3). Of course, in his self-conscious duplicity, the actor of the *Letter* is only the developed expression of the dissembling man of the *Second Discourse*.[13] Caring more for gain than virtue, such actors and citizens forfeit the esteem of more discerning judges; hence Smith notes that actors are held in disrepute as their exertion "for the sake of gain is considered, whether from reason or prejudice, as a sort of public prostitution" (WN I.x.b.25; cf. L, 76/OC V, 69–70; L, 83/OC V, 76). Even if their profession is useful, this alone cannot make it appear noble (L, 77/OC V, 70; WN II.iii.2).

But this brings a problem of its own: if actors are debased, why do audiences still cram theaters and enthusiastically applaud them? In truth, fault seems to lie not only with authors and actors but with spectators. Spectators, both explain, always prefer dazzling spectacles of greatness to more humble portraits of goodness. Thus Rousseau's lament: "Victims of our own mad applause, will we never learn how much contempt and hate are deserved by any man who abuses the genius and the talent that nature gave him, to the hurt of humankind?" (L, 29/OC V, 27)[14] Spectatorship, seen in this way, seems more likely to corrupt than purify moral judgment. The popularity of the stories of Medea, Phaedra and Cataline all testify to the theater's capacity to bestow upon "clever knaves" (*méchans habiles*) the "benefits of the public esteem owed to the virtuous" and thereby render its audience insensitive to the distinction between praise and praiseworthiness (L, 23/OC V, 21; L, 29/OC V, 27). And Smith too laments that the "artful knave" in the splendor of "dexterity and address" is "too often received in the world with an indulgence which he by no means deserves" (TMS VI.i.16). With Rousseau he agrees that both on the stage and in common life spectators mistake greatness for goodness. Dazzling displays of virtue seem beautiful, and seduced by this beauty spectators never attend to the dubious effects of such spectacles, but instead find "the most worthless men" praiseworthy (TMS VI.iii.8; VI.conc.7).

Smith finds a parallel in our fascination with wealth. The same disposition that leads us to marvel at crimes also leads spectators to admire and worship the most "gaudy and glittering" displays of riches and prefer them to more praiseworthy but more humbly-clad displays of virtue (TMS I.iii.3.2). Smith's fascination with our love of vulgar beauty and its affect on our imagination is indeed a central theme of his writings (EPS, 183–84; WN I.xi.c.31; TMS V.1.2). His economics in fact relies on this "deception" of the imagination: namely, that what appears beautiful is in fact good and worthy of our exertion (TMS IV.i.9–10). Nature has implanted in us both a "fascination of greatness" and a solicitude for esteem in order to stimulate our vanity and thereby encourage us to do our part in promoting universal prosperity: this is the foundation of his system of natural liberty (TMS VI.ii.1.20; I.iii.2.2–3; I.iii.3.2; VI.iii.30).[15]

Now, in claiming that the illusions of the vain modern imagination are the key to universal opulence, Smith seems to part sharply from Rousseau. But elsewhere he calls attention to a darker side of this scheme for peace and prosperity. In observing that our admiration for the great makes kings and nobles the proper subjects of tragedy (see also LRBL, 44–45; TMS I.iii.2.2; cf. L, 116/OC V, 106), he notes that the propensity to worship our superiors also has less happy consequences:

> There is in human nature a servility which inclines us to adore our superiors and an inhumanity which disposes us to contempt and trample under foot our inferiors. We are too much accustomed to the misfortunes of people below or equal with ourselves to be greatly affected by them. But the misfortunes of the great both as they seem connected with the welfare of a multitude...we are apt to pay great respect and attention to our superiors however unworthy...Nay such is the temper of men, that we are rather disposed to laugh at the misfortunes of our inferiors than take part in them (LRBL, 124).

Smith's language here is not that of optimism, but that of warning and caution: "we are rather apt to make sport of the misfortunes of our inferiors than sympathize with them" (LRBL, 124). Like Rousseau, Smith is no stranger to the tragic awareness that the same predisposition that makes prosperity possible encourages indifference and condescension towards those who have dropped out of the sight of mankind.

With this observation we come to the political tragedy at the heart of both commercial society and the theater. In their ideal forms, both the market and the theater are said to encourage sociability and the softening and civilizing of manners. But Rousseau suggests and Smith develops the counter-argument that the sociability and civilizing supposedly encouraged by both markets and theaters are only masks for a more insidious atomistic egoism. Thus Rousseau's famous claim: "People think they come together in the theatre, and it is there that they are isolated. It is there that they go to forget their friends, neighbors, and relations in order to concern themselves with fables" (L, 16–7/OC V, 16). Markets and theaters alike feed the selfishness that encourages us to attend to the trivial and fantastic and in so doing lead us to neglect our real duties to others. To push the parallel further: our very love of the theater and its entertainments seems born of the same "discontent with one's self" and restive desire for escape that is at once the stimulus and scourge of commercial life (L, 16/OC V, 15; L, 126n/OC V, 115n; TMS III.3.31). Both markets and theaters encourage consumers to rush towards the "self-forgetting" and "annihilation" which are the emancipation of their selfishness.[16] Thus the vanity that originally led the opinion-loving pleasure-seekers to seek out others degenerates into self-indulgence and self-absorption. The fate of civilized man is thus a lonely narcissism; the search for sympathetic spectators ends in solitude, before the mirror (EPS, 186).[17] The road to the most perfect form of sympathetic identification leads not towards but away from the city; only when we are alone can we be sure of being perfectly understood.

The theater, in sum, seems to draw on and encourage several of the same passions and propensities encouraged by commercial society. For this reason Smith and Rousseau resisted the claim that the corruptions of commerce might be countered by transforming the theater into a school of virtue, dedicated to presenting the most ennobling characters and edifying lessons.[18] Rousseau's challenge to this common view begins with his study of the nature of comedy. Comedy, he insists, could never teach virtue since its aim is to mock it.[19] Thus Molière: "His greatest care is to ridicule goodness and simplicity and to present treachery and falsehood so that they arouse our interest" (L, 34/OC V, 32). Comedy achieves this goal via the actions it portrays. In comedy the vicious are not only cleverer but also more successful than the virtuous; the latter only talk while the former act. Properly understood comedy is then not so much a school of virtue as a school of utility in which success is made to seem more attractive than virtue. This reversal of the low and the high is in fact the very foundation of comedy; Smith too notes that comedy exploits our propensity to laugh whenever "what we expect to find great and noble turns out otherwise" (LRBL, 45). Smith, to be sure, has some hope for comedy's reformative potential (see LRBL, 47), but he can offer no guarantee that the comic poets will stay within their boundaries and not pander to "superficial minds" who despise the "virtues of the inferior ranks of people" and delight in the vices of the great (TMS V.2.3). The virtues of the sober and temperate hardly play well on the stage, and thus comedy inclines to celebrate extremes and to disparage moderation. And lest the comedians defend their trade by insisting that their scripts allow the virtuous to win in the end, Rousseau reminds his readers that the forced and facile "lessons" taught in final scenes are quickly forgotten, and that the knavery that dominates the rest remains impressive long after the audience departs (cf. E, 112–16).

Comedy thus elevates the vicious at the expense of the virtuous. But Rousseau is also careful to point out that comedy directly assaults virtue as well, and indeed does so in a particularly political way. The chief target of the comic poet, he explains, is custom both ancestral and local. Tragedy portrays the aged not as wise but tyrannical, and comedy paints them as jealous, avaricious and petty: "this is the honorable view given of old age in the theater; this is the respect for it with which the young are inspired" (L, 50/OC V, 46; cf. TMS II.ii.3.8). But the theater, and comedy in particular, also ridicules local custom. Under the guise of cosmopolitanism the theater allows its patrons to become imbued "with foreign objects" (L, 58/OC V, 53). Yet it is Rousseau's conviction that "it is not good that we be shown all sorts of imitations, but only those of things that are decent and befitting free men" (L, 120/OC V, 109).

The limits of comedy as a school for virtue are obvious. But what about tragedy? Neither Rousseau nor Smith find much reason for greater optimism here. Tragedy may be well-intended, yet it is weak; if comedy hastens towards vulgarity, tragedy only inches towards nobility. Tragedy shapes the emotions of its audience by eliciting pity, but neither Smith nor Rousseau thinks that such pity alone can actuate mere spectators to acts of moral nobility. "What is this pity? A fleeting and vain emotion which lasts no longer than the illusion which produced it…a sterile pity which feeds on a few tears and which has never produced the slightest act of humanity" (L, 24/OC V, 23). It is less virtue than vanity that Rousseau finds in the spectacle of the pathetic weeping matrons at their opera boxes, "proud of their tears" (L, 25). The sterility of this disposition is even less excusable than its vanity. Crying spectators deceive themselves into thinking that they have satisfied their duties to the suffering, while "unfortunate people in person would require attention from us, relief, consolation, and work, which would involve us in their pains and would require at least the sacrifice of our indolence" (L, 25/OC V, 23). So far from promoting virtue, tragedy substitutes for duty "some passing and sterile emotions that have no consequences" (L, 26/OC V, 24).[20]

Smith was not unfamiliar with the phenomenon here described. His own moral system sought to encourage "fellow-feeling" or sympathy, yet this hardly blinds him to the vulgarity of those affected displays that Rousseau condemns. Thus even in noting that we often "weep even at the feigned representation of a tragedy," Smith knows that not all tears are equally telling (TMS I.ii.5.4). In our compassion we may be moved on hearing the misfortunes of our friend, "and perhaps, on that account, work ourselves up into an artificial sympathy, which, however, when it is raised, is always the slightest and most transitory imaginable; and generally, as soon as we have left the room, vanishes, and is gone forever" (TMS I.iii.1.12). A true friend, however, knows that "sympathetic tears" are "but a small part of the duty" we owe others. Only when our "indolent and passive fellow-feeling" gives way to a "more vigorous and active sentiment" that leads us to act do we do our friends justice (TMS II.i.2.5; II.iii.3.3). Like Rousseau, Smith thinks this "artificial commiseration" is "perfectly useless" (TMS III.3.9). Smith and Rousseau, we might conclude, little esteem the spectators who remain mere spectators and never become actors in their own right and who consider good-feeling sufficient to exempt them from good-doing. Cosmopolitan consciousness of universal suffering does not enlighten but enfeebles; better not to pity at all if pitying prevents us from benefiting anyone (PN, 99/OC II, 967). So too Smith: Nature in her wisdom knew when loading us with our own sorrows not to "command us to take any further share in those of others, than what was necessary to prompt us to relieve them" (TMS I.iii.1.12). Tragedy, however, seems unlikely to further this goal. Theatrical imitations elicit only imitations of passions. True sympathy is only realized by real and not imagined spectators.

I have attempted above to state as forcefully as I could Rousseau's and Smith's critiques of both modern theatricality and modern theater. That critique again is this: in his dependence on recognition, civilized modern man is led on the one hand to a slavish need for approbation (which culminates in the obliteration of the self) and on the other to seek a radical emancipation (which culminates in the obliteration of concern for others). Both paths are inimical to the possibility of decent political life. The theater in its various forms then furthers this attack on political decency: comedy by loosening the attachment of the citizens not only to what is decent but also to what is historically and locally customary, and tragedy by elevating sentiment over duty and good-feeling over good-doing. But how did Rousseau and Smith think such challenges should be met? Their answer was both moderate and modern, and hence a rejection of solutions both extreme and ancient.

Their moderation is partly evident in the methods they use to present their works. The rhetoric of the *Letter* is meant as a counter-example to that of Voltaire and Molière. Interestingly the *Letter* begins not with d'Alembert's proposal for a theater but with his thoughts on Geneva's religion. The aim of this opening is to reveal the actual intolerance of religion espoused by the champions of liberal religious toleration. But Rousseau will not allow himself to be so guilty; he promises "to respect the secrets of consciences" (L, 14/OC V, 13). Respect for the beliefs of his fellow citizens indeed animates the *Letter*. Always conscious of their needs and the good of their city, Rousseau avoids teachings capable of harming the decent but unenlightened.[21] This commitment to respecting the beliefs of the decent is perhaps what he has in mind when he twice insists in the *Confessions* that the *Letter* was composed in a spirit of tenderness and "gentleness of soul" (C, 415/OC I, 495; C, 420/OC I, 502).[22] Smith is animated by the same conviction, and this often-overlooked aim allies him with Rousseau, against satirizing enlighteners from the age of Socrates down to that of "Dr. Swift and Voltaire." Smith disdains those who "have too often distinguished themselves by the most improper and even insolent contempt of all the ordinary decorums of life and conversation, and who have thereby set the most pernicious example to those who wish to resemble them" (TMS VI.i.10).

Respect for audiences is one sign of Rousseau's and Smith's moderation. Yet the moderation and sophistication of their response to the challenges of commercial society also shows itself in another way. Their answer is predicated on the belief that the means best suited to the remedy of modern morals emerge from the very conditions of modern morality itself. The "realistic" character of such a remedy distances it from the idealism of remedies both modern and ancient. Now, the modern remedy is the one proposed by d'Alembert; the idealism of his remedy lies in its cosmopolitanism. The excerpt from his article included in the Preface to the *Letter* suggests that Geneva's best interest is hardly the only good that he has in mind. His ostensible aim is to enable Geneva to realize Athens' urbanity and Sparta's prudence together, but his goal is less to improve Geneva than to refine Europe. Building a theater will allow Geneva to shine on the European stage: foreigners will come to see its politeness, its actors "would serve as a model to the actors of other nations," and the collective amour-propre of its citizens would be gratified in the "glory of having reformed Europe on this point" (L, 5/OC V, 5). But from these prospects Rousseau returns his readers to consider the real interests of their city; against the member of the academies of France, Prussia, London, Sweden and Bologna, the citizen of Geneva calls for a reorientation of perspective.[23] Thus he reminds his fellow citizens that the question of whether Geneva's theater will be good for Europe is far less pressing than the question of whether it will be good for Geneva; in all such deliberations it is far more important in the first instance "to establish what will result in our particular situation" as a consequence of the innovation than to judge that innovation itself (L, 92/OC V, 84–85).

Rousseau's argument against modern idealism also informs his argument against ancient political idealism. Rousseau is often assumed to have taken Sparta as his model. But Sparta only serves as a standard to judge the distance of modernity's departure from antiquity. As a guide to solving modern problems it is worthless; Rousseau knows that solutions to today's problems can only be discovered by those living today. This point is important for his treatment of the theater. The modern champions of the theater insist on its utility as a school of virtue, which Rousseau of course rejects. But what alternative is to be found? Sparta had no theater, he insists (wrongly, it turns out); morality there was instead regulated by law. But will modern lawgivers find Sparta's methods practical? Can "severe" or "well-executed" laws today be trusted to do the job? (L, 66/OC V, 60) More than once he answers with a resounding "no": "never do good laws change the nature of things; they only follow it" (L, 79/OC V, 72). Again: "laws are everywhere insufficient to repress the vices which arise out of the nature of things" (L, 122/OC V, 111). But if laws are insufficient, what alternative might be proposed? The *Letter* notes that three instruments are available to legislators who wish to work on the morals of a people: "the force of the laws, the empire of opinion, and the appeal of pleasure" (L, 22/OC V, 20–21). But laws and argument rule only in the city ruled by reason, and from the *Republic* he knows that the third course is proper where the taste for poetry has given rise to the ascendancy of pleasure and pain.[24] But in a Geneva that is no longer a Sparta and almost but still not quite a Paris – that is to say, a city no longer so pure as to be directed by law alone and not yet so corrupt as to be led only by pleasure – a middle way is likely to be most effective at shaping the morals of this middle state:

> By what means can the government get a hold on morals? I answer that it is by public opinion. If our habits in retirement are born of our own sentiments, in society they are born of others' opinions. When we do not live in ourselves but in others, it is their judgments which guide everything (L, 67/OC V, 61–62).

Thus Rousseau moves beyond the diagnosis set forth in the *Second Discourse* and begins to work towards a cure. Here the very vice that separates the ancients from the moderns, the love of opinion, is proposed as a remedy for the ills it engenders.[25]

The *Letter* thus might be read as providing an education in prudence to statesmen. Its lesson is that those who would shape the morals of the city must carefully examine the conditions of that city to determine the most fitting course of action. Thus while Smith is more famous for his "science of the legislator," Rousseau too is concerned in the *Letter* to establish the methods of the "true legislator's science" for the benefit of "real statesmen" (L, 66/OC V, 60–61). And on at least one point Smith's and Rousseau's political sciences agree: the aim of the legislator is not to establish the ideal, but to establish the best possible in light of the limitations of current conditions: "let us not seek for the chimera of perfection but for the best possible according to the nature of man and the constitution of society" (L, 110/OC V, 101). Wise legislators do not disdain perfection, but suit their imitations of perfection to the tastes of ordinary citizens.[26] The best example is Solon, concerned to establish "less the best laws in themselves than the best of which it admits in the given situation" (L, 66/OC V, 61).[27] Solon is also Smith's ideal statesman. The man of system imposes his imaginary constructions on the state to its detriment. But the humane and benevolent statesman

> will accommodate, as well as he can, his public arrangements to the confirmed habits and prejudices of the people; and will remedy as well as he can, the inconveniences which may flow from the want of those regulations which the people are averse to submit to. When he cannot establish the right, he will not disdain to ameliorate the wrong; but like Solon, when he cannot establish the best system of laws, he will endeavour to establish the best that the people can bear (TMS VI.ii.2.16; cf. WN IV.v.b.53).

Both Rousseau and Smith insist on the necessity of meeting people where they stand, and their practical politics are similarly impressed with a spirit of moderation. Each author considers compromise superior to both the idealism of the utopian and the twice-removed imitations of the poets. This method in turn leads them to agree that modernity will never achieve a recovery of antiquity. To think otherwise is futile: "let us not flatter ourselves that we shall see Sparta reborn in the lap of commerce and the love of gain" (L, 67/OC V, 61).[28] Geneva's imitation of Sparta would be a political disaster. Yet attention to Geneva's ills will prevent it from suffering Paris's fate.

The use of opinion to regulate popular morals is the great theme of Smith's morality of spectatorship, at least in its foundations. The concept for which his system is today most famous is the "impartial spectator." Less frequently noted are his many hints that this spectator is more imaginary than real, and hence his repeated qualifications of the impartial spectator as the "*supposed* impartial spectator."[29] But less illusory is the real presence of others and the benefits afforded by a consciousness of their gazes, which prompts Smith's reminder that virtue is not to be discovered in the "abstruse syllogisms of a quibbling dialectic" but in "a regard to the sentiments of the real or supposed spectator of our conduct" (TMS III.3.21). In this manner, regard for the esteem of others, that most modern of obsessions, is raised to the level of the morally salutary.

Smith and Rousseau both recognize that the highest excellence disdains solicitude for the opinions of others. But for those who aspire not to excellence but to competence, their limitations hold the key to their improvement. Thus to reproach the narcissist for succumbing to the "universal vice of his age" is less useful than helping him to recognize this vice and encouraging him to employ it as the first step in its overcoming (OC II, 995; TMS VI.iii.46). Thus like Smith, Rousseau insists that opinion is to be used to regulate morals in the world in which opinion is valued above reason; here "the same causes that have corrupted peoples sometimes help prevent a greater corruption."[30] Such an approach may seem to "destroy virtue," yet in a second-best world it alone can "preserve its public semblance, and this at least is a fine thing to do." For this reason Rousseau suggests that we substitute "politeness and propriety" for virtue (PN, 103/OC II, 972). Smith does the same. He begins his *Theory* with an inquiry into "the sense of propriety" and turns to "the character of virtue" only in the sixth part. Now, neither Smith nor Rousseau thinks that propriety and politeness alone are sufficient; Rousseau later condemns the latter as "lying and false" (L, 45/OC V, 41). As he builds his argument, Smith also distinguishes "a considerable difference between virtue and mere propriety": the latter consists in "mediocrity," but the former is "something uncommonly great and beautiful" (TMS I.i.5.6–7). Yet both Rousseau and Smith consider propriety's imitation of virtue as an indispensable first step in virtue's pursuit.

Both Rousseau and Smith use spectatorship to encourage the propriety on which modern morals are founded. Each of their systems relies on the propensity of the decent man to act differently in situations where real spectators are present.[31] Not only do both think that the love of praise encourages its possessor to act in a praiseworthy manner, but both agree that bashfulness, or the fear of shame that comes from a consciousness of the opinions of others, can restrain blameworthy conduct. Each writer believes that "vice is a friend of shadows" and anonymity a recipe for immorality (L, 129/OC V, 117). Hence Rousseau claims that in the "big city" morals suffer "because each, easily hiding his conduct from the public eye, shows himself only by his reputation and is esteemed only for his riches," whereas individuals who live in "small cities" have more regular morals since their inhabitants "always in the public eye, are born censors of one another" and "the police can easily watch everyone" (L, 58–59/OC V, 54).[32] So too Smith: in a "country village" even the most humble individual can expect that "his conduct may be attended to, and he may be obliged to attend to it himself." Yet "as soon as he comes into a great city" and finds himself "sunk in obscurity and darkness," his "conduct is observed and attended to by nobody," and he is likely "to abandon himself to every sort of low profligacy and vice" (WN V.i.g.12).

A principal aim of the *Letter* is then to distinguish proper and useful spectatorship from theatrical spectatorship. By establishing the conditions for the former it shows how the same disposition that corrupts in the "dark prison" and "gloomy cavern" of the theater improves us in the streets, "under the sky" (L, 78/OC V, 72; L, 125/OC V, 114). All of the social institutions and civic rituals described in the *Letter* in fact depend on a well-regulated spectatorship for their effectiveness. As has been frequently noted, particularly with regard to Rousseau's famed account of the spontaneous festival of the Saint-Gervais regiment, these practices substitute genuine transparency for the opacity of the theater.[33] Thus courts of honor combat "secret challenges" by making it possible for courage to "show itself on the field of honor" and casting suspicion on "those who had hidden themselves to fight" (L, 70/OC V, 64). The circles of the men preserve the image of ancient morals insofar as they "neither wish nor are able to be hidden" and make it easier for the police to carry out their "inspection" of citizens' private lives (L, 104–105/OC V, 96; L, 108/OC V, 99; L, 110/OC V, 100–101).[34] The gossip societies of the women are filled with "severe observers" who "almost perform the function of censors" in their imitations of Roman citizens "watching one another" (L, 106/OC V, 97). Marriage balls allow the young to "show themselves off" but also use this same desire to be noticed to encourage "propriety and circumspection," the product of their consciousness of "the eyes of the public" forcing them "to watch themselves most carefully": "the spectator imposes a gravity out of which they would not dare to step for an instant" (L, 128/OC V, 117).

Smith, following Rousseau, likewise distinguishes proper from theatrical spectatorship and insists that the watchful eye of others is a key to improvement. Thus Smith notes that "obscure strangers who visit foreign countries" are more likely to ruin themselves through spending than those who live among peers (TMS VI.iii.37). Thus too he notes that the young gentleman on the Grand Tour "at a distance from the inspection and controul of his parents and relations" commonly loses all his former good habits, and returns home conceited, unprincipled and lazy (WN V.i.f.36; TMS VI.ii.1.10). Obscurity and anonymity lend themselves to vice, and typically their only remedy is to remind one of his reputation by surrounding him with real spectators. Conscience is rarely enough: "the man within the breast, the abstract and ideal spectator of our sentiments and conduct, requires often to be awakened and put in mind of his duty, by the presence of the real spectator" (TMS III.3.38). And herein lies the only remedy for the stranger lost in the city. He "never emerges so effectually from this obscurity" as when he becomes "the member of a small religious sect" in which he gains "a degree of consideration which he never had before" and his brother sectaries become "interested to observe his conduct" (WN V.i.g.12). Around the corner Smith will insist that such a cure is potentially worse than the disease, but the limited point is clear: a sense of honor or shame is the only cure for the moral ills of obscurity.

Each of these institutions clearly depends on "spectatorship" to be effective. But what separates this spectatorship from spectatorship in the theater is that the latter lacks reciprocity; at the theater spectators are separated from actors, and for all the importance invested in how the former see the latter it matters not at all how the latter see the former. But the spectatorship that both Rousseau and Smith admire is not a one-way process; for spectatorship to be truly useful the spectators must themselves become actors who are in turn observed by others. Both thinkers can envision this transformation occurring in the theater itself. Rousseau recounts Plutarch's story of the old Athenian theater-goer teased by boys who would not offer him a seat. The prank's victim finds relief only when the ambassadors from Sparta rise to give him a place of honor among them. "This action was observed by the whole audience and universally applauded": thus the spectator is transformed into a spectacle more edifying than that performed on stage (L, 32/OC V, 30). Smith likewise claims that what edifies at the theater is not the audience's apprehension of the action onstage but their apprehension of each other. Self-command is learned not by seeing staged imitations of it, but in our own exercising of it before other spectators. When we see a tragedy, he explains, we struggle against our sympathy as long as we can, and "give way to it at last only when we no longer can avoid it: we even then endeavour to cover our concern from the company. If we shed any tears, we carefully conceal them, and are afraid, lest the spectators, not entering into this excessive tenderness, should regard it as effeminacy and weakness" (TMS I.iii.1.9).[35] Spectatorship is efficacious only when the spectator's gaze is reversed, and true change comes about only when we become "the spectators of our own behavior" (TMS III.1.5; cf. I.i.4.8).

The rehabilitation of the characteristic vice of modern commercial society, the love of appearances, is thus at the heart of Rousseau's and Smith's attempts to encourage a morality of spectatorship. But does their rehabilitation of spectatorship also extend to a rehabilitation of theatrical performances or "spectacles" themselves?[36] Smith's advocacy of the theater in the *Wealth of Nations* seems to provide an answer. But is his advocacy a renunciation of

Rousseau's position as set forth in the *Letter* and his own as reflected in his actions of 1762, or is this position in 1776 commensurate with his earlier principles?

An answer to this question requires reexamining the intentions of the *Letter*. Its obvious theme is to argue against the theater, yet we know that the *Letter* also has a more subtle side, evident in its effort to train legislators to consider not "what is good for men in general" but "only what is good for them in this time or that country" (L, 17/OC V, 16). This is of the greatest significance for Rousseau's final teaching on the theater. The standard by which the theater is to be judged good or bad has less to do with the nature of the theater than with the nature of those who attend it. Before we can pronounce whether the theater is good or bad for a particular people, "we must know in the first place if the morals are good or bad there." With this idea in mind Rousseau revises his provisional conclusion that the theater is good for those who are good and bad for those already bad. Now we learn the truth: "when the people is corrupted, the theater is good for it, and bad for it when it is itself good" (L, 65/OC V, 59–60; cf. PN, 104/OC II, 973–74).[37]

The question of the current moral state of Geneva is then central to resolving the theater question.[38] The assumption in the *Letter* seems to be that Geneva is an island of purity in a sea of corruption, but more than once Rousseau undermines that assumption. Already he has distinguished Geneva from Sparta as the lap of commerce and the love of gain, and the distinction is drawn more sharply as he continues. Thus he claims that Geneva's "lavishness" and "abundance" prevent it from appearing to be "the image of Lacedaemon" (L, 127/OC V, 116). Thus too he admits that whatever esteem he may feel for his fellow citizens, he knows "too well how far it is from them to the Lacedaemonians." They had "strength of soul," but Genevans are "only decent" (L, 134/OC V, 122). Truth be told, the decent Genevans seem to have less in common with Spartans than with Parisians. In Paris vanity and an obsession with productivity leave no time for leisure. But what distinguishes Rousseau's Geneva? Geneva too has no indolence, and prodigious amounts of industry (L, 93/OC V, 85). Like the Parisians, its people know "too well the value of time and money" (L, 110/OC V, 101). And the virtues considered the "treasures of Geneva" ("its use of time, its vigilance, its austere parsimony") would seem more Parisian than Spartan (L, 93/OC V, 85). The decent Genevans, in short, are good bourgeois, and theirs the sort of town in which Smith's bourgeois would feel right at home. His "prudent man," distinguished by the "regularity of his temperance" and the "steadiness of his industry" and the "strictness of his frugality" and his ardent desire to be "an exact observer of decency," is indeed at once a perfect image of the commercial man and also of Rousseau's good Genevan (TMS VI.i.9–10). From this similarity we might conclude that so far from resisting commercial modernity, the Genevans have already gone further down the road to Paris than its proud citizens might be prepared to admit: "One must not dissemble: the intentions are still upright, but the morals already noticeably incline toward decadence, and we follow, at a distance, in the tracks of those same peoples whose fate does not fail to cause us anxiety" (L, 111/OC V, 102).

Rousseau's description of Geneva, in conjunction with his standard for theater as bad for the good but good for the bad, entitles us to wonder: if Geneva is already closer to Paris than Sparta, is it not also close to the point at which the theater will be good for it? Put differently, is the more significant intention of Rousseau's polemic against the theater to warn readers that their corruption will soon render the theater (and much else) necessary in their city? This conclusion, invited by Rousseau, finds its full explication in Smith's work. Thus the *Wealth of Nations* makes explicit the implicit teaching of the *Letter*: a need for a theater is both evidence of and the consequence of commercial corruption.

Smith's advocacy of the theater in the *Wealth of Nations* is based precisely on the Rousseauian conviction that theater is good for the bad. But it is also evident from the *Lectures on Rhetoric* that Smith agrees with the other half of Rousseau's formula. Rousseau regards Athens as the best example of how theater is bad for the good: "it was by the violence of the theater that Athens was lost" (L, 121/OC V, 111). Smith took the same position in a lecture delivered in the term that the faculty committee on the Glasgow theater convened. In it he recounts the story of Eubulus the Athenian and his law for public subsidy of theater patronage. In a manner reminiscent of Rousseau, Smith describes the decision to support attendance of the theater with public funds, the famed *theôrika*, as the beginning of the end of Athens. "This was the foundation of all their disorders," he insists:

> From this time the people became altogether idle and inactive; they received the same pay for sitting at home and doing nothing but attending the public diversions as they did for serving their country abroad…Military glory then had no weight; the orators ruled the people coaxing them with new schemes of additional wealth and often overruled the most experienced commanders, turning them, continuing them or changing them as they thought fit. Levies were then seldom voted and where they were, as seldom made. The Athenians from being the most enterprising people in Greece were now become the most idle and inactive (LRBL, 151).

Smith's argument is precisely Rousseau's: Athens' support of theater encouraged luxury and decadence in which self-interest was emancipated and public spirit crushed. The law of Eubulus was thus the cause of its fall: the war was upon them but as none could see "any advancement of their fortunes" or "private advantage" in participating, even Demosthenes could not rouse them from their luxurious lethargy (LRBL, 152).

Smith's pronouncement on the Athenian theater in his rhetoric lectures explains his position on the Glasgow theater question in that same year. Yet this defense prompts an obvious question: what happened between then and 1776 to elicit what appears to be a categorical reversal of his position? One suggestion is that this seeming reversal owes less to Smith's reconsideration of the merits of the theater than to his reconsideration of the merits of his fellow Glaswegians in the intervening years. The middle decades of the eighteenth century in fact brought great change to both Glasgow and the Glaswegians as the city experienced a tremendous commercial boom. Smith himself notes with pride that between 1750 and 1765 Glasgow's total trade doubled in size thanks largely to the city's expanding cotton and tobacco markets, and he also emphasizes the city's industriousness as compared to rival Edinburgh's (WN II.ii.41; II.iii12). Yet Smith also would have been among the first to see that Glasgow's commercial explosion coincided with a deterioration of social conditions that in time gave rise to Europe's most profound case of urban destitution.[39] Smith's city indeed might be said to have experienced precisely the fate that made Rousseau tremble, and the professor at Glasgow would not have needed to look far to see evidence of the truth on which the citizen of Geneva insists: that wealth and viciousness travel together.

The Glaswegians thus provide a classic instance of a good people gone bad at the hands of commerce. But so far from indifferent to this fact, Smith describes the nature of this corruption and proposes a scheme for the amelioration of the worst of these vices. His proposed therapy for the vices of commerce is the principal subject of two writings: Book V of the *Wealth of Nations* and Part VI of *The Theory of Moral Sentiments*. The former deserves our particular attention as it is here, in the course of describing his therapy for the feverish city, that he reconsiders his original position on the theater.

Smith begins by describing what commercial society has lost, and readers of Rousseau will find in his description several familiar suggestions. His enumeration of the "disadvantages of a commercial spirit" begins with the claim that the love of gain "sinks the courage of mankind, and tends to extinguish martial spirit." Later he insists that "military courage diminishes" in a commercial people because "by having their minds constantly employed on the arts of luxury, they grow effeminate and dastardly." Where "our ancestors were brave and warlike, their minds were not enervated by cultivating arts and commerce," modern men are vitiated (LJ(B) 331–3; cf. L, 101). In short, commercial modernity leaves no time to cultivate the "noblest of all arts," that of war (WN V.i.a.14).

But corruption of martial spirit is not the only, or even the worst, consequence of the commercial spirit. Even more threatening to political stability is the "mental mutilation" that the division of labor encourages.[40] So far from insisting on a necessary connection of wealth and virtue, Smith insists that wealth and stupidity are more likely to run hand in hand: "in every commercial nation the low people are exceedingly stupid" (LJ(B) 329). Their stupidity is the famous effect of the division of labor, which by confining the activities of all to a few simple operations, promotes "drowsy stupidity" or "gross ignorance and stupidity" and finally leaves minds "mutilated and deformed" (WN V.i.f.51; V.i.f.61). In his 1762 jurisprudence lectures Smith countered this description of economic productivity and intellectual torpor with his description of the considerable moral benefits of the system of household manufacturing that precedes labor specialization: "When the mind is employed about a variety of objects it is some how expanded and enlarged, and on this account a country artist is generally acknowledged to have a range of thoughts much above a city one." The latter is "perhaps only a cabinet maker," whereas the former is "perhaps a joiner, a house carpenter, and a cabinet maker all in one" (LJ(B) 328–29). But here again the point is directly anticipated by Rousseau. It is not difficult for a reader of the *Letter* to hear in Smith's description of the country artist Rousseau's celebration of mountain life outside Neufchatel, where specialization is still to arrive and even complex tasks know no division of labor – a place where "each joins in himself all the various crafts into which watchmaking is subdivided and makes all his tools himself." Thus its greatness: "never did carpenter, locksmith, glazier, or turner enter this country; each is everything for himself, no one is anything for another" (L, 61/OC V, 56).[41]

Commerce thus seems to encourage stupidity. But what is it about this stupidity that makes it a political problem, and why does Smith insist that to remedy these defects "would be an object worthy of serious attention" from wise men and from government? (LJ(B) 333) Benevolence alone does not explain his reasons. Rather, Smith thinks that commercially-induced stupidity is a political problem not simply because it is ignoble, but because stupidity is a breeding ground for faction, and for religious faction in particular. His thoughts on the political consequences of faction are unambiguous: "Of all the corruptors of moral sentiments, therefore, faction and fanaticism have always been by far the greatest" (TMS III.3.43). The superlative is also used to describe the problem of faction in the *Wealth of Nations*: "the most essential circumstance in the public morals of a free people," he explains, is "the good temper and moderation of contending factions" (WN V.i.f.40). Thus his support of public education: the more instruction pupils receive, "the less liable they are to the delusions of enthusiasm and superstition, which, among ignorant nations, frequently occasion the most dreadful disorders" (WN V.i.f.61). Organized religion, Smith insists, has at all times attempted to exploit this popular stupidity to further its private ends. Thus he adduces a quotation from Hume's *History of England* in which the clergy appear like nothing so much as the poets whose amour-propre leads them to go to any lengths necessary to elicit approval, irrespective of their effects. To "render himself more precious and sacred in the eyes of his retainers" the clergyman will "continually endeavor, by some novelty, to excite the languid devotion of his audience. No regard will be paid to truth, morals, or decency in the doctrines inculcated" (WN V.i.g.6). Like the poet, he is led to all sorts of dangerous extremes for the sake of eliciting "the respect and veneration of the common people" (WN V.i.g.11; V.i.g.29; V.i.g.34–35). Here again the desire for esteem is the root of disorder. Such an analysis is particularly congenial to the author of the *Letter*, who likewise presents himself as the "friend of every peaceful religion" and enemy of the "interest, pride, and opinionation" which fuel the "dissensions of the priests and the philosophers" (L, 11 and n/OC V, 11 and n).[42]

Smith's diagnosis of the corruption of modern morals by commerce thus runs as follows: commercial wealth requires the division of labor. The division of labor brings opulence but also stupidity. Popular stupidity in turn renders men susceptible to religious zeal. Religious zeal in its turn promotes the worst of all political ills, the faction which is the herald of political collapse. And it is with this apocalyptic vision in mind that we are returned to the consideration of the theater. Smith's call for theater is presented as one of "two very easy and effectual remedies" he proposes to "correct whatever was unsocial or disagreeably rigorous in the morals of all the little sects" into which a country is divided (WN V.i.g.13). The first is the study of natural science, "the great antidote to the poison of enthusiasm and superstition" (WN V.i.g.14; cf. V.i.f.24). The second remedy is "the frequency and gaiety of public diversions," among which he numbers painting, poetry, music, dancing, and "all sorts of dramatic representations and exhibitions" which might "amuse and divert the people." His justification is that such diversions would

> easily dissipate, in the greater part of them, that melancholy and gloomy humor which is almost always the nurse of popular superstition and enthusiasm. Public diversions have always been the object of dread and hatred, to all the fanatical promoters of those popular frenzies. The gaiety and good humor which those diversions inspire were altogether inconsistent with that temper of mind, which was fittest for their purpose, or which they could best work upon (WN V.i.g.15).

Such a defense of the theater hardly rests on the conventional defense that it might serve as a "school for virtue." To the degree that the theater is a "valuable moral resource in a community,"[43] it is so not because it teaches the bad to be good, but because it prevents the bad from doing evil; thus five times in five sentences Smith insists that the theater is to be valued as a "diversion" which channels the energies of the vicious away from the sorts of actions in which they would find their natural expression.

So far from constituting a renunciation of Rousseau, Smith's stance on the theater in the *Wealth of Nations* is ultimately in full agreement with the claim of the *Letter* that "reason dictates the encouragement of the amusements of people whose occupations are harmful, and the turning-away from the same amusements of those whose occupations are beneficial" (L, 58/OC V, 53). Both thinkers insist that it is necessary to encourage amusements "that might to some extent distract men's wickedness, and prevent them from spending their idleness in more dangerous pursuits" (PN, 104/OC II, 972). The theater's only justification is that we should let men drink if by forbidding it we would encourage them to do worse (L, 108/OC V, 99). For both Smith and Rousseau the theater is the elixir of the masses, and their defense of it partakes less of an enlightened faith in man's capacity to improve man, and more of the prudent conviction that it is necessary for modern men to seek to manage what they cannot fully control.

NOTES

Earlier versions of this essay were presented at the Annual Meeting of the American Political Science Association, Philadelphia, PA, August 2003; and at the Annual Meeting of the American Society for Eighteenth Century Studies, Boston, MA, March 2004. I am grateful for comments offered by both audiences, and wish to express a particular debt of gratitude to Robert Wokler for his comments on an earlier draft, and to John Scott and the Rousseau Association for organizing the ASECS panel.

1. See Ian Ross, *The Life of Adam Smith* (Oxford: Clarendon Press, 1995), 148. The reports of the committee's meetings have been collected in W. R. Scott, ed., *Adam Smith as Student and Professor* (Glasgow: Jackson, Son and Co., 1937), 164–66. It is at least amusing to note that several of the committee's meetings would have fallen on the same days as the delivery of Smith's lectures: 3 December 1762, the committee's second meeting, was the day of the eighth rhetoric lecture (LRBL, 40–47); 6 January 1763, the sixth committee meeting, was the day on which he delivered the jurisprudence lecture reprinted as LJ(A) i.90–115; 16 March 1763 saw the seventh meeting of the committee and the jurisprudence lecture reprinted as LJ(A) v.72–84.

2. On Smith's enthusiasm for theater and his attendance while in France from 1764–66, see John Rae, *The Life of Adam Smith* (London: Macmillan, 1895), 82, 213–14.

3. Adam Smith, *An Inquiry into the Nature and Causes of the Wealth of Nations*, ed. R. H. Campbell and A.S. Skinner (Indianapolis: Liberty Fund, 1981), V.i.g.15. I treat this passage at greater length below. Hereafter references to Smith's works will be to the Glasgow edition published by Oxford and reissued in paperback by the Liberty Fund (1981–84). The following abbreviations have been used: CAS = *Correspondence*; EPS = *Essays on Philosophical Subjects*; LJ = *Lectures on Jurisprudence*; LRBL = *Lectures on Rhetoric and Belles-Lettres*; TMS = *The Theory of Moral Sentiments*; WN = *An Inquiry into the Nature and Causes of the Wealth of Nations*. Numerical references to LJ, TMS, and WN are to the standard paragraph numbering system of the Glasgow edition; all other references are to pages. Wherever possible I have used standard English translations of Rousseau's works: E = *Emile*, trans. Allan Bloom (New York: Basic Books, 1979); FD = *Discourse on the Arts and Sciences* (first *Discourse*) in *The Discourses and Other Early Political Writings*, trans. Victor Gourevitch (Cambridge: Cambridge University Press, 1997); L = *Letter to d'Alembert*, translated by Bloom as *Politics and the Arts: Letter to d'Alembert on the Theatre* (Ithaca: Cornell University Press, 1968); PN = *Preface to 'Narcisse'* in Gourevitch, *Discourses*; SD = *Discourse on the Origins of Inequality* (second *Discourse*) in Gourevitch, *Discourses*. References to other of Rousseau's works are to the *Oeuvres complètes*, ed. Bernard Gagnebin and Marcel Raymond, 5 vols. (Paris: Gallimard, 1959–95), and are cited by volume and page number.

4. For the influence of the contemporary French stage on Smith's thought see Deidre Dawson, "Is Sympathy So Surprising? Adam Smith and French Fictions of Sympathy," *Eighteenth-Century Life* 15 (1991): 147–62. On the theatrical elements of Smith's moral philosophy, see especially David Marshall, *The Figure of Theater: Shaftesbury, Defoe, Adam Smith and George Eliot* (New York: Columbia University Press, 1986), 167–92; and Charles Griswold, *Adam Smith and the Virtues of Enlightenment* (Cambridge: Cambridge University Press, 1999), 65–70.

5. Dugald Stewart, "Account of the Life and Writings of Adam Smith, LL.D.," III.15, in *EPS*, 305–06.

6. As suggested by Scott in *Adam Smith as Student and Professor*, 163n3 – a suggestion Ross calls "a lame excuse" (*Life of Adam Smith*, 148). But the suggestion is not without merit given the actual history of the theater in Glasgow. In 1764 its supporters, having been denied permission to build within the city, built west of town and outside the city's jurisdiction. The night before the initial performance it was set

ablaze by a mob inspired by George Whitefield, the famed Methodist revivalist; see John Jackson, *The History of the Scottish Stage* (Edinburgh, 1793), 97–102; Walter Baynham, *The Glasgow Stage* (Glasgow: Robert Forrester, 1892), 8–17; Rae, *Life of Adam Smith*, 79–80. Given the topics of the present essay, it should also be noted that the theater ultimately built in Geneva in 1766 was likewise the target of arson soon after its completion; see Jeffrey Ravel, "Rousseau and the Construction of French Provincial Playhouses," in *Rousseau on Arts and Politics: Autour de la Lettre à d'Alembert*, ed. Melissa Butler (Ottawa: North American Association for the Study of Jean-Jacques Rousseau, 1997), 184; and John Hope Mason, "The *Lettre à d'Alembert* and its Place in Rousseau's Thought," in *Rousseau and the Eighteenth Century*, ed. Marian Hobson, J. T. A. Leigh, and Robert Wokler (Oxford: Voltaire Foundation, 1992), 253n12.

7. The *Douglas* controversy began as a debate over the propriety of clergymen writing for the stage, and its participants included the Scottish Enlightenment's most eminent literati. After a vicious denunciation by the Edinburgh clergy (who compelled him to tender his resignation to the Haddington presbytery), Home received public defenses from, among others, Adam Ferguson in *The Morality of Stage-Plays Seriously Considered* (Edinburgh, 1757) and David Hume, whose open letter to Home was appended to the 1757 printing of his *Four Dissertations*.

8. Hume to Smith, March 1757 in CAS, 20.

9. Edward Duffy notes the prominence of the *Letter* in Britain in the late 1750s and 1760s in his *Rousseau in England* (Berkeley: University of California Press, 1979), 10–12. At 160n12 Duffy also calls attention to the fact that the *Letter* was widely reviewed in England soon after its initial publication. One of the most important English reviews appeared in Edmund Burke's *Annual Register*, which praised Rousseau's *Letter* as "by far the most ingenious, spirited, and philosophical performance that ever appeared on theatrical entertainments." This review, interestingly, was directly followed by an important review of Smith's just-published *Theory of Moral Sentiments* (the review of the *Letter* can be found at *Annual Register* 2 (1759): 479–84, with the review of *TMS* following at 484–89). It is easy to imagine that Smith, who had himself reviewed Rousseau's *Discourse on Inequality* three years previously (see EPS, 242–54), would have been keenly interested in both reviews. But more importantly, Smith's library catalogue lists two copies of the *Letter*, one of indeterminate date and a second in a 1760 edition of Rousseau's collected works [see Hiroshi Mizuta, *Adam Smith's Library: A Catalogue* (Oxford: Oxford University Press, 2000), 217; of course, when these copies were acquired is not known]. And Smith's familiarity with the *Letter* is not anomalous, for he seems to have followed Rousseau's writings of the late 1750s and early 1760s with great care. In addition to the two copies of the *Letter*, Smith also owned early editions of *Julie* (1761), *Emile* (1762), and the *Letters from the Mountain* (1764). This suggests that his interest in Rousseau did not end with his famed review and translation of sections of the *Discourse on Inequality* but continued well into the 1760s, an important fact given that this period witnessed several of his own most significant endeavors, including publication of the first (1759) and second (1760–61) editions of the *Theory of Moral Sentiments* and the *Dissertation on the Origin of Languages* (1761), the delivery of the *Lectures on Rhetoric* and *Jurisprudence* (1762–

63) and the composition of the "Early Draft" of the *Wealth of Nations* (pre-1764).

10. In this respect the present essay seeks to complement several studies of Rousseau's influence on Smith which have tended to focus on the latter's engagement with the *Discourse on Inequality* rather than the *Letter to d'Alembert*. Particularly important treatments of this connection include Michael Ignatieff, *The Needs of Strangers* (London: Picador, 1984), 107–31; Donald Winch, *Riches and Poverty: An Intellectual History of Political Economy in Britain, 1750–1834* (Cambridge: Cambridge University Press, 1996), esp. 60, 66–75; and Pierre Force, *Self-Interest Before Adam Smith: A Genealogy of Economic Science* (Cambridge: Cambridge University Press, 2003), 20–47, 121–25 and 154–68.

11. For excellent recent discussions of the sensitivity of Rousseau's legislative proposals to political context, see Fonna Forman-Barzilai, "The Emergence of Contextualism in Rousseau's Political Thought: The Case of the Parisian Theatre in the *Lettre à d'Alembert*," *History of Political Thought* 24 (2003): 435–63; and Christopher Kelly, *Rousseau as Author: Consecrating One's Life to the Truth* (Chicago: University of Chicago Press, 2003), 62–66.

12. Smith translated this line as part of his "Letter to the Edinburgh Review"; see EPS, 252.

13. A point nicely made by John Hope Mason in "The *Lettre* and its Place in Rousseau's Thought," 262; see also Marshall's treatment of amour-propre as a "theatrical problem" in *The Surprising Effects of Sympathy: Marivaux, Diderot, Rousseau and Mary Shelley* (Chicago: University of Chicago Press, 1988), 138. A suggestive treatment of several other possible connections between theater and commerce in the late eighteenth century beyond those examined in the present essay is provided in Jean-Christophe Agnew, *Worlds Apart: The Market and the Theater in Anglo-American Thought, 1550–1750* (Cambridge: Cambridge University Press, 1986), 149–94.

14. See *Gorgias* 502b and Rousseau's transcription in "Of Theatrical Imitation" at OC V, 1204.

15. This theme has been particularly emphasized by Griswold; see his *Adam Smith and the Virtues of Enlightenment*, 262–66. Samuel Fleischacker provides an important response to Griswold in his *On Adam Smith's "Wealth of Nations": A Philosophical Companion* (Princeton: Princeton University Press, 2004), 104–20.

16. On such "self-forgetting and self-alienation" and "self-annihilation," see especially Marshall, *Surprising Effects*, 145.

17. But cf. TMS III.1.3 and OC IV, 1092. See also Marshall's depiction of the mirror as a "metaphor" for "the double reflection that contains both sympathy and *amour-propre*" (*Surprising Effects*, 153).

18. See the 1758 responses to the *Letter* by Ximines, d'Alembert, and Marmontel. The seventeenth and eighteenth-century background to the theater controversy in France is helpfully reviewed in M. Barras, *The Stage Controversy in France from Corneille to Rousseau* (New York: Institute of French Studies, 1933).

19. A fact known not only to the citizen of Geneva but also to the author of *Narcisse*: *"Le prétexte est de corriger Valére: mais le vrai motif est de rire à ses dépens"* (OC II, 981).

20. For discussions of Rousseau's critique of the theater as absolving spectators from their ethical responsibilities, see Amal Banerjee, "Rousseau's Concept of Theatre," *British Journal of Aesthetics* 17 (1977): 173-76; Benjamin R. Barber, "Rousseau and

the Paradoxes of the Dramatic Imagination," *Daedalus* 107 (1978): 85; Victor Gourevitch, "Rousseau on the Arts and Sciences," *Journal of Philosophy* 69 (1972): 742-46; Christopher Kelly, "Rousseau and the Case Against (and for) the Arts," in Clifford Orwin and Nathan Tarcov, eds., *The Legacy of Rousseau* (Chicago: University of Chicago Press, 1997), 24; C. N. Dugan and Tracy Strong, "Music, Politics, Theater and Representation in Rousseau," in Patrick Riley, ed., *The Cambridge Companion to Rousseau* (Cambridge: Cambridge University Press, 2001), 333-34; Marshall, *Surprising Effects*, 142-43, 148-50. Particularly useful is John Hope Mason's analysis of Rousseau's belief that theatrical spectatorship promotes "psychological satisfaction instead of social amelioration" ("The *Lettre* and its Place in Rousseau's Thought," 256).

21. See *Republic* 605c and Rousseau's transcription in "Of Theatrical Imitation" at OC V, 1207–08.

22. The *Confessions* also note that the *Letter* was written not to bring its author honor, but to provide evidence that he was praiseworthy and deserved honor; see C, 416. This is nicely treated by Pamela Jensen in "The Philanthrope: The Place of Religion in the *Letter to d'Alembert*," in Butler, ed., *Rousseau on Arts and Politics*, 159.

23. The title-page of the *Letter* is often rightly regarded as Rousseau's attempt to frame his conflict with d'Alembert as that of the citizen against the *philosophe*, but the litany of cities suggests that it is a conflict of the local and the cosmopolitan as well as a clash of the humble and the great. To this one might add Rousseau's remark in the "Preface to *Narcisse*": "Everything that facilitates communication between nations transmits not the virtues, but the crimes of each to the others, and adulterates the morals appropriate to the climate of each and to the constitution of its government" (PN, 96n/OC II, 964).

24. See *Republic* 607a and Rousseau's transcription in "Of Theatrical Imitation" at OC V, 1210.

25. A point nicely made by Benjamin Barber ("Rousseau and the Paradoxes of the Dramatic Imagination," 88): "the imagination by virtue of which we pervert our innocence and deprave our natural simplicity is also the faculty by virtue of which we overcome our perversity and transform our nature."

26. See Gourevitch's claim that in the political writings, "the political problem assumes precedence and defines the horizon within which all other problems must be viewed" ("Rousseau and the Arts and Sciences," 737). This would seem to hold for the group of works that Rousseau consciously associated with this perspective; see Jensen, "The Quarrel Between Philosophy and Poetry Revisited: Rousseau's 'On Theatrical Imitation'," in *Rousseau and Criticism*, ed. Lorraine Clark and Guy Lafrance (Ottawa: North American Association for the Study of Jean-Jacques Rousseau, 1995), 183–84.

27. Forma-Barzilai offers a thorough and nuanced reading of Rousseau's "Solonian" approach to moral reformation via palliation in the *Letter* in her "Emergence of Contextualism in Rousseau's Political Thought"; see esp. pp. 445–50. For Smith's use of Solon, see Winch, *Riches and Poverty*, 96–97, 104–105.

28. For the claim that Rousseau thinks Geneva a modern Sparta, see Jonas Barish, *The Antitheatrical Prejudice* (Berkeley: University of California Press, 1981), 287;

for a helpful corrective, see John Scott, "The Play of the Passions: Music, Mores, and Rousseau's *Lettre à d'Alembert*," in Butler, ed., *Rousseau on Arts and Politics*, 88.

29. I owe this point to Emma Rothschild; see her "Dignity or Meanness," forthcoming in the *Adam Smith Review*, especially ms p. 8 and ms p. 35n7; cf. Orwin, "Rousseau and the Discovery of Political Compassion," in Orwin and Tarcov, eds., *The Legacy of Rousseau*, 303. In a similar vein, compare Smith's awareness of our "secret consciousness" that sympathy depends upon "an imaginary change of situation" (TMS I.i.4.7) to Rousseau's exposure of the complacency of our sympathy with the suffering (SD 153–54/OC III, 154–55).

30. A particularly nice treatment of Rousseau's appeals to amour-propre is provided by Zev M. Trachtenberg in *Making Citizens: Rousseau's Political Theory of Culture* (London: Routledge, 1993), esp. at 193, 203, 209. Marshall similarly notes that "what is deplored in the second *Discours* (as well as in the *Lettre* itself) is here recommended to the state for exploitation" (*Surprising Effects*, 164).

31. See *Republic* 604a and Rousseau's transcription in "On Theatrical Imitation" in OC V, 1206.

32. For a vivid example of the follies of the life of urban anonymity, see Rousseau's account of life in Lausanne as Vaussore de Villeneuve in C, 124–25.

33. See especially Jean Starobinski, *Jean-Jacques Rousseau: Transparency and Obstruction* (Chicago: University of Chicago Press, 1988), 92-97; Marshall, *Surprising Effects*, 159; Dugan and Strong, "Music, Politics, Theater and Representation," 335; and Paul Thomas, "The Revolutionary Festival and Rousseau's Quest for Transparency," *History of Political Thought* 18 (1997): 666-70

34. Trachtenberg's nice discussions of the circles and the balls (*Making Citizens*, 179–88, 200–05) emphasize that such institutions, in Rousseau's formulation, have an "undeniable totalitarian cast" (277n5).

35. See also *Republic* 605d, and Rousseau's transcription in "Of Theatrical Imitation," OC V, 1207.

36. I follow Allan Bloom and David Marshall in thinking that Rousseau's reference to "*spectacles*" is meant to put readers in mind not only of stage plays but also the familiar act of observation and judgment outside of the theater; see Bloom's introduction to his translation of the *Letter* at 150n12; and Marshall, *Surprising Effects*, 258n3.

37. Benjamin Barber and Janis Forman nicely call attention to Rousseau's emphasis on "the theater's palliative role in already corrupt societies" in their introduction to their translation of the "Preface to *Narcisse*" in *Political Theory* 6 (1978): 539; see also Forman-Barzilai, "Emergence of Contextualism," 462–63.

38. Rousseau's assessment of the current moral state of Geneva has received careful attention from several quarters. The republican aspects of his perspective are emphasized by John Hope Mason (see esp. 253-54 and 267, though he too notes at 259-60 that Rousseau understood that Geneva was "*not yet* Paris," though already well on its way). Helena Rosenblatt similarly reads the *Letter* as driven by a republican agenda, insisting that it provides a "continuation of Rousseau's argument against *doux commerce* theory"; see her *Rousseau and Geneva: From the First Discourse to the Social Contract, 1749-1762* (Cambridge: Cambridge University Press, 1997), 225. My own interpretation of Rousseau's intentions sides more closely with both Marshall's

claim that in the *Letter* Rousseau "sets out to reform a corrupt society and prevent Geneva from becoming like Paris rather than like Sparta" (*Surprising Effects*, 157), and Trachtenberg's claim that Rousseau appreciated Geneva's "decidedly un-Spartan commercial spirit," which itself forbid the revival of ancient conceptions of virtue there; see Trachtenberg, "Theater as an Economic Institution: An Aspect of Rousseau's Rhetoric in the *Letter to d'Alembert*," in Butler, ed., *Rousseau on Arts and Politics*, 136-39. Kelly also helpfully illuminates Rousseau's use of Neufchatel and Paris as "two extremes of a continuum" in *Rousseau as Author*, 131-33.

39. On the social effects of Glasgow's commercial boom, see especially T. M. Devine, "The Urban Crisis," in *Glasgow*, ed. Devine and Gordon Jackson (Manchester: Manchester University Press, 1995). In his review of Glasgow during the 1750s and 60s, Scott observes that "the picture of the times is one of strong lights and some deep shadows," noting that rises in graft, theft, arson and violent crime all accompanied the rapid progress of opulence during these decades (*Adam Smith as Student and Professor*, 79). Helena Rosenblatt also calls attention to contemporary perceptions of "moral decline" among Genevans even in "the 'golden age' of Genevan capitalism" (*Rousseau and Geneva*, 22–24).

40. Not to mention the neglect of education that Smith thinks is a consequence of enforced child labor. If space permitted, one might inquire into Smith's and Rousseau's understandings of the merits of ancient and modern education. To remedy the defects of modern education Smith looks back to ancient education in both arms and music (LRBL, 139). The superiority of ancient to modern education seems to consist in its ability to cultivate through this balance of arms and music both the awful and the amiable virtues (to use Smith's language) or to join the ferocity of the Spartans to the urbanity of the Athenians (to use Rousseau's). But for all his conscious recognition of the excellence and success of the balanced Greek education in which the hardiness of the gymnastic education was tempered by the softness of musical education (WN V.i.f.39; LRBL, 138), Smith recommends to his modern audience not the Greek education but the Roman, which is precisely the education which neglects music and concentrates only on war (WN V.i.f.40).

41. An echo of Rousseau's insistence that the mountain people of Neufchatel still enjoy the benefits of leisure to make inventions and improvements perhaps also can be heard in Smith's insistence that prior to the advent of the division of labor "invention is kept alive" (WN V.i.f.51).

42. Pamela Jensen reads the *Letter* as a plea for toleration: "the *Letter* demonstrates Rousseau's own commitment to the development of a humane and tolerant society that will eradicate superstition and religious fanaticism and ameliorate the righteous indignation characteristic of the current debates" ("The Philanthrope," in Butler, ed., *Rousseau on Arts and Politics*, 151). Jensen further develops this thought elsewhere in suggesting that Rousseau's attack on the poets is at once a critique of the priests; see "The Quarrel Between Philosophy and Poetry Revisited," in Clark and Daston, ed., *Rousseau and Criticism*, 186. For Rousseau on the dangers of atheism, see Gourevitch, "Rousseau on the Arts and Sciences," 748.

43. Ross, *Life of Adam Smith*, 148.

Faux savants, femmes philosophes, & philosophes amoureux: Foibles of the *philosophe* on the Eighteenth-Century French Stage

ANNE VILA

Of all the terms that are commonly evoked to discuss the eighteenth century, none may be more banal or as vague as the word *philosophe*. Although some scholars seem content to employ *philosophe* as a handy catch-all term applicable to a wide swath of intellectuals who wrote during the eighteenth century, others embrace a more constrained usage that restricts it to those associated with the Encyclopedist movement, an approach that has the virtue of anchoring the term in a specific discursive and ideological context in which *philosophe* was sometimes less a badge of honor than a smear word. Thanks to recent efforts to reconstruct the particular social and professional frameworks within which members of early modern French society used such titles as *auteur*, *écrivain*, and *homme de lettres*, we now have a more rigorous understanding of the image and self-image of those who held them at the time.[1] The case of *philosophe* is, however, somewhat more problematic: because the term was both multifaceted and highly charged, pinning down its meanings is a more delicate enterprise, one that is probably best conducted on a local, author-by-author (or at least field-by-field) basis. Although we now have available Dinah Ribard's masterfully detailed account of the ways in which the term and persona of the *philosophe* were defined in and through the period's biographical literature, we still lack focused studies of what being a *philosophe* implied in other, equally influential discursive arenas, especially the theater.[2]

We are not, of course, lacking in studies of theater, per se: others have explored the theater's crucial role as a forum for the promotion of the "philosophic" movement, as a proving ground for authors who sought to achieve fame and fortune in the Republic of Letters, and as a space in which the very idea of the public was shaped and debated in various ways.[3] It is, by now, well established that theater was central to both the aesthetic theory and the social agenda of Voltaire (François-Marie Arouet), Denis Diderot, and other literary writers who went by the title of *philosophe*.[4] Yet we know far less about what the theater of the day had to say about them and their brethren, beyond a few notorious works like Charles Palissot de Montenoy's *Les Philosophes* (1760); and our sense of how *philosophes* were theatrically represented in the early decades of the century is scantier still. It was, however, during those early decades that theater may have done the most to redefine the *philosophe* and to create a climate more sympathetic to the sort of intellectual to whom we commonly ascribe the name.

As Ira Wade observed decades ago, the eighteenth century produced approximately two hundred and twenty-five plays in which a *philosophe* appeared—an estimate to which we can now add greater precision thanks to the data compiled on CESAR, acronym for the web site "Calendrier électronique des spectacles sous l'ancien régime et sous la révolution."[5] In addition to providing invaluable information about the authors, theaters, and troupes that were involved in staging various figures of the *philosophe*, CESAR offers a rich overview of pertinent titles: it lists seventy-five plays produced between 1700 and 1798 that include the word *philosophe* in their title, twenty-four that feature a *savant* or *savante*, nineteen that star a *pédant*, and three that headline an *homme* or *gens de lettres*. Not all of the heroes announced by these play titles are intellectuals: approximately fourteen of the *philosophes* are peasants, gardeners, shepherds, cobblers, jewelers, soldiers, or valets; and eight of the *savants* are horses, dogs, pigeons or wigs.[6] On the whole, however, the focus of interest evinced by these titles is centered squarely on a particular set of humans, those whose beliefs, vocabulary, and comportment connected them with philosophy, however the playwright construed it.

Some intriguing patterns emerge when one peruses the sorts of characters who appeared before eighteenth-century theater audiences in the guise of a *philosophe* or a *savant*. First, judging from the dates on the CESAR lists, *philosophes* and *savants* were ambivalent stage personae from the very beginning of the century, their intellectual status sometimes cast into doubt through pejorative qualifiers like *faux*, *petit*, *soi-disant*, or *ridicule*. In other words, satires of the *philosophe* were standard theatrical fare well before the Encyclopedist movement emerged and triggered a small flood of counter-Enlightenment comedies like Palissot's *Les Philosophes* and Jean-Jacques Rutlidge's *Le Bureau de l'esprit* (1776), where *philosophe* became an epithet applied to members of an irreverent, free-thinking, elitist Parisian cabal.[7] Second, male scholars or pseudo-scholars are the principal targets of the plays listed on CESAR: although *femmes savantes* or *femmes philosophes* remained popular comic targets in the wake of Molière's celebrated satires of women who aspired to learning, their virile counterparts were more likely to be lampooned on the eighteenth-century French stage.[8] Finally, love themes predominate in most of the plays that feature a *philosophe* or scholarly type, suggesting that even playwrights who were more preoccupied with the selfishness or charlatanism they imputed to *philosophes* found sentiment to be the easiest mechanism for tripping up their target.

Indeed, from Germain-François Poullain de Saint-Foix's *Le Philosophe dupe de l'amour* (1726) to Pierre-Antoine-Auguste de Piis's *Aristote amoureux, ou le philosophe bridé* (1780), the *philosophe* was regularly played for a fool in love; in the case of Piis's comic opera, the once haughty Aristotle ends up allowing himself to be fitted with a bridle and hooked to the front of a cart carrying the gorgeous young Indian maiden with whom he has become smitten.[9] To add insult to injury, comic playwrights often associated the figure of the *philosophe* with voluntary or involuntary celibacy, if not outright impotence. Given the degree to which prominent *philosophes* like Charles-Louis de Secondat de Montesquieu, Voltaire and Diderot were integrated into worldly society, it may seem paradoxical that the stage persona of the *philosophe* retained this particular vestige of the pedant of centuries past, often appearing to be an eminently dupable, romantically incompetent figure.[10] However, despite the best efforts of many *philosophes* to fashion themselves as urbane, salon-loving, and even gallant, a general perception persisted in French culture that "philosophy," or the love of knowledge, was inherently incompatible with carnal love.[11] The comic theater of the day provides a revealing window into both the assumptions that grounded this perception and the manner in which it evolved as the tastes of theatergoers changed. This shift occurred, interestingly enough, in the 1720s and 30s, a few decades before *philosophes* took to writing plays to defend themselves, their moral character, and their place in contemporary society.

* * *

As Herbert Dieckmann has noted, the figure of the *philosophe* as a distinctly new kind of intellectual was identified early in the century, not so much by self-defined *philosophes* as by conservative authors who opposed the figure on religious and social grounds.[12] Some of the early plays that featured a *philosophe* were, in fact, written by Jesuit priests in order to be performed or seen by their pupils: for example, *Le Philosophe à la mode* (1720) was composed by Father Jean-Antoine du Cerceau to teach his students at the Collège de Louis Le Grand to beware of the "wickedness and corruption" of fashionable thinkers like his title character, symbolically named Narcisse.[13] Other plays, however, aimed less to preach about the dangers of the intellectual than to poke fun at his peculiarities by setting them under the harsh glare of polite society, the refined milieu that dictated standards of good taste in matters of thought as well as sentiment.

The theme of the *philosophe* as out of step with love and society was not, of course, unique to the eighteenth-century French stage: one version of it dates back to the medieval fabliau *Le Lai d'Aristote*,and other variants abound in seventeenth-century literature.[14] Many of the eighteenth-century comedic authors who satirized thinkers did little more than recycle the devious tutor of *Le Pédant joué* (written by Savien de Cyrano de Bergerac in the 1650s) or one of Molière's hypocrites or pedants, like the scheming *dévot* Tartuffe, the jealous tutor Arnolphe, or the pretentious s*avante* Philaminte.[15] Other playwrights who presented a *philosophe* or *savant* merely adapted the *docteur* character of Italian comedy and the Foire—a figure who, ridiculous by dint of his age, his pomposity, and his suspicious nature, invariably interfered in the efforts of two young lovers to achieve happiness via amorous contentment.[16] Still others plays satirizing the *philosophe* were thinly veiled dramatizations of the tale of Socrates included in Marie-Catherine de Villedieu's short story collection, *Les Amours des grands hommes* (1671), itself an adaptation of biographical details gleaned from Plutarch's *Lives,* where Socrates is cast as a Stoic who falls in love with his young charge Timandra, claims to be interested only in making her a "philosophical" woman, and eventually loses her to his handsome, wily young disciple Alcibiades.

Of all of those historical sources, it was probably Villedieu who set the stage for the more sympathetic view of the amorous *philosophe* which came into favor among French theatergoers during the 1720s and 1730s. The basic plot of Villedieu's novella was not, in and of itself, favorable to the philosopher in love. Her protagonist is an ugly fellow who preaches contempt for the passions while burning with desire for the young beauty he has secreted away in the woods of Athens, while her Alcibiades has no more trouble in shaking Socrates's confidence in Stoic philosophy than in sweet-talking her gullible duenna, the "astrologess" Aglaonice, in order to gain access to Timandra's ear and heart.[17] Among the eighteenth-century plays that appropriated elements of Villedieu's tale of Socrates, many did little more than mock the figure of the love-struck pedant and/or a deluded *femme philosophe* modeled after Villedieu's character Aglaonice.[18] The exception to that rule is Pierre Carlet de Chamblain de Marivaux's *Le Triomphe de l'amour* (1732), a play that borrowed from Villedieu not just in its plot line, but also in its nuanced, humane view of a *philosophe* grappling with the eternal "surprise" of love.[19] It could be argued that the psychology of love which underlies this particular amorous *philosophe* comedy is so distinctly Marivaudian that it defies comparison to works by other authors.[20] There is, however, such a striking resonance between Villedieu's conception of love in relation to philosophy and that which Marivaux presents in *Le Triomphe de l'amour* that a short detour through *Les Amours des grands hommes* seems in order.

Villedieu's view of what love implies for the philosopher is only partly apparent within the pages of "Socrate": the moral of this story seems simply to be that love can overtake the heart of even those most ill-suited to be lovers, including the unattractive, uncourtly, austerely virtuous Socrates.[21] "Socrate" is not, however, a freestanding piece of fiction; rather, it functions as a pendant to "Solon," the tale of another amorous philosopher which opens *Les Amours des grands hommes*. Reading back to "Solon," one finds a wealth of moral reflections that reveal Villedieu's underlying purpose as a narrator /historian: Villedieu aims, as Nancy D. Klein puts it, to rectify the "larger-than-life" portrayal which official historians have put forth of famously wise or virtuous men by telling "the other story of their lives, a private and personal version that represents these illustrious men in more realistic terms."[22] To that end, Villedieu begins "Solon" by correcting the austere Stoic view of wisdom: that quality, her title character insists, "consists not in a brutish fierceness: Those who described her so, never knew her well; she was made for Man, and should be a sociable Vertue" (9). True to the humanist conception of wisdom, Villedieu's ideal man is wise not because he is learned, but because he has undergone a moralizing process that transforms his wisdom from knowledge to virtue.[23] What most distinguishes her use of this idea is the emphasis she places on love in accomplishing that transformation: a few pages later, the narrator of "Solon" observes that "the love of those who make Profession of Wisdom is much more ardent than that of ordinary Lovers; it is not dispelled by any exterior ceremony, but as it reserves itself inward and intire for great occasions, so it ordinarily breaks forth to advantage" (19–20). The usually grave Solon thus exults without reserve once he is reunited with his beloved Orgina after a long and painful separation, and he strives from that point on to balance his public service to the State with private service to his love (20–21). Villedieu's insistence that love exerts a transformative, redemptive power over "those who make Profession of Wisdom" clearly signals a shift away from the stereotype of the *philosophe* as a hopelessly anti-social pedant.

Villedieu's emphasis on the amorous motivations that drove antiquity's great philosophers should, of course, be situated within the context of *préciosité*, a seventeenth-century cultural movement that sought to create greater respect for love and the tender feelings cultivated by women of refinement.[24] Yet it can also be connected to the broader interest in the private lives of great thinkers and statesmen which emerged during the early modern period, finding expression in such forms as collective biographies, academic eulogies and, pertinently, stage depictions of the *philosophe*.[25] The Athenian philosopher Hermocrate whom Marivaux invents for his play *Le Triomphe de l'amour* has not, generally speaking, been seen as a great thinker by twentieth-century critics; quite the contrary, some have gone so far as to brand him and his *savante* sister Léontine as "self-deluded imposters blinded by their narcissism."[26] I would argue, however, that Marivaux designs Hermocrate to be the real thing, and that, much like Villedieu, he seeks to make his fictional *philosophe* sympathetic, if not exactly exemplary, in the ardor he exhibits when he finally yields to love after it surprises him in his isolated woodland retreat.

Many recent interpretations of *Le Triomphe de l'amour* have been predicated on the assumption that Marivaux's sympathies lie primarily with Léonide, a Spartan princess who, Alcibiades-like, falls in love with Hermocrate's handsome young charge Agis, masks her identity, and presents herself at the door to Hermocrate's garden in the guise of Phocion, a young man ostensibly drawn there only by the much-reputed wisdom of a great philosopher.[27] However, while Léonide-Phocion is unquestionably the play's protagonist, she is not an unambiguously positive character: in addition to serving the function of beautiful young heroine, she is also a dubiously established ruler (in that she has inherited a throne usurped from Agis's father by her uncle) and the author/director of the sham seductions by which Hermocrate and Léontine are fooled into believing that they, not Agis, are the objects of her ardor.[28] Although Léonide is unquestionably masterful in manipulating the play's other characters, her actions are driven not just by an "equitable" desire to right the wrongs committed by her uncle by restoring Agis to the throne (I, 1), but also by the disquieting belief that she must spare no one to win the heart of a young man who has every reason to hate her.[29]

Nor, for that matter, is Hermocrate a sinister or ridiculous figure: far from being the heavy of the play, as is the case in most amorous pedant comedies of the period, he, like his sister, comes across as a hapless victim of a ruthless con artist.

There is, therefore, something problematic about the contention (advanced by Robert Tomlinson in an otherwise astute reading of the play) that Hermocrate is a false philosopher simply because he succumbs to desire and that Léonide-Phocion, conversely, embodies the more authentic, life- and love-affirming moral philosophy which Marivaux is intent on promoting in *Le Triomphe de l'amour*.[30] Not only does that interpretation finesse the darker side of Léonide-Phocion's character, it also implies that Hermocrate is nothing more than a vain-glorious pretender to the title *philosophe* who gets his just desserts when he is tripped up by love.[31] Although *faux philosophes* did, indeed, abound on the eighteenth-century French stage, the characterization does not fit Hermocrate as Marivaux constructs him.[32] Rather, Hermocrate's temperament and comportment are closer to those exhibited by Villedieu's philosophers: he falls in love while at the height of his justly earned fame as a sage, and he undergoes his amorous adventure in the midst of a political situation that has life-and-death repercussions for his young charge Agis (whom Hermocrates and his sister bravely rescued as an infant, and whom they also seek to restore to the throne of Sparta).

Not only is Hermocrate remarkably prescient about Léonide /Phocion's real designs (I, 8), he is also exceptionally lucid about the trap into which he is falling. If, as Raymond Joly has put it, the general rule for Marivaux's heroes and heroines is to feel love as a form of humiliation, then Hermocrate may be more heroic than most.[33] Humiliation is, indeed, the order of the day for Hermocrate as he succumbs to the charms of the irresistible Aspasie (the name that Léonide assumes once Hermocrate sees through her masculine disguise). Recognizing that his cherished wisdom has not made him any less vulnerable to "tous les ravages que l'amour fait dans le coeur des autres hommes," he unsparingly compares himself in his jealous agitations to "l'âme la plus vile, les amants les plus vulgaires, la jeunesse la plus folle [. . .] Reconnaissez-vous Hermocrate à ce portrait? L'univers est plein de gens qui me ressemblent" (170).[34] Love, however, does not merely reduce Hermocrate to an ordinary man: it also redeems him by converting his formerly dispassionate wisdom into an active, human virtue.

Although Hermocrate does not end up marrying in the end, both he and his spinster sister Léontine exuberantly embrace the possibility of marriage and full social engagement once the seductive Phocion-Léonide dupes them into believing that she is enamored of them. The most poignant illustration of this aspect of their characters is found in the sweetly comic scene between the love-besotted siblings which ends Act II. Hermocrate and Léontine, both giddy at the thought of eloping with Phocion/Léonide but unaware of her real identity (or of their sibling's plans), gallantly recognize each other's loveable qualities and admit the shortcomings of the austere mode of life they have followed. When Léontine remarks that poor Agis "vit dans une solitude dont on se rebute quelquefois à son âge," Hermocrate replies "Quelquefois à tout âge"; and when Léontine summons the courage to admit that she has often found herself bored and melancholic in their philosophical retreat, Hermocrate rejoins: "Qu'appelez-vous courage? Et qui est-ce qui ne s'y ennuierait pas? N'est-on pas né pour la société?" (176). This dual confession of discontent with a purely "philosophical" existence emboldens both siblings to hint that they intend to give it up in favor of marriage, and to venture the opinion that they are both perfectly suited for matrimony. After Léontine intimates that she has some romantic prospects (and Hermocrate more evasively mentions that he might, too), the siblings part company, leaving Hermocrate alone on stage to utter an extraordinarily astute, slightly melancholic comment on the situation: "A ce que je vois, nous sommes tous deux en bel état, Léontine et moi. Je ne sais à qui elle en veut; peut-être est-ce à quelqu'un aussi jeune pour elle que l'est Aspasie pour moi. Que nous sommes faibles! mais il faut remplir sa destinée."[35]

In the end, it may well be the destiny of Hermocrate, rather than Princess Léonide, to give the fullest expression of Marivaux's vision of love, life, and authentic wisdom: wisdom, this play suggests, must be sociable, but it must also be compassionate, generous, and humble (qualities sorely lacking in Léonide-Phocion).[36] Although, in the words of the valet Arlequin, the solitary *sagesse* in which Hermocrate and his entourage live at the outset of the play is "incivile pour l'amour," one could just as easily invert the relationship and say that love proves distinctly uncivil toward philosophy in this comedy.[37] True to the irreducible ambiguity of all of Marivaux's plays, *Le Triomphe de l'amour* makes it hard to determine whether the punishment meted out to Hermocrate and his sister is justifiable—not just because the two recluses are simultaneously sympathetic and laughable, but because Phocion-Léonide is an irreducibly mixed character, on the one hand attractive and unquestionably equitable toward Agis, yet on the other hand cruel in her quest to possess her heart's desire.[38] Significantly, perhaps, the Parisian audiences who saw this comedy when it was performed in 1732 seem to have viewed Phocion-Léonide not as a positive embodiment of love in all its glory, but as a scandalous trickster who victimizes an undeserving Hermocrate. As one contemporary put it, "on trouva mauvais qu'une Princesse de Sparte se déguise pour venir trouver un jeune homme, dont elle n'est pas certaine d'être aimée, et qu'elle abuse un Philosophe par une fourberie impardonnable à tout autre qu'à Scapin."[39]

Interestingly, five years before *Le Triomphe de l'amour* received this unfavorable public reception, another play featuring a *philosophe* fared much better at the box office: that work was Philippe-Néricault Destouches's *Le Philosophe marié* (1727), the most well attended and frequently performed French comedy of the first half of the century.[40] It is the play's subtitle, *Le Mari honteux de l'être,* that truly expresses the dilemma around which this comedy is constructed: Ariste, a well-born, bookish fellow who seems reluctant to leave the "cabinet de livres" in which much of the action initially takes place, has secretly married Mélite, a modest, dignified beauty with an impeccable pedigree but no dowry. Ariste is ashamed of being married for a number of reasons. First, he regards love as a weakness and married life as a threat to the freedom he savors when alone with his Muses in his *cabinet*.[41] Second, realizing that contemporary mores have made the name "spouse" ridiculous, he dreads becoming the laughingstock of Paris, a well-founded fear, given that he himself delighted in poking fun at husbands when he was a carefree bachelor (378, 425–26). Finally, he realizes that, if his marriage becomes publically known, he might lose the inheritance promised to him by his uncle Géronte, a rich but cantankerous *financier* who is set on marrying Ariste to his step-daughter (384, 420). Ariste is thus tormented by the thought that someone in his entourage might reveal the secret, which is, of course, exactly what happens by the end of Act IV, thanks to the indiscretion of Mélite's loquacious, vain sister Céliante (a character modeled, apparently, after the author's own sister-in-law).[42]

For my purposes, what is most intriguing about this play is that it begins by depicting the "philosophical" and married modes of life as mutually incompatible, but ends by presenting a virtuous, love-based marriage as the ultimate proof of a *philosophe*'s character and moral fortitude. The initial tension is made abundantly clear in Act I, which begins with a monologue in which Ariste, surrounded by his books, his pens, his mathematical instruments and his globe, exults in the solitary pleasures of his scholarly retreat, until he remembers that a very different existence awaits him in the next room: "Ma retraite est mon Louvre, et j'y commande en roi./ Mais je n'use qu'ici de mon pouvoir suprême;/ Hors de mon cabinet je ne suis plus le même/ Dans l'autre appartement, toujours contrarié:/ Ici, je suis garçon, là, je suis marié" (374).[43] After venting his remorse for having allowed himself to be captivated by the fair sex, Ariste tries to return to his reading but is repeatedly interrupted, first by his friend Damon and then by the soubrette Finette, who in Scene 4 barges into his study, mutters a dismissive "toujours lire!" and loudly announces that

"Madame votre femme" wishes to come and speak to him (381). When Ariste rejects both this request and Finette's argument that he should make his marriage public, the exasperated Finette blurts out a wisecrack regarding Ariste's procreative capacity: "On dit qu'on n'a jamais tous les dons à la fois,/ Et que les grands esprits, d'ailleurs très estimables, / Ont fort peu de talent pour former leurs semblables" (385–6).[44] Although Ariste is visibly piqued by this insult to his virility, he says nothing much to counter it: rather, he simply begs Finette to keep Mélite from bothering him for an hour or two so that he can philosophize in peace.

Finette's salty intimation that Ariste may not be able to rise to his conjugal duties, if he ever fully accepts them, is a curious moment in a play that prefers to dwell on other reasons to explain why *philosophes* are generally ill-suited for the state of marriage: for example, that they value their independence too highly; that they are reclusive sorts who disdain worldly conventions and women's idle chit-chat; or that they are deluded by their Stoic principles into thinking that they are above the human passions. Although *Le Philosophe marié* contains no more references to Ariste's possible physical inadequacy as a husband, Finette's remark evokes an emerging leitmotif in both the biographical and the medical representation of great male thinkers: namely, the notion that the trade-off for their extraordinary intellectual creativity was a lack of interest in or capacity for sex and procreation, or (to cite a variation on that theme) that the scholarly propensity for *voluptés de l'esprit* made thinkers fundamentally solitary beings.[45]

Fortunately, events conspire in Destouches's comedy to cure poor Ariste of his reluctance or inability to accept the public and private duties of a married man. The first step is to get him out of his *cabinet*, an operation whose steady progress is underscored by the play's gradual shift in tone and setting. At the outset of *Le Philosophe marié*, Ariste's study is a sanctum, a place where only like-minded men may join him. He is thus dismayed when Mélite enters it in scene 6 of Act 1, and even more aghast when, between the Second and Third Acts, his uncle Géronte rudely interrupts a conversation that Ariste is having with the Marquis du Lauret, a friend and fellow wit who, not knowing that Mélite is Ariste's wife, persistently tries to woo her. By Act IV, however, Ariste has largely left his beloved *cabinet* for the more sociable rooms of his Parisian hôtel. The second step is to test Ariste's mettle by pitting him against characters like Géronte, who takes the conventionally dim view of thinkers and the contemplative mode of life.[46] To counter Géronte's portrait of intellectuals as foolish, socially useless prattlers (461), Ariste praises the ideal *philosophe* as a man of action rather than words, a true, fair and compassionate man whose greatness shines in adversity (462). However, Ariste has no sooner defended his ideal than he contradicts it by his evasive behavior. It is not until Géronte threatens to break up the marriage and Mélite's honor is in peril that Ariste finds the moral backbone to defend her before his powerful, quarrelsome uncle (485). Even then, Artiste's courageous demonstration of philosophical character does not suffice to bring about a happy ending: the play's resolution also depends on Mélite's tearful, touching appeal to Géronte (497) and on the Marquis's noble offer to marry Géronte's stepdaughter without accepting her dowry, thereby allowing Ariste to keep his uncle's fortune (499–500).

Le Philosophe marié thus solves the conflict between the temperament of the *philosophe* and the state of marriage by enlisting all the sympathetic characters in the effort to soften the heart of the play's true villain: Géronte, a venal, ill-mannered fellow who comes dangerously close to ruining Ariste and his wife. Destouches's ultimate end in this play is not to lampoon *philosophes* but to socialize them, and to draw attention to the ways in which the so-called polite society that ridicules them has been corrupted by forces ranging from greed and foppishness to aristocratic idleness and anti-intellectualism.[47] True to the tradition of the "comédie de moeurs," *Le Philosophe marié* offers a corrective to *philosophes* who are not living up to the name, along with edifying instructions for everyone on how to be a good spouse and citizen. It locates manly virtue not in Stoic disdain for society, but in the wholehearted embrace of matrimony and the courage to brave the heady dangers posed by love and women. Seen in the light of later works like Michel-Jean Sedaine's popular drama *Le Philosophe sans le savoir* (1765), Destouches's comedy might even be called trend-setting, in that the campaign to reconcile philosophy and family life became a prominent theatrical and poetic theme, from the *drame bourgeois* to the 1773 poetry competition which the Académie Française launched to combat celibacy among men of letters.[48]

When we remember that Destouches's comedy was packing the Comédie Française at the same time that Marivaux's was getting a tepid public response, we might conclude that Parisian theater audiences of 1732 no longer wanted to see a *philosophe* played for a fool on the stage. And when we note that, two years later, Barthélemy-Christophe Fagan's comedy *La Pupille* won acclaim and popularity by reversing the standard "duped philosopher" plot line and depicting a lovely young heroine who pines away passionately for her 45-year-old tutor, we find ourselves on the trail of an interesting mutation in mentalities that manifested itself both on the stage and off.[49] Although mocking satires of the amorous pedant would continue to appear in French theaters until the end of the century, they were generally produced for the

Foire or Opéra Comique, whereas the stages of "high" theater were given over to plays that depicted the *philosophe* as an exemplary family man or that justified the *philosophe*'s seemingly inborn urge to retreat, if only occasionally, from a world that seemed dominated by vanity, venality, and other destructive social passions.[50] Of all the stage depictions of the *philosophe* that abounded in eighteenth-century France, this was the one that coincided most harmoniously with the conception of the figure found in the writings of Montesquieu, Voltaire and Diderot, authors who championed the love of humanity, but who also delighted in giving themselves over to the private, inward-turning pleasures of study, writing and reflection.

NOTES

1. See for example, the essays assembled in G.R.I.H.L (Groupe de recherches interdisciplinaires sur l'histoire du littéraire), *De la publication: Entre Renaissance et Lumières*, ed. Christian Jouhaud and Alain Viala (Paris: Fayard, 2002); Nicholas Schapira, *Un Professionnel des lettres au XVIIe siècle* (Seyssel: Champ Vallon, 2003); Geoffrey Turnovsky, "The Enlightenment Literary Market: Rousseau, Authorship and the Book Trade," *Eighteenth-Century Studies* 36:3 (2003), 387–410; and Gregory S. Brown, *A Field of Honor: Writers, Court Culture and Public Theater in French Literary Life from Racine to the Revolution* (New York: Columbia University Press/ EPIC, 2002; electronic resource available from www.gutenberg-e.org).

2. See Dinah Ribard, *Raconter, vivre, penser: histoire des philosophes, 1650–1766* (Paris: Vrin, 2003). As Ribard demonstrates, the immense amount of biographical literature on *philosophes* produced during the seventeenth and eighteenth centuries played a decisive role in shaping perceptions of both the *philosophe* and *philosophie*: among other things, it created the history of philosophy as a distinct genre and imbued eighteenth-century French philosophy with a pronounced literary cast. See also Ribard, "Philosophe ou écrivain? Problèmes de délimitation entre histoire littéraire et histoire de la philosophie en France, 1650–1850" in *Annales H.S.S.* (March-April 2000), 355–88.

3. On theater as an authorial proving ground, see Brown, *Field of Honor*. On its relationship to emerging notions of the public, see Jeffrey S. Ravel, *The Contested Parterre: Public Theater and French Political Culture, 1680–1791* (Ithaca, N.Y.: Cornell University Press, 1999); David Trott, *Théâtre du XVIIIe siècle : jeux, écritures, regards : essai sur les spectacles en France de 1700 à 1790* (Montpellier: Espaces 34, 2000); and Antoine Lilti, "Public ou sociabilité? Les théâtres de société au XVIIIe siècle" in G.R.I.H.L, *De la publication*, 281–300.

4. On Voltaire's dramatic writings, see (among others) R.S. Ridgway, "Voltaire and Tragedy," *Humanities Association Review/La Revue de l'Association des*

Humanités 13 (1962–63), 26–36; Ahmad Gunny, "Tragedy in the Service of Propaganda: Voltaire's *Mahomet*" in Alan Howe and Richard Waller, eds., *En marge du classicisme : Essays on the French Theatre from the Renaissance to the Enlightenment* (Liverpool: Liverpool University Press, 1987), 227–42; and Marie Wellington, *The Art of Voltaire's Theater: An Exploration of Possibility* (New York: Lang, 1987). On Diderot's views on theater, see Julie Candler Hayes, *Identity and Ideology: Diderot, Sade, and the Serious Genre* (Amsterdam and Philadelphia : J. Benjamins Pub. Co., 1991); Jay Caplan, *Framed Narratives: Diderot's Genealogy of the Beholder* (Minneapolis: University of Minnesota Press, 1985) and Pierre Frantz, *L'Esthétique du tableau dans le théâtre du XVIIIe siècle* (Paris: Presses universitaires de France, 1998).

5. Ira Wade divides eighteenth-century French plays containing a *philosophe* as a character into four categories: those that revolved around a philosopher of antiquity, like *Aristote amoureux* or *Socrate* (40 plays); those that depicted the *philosophe* in love, like Destouches's *Le philosophe marié* (about 30); those that portrayed the philosophe as a bourgeois character or *honnête homme*, like Sedaine's *Le Philosophe sans le savoir* (about 20); those that showed the *philosophe* in meditative retreat from the world (approximately 25); and hostile comedies like Palissot's *Les Philosophes* which cast the *philosophe* as a cheat and a fake (approximately 50); *The Structure and Form of the French Enlightenment* (Princeton: Princeton University Press, 1977), vol. 1, 14. See also Wade's earlier study *The "Philosophe" in the French Drama of the Eighteenth Century* (Princeton: Princeton University Press, 1926). The CESAR Web site can be found at www.cesar.org.uk.

6. Works in this vein include Thiroux d'Arconville, *Le Bijoutier philosophe* (n/d); Pompigny, *Le Riche laboureur ou le paysan philosophe* (1789); Taconet, *Le Savetier philosophe ou l'esprit tiré à cheveux* (1766); Lizarde de Radonvilliers, *Le Valet philosophe* (1741); Veronese, *Les philosophes militaires* (1752); Quensley, *Le Cheval savant* (1708); anon., *Le Chien savant ou les métamorphoses de l'amour* (1786); Guérin, *Le Pigeon Savant* (1717); and Montorcier, *La Perruque savante* (1772).

7. Jean-Claude Bonnet underscores that the theater was used as an instrument of propaganda by both sides of the pro- vs. anti-*philosophe* polemic, especially from the 1760s on; see *Naissance du Panthéon: Essai sur le culte des grands hommes* (Paris: Fayard, 1998), 122–27. For detailed summaries of plays involved in those propaganda efforts, see Wade, *The "Philosophe" in French Drama*, 97–127. On the figures and strategies involved in the counter-Enlightenment movement in France, see Rémy G. Saisselin, *The Literary Enterprise in Eighteenth-Century France* (Detroit: Wayne State University Press,1979, 98–121; Didier Masseau, *Les Ennemis des philosophes: l'antiphilosophie au temps des Lumières* (Paris: Albin Michel, 2000); and Darrin M. McMahon, *Enemies of the Enlightenment: The French Counter-Enlightenment and the Making of Modernity* (Oxford: Oxford University Press, 2001).

8. Numerous eighteenth-century playwrights appropriated elements of Molière's comedies *Les Précieuses ridicules* (1659) and *Les Femmes savantes* (1672): see,

for example, Teisserenc, *La Femme philosophe* (1759), Palissot, *Les Philosophes*, and Rutlidge, *Le Bureau de l'esprit*. On the longer tradition of *femme savante* satires, see Linda Timmerans, *L'Accès des femmes à la culture (1578–1715): Un débat d'idées de Saint François de Sales à la Marquise de Lambert* (Paris: Champion, 1993), 320–5.

9. Pierre-Antoine-Augustin de Piis, *Aristote amoureux ou le philosophe bridé* (Paris: Vente, 1780); see especially scenes 11–14. Piis's comedy draws on two medieval precedents: Chrétien de Troyes's twelfth-century romance, *Lancelot, ou le Chevalier à la charrette*, which probably inspired Piis's scene of a lover pulling a cart in which his sweetheart is riding; and the thirteenth-century fabliau *Le Lai d'Aristote* (discussed below, note 14).

10. On the glorification and self-glorification of thinkers in eighteenth-century France, see Jean-Claude Bonnet, *Naissance du Panthéon*; David A. Bell, "National Memory and the Canon of Great Frenchmen" in *The Cult of the Nation: Inventing Nationalism, 1680–1800* (Cambridge, Mass.: Harvard University Press, 2001), 107–39; and Daniel Brewer, "Constructing Philosophers" in *SVEC* 2002:05, 21–35. On the role of sociability in eighteenth-century French learned society, see Roger Chartier, "L'homme de lettres" in Michel Vovelle, ed., *L'Homme des lumières* (Paris: Editions du Seuil, 1996), 159–209; Dena Goodman, *The Republic of Letters: A Cultural History of the French Enlightenment* (Ithaca: Cornell University Press, 1994); and Daniel Gordon, *Citizens Without Sovereignty: Equality and Sociability in French Thought, 1670–1789* (Princeton: Princeton University Press, 1994).

11. For examples of the socially integrated image of the eighteenth-century French intellectual, see Voltaire's article "Gens de lettres" in Denis Diderot and Jean d'Alembert, eds. *Encyclopédie, ou Dictionnaire raisonné des sciences, des arts et des métiers* (Paris, 1751–65; reprint, New York: Pergamon Press, 1969), vol. 7, 599; and the chapter "Gens de lettres" in Charles Duclos, *Considérations sur les moeurs de ce siècle (1751), in Oeuvres complètes de Duclos* (Paris: Janet et Cotelle, 1820), vol. 1, 135–47. Alain Viala describes a decidedly less harmonious relationship between *gens de lettres* and *gens du monde* in the seventeenth century: see *Naissance de l'écrivain: sociologie de la littérature à l'âge classique* (Paris: Editions de Minuit, 1982), esp. 271–72. See also Christian Jouhaud, *Les Pouvoirs de la littérature* (Paris: Gallimard, 2000) and Schapira, *Un Professionnel des lettres au XVIIe siècle*.

12. Herbert Dieckmann, *Le Philosophe: Text and Interpretation*, *Washington University Studies* 18 (1948), 69.

13. Dieckmann notes that the only remaining trace of this play is found in a review published in the *Mercure de France* of June, 1720; on the basis of that review, he provides the following plot summary: "Narcisse … discredits and undermines by his examples and teaching the highest virtues, such as love of one's country, devotion to one's parents and friends, self-sacrifice for a common, noble cause"; *Le Philosophe: Text and Interpretation*, 71.

14. *Le Lai d'Aristote,* written sometime in the thirteenth century, depicts a *philosophe* who becomes ridiculous when he falls in love with a young girl; see Henri d'Andeli, *Le Lai d'Aristote*, intro. A. Héron (Rouen: Imprimérie Léon Gy, 1901).

Henri Coulet and Michel Gilot cite this fabliau as a possible source of Marivaux's *Le Triomphe de l'amour* in their introduction to that play; in Marivaux, *Le Prince travesti /Le Triomphe de l'amour* (Paris: Honoré Champion, 1983), 124. As Ira Wade points out, the plot of *Le Lai d'Aristote* was repeated in Marmontel's *Le Soi-disant Philosophe* (1759), a *conte moral* that was dramatized at least nine times between 1760 and 1790, and in such plays as Piis's *Aristote amoureux* and Saint-Foix's *Oracle* (1740); Wade, *The "Philosophe" in the French Drama of the Eighteenth Century*, 83–87.

15. For those characters, see respectively Molière's *Tartuffe* (1664), *L'Ecole des femmes* (1662), and *Les Femmes savantes* (1672).

16. See Isabelle Martin's detailed typology of the characters that appeared in productions of the Théâtre de la Foire, in *Le Théâtre de la Foire: des tréteaux aux boulevards*, *SVEC* 2002:10, 252–307.

17. Marie-Catherine Desjardins (Madame de Villedieu), "Socrate" in *Amours des grands hommes*, translated as "Socrates" in *The Loves of sundry philosophers and other great men* (London: Herringman and Starkey, 1673), 29–62.

18. See, for example, Saint-Foix's *Le Philosophe dupe de l'amour* (1726), Philippe Poisson's *Alcibiade* (1731), Charles-Simon Favart's *La Fille mal gardée, ou le pédant amoureux* (1758); and Tesseirenc's *La femme philosophe* (1759).

19. It was Jean d'Alembert who coined the expression "*l'éternelle surprise de l'amour*" to describe the fundamental theme of all of Marivaux's plays; see d'Alembert, "Eloge de Marivaux," in Pierre Carlet de Chamblain, dit Marivaux, *Théâtre complet* (Paris: Editions du Seuil, 1964), 20.

20. This is the position ultimately taken by Coulet and Gilot in their introduction to the play; Marivaux, *Le Prince travesti /Le Triomphe de l'amour,* 124.

21. "The best Descriptions the World has given us of *Socrates* containe little answerable to the qualities of a *Lover*. He was neither of a Courtly Humour, nor of taking Shape or Feature. He made Profession of an *Austere Philosophy*, and yet for all this he was in *Love*"; "Socrates," 29, Villedieu's emphasis.

22. Nancy D. Klein, "Inscribing the Feminine in Seventeenth-Century Narratives: The Case of Madame de Villedieu," in Roxane Decker Lalande, ed., *A Labor of Love: Critical Reflections on the Writings of Marie-Catherine Desjardins (Mme de Villedieu)* (Madison/ Teaneck: Farleigh Dickinson University Press, 2000), 87–100, here 95. See also Henriette Goldwyn's essay "Men in Love in the Plays of Mme de Villedieu," 64–83 in the same volume.

23. See Eugene F. Rice, Jr., *The Renaissance Idea of Wisdom* (Cambridge, Mass: Harvard University Press, 1958).

24. To support this interpretation, Klein cites the following passage from Villedieu's dedicatory letter to Louis XIV: "Il est permis aux dames de chercher des endroits sensibles dans les coeurs les plus illustres"; "Inscribing the Feminine," 95.

25. On the popularity of academic eulogies and collective as well as individual biographies, see Bonnet, *Naissance du Panthéon*, 53–111, Bell, *The Cult of the Nation in France*, 107–39; and Ribard, *Raconter, vivre, penser*.

26. Guillaume Ansart, "*Le Triomphe de l'amour*: Cross-Dressing and Self-Discovery in Marivaux," *MLN* 117:4 (2002), 908–918, here 913. On the theme of

narcissicism in *Le Triomphe de l'amour*, see also Robert Tomlinson, "Marivaux dans les jardins de Socrate ou l'Anti-Banquet," in *Etudes littéraires* 24:1 (1991), 39–49, and Raymond Joly, "La Haine du philosophe: notes pour une lecture psychanalytique du *Triomphe de l'amour*," 51–62 in the same volume.

27. Marivaux, *Triomphe*, Act I, scene 1, 136.

28. In the opening dialogue, Léonide/ Phocion explains to her *suivante* Corine (herself disguised for most of the play as the manservant Hermidas) why she is determined to pursue her plan even though she regrets having to dupe Hermocrate and his sister: "il me vengera d'Hermocrate et de sa soeur qui méritent que je les punisse; qui, depuis qu'Agis est avec eux, n'ont travaillé qu'à lui inspirer de l'aversion pour moi, qu'à me peindre sous les traits les plus odieux, et le tout sans me connaître, sans savoir le fond de mon âme, ni tout ce que le ciel a pu y verser de vertueux. C'est eux qui ont soulevé tous les ennemis qu'il m'a fallu combattre, qui m'en soulèvent encore de nouveaux" (Marivaux, *Triomphe*, 136–7).

29. Hermocrate has instilled in Agis not only hatred for the princess who currently reigns over Sparta, but also the belief that he must make himself impervious to love to avoid his father's unhappy fate. When Léonide, still disguised as Phocion, but soon to reveal to him that she is a woman, supposedly named Aspasie, tries to persuade Agis that he should see love in a more sympathetic light, he replies: "Moi, de l'amour, Phocion! Fasse le ciel que votre âme lui soit aussi inaccessible que la mienne! Vous ne me connaissez pas; mon éducation, mes sentiments, ma raison, tout lui ferme mon coeur; il a fait les malheurs de mon sang, et je hais, quand j'y songe, jusqu'au sexe qui nous l'inspire" (*Triomphe*, 157).

30. Tomlinson, "Marivaux dans les jardins de Socrate," 46–47.

31. Tomlinson, citing Michel Deguy, characterizes Hermocrate as a mere "pseudo-maître de philosophie"; "Marivaux dans les jardins de Socrate," 46. See Deguy, *La Machine matrimoniale ou Marivaux* (Paris: Gallimard [Tel], 1986 [1981]), 105.

32. Examples of stereotypical false philosophers include the charlatan Polimatte of Jacques Du Vaure's comedy *Le Faux savant* (1728), the pretentious social climber Ariste of Mlle de Maestricht's adaptation of Marmontel, *Le philosophe soit-disant [sic.]* (1767), and the various *philosophe* characters which Palissot and Rutlidge created for the stage.

33. Joly, "La Haine du philosophe," 59. Joly points out that Hermocrate and Léontine are not nearly as grotesque as they might have been: unlike typical stage pedants, they have no obvious vice, infirmity, tic, mania, or *idée fixe*, and they do not lust after the young and appetizing stranger who intrudes into their solitary retreat; quite the contrary, "ils se protègent contre l'amour, il redoutent cette passion ennemie de la sagesse et du repos, ils la fuient dans la retraite, fidèles en cela à l'enseignement invariable des moralistes. S'ils succombent enfin, ce n'est pas que leur nature libineuse renverse le garde-fou de l'hypocrisie, c'est qu'ils ont un coeur et un corps comme tout le monde, et, surtout, que Phocion leur a tendu un piège diabolique" (56).

34. See also Hermocrate's lament in the portrait scene of Act II, where he gives himself over to the illusion that "Aspasie" adores him and kisses the portrait she has just given him: "Me trouvez-vous assez humilié? Je ne vous dispute plus rien" (*Triomphe*, 174).

35. Prior to this point, Hermocrate typically insists that he is unlovable; see, for example, his remark to "Aspasie" in Act I, scene 8: Suis-je fait pour être aimé? Vous attaquez une âme solitaire et sauvage, à qui l'amour est étranger; ma rudesse doit rebuter votre jeunesse et vos charmes, et mon coeur en un mot ne pourrait rien pour le vôtre" (*Triomphe*, 149).

36. Léonide shows a bit of remorse at the end of the scene that precedes this dialogue: having persuaded Hermocrate that she and he will soon be married, she declares in an aside "J'ai pitié de sa faiblesse, ô ciel! pardonne mon artifice! (*Triomphe*, 176). There is, however, a far more brutal and dismissive tone to the remark she makes about these characters in the scene that follows the siblings's conversation: "Hermocrate et sa soeur m'ont obsédée tour à tour; ils doivent tous deux m'épouser en secret: je ne sais combien de mesures sont prises pour ces mariages imaginaires. Non, on ne saurait croire combien l'amour égare ces têtes qu'on appelle sages" (178). On the importance of compassion in Marivaux's moral philosophy, see Jean Sgard, "Trois 'philosophes' de 1734: Marivaux, Prévost, et Voltaire" in *Etudes littéraires* 24:1 (1991), 31–38.

37. "Malepeste! de l'amour dans cette maison-ci? ce serait une mauvaise auberge pour lui; la sagesse d'Agis, d'Hermocrate et de Léontine, sont trois sagesses aussi inciviles pour l'amour qu'il y en ait dans le monde"(*Triomphe*, 138).

38. Arguing that Marivaux's comedies support both an "aristocratic" reading (emphasizing the erotic) and a "bourgeois" one (underscoring the sentimental), Lionel Gossman comments: "the nature of desire is shrouded in ambiguity by his art, and this ambiguity itself is also socially significant . . . many of the plays would be destroyed if we plumped for one or the other [reading], for they depend on nothing so much as the bracketing of any single 'real'meaning"; "Literature and Society in the Early Enlightenment: The Case of Marivaux," in *MLN* 82:3 (1967), 306–33, here 331.

39. This comment is related in the *Annales du théâtre* of March 12, 1732, transcribed on the CESAR Web site page for *Le Triomphe de l'amour*. The *Comédiens Italiens* performed the play only six times that year (once before the court); although it would not be staged again until 1912, it did appear in print from 1732 on. See Bernard Dort's note on the play in Marivaux, *Théâtre complet* (Paris: Seuil, 1964), 301. David Trott offers an interesting alternative explanation of the relative unpopularity of *Le Triomphe de l'amour* and other Marivaux comedies during the 1730: public audiences of this period, Trott maintains, disliked Marivaux's overt theatricality and preferred plays that developed a resolutely non-theatrical theme, like Voltaire's *Zaïre* and Destouches's *Le Glorieux*; Trott, "Marivaux et la vie théatrale de 1730 à 1737" in *Etudes littéraires* 24:1 (1991), 19–30.

40. According to Aleksandra Hoffmann-Lipoñska, *Le Philosophe marié* attracted 80,000 spectators to the Comédie Française and was performed approximately 163 times from 1727 and 1754; Hoffmann-Lipoñska, "Destouches et Voltaire, relations et correspondance" in *Cahiers de Varsovie* 10 (1982), 251–58, here 252. On Destouches's very successful dramatic career, see John Dunkley's introduction to *l'Irrésolu* (Paris: Société des Textes Français Modernes, 1995), v–xcvi; Jean Hankiss, *Philippe Néricault Destouches: L'homme et l'oeuvre* (Debreczen: François de Csáthy, 1918); A. Burner, "Philippe Néricault-Destouches (1680–1754): Essai de biographie"

in *Revue d'histoire littéraire de la France* 38 (1931), 64–70; and Aleksandra Hoffmann-Lipoñska, *Philippe Néricault Destouches et la comédie moralisatrice* (Poznan: UAM, 1979). Beyond these essays and monographs, little scholarly research currently exists on Destouches, although he did share top billing with Nivelle de la Chaussée at a conference held at the Sorbonne in March 2004 (see http://www.cometes.org). Nor are there any focused studies of *Le Philosophe marié*, despite the fact that this comedy continued to be staged annually or even semi-annually by Parisian theater troupes until 1799 and was published multiple times well into the nineteenth century, either on its own or as part of a collection of Destouches's works (twenty-six editions of *Le Philosophe marié* appeared from 1727 to 1887, and forty-seven editions of his *Oeuvres* were produced from 1727 to 1872).

41. Destouches, *Le Philosophe marié, ou le Mari honteux de l'être* in *Oeuvres dramatiques de N. Destouches* (Paris: Crapelet, 1822), vol. 2, 374, 276.

42. This biographical interpretation, repeated by subsequent Destouches critics like Burner, was first advanced by Jean d'Alembert in his "Eloge de Destouches"; see *Oeuvres de d'Alembert* (Paris; Belin, 1821), vol. 3, 412.

43. On the centrality of the secluded study to the image of the early modern European scholar, see Gadi Algazi, "Scholars in Households: Refiguring the Learned Habitus, 1480–1550," *Science in Context* 16:1/2 (2003), 9–42.

44. The nineteenth-century medical popularizer Julien-Joseph Virey cited Finette's wisecrack in *Le Philosophe marié* to support his theory that great scholars like Newton were tepid lovers and poor sires because their vital fluids had to concentrate on a higher calling; see Virey, *De la femme sous ses rapports physiologique, moral et littéraire* (1823; 2nd edition Brussels: Wahlen, 1826), 437.

45. As Voltaire's *Lettres philosophiques* (1734) attest, this notion often appeared in biographies of Isaac Newton, who was widely considered to be the world's greatest genius at the time, and whose death in 1727 (the same year, coincidentally, that *Le Philosophe marié* was first performed) inspired a veritable craze of Newtonianism in European culture for decades afterward. On the concern emerging among French physicians over the effects of intense thinking on men's sexual capacities, see Anne C. Vila, "Sex, Procreation, and the Scholarly Life from Tissot to Balzac," *Eighteenth-Century Studies* 32:2 (2002), 239–46. On the studious life as a perceived medical problem elsewhere in eighteenth-century Europe, see John Mullan, *Sentiment and Sociability: The Language of Feeling in the Eighteenth Century* (Oxford: Clarendon Press, 1988), 201–40; Anita Guerrini, *Obesity and Depression in the Enlightenment: The Life and Times of George Cheyne* (Norman: University of Oklahoma Press, 2000), 119–25; and the chapter "Kant's Hypochondria" in Susan Meld Shell, *Embodiment of Reason: Kant on Spirit, Generation, and Community* (Chicago: University of Chicago Press, 1996), 264–305.

46. Lisimon is a poor gentleman who, unlike his brother Géronte, refused to debase himself by becoming a *riche roturier* (*Le Philosophe marié,* 451). Ariste thus depends on Géronte, rather than his father, for his fortune.

47. Destouches returned to the theme that the love of scholarship is misunderstood by aristocrats, whether old-style, idle *gentilshommes* or capitalists of the new generation, in *Les Philosophes amoureux* (1729), a play that met with far less success on stage

than did *Le Philosophe marié*, although it did appear in print in many editions of Destouches's works.

48. In 1773, the Académie Française organized a rather odd poetry competition on the theme of celibacy's disadvantages; see on that event Eric Walter, "Le complexe d'Abélard ou le célibat des gens de lettres" in *Dix-huitième siècle* no. 12, 1980, 127–52.

49. Fagan's sympathetic depiction of the *philosophe* is, however, tempered by a passing evocation of the theme of scholarly impotence. In an early scene of *La Pupille*, Ariste scoffs at the idea of marrying, and his friend Orgon replies: "il est vrai que vous avez toujours été un peu philosophe, et par conséquent peu curieux d'engendrement"; *La Pupille* (1734), in Jacques Truchet, ed., *Théâtre du XVIIIe siècle* (Paris: Gallimard, Bibliothèque de la Pléaide, 1972), vol. I, 990.

50. Diderot's *Le Fils naturel* (1757) exemplifies both trends, as do dramas like Voltaire's *Socrate* (1759) and Mercier's *Montesquieu à Marseille* (1784). Marivaux himself should be included among eighteenth-century authors drawn to philosophical retreat from society: that is the position of the mature Marianne who narrates his novel *La vie de Marianne* (1731–1737) and of the Hermocrate character who appears in his journal *Le Spectateur français* (1721–24). As Michel Gilot points out, a distinct pessimism regarding contemporary society haunted Marivaux at various points in his life; Gilot, "Du *Jeu de l'amour et du hasard* aux *Fausses confidences*: Remarques sur l'évolution du théâtre de Marivaux" in *Etudes littéraires* 24:1 (1991), 9–18, at 15.

The New Paris in Guise of the Old: Louis Sébastien Mercier from Old Regime to Revolution

JOANNA STALNAKER

> "Sous le Paris actuel, l'ancien Paris est distinct, comme le vieux texte dans les interlignes du nouveau."
> —Victor Hugo, "Paris"[1]

The writings of Louis Sébastien Mercier have received increasing attention in recent years, thanks to the outstanding critical editions published by Jean-Claude Bonnet over the past decade.[2] Prior to this renewal of interest, Mercier suffered from the neglect that so often strikes writers who fall between two traditionally distinct periods in literary historiography. Born in 1740, Mercier belongs properly neither to the intellectual movement of the Enlightenment, nor to the self-proclaimed literary era of the *dix-neuvième siècle*. Although he was directly influenced by the major figures of the Enlightenment, he also lived to see the 1789 Revolution and the rise and fall of the Napoleonic Empire, dying in 1814 the day after Louis XVIII left England to take the French throne. His lifespan thus granted him an ideal vantage point from which to describe both Old Regime and revolutionary Paris, and to ponder the strange gulf that seemed to separate the two. This he did in two of his most important works, the *Tableau de Paris*, a twelve-volume description of the physical and moral physiognomy of the city published between 1781 and 1788, and *Le Nouveau Paris,* a six-volume account of revolutionary Paris published in 1798 or early 1799. A comparison of these two works reveals differing writing strategies that reflect a distinct shift in the author's perceptual position with respect to the city of Paris.

* * * *

Mercier begins his account of revolutionary Paris, *Le Nouveau Paris*, with a strangely paradoxical statement: "Je ne marche plus dans Paris que sur ce qui me rappelle ce qui n'est plus. Bien m'a pris de faire mon tableau en douze volumes. Car s'il n'était pas fait, le modèle est tellement effacé qu'il ressemble au portrait décoloré d'un aïeul mort à l'hôpital et relégué dans un galetas."[3] In 1795, when this passage was written, Mercier finds himself in a new and unfamiliar Paris. The model on which he had based his previous 'painting' seems so faded, literally *erased*, as to be nearly unrecognizable. Thus the opening lines of *Le Nouveau Paris* emphasize the newness of revolutionary Paris, and imply a radical break with the past. At the same time, the new Paris appears within these lines in the guise of the old: at three removes from the purported newness of revolutionary Paris, the city is compared to the faded portrait of a grandparent who was abandoned in a garret and died miserably in a hospice.

A similarly paradoxical relationship between old and new can be seen in Mercier's formal choices as a writer. On a formal level, the *Tableau de Paris* is innovative, even revolutionary: brief chapters of a few pages each describe a remarkable variety of things, people, places, customs and scenes one might encounter in Old Regime Paris. For example, a chapter entitled "Balcons" gives a view of a Parisian traffic jam from up above; another, called "Faux cheveux," takes a somewhat distastefully close look at an elegant lady's hairpiece stuck full of pins; a chapter on the "Quai de la Vallée," where fowl markets were located, describes the practice of force-feeding pigeons to keep them plump and attractive to prospective buyers.[4] Because the chapters are brief, have descriptive titles, and are organized in no easily discernible order, the reader is granted as much freedom to wander within the text as Mercier himself had to wander through the city. Through its formal innovations, thus, the *Tableau de Paris* recreates the "croisement [des] innombrables rapports" that Baudelaire would subsequently associate with big cities in the preface to his prose poems.[5]

At the same time, patterns of repetition and parallelism between various chapters published over a period of eight years create a sense of time passing, as Old Regime Paris seems to change slowly before the reader's eyes. The insalubrious cemeteries are moved to the outskirts of the city, the hazardous houses on the bridges of the Seine are destroyed, the church of the Quinze-Vingts falls into ruin.[6] Other changes are more gradual and exist on a smaller scale, but nonetheless contribute to the sense of time passing: eight years after describing how the *engaveur* uses his own mouth to stuff grain down pigeons' gullets, Mercier reports that the same man has developed a cancer and had his tongue cut out due to the unhealthy practice.[7]

The rapid changes and heightened contrasts of revolutionary Paris are of an entirely different nature, and one might thus expect new formal innovations to accompany the new title Mercier chooses for *Le Nouveau Paris*. And yet, despite his conviction that a new work is needed to describe revolutionary Paris, Mercier keeps the literary form he had invented to describe Old Regime Paris. Short, titled chapters arranged in no discernible order make *Le Nouveau Paris* appear as a mere continuation of the *Tableau de Paris*, albeit in an entirely new context. Once again, on the level of formal innovation, the new Paris appears in the guise of the old.

Yet *Le Nouveau Paris* is not simply a rewriting of the *Tableau de Paris* in the revolutionary context. It is a radically experimental work, which Baudelaire called "merveilleux" and which perfectly exemplifies Hermann Hofer's characterization of Mercier as "peut-être le plus moderne de tous les auteurs du XVIIIe siècle, un moderne pour qui la littérature a un caractère expérimental: il s'intéresse aux extrêmes des formes et des contenus."[8] Arguably Mercier's most modern work, *Le Nouveau Paris* engages with political and literary problems that he could not even have imagined as author of the *Tableau de Paris*.[9] At the same time, through its connection to the *Tableau de Paris*, *Le Nouveau Paris* can be seen as a literary project built on the ruins of the Enlightenment ideal of seeing and describing all. Thus, in addition to representing the shift from old Paris to new, *Le Nouveau Paris* can help us to understand the complex relationship of continuity and rupture between two periods in literary history that we tend to treat as distinct. The Directory, depicted in *Le Nouveau Paris* as a period that both preserves and erases memories of the Terror through its relentless quest for pleasure, embodies that complex relationship and serves as a perilous bridge between the pre- and post-revolutionary periods.

* * * *

When choosing a title for his description of Old Regime Paris, Mercier settled on the singular form of *tableau*, rather than the plural as is often mistakenly assumed. This choice reflects his overriding aesthetic purpose in writing the *Tableau de Paris*: to create not a series of paintings, but rather a *single* painting of Paris, which incorporates both discontinuity and temporal change into a unified representation. Presenting his work to the reader in his preface, Mercier writes "le voici, tracé tel qu'il est sorti de dessous ma plume, à mesure que mes yeux et mon entendement en ont rassemblé les parties."[10]

The author has brought the disparate parts of Paris together into one work, and so too must the reader compose and recompose a unified vision of Paris based on Mercier's descriptions. The term *tableau* also connects Mercier's project to the encyclopedic and descriptive aspirations of the Enlightenment: like Diderot and d'Alembert's *Encyclopédie* for the realm of human knowledge, and Buffon's *Histoire naturelle* for the realm of nature, the *Tableau* aims through its accumulation of individual descriptions to provide a global representation of the city, characterized by its completeness and comprehensiveness.[11]

Thus the very fact that Mercier gives a new title to his description of revolutionary Paris, rather than presenting it as a continuation of his best-selling *Tableau de Paris*, signals the radical nature of the break he perceives between the old Paris and the new.[12] For him, the changes of revolutionary Paris are too great to be incorporated into a unified *tableau*. But in addition to connoting the *newness* of revolutionary Paris, the new title also drops the pictorial referent *tableau*, thereby collapsing the representational project and the object described into one. Instead of a new painting of Paris, we have simply the new Paris, cut loose not only from the old Paris but also from the Enlightenment model of a comprehensive, descriptive *tableau*. Mercier also chooses not to include the definite article "le" in his first title, *Tableau de Paris*, but does in his second, *Le Nouveau Paris*, as if to suggest that whereas the first work is but one painting among many, the second is unique and definitive, the first and last of its kind. Subsequent writers appear to have picked up on this distinction, for the *Tableau de Paris*, unlike its revolutionary counterpart, inspired numerous imitations with the same or similar titles throughout the first half of the nineteenth century, to such an extent that the *tableau de Paris* has even been considered by some critics as a minor literary genre.[13]

* * * *

Thus the change in title from the *Tableau de Paris* to *Le Nouveau Paris* implies not only the transformation of Paris itself, but also a fundamental reorientation of Mercier's representational project. A seminal chapter in *Le Nouveau Paris*, entitled "La ville de Paris en relief (monument qui voit au Palais-Égalité)," reveals that Mercier himself understood the two projects as quite distinct in their representational goals.[14] In this chapter, Mercier offers a lengthy description of an immensely detailed three-dimensional scale model of Paris, made out of wood and cardboard by the Citoyen Arnauld and displayed in the Palais-Égalité (formerly the Palais-Royal) in 1797. Mercier expresses great admiration for this miniature version of Paris, and draws an explicit parallel between Arnauld's artistry and his own work of description in the *Tableau de Paris*, writing "il a fait au physique sur Paris ce que j'ai tenté de faire au moral dans mon *Tableau.*"[15] In fact, the scale model can be seen as an implicit metaphor for the *Tableau de Paris* embedded within *Le Nouveau Paris*. As such, it provides a rare opportunity for us to see how Mercier viewed his previous work from a revolutionary perspective. On the one hand, the chapter demonstrates how the *Tableau de Paris* can be revisited and reread in light of revolutionary events; on the other, it suggests that the work has been made obsolete by the Revolution, thereby justifying the writing of *Le Nouveau Paris*.

Like the *Tableau de Paris*, the scale model participates in the encyclopedic ideal of the Enlightenment, in its attempt to achieve a complete representation of Paris. Mercier shows his admiration for this aspect of the topography when he urges viewers to stand up on a chair and get a bird's eye view, just as he had urged readers of the *Tableau de Paris* to climb to the top of Notre-Dame for the same reason.[16] He also suggests that viewers use a magnifying glass to bring the scale of the miniature city up to size, thereby mirroring his own tendency in the *Tableau de Paris* to zoom in on certain details like the hairpins sticking into an elegant lady's scalp.[17] Both suggestions emphasize the fact that the viewer's perspective on the city is not controlled or oriented in any single direction: like the reader of the *Tableau de Paris*, he or she has the freedom to survey the topography from many different angles and in any order.

But Arnaud's scale model also provides an occasion for Mercier to reflect on how much, or rather how little, the physical topography of Paris has changed since the Revolution, in the face of dramatic social and political changes:

> Tel est ce plan curieux et instructif qui remet Paris sous nos regards, tel qu'il était en 1789, sans aucune dégradation, et dans tous ses accroissements successifs. On voit que la révolution, si elle a fait tomber des milliers de têtes, n'a point endommagé sa masse physique, qu'elle est la même, absolument la même, et cette réflexion qui nous dit que l'oiseau passe et que le nid demeure, se creuse encore lorsqu'on contemple tant de palais et de maisons que n'habitent plus leurs propriétaires, ni leurs possesseurs encore vivants.[18]

As a physical entity, Paris has remained absolutely the same between 1789 and 1797, even as the lives of its inhabitants have changed drastically. What then can this topographical model of Paris, which focuses solely on physical structures, have to say about the Revolution? This is where revolutionary memory, one of the central themes of *Le Nouveau Paris*, comes into play.

For according to Mercier, Arnaud's scale model allows each spectator to revisit his or her personal memories of the Revolution, in connection with various places depicted on it. In fact, Mercier spends most of the chapter describing not the scale model itself, but rather the memories it evokes in a wide variety of viewers. What we see in the chapter, then, is an individuation and fragmentation of the viewing public. This becomes particularly apparent when one of the viewers, a *bonnet rouge* or radical revolutionary, is marginalized from the viewing public. His exclusion is orchestrated by a mysteriously impersonal pointer which suddenly materializes in Mercier's text, to designate the site where Sanson, an executioner during the Terror, chopped off heads, or as Mercier puts it, minted fresh coins: "l'ancien bonnet rouge lui-même frémit quand le bout de la baguette marque la place où Sanson battit monnaie [...] et il s'éloigne un peu de côté pour ne pas entendre la réflexion qui suit, et qui le regarde."[19] The accusing gesture of the pointer is reinforced by a comment made by an unidentified speaker, who effectively excludes the radical revolutionary from what now appears as a collective viewing experience, a sort of ideologically motivated tour of Arnaud's topography.

The question then becomes whether this unidentified voice making an accusatory remark in fact reflects the position of the author in *Le Nouveau Paris*. This is a complicated question: on the one hand, *Le Nouveau Paris* is clearly a work of political polemic, an accusation against the radical Montagnard members of the Convention for their condemnation and execution of the more moderate Girondins. At times, indeed, Mercier gives the impression that proving the guilt of the Montagnards is his overriding purpose in writing *Le Nouveau Paris*: "Trente à quarante scélérats encore plus ineptes que barbares sont venus décomposer tout ce que le génie et le courage avaient formé de grand et de solennel. Ces trente à quarante scélérats sont les chefs montagnards. C'est ce que je démontrerai dans la suite de cet écrit."[20] Clearly Mercier no longer appears here as the impartial observer and describer of the *Tableau de Paris*; for some critics, indeed, the overtly political nature of *Le Nouveau Paris* makes it an inferior work when compared to its Old Regime counterpart.[21]

Yet Mercier does acknowledge the subjective nature of his view of the Revolution, when he includes a veiled reference to the thirteen months he spent in prison, from October 1793 to October 1794, for his defiant support of the Girondins: "Là l'épouse de l'ex-conventionnel montre à sa fille la prison où son malheureux père abandonné de la nation entière, et toujours républicain, attendit la mort qu'il avait bravé pour l'intérêt de la liberté, et par haine pour l'anarchie, et l'attendit pendant treize mois à chaque instant du jour et de la nuit."[22] With this indirect reference to his own life, Mercier implicitly acknowledges the extent to which his description of revolutionary Paris is informed by his personal memories of the Revolution. No longer can he play the role of the Enlightenment describer, stepping up onto a chair to "embrasse[r Paris] d'un seul regard" and aiming to provide a comprehensive *tableau* of Paris.[23] Nor can he occupy the impersonal and curiously disembodied position of the anonymous tour guide, who accuses the *bonnet rouge* without situating himself with respect to his own experience of the Revolution. On the contrary, the fragmentation of the viewing public in the "Ville de Paris en relief" chapter suggests that any view of the Revolution will be partial and fragmentary, driven by the vagaries of memory and individual experience.

* * * *

For Mercier, then, a description of revolutionary Paris cannot be simply a record of things seen: it must reproduce the multi-layered experience of walking through the new Paris while remembering the old. A further layer of memory is added when one considers the way the work was composed: while the initial project and some chapters date from the early years of the Revolution, it was only after his release from prison in 1794 that Mercier began a regular chronicle of revolutionary Paris in the journal *Les Annales patriotiques et littéraires*, and only in 1797 that he began gathering articles to compose *Le Nouveau Paris*. It is thus, as Shelly Charles puts it, that Mercier's *tableau* of Revolutionary Paris is written not so much in the "j'ai vu" mode of a chronicle, but rather in the "je me souviens" mode of remembrance.[24] In addition to the old Paris, it is the most turbulent years of the Revolution that Mercier remembers as he walks through the new Paris of the Directory.

But when it comes to the events of the Terror, those memories are obscured by the frenzied quest for pleasure that characterizes the Directory period. Thus, in a passage that beautifully suggests how much description has become an act of unveiling, Mercier writes: "Si tous les événements désastreux ne sont pas oubliés au milieu de nos fêtes et de nos plaisirs, ils sont couverts d'un rideau ou que l'on craint de soulever, ou que l'on soulève rarement."[25] Yet even the image of lifting a curtain to reveal hidden memories does not do justice to the subtlety of Mercier's descriptive approach in *Le Nouveau Paris*. For in some cases, it is the curtain itself that he chooses to describe, in a way that reveals the very horrors it was intended to hide. This can be seen in a chapter entitled "Les bals d'hiver," in which Mercier describes the frenzied dancing, gastronomic excess and unchecked lubricity that overtook men, and especially women, during the Directory:

> On danse *aux Carmes* où l'on égorgeait ; on danse *au noviciat des jésuites* ; on danse *au couvent des carmélites du Marais* ; on danse *au séminaire Saint-Sulpice* ; on danse *aux Filles de Sainte-Marie* ; on danse dans trois églises ruinées de ma section, et sur le pavé de toutes les tombes que l'on n'a point encore enlevées : le nom des morts est sous les pieds des danseurs qui ne l'aperçoivent pas, et qui oublient qu'ils foulent des sépulcres.[26]

By dancing wildly in churches and convents, the ball-goers trample their ancestors' tombs, thereby erasing the collective memory of the dead traditionally preserved by religious institutions.[27] Unlike Mercier, who traverses Paris in order to remember, the ball-goers turn ceaselessly upon themselves, seeking to forget the past through the rapid movement of their feet. Like so many other pleasure seekers in *Le Nouveau Paris*, they seem to rise above time itself, "Oubliant le passé, tuant le présent, ne songeant pas à l'avenir."[28] In this respect, Mercier's beautifully rhythmic depiction of the dancers mirrors his view of the Jacobin extremists who orchestrated the atrocities of the Terror. For they too, according to Mercier, seek to rise above time by erasing the past and refusing to consider the future: "Des hommes ineptes avaient dit *qu'en révolution il ne faut jamais regarder derrière soi*. Cette maxime est très fausse. Les révolutions se conduisent et s'achèvent par ceux qui mesurent et comparent ce qui est fait, et ce qui reste à faire."[29] This remark makes it strikingly clear that for Mercier, the revolutionary phenomenon implies neither a radical rupture nor a complete erasure of the past; on the contrary, the notion that revolutions are best conducted by those who look both backwards and forwards demonstrates his preoccupation with preserving some level of continuity in the face of dramatic social and political change.

* * * *

On several levels, then, *Le Nouveau Paris* can be understood as a meditation on the possibilities for continuity in the face of radical change. On a political level, this can be seen in Mercier's position on the execution of Louis XVI. As deputy to the Convention from 1792 until his arrest in October of 1793, Mercier voted against the execution of the king, but in favor of his lifetime imprisonment. While this position is consistent with what he calls his "modérantisme," it is not simply a middle-of-the-road compromise.[30] What is most interesting about Mercier's position, in fact, is his argument that the lifetime imprisonment of the king would serve as a guarantor of continuity between the Old Regime and the young Republic, invalidating any attempts to erase the progress of the Revolution through counterrevolution and Restoration.[31] This argument rests not on a paradox, but on a difference in perception between France and the rest of Europe. In the eyes of the French nation, according to Mercier, the king is already politically and symbolically dead, having been executed not by the guillotine but by the political laws of the nation: "Je soutiens que le roi est mort, qu'il est enseveli; il n'a plus d'existence politique. [...] les lois politiques ont tué l'être politique; [...] Le roi n'est plus qu'un fantôme; et avoir placé sa tête sous la hache de la loi, c'est comme si elle était tombée."[32] For the rulers of Europe, on the contrary, Louis XVI preserves his political identity as the king of France, and for this reason, he guarantees that no other ruler can take the throne. Thus Mercier does not merely argue that it is not politically necessary to kill the king, he asserts on the contrary that it is politically necessary to keep him alive as long as possible, or at least until the stability of the young Republic has been ensured.

Of course, Mercier's bid for the lifetime imprisonment of a political phantom failed, and in January of 1793 the former king was guillotined in what Mercier describes as a badly botched decapitation. The guillotine itself, introduced in 1792 as a more humane form of execution, became a compelling symbol of the radical political rupture Mercier had sought to avoid. In a chapter entitled "Est-ce un supplice doux que celui de la guillotine?," he addresses the widespread fear that the severed head of a guillotine victim may experience pain in the moments following execution.[33] Considering the question from a purely physiological point of view, Mercier rules out the possibility that there may be any continuity of sensation after the separation of head and body. As a revolutionary machine, indeed, the guillotine functions perfectly, realizing the complete severance and erasure of continuity that for Mercier is so problematic from a political point of view.

Yet Mercier also traces human efforts to restore a macabre form of continuity in the face of the revolutionary machine's complete severance. In "Chevelures blondes," he cites a Convention member's cruelly ironic proposal that old women cover their bald spots by wearing wigs made from the hair of the guillotine's victims, and concludes: "Qui croirait qu'un tel discours a été tenu? Ce fut à cette époque que commença le règne des perruques blondes; comme si les femmes avaient voulu braver par ces représailles ces ironies sanglantes."[34] Generally hostile to counterrevolutionaries, Mercier appears here to view their gesture of donning blond wigs as a courageous reprisal against the violent irony of the Convention member. Although they are unable to combat the actual physical decapitation of the guillotine, the women resist that severance with a symbolic image: it is an image of continuity, an image of the living carrying the dead on their shoulders rather than dancing on their tombs.

Mercier's own powerful symbol of continuity can be found in a brief chapter entitled "Rubans." The chapter begins with a dictionary-style definition of the ribbons used by royalty during the Old Regime to decorate and honor their courtiers. These servile Old Regime ribbons, likened to a harness with which the king controls his subjects, are then contrasted with the tri-colored revolutionary ribbons or *cocardes*, a symbol of the new freedom enjoyed by the French people. Thus Mercier takes the same object, one that might appear insignificant in the context of full-scale political and social revolution, and traces a radical discontinuity in its symbolic meaning from Old Regime to new.

Yet the chapter does not end there. For Mercier concludes with a third image of the ribbon, and this time it is not a short cut of ribbon gracing the apparel of a servile Old Regime courtier or a freed French citizen. Rather, it is a long, continuous ribbon that stretches across the entire terrace bordering the Tuileries palace garden:

> Pour séparer le jardin du château des Tuileries qu'occupait Louis le traître, de la terrasse des Feuillants où le public se rassemblait, le peuple tendit le long de cette terrasse un simple *ruban*, et cette barrière fut respectée ; personne ne la franchit. Du canon n'aurait point produit cet effet. C'est que le peuple obéissait à une loi qu'il s'était lui-même imposée.[35]

Here, the long ribbon, which can be seen as a symbol of continuity, marks neither the servitude nor the absolute freedom of the people, but rather the restrictions on their freedom that they themselves have chosen. What the ribbon seems to represent, then, is a peaceful and harmonious transition between monarchical and national sovereignty: the people do not take over the palace, but their freedom is limited only by the sovereignty of a self-imposed law, and not by the arbitrary power of a monarch.[36]

History would prove the ribbon illusory when in June 1792 the Tuileries Palace was invaded, leading to the end of the monarchy in August and the execution of the king in January of the following year. Despite his bid for lifetime imprisonment, Mercier accepted the execution of the king in order to avoid a split in the Convention, even declaring, significantly, "s'il le faut, je danserai politiquement sur ses cendres."[37] But for him, the king's execution represented the negation of the political continuity he had sought to preserve, the cutting of the ribbon that stretched from the Old Regime to the new Republic. Mercier's ribbon, like the wigs of the counterrevolutionaries, illustrates the importance of figurative and symbolic responses in the face of very real historical and political rupture. As such, it is a testament to the place of literature in modern life.

Throughout *Le Nouveau Paris*, Mercier uses both metaphor and political polemic to resist the efforts, on the part of Jacobins, royalists and Directory pleasure seekers alike, to erase the past. One of the most striking aspects of *Le Nouveau Paris*, indeed, is the extent to which Mercier's political preoccupations are mirrored by his literary approach. For if he represents the new Paris as a faded portrait of its former self, it is because he sees the Revolution, in its most extreme form, as a force that erases the collective memories of the French nation. His awareness that such memories may not always be transmitted continuously from generation to generation as they were during the Old Regime, and his struggle to resist the force of erasure even as he welcomes the progress of Revolution, are among the most remarkable aspects of *Le Nouveau Paris*. Above all, the complex intertextual relationship between Mercier's twin descriptions of Paris reflects his subtle understanding of the nature of revolutionary change: while the formal resemblance between the two works preserves some level of continuity, the experimental newness of *Le Nouveau Paris* marks an important departure from a project originally conceived within the framework of the Enlightenment.

* * * *

If *Le Nouveau Paris* can indeed be considered more experimental than the *Tableau de Paris*, even testing the limits of representation, it is in large part due to a significant shift in the position of the observer. For one of Mercier's most cited claims about the *Tableau de Paris* is that he wrote it with his legs: "J'ai tant couru pour faire le *Tableau de Paris*, que je puis dire l'avoir fait avec *mes jambes*; aussi ai-je appris à marcher sur le pavé de la capitale, d'une manière leste, vive et prompte. C'est un secret qu'il faut posséder pour tout voir."[38] In order to complete a work of encyclopedic proportions, Mercier developed a particular way of walking, an agile and rapid step that allowed him to cover the entire city, to *see all*. Implicit in this formulation is the image of a relatively stable city: it is the observer who must traverse the city, moving rapidly and exploring even the most hidden places in order to complete his work of description. Although the *Tableau de Paris* does convey a sense of time passing, Mercier's rapid step seems designed to overtake the somewhat slower passage of time. Thus despite the incorporation of temporal change and shifts in perspective, something entirely new with respect to descriptive technique of the Enlightenment, the observer in the *Tableau de Paris* retains an Enlightenment mastery over the object described.

This is no longer the case in *Le Nouveau Paris*. Although Mercier remains loyal to the principle of first-hand observation, the position from which he observes Paris has changed radically: "Comment peindre tant de faits et d'événements? Je dirai ce que j'ai vu. Porté sur tous les flots orageux, n'ayant pas perdu un coup de vent, mon œil a distingué dans la tempête quelques accidents particuliers."[39] Rather than circulating freely within the object of his description (rather than writing with his legs), Mercier is now carried along by the stormy waves he seeks to describe. He no longer chooses his own trajectory as he did in the *Tableau de Paris*. In *Le Nouveau Paris*, as in the *Tableau de Paris*, Mercier describes a city in flux; the difference is that he is no longer able to keep pace with those changes through the rapidity of his step. Despite the acuity of his observing eye, he can no longer hold onto the encyclopedic ideal of seeing and describing all.

Thus in a key chapter called "Tout est optique," Mercier reflects on the impossibility of reproducing even his own perspective on revolutionary events. While the title "Tout est optique" asserts that everything is a matter of perspective, the first sentence of the chapter, "Ou jeu d'optique," undercuts that assertion. Is everything a matter of perspective, or an interplay of various perspectives? Will the writer give us his own coherent perspective on the Revolution, or a bewildering kaleidoscope of different points of view?

The chapter as a whole is deeply skeptical about the possibility of reproducing any single point of view on revolutionary events, even one based on Mercier's own first-hand observations. Of the session that determined the fate of Louis XVI, he writes "de tout ce que j'ai vu là, rien ne peut se dire comme il s'est passé; il est impossible de se figurer ce qui est; l'histoire ne pourra y atteindre."[40] Like Fabrice in Stendhal's *La Chartreuse de Parme*, who finds himself in the midst of the battle of Waterloo without even understanding he is on a battlefield, Mercier was present for some of the most memorable days of the Revolution without realizing it until after the fact: "il en est de même de toutes les journées mémorables; j'y étais, et je n'ai jamais su où j'étais, c'est-à-dire, comprendre ou le péril où je me trouvais, ou toutes les singularités qui m'environnaient."[41] The very idea that the 13 Vendémiaire, when a royalist insurrection against the Thermidorian Convention was suppressed by the young general Bonaparte, was a memorable day reveals the interplay of various perspectives at work in *Le Nouveau Paris*: this day has been remembered, in hindsight, as one of the important days of the Revolution, and so Mercier will write about it in *Le Nouveau Paris*, even though on the day itself, he was completely unaware of what was happening.

Similarly, despite the skill for observation he acquired in writing the *Tableau de Paris*, Mercier suggests that the secret workings and causes of the Revolution escaped even his perceptive eye. Like all first-hand witnesses, he lacked the distance necessary to separate the memorable from the unmemorable, the causes from the results.

In the same chapter, however, Mercier argues that the historian's more distant perspective on the Revolution will be equally distorted. For unlike the observer who is too close to the events to understand their significance, the historian is too far away to perceive the infinitely small factors that in revolutionary times "forment la base essentielle de tous les événements."[42] Hence the problem of historiography brings Mercier back to the challenge of his own project in *Le Nouveau Paris*. How can the historian explain the causes of the most unexpected events of the Revolution, "lorsque les hommes les mieux exercés à voir ont eu peine à saisir un point de vue, et à fixer un objet dans cette extrême et continuelle mobilité d'optique?"[43] As one of the men most practiced in the art of observation at the dawn of the Revolution, Mercier suggests that even he was unable to focus clearly on his object amidst the extreme and continual mobility of shifting perspectives. His project of 'painting' Revolutionary Paris, like the historian's project of explaining the causes of Revolutionary events, is in conflict with these constant shifts in perspective, which are both visual and temporal. It is perhaps for this reason that Mercier chooses not to include the word *tableau* in the title of *Le Nouveau Paris*, despite his continued reliance on the ekphrastic metaphor. Long before Baudelaire, who according to Karlheinz Stierle realized that the genre of the *tableau de Paris* had been exhausted by the time he wrote his "Tableaux parisiens" for the *Fleurs du mal*, Mercier understood that a unified *tableau* of Paris had been made obsolete by the Revolution.[44]

Thus in "Tout est optique," Mercier favors neither the perspective of the contemporary observer nor that of the temporally distant historian. His subtle appreciation for the inevitable distortion of any given historical perspective sets him apart from Alexis de Tocqueville, who would claim some fifty years later to occupy "ce point précis d'où l'on peut le mieux apercevoir et juger ce grand objet. Assez loin de la Révolution pour ne ressentir que faiblement les passions qui troublaient la vue de ceux qui l'ont faite, nous en sommes assez proches pour pouvoir entrer dans l'esprit qui l'a amenée et pour le comprendre."[45] Unlike Tocqueville, who characterizes his own historical moment as the single most ideal vantage point from which to analyze the Revolution, Mercier offers the distinctly poetic solution of a "jeu d'optique," a formula that perfectly characterizes the composition of *Le Nouveau Paris* as a whole. Rather than a single perspective or painting of Revolutionary Paris,

Le Nouveau Paris will present a kaleidoscopic interplay of various perspectives, in which Mercier's contemporary perceptions of Revolutionary events are intermingled with his subsequent judgments and interpretations of them. Tiny details are recorded alongside what have since been deemed the most memorable days, and no hierarchical structure is established to sift the significant from the insignificant. Personal memories of the most intimate kind are placed alongside public events, and are seen to have the same significance for understanding the Revolution as a whole. It is no wonder that so many readers of *Le Nouveau Paris* have been disconcerted, and even disappointed by this work. For they are unceremoniously placed in the center of a kaleidoscope, that of Mercier's mixed perspectives on the Revolution, but also that of *Le Nouveau Paris* as an unstable and experimental work of literature which tests the limits of literary coherence.

* * * *

It should now be possible to measure the distance traveled from the *Tableau de Paris* to *Le Nouveau Paris*, both in Mercier's conception of Paris, and in his understanding of his own representational project. The abandonment of a certain Enlightenment ideal is indicated by the fact that in *Le Nouveau Paris*, the observer is no longer in a position to guarantee coherence. Unlike the spectator of Arnaud's topographical map, he can no longer stand up on a chair and "embrasse[r Paris] d'un seul regard."[46] Although he remains loyal to the Enlightenment principle of first-hand observation, he is surrounded by a "jeu d'optique," an interplay of various perspectives that cannot, and should not, be organized into a coherent vision or *tableau*. Similarly, despite his focus on revolutionary memory and his various attempts to figure the new in guise of the old in *Le Nouveau Paris*, Mercier finds himself unable to guarantee the continuity between old and new, between past and present. In fact, the only thing that guarantees continuity and stability, the only ribbon that stretches from the Old Regime into the new, is now the city of Paris itself:

> Au sein des tempêtes de la révolution et de la sanglante anarchie, elle a gardé une assiette immobile; ses propres fureurs, les excès jacobites n'ont pu la détruire, et les armées innombrables des rois conjurés qui voulaient la dévorer ont passé comme l'ombre; leurs forteresses lointaines sont tombées, et Paris subsiste tout entier.[47]

Paradoxically, Mercier suggests here that Paris remained steady, even as its own revolutionary furors threatened to destroy it. Yet he is not claiming that the city has simply remained unchanged while everything, including himself, has changed around it. Rather, he suggests that Paris itself is the force of revolutionary change, and as such, guarantees the continuous transition from past to present and from old Paris to new:

> Là, est le cerveau puissant qui crée, forme et dissémine les républiques, qui les fera germer sur le sol opprimé par des rois ou des oligarques; là, est le bras qui exécutera les projets les plus hardis, qui jettera un pont de la Seine à la Tamise; il a déjà changé la face féodale de l'Europe, et plus la résistance aux droits de l'homme et de la liberté sera grande, plus le torrent régénérateur couvrira de plus large surface. Tel un rocher au milieu des mers voit arriver les vagues du pôle, il les repousse; elles fondent du bout de l'horizon, et il résiste à leurs efforts. Il tient au fondement du monde, il verra mille naufrages, et subsistera dans toute sa gloire, dans cette gloire que donnent la force de la pensée et le courage des armes.[48]

According to Mercier's formulation, Paris is both a rock that remains steady amidst stormy seas, and a torrential force of regeneration that will gradually encompass a greater and greater portion of the globe. The city is able to occupy this untenable position, in a way that no individual actor in the Revolution can do, because it is itself the agent of change, containing within itself all of the minds and arms which propel the Revolution forward.

With this strikingly modern conception of the city, Mercier prefigures the remarkable homage to Paris that Victor Hugo would write from exile as a preface to the *Paris-Guide* for the Universal Exhibition of 1867.[49] For if Hugo considers Paris as the natural capital for a future nation called Europe, it is above all because he, like Mercier, attributes both will and agency to this city where the very face of history is continually being transformed:

> Vouloir toujours; c'est le fait de Paris. Vous croyez qu'il dort, non, il veut. La volonté de Paris en permanence, c'est là ce dont ne se doutent pas assez les gouvernements de transition. Paris est toujours à l'état de préméditation. Il a une patience d'astre mûrissant lentement un fruit. Les nuages passent sur sa fixité. Un beau jour, c'est fait. Paris décrète un événement. La France, brusquement mise en demeure, obéit.[50]

In 1867, Hugo warns transitional governments of the city's enduring will to effect change, thereby extrapolating from Mercier's earlier claim that Paris had the power to form and disseminate republics. For Hugo, indeed, the series of revolutions that shook the various regimes of the nineteenth century was a continuing testament to the city's ability to overcome the power of governments and individuals and lead Europe to its destiny as a liberated nation. For both writers, thus, revolution is a phenomenon engendered and propelled by the city. Hugo puts it most succintly when, in response to the question "Qui a fait le 14 juillet?," he responds simply, "Paris."[51]

Hugo's 1867 homage to Paris is a remarkable text, and one which, according to Priscilla Parkhurst Ferguson, "alters the very conception of the city" through its "assimilation of Paris and the Revolution."[52] It is thus striking to see how much this text, written during the Second Empire after nearly a century of political upheaval, owes to *Le Nouveau Paris*. Mercier's determining influence on Hugo is even more apparent in other works, most notably *Quatre-vingt treize* in which several anecdotes and passages are borrowed directly from *Le Nouveau Paris*.[53] But Hugo was by no means the only major figure of the nineteenth century to have been inspired by Mercier. In a letter written to his mother in 1862, Baudelaire not only describes *Le Nouveau Paris* as a marvelous work, but also alludes to "un gros travail" he is preparing on the subject. Although this project may never have been completed, the urban poetics elaborated in both the prose poems and *Les Fleurs du mal* clearly owes much to Mercier. Balzac too was a great reader of Mercier, and Rastignac's last words in *Le Père Goriot*, "À nous deux maintenant," are addressed to a city that Mercier would have recognized as his own. And well before Hugo affirmed the link between Paris and revolution in his "Paris" text, Michelet had placed Paris at the center of his vast fresco of the French Revolution, portraying the city as an agent of historical change.[54]

* * * *

Mercier's influence on the representation of Paris throughout the nineteenth century is undeniable, and for this alone he should be acknowledged as one of the architects of modern French literature. Yet it should not be forgotten that his initial project of describing Paris in its multiple dimensions grew directly out of the encyclopedic and descriptive aspirations of the Enlightenment. If, indeed, *Le Nouveau Paris* can serve as a bridge between the literature of the Old Regime and that of the modern era, it is because this work marks a definitive departure from the Enlightenment, even as it remains attached, by its formal resemblance to the *Tableau de Paris*, to the literary and social ideals of an age made obsolete by the Revolution. At the same time, *Le Nouveau Paris* is clearly much more than an endpoint. For in addition to transforming the representation of the city for modern times, it embodied a revolution in the individual writer's position within the city and capacity to represent it. Whereas prior to the Revolution Mercier saw Paris as an object of exhaustive description, in *Le Nouveau Paris* he sees the city as a force that takes over his own representational goals: it is Paris that preserves memories of the past, it is Paris that assures the continuity between the Old Regime and the new, and it is Paris that is reflected in the kaleidoscope of revolutionary events that confound the individual observer. Rather than a total description of Paris, *Le Nouveau Paris* is a testament to the city's ability to surpass the limitations of individual perception and representation: it is Paris seen as it can no longer be described.

NOTES

Many thanks to Philippe Roger, Jeffrey Ravel, and the anonymous readers of *SECC* for their invaluable comments on earlier versions of this article.

1. Victor Hugo, "Paris," *Oeuvres completes. Politique* (Paris: Robert Laffont, 1985), 11.

2. These editions include: Louis Sébastien Mercier, *Tableau de Paris*, 2 vols., ed. Jean-Claude Bonnet (Paris: Mercure de France, 1994), *Le Nouveau Paris*, ed. Jean-Claude Bonnet (Paris: Mercure de France, 1994), *Mon bonnet de nuit. Du théâtre*, ed. Jean-Claude Bonnet (Paris: Mercure de France, 1999). See also Jean-Claude Bonnet, ed., *Le Paris de Louis Sébastien Mercier. Cartes et index* (Paris: Mercure de France, 1994) and *Louis Sébastien Mercier un hérétique en littérature* (Paris: Mercure de France, 1995). All quotations from the *Tableau de Paris* and *Le Nouveau Paris* refer to these editions. For a translation of selections of the *Tableau de Paris*, largely a reprint of previous English language translations of the *Tableau* from earlier in the century, see Jeremy D. Popkin, *Panorama of Paris. Selections from* Tableau de Paris (University Park, PA: Penn State University Press, 1999).

3. Mercier, *Nouveau Paris* 31.

4. See Mercier, *Tableau* 1:916–21 and 1:182–84.

5. Charles Baudelaire, *Le Spleen de Paris. Petits poèmes en prose* (Paris: Flammarion, 1987), 74.

6. See the chapter "Il fait bon crier un peu," Mercier, *Tableau* 2:1031–33, which makes reference to these and other changes in Paris.

7. See Mercier, *Tableau* 2:1356–59.

8. Hermann Hofer, "Mercier devant la Révolution," *L'écrivain devant la Révolution. 1780–1800*, ed. Jean Sgard (Grenoble: Université Stendhal, 1990), 206. On Baudelaire's admiration for *Le Nouveau Paris*, see Jean-Claude Bonnet, "Introduction," Mercier, *Nouveau Paris* I–II.

9. Daniel Rosenberg's perceptive analysis of Mercier's 1801 neological dictionary, *La Néologie*, effectively demonstrates the modern and experimental nature

of this work as well. See "Louis-Sébastien Mercier's New Words," *Eighteenth-Century Studies* 36:3 (2003): 367–86.

10. Mercier, *Tableau* 1:14.

11. To varying degrees, these works do acknowledge the elusive nature of complete representation. Nevertheless, achieving the most comprehensive *tableau* possible remains the explicitly stated goal of all three works. Mercier makes his debt to Buffon clear when he writes: "lisez ces belles pages de Buffon, et sentez une fois que ce n'est que dans la parole écrite que réside l'imitation au souverain degré du cheval, de l'âne, du lion, du chat, du colibri." See Mercier, "Musées, Jardins et Fêtes," *Nouveau Paris* 964–65.

12. On the best-selling status of the *Tableau de Paris*, see Robert Darnton, *Édition et sédition: L'Univers de la littérature clandestine au XVIIIe siècle* (Paris: Gallimard, 1991), 165–69.

13. On the tradition of the *tableau de Paris* in the nineteenth century, see Karlheinz Stierle, "Baudelaire and the Tradition of the *Tableau de Paris*," *New Literary History* 11:2 (1980): 345–61.

14. See Mercier, *Nouveau Paris* 478–95.

15. See Mercier, *Tableau* 1:495.

16. See Mercier, *Tableau* 1:34.

17. See Mercier, *Tableau* 1:916–21.

18. Mercier, *Nouveau Paris* 491.

19. Mercier, *Nouveau Paris* 483–84.

20. Mercier, *Nouveau Paris* 32.

21. For Priscilla Parkhurst Ferguson, "*Le Nouveau Paris* in 1798 has less to do with customs than with politics and is a decided disappointment after the *Tableau*." Ferguson also cites a contemporary rival of Mercier, J.B. Pujoulx, for whom "Mercier's political role makes *Le Nouveau Paris* the work of a political historian rather than that of a man of letters." See Priscilla Parkhurst Ferguson, *Paris as Revolution. Writing the Nineteenth-Century City* (Berkeley: University of California Press, 1994), 237.

22. Mercier, *Nouveau Paris* 481–82.

23. Mercier, *Nouveau Paris* 486.

24. Shelly Charles, "Histoire du texte: Des nouvelles de Paris au *Nouveau Paris*," *Le Nouveau Paris*, ed. Jean-Claude Bonnet (Paris: Mercure de France, 1994), CLXXXVI–IX.

25. Mercier, *Nouveau Paris* 26.

26. Mercier, *Nouveau Paris* 401.

27. While this chapter does not make specific reference to the notorious *bals des victimes*, at which relatives of guillotine victims purportedly paid macabre homage to victims through hairstyles and dance steps imitating the ceremonial of decapitation, Mercier does mention these balls in another chapter entitled "Bals à la victime." Yet according to Ronald Schechter, despite Mercier's passing reference and "[d]espite the common agreement of historians over a period of more than 160 years, there is little if any contemporary evidence that the *bals des victimes* in fact existed." Schechter instead interprets the persistent myth of the *bals des victimes* as a collective *aide-mémoire* that helped post-Terror generations to remember and make sense of a

troubling past. See "Gothic Thermidor: The *Bals des victimes*, the Fantastic, and the Production of Historical Knowledge in Post-Terror France," *Representations* 61 (Winter 1998): 78–94, and Mercier, *Nouveau Paris* 337–40.

28. Mercier, *Nouveau Paris* 423.

29. Mercier, *Nouveau Paris* 18.

30. On Mercier's *modérantisme*, see "Je suis un modéré," Mercier, *Nouveau Paris* 694–702, and Bonnet, "Introduction," Mercier, *Nouveau Paris* XVII.

31. Mercier was not the only writer to take this position. In her defense of Louis Capet, for example, Olympe de Gouges made a similar argument. See Olympe de Gouges, *Écrits politiques*, ed. Olivier Blanc (Paris: Côté-Femmes, 1993), 191–94.

32. Mercier, *Nouveau Paris* 316.

33. See Mercier, *Nouveau Paris* 205–10.

34. Mercier, *Nouveau Paris* 250.

35. Mercier, *Nouveau Paris* 288.

36. Mercier was not the only writer whose imagination was captured by this ribbon. Germaine de Staël refers to it in characterizing the tenuous power of the Constituent Assembly: "L'assemblée constituante a toujours cru, bien à tort, qu'il y avoit quelque chose de magique dans ses décrets, et qu'on s'arrêteroit, en tout, juste à la ligne qu'elle auroit tracée. Mais son autorité, sous ce rapport ressembloit à celle du ruban qu'on avoit tendu dans le jardin des Tuileries, pour empêcher le peuple de s'approcher du palais : tant que l'opinion fut favorable à ceux qui avoient tendu ce ruban, personne n'imagina de passer outre ; mais, dès que le peuple ne voulut plus de la barrière, elle ne signifia plus rien." See Germaine de Staël, *Considérations sur la Révolution française*, ed. Jacques Godechot (Paris: Tallandier, 1983), 243.

37. Cited by Bonnet, "Introduction," Mercier, *Nouveau Paris* XVIII.

38. Mercier, *Tableau* 2:1309.

39. Mercier, *Nouveau Paris* 32.

40. Mercier, *Nouveau Paris* 880.

41. Mercier, *Nouveau Paris* 880.

42. Mercier, *Nouveau Paris* 881.

43. Mercier, *Nouveau Paris* 882.

44. See Stierle 345–61.

45. Alexis de Tocqueville, *L'ancien régime et la Révolution*, ed. J.-P. Mayer, Collection Folio/Histoire (Paris: Gallimard, 1967), 61.

46. Mercier, *Nouveau Paris* 486.

47. Mercier, *Nouveau Paris* 493–94.

48. Mercier, *Nouveau Paris* 494.

49. On Hugo's introduction to the *Paris-Guide*, see Ferguson 69–75. On the important intertextual relationship between Hugo and Mercier, see Helen Temple Patterson, *Poetic Genesis: Sébastien Mercier into Victor Hugo*, Studies on Voltaire and the Eighteenth Century (Geneva: Institut et Musée Voltaire, 1960).

50. Hugo 21.

51. Hugo 22.

52. Ferguson 73. Ferguson, who eloquently analyzes a conception of the city that owes so much to *Le Nouveau Paris*, chooses to focus on the *Tableau de Paris* rather than *Le Nouveau Paris*, and characterizes the latter work as a disappointment.

53. See, for example, the beginning of the second part of the novel, entitled "Les rues de Paris dans ce temps-là." In addition to more direct borrowings, this chapter includes a sentence reminiscent of Mercier's rhythmic description of the Directory ball-goers: "On dansait dans les cloîtres en ruine, avec des lampions sur l'autel, à la voûte deux bâtons en croix portant quatre chandelles, et des tombes sous la danse." Victor Hugo, *Quatre-vingt treize*, ed. Judith Wulf (Paris: Flammarion, 2002), 145.

54. On Mercier's influence in the nineteenth century, see Hermann Hofer, ed., *Louis-Sébastien Mercier précurseur et sa fortune* (Munich: Fink Verlag, 1977).

Carriages, Conversation, and A Sentimental Journey

DANIELLE BOBKER

> At Whitehall inquiring for a coach, there was a Frenchman with one eye that was going my way, so he and I hired the coach between us . . . Strange how the fellow, without asking, did tell me all what he was . . .
> —Samuel Pepys[1]

> This day, set up my Carriage,—new Subject of heartache, That Eliza is not here to share it with me—
> —Laurence Sterne[2]

> What if we saw [intimacy] emerge from much more mobile processes of attachment?
> —Lauren Berlant[3]

Sterne's Post-Chaise

Intimate space was on Laurence Sterne's mind in the summer of 1767 when he began writing *A Sentimental Journey*. He was making improvements to his Yorkshire cottage, and indulging fantasies of future domestic bliss with Eliza Draper, a young married woman he had met in London several months before, while soliciting subscriptions for his second novel. "I have this week finish'd a sweet little apartment which all the time it was doing, I flatter'd the most delicious of Ideas, in thinking I was making it for you—," he wrote in his *Bramine's Journal* addressed to her as she traveled back to her husband in Bombay. "Tis a neat little simple elegant room, overlook'd only by the Sun—just big enough to hold a Sopha,—for us—"(June 7:196–7). In three weeks' time the apartment fantasy had grown considerably: "I . . . am projecting a good Bed-chamber adjoining [the sitting room], with a pretty dressing room for You, which connects them together—the Sleeping room will be very large—The dressing room, thr' w[ch] You pass into y[r] Temple, will be little— . . . but if ever it holds You & I, my Eliza—the Room will not be too little for us—but We shall be *too big* for the Room" (June 29: 209 original emphasis). Around the same time Sterne acquired his first carriage, a second-hand post-chaise. In a letter to a friend, he adored it unequivocally: "when I say my Lord's prayer, I always think of it," he joked.[4] But in his *Journal* to Eliza, the coach, like the dressing room, gives shape to his longing: "—I have a thousand things to remark & say as I roll along—but I want You to say them to—I could sometimes be wise—& often Witty—" (June 9: 198). Whereas Sterne pictures being together in Eliza's dressing room as an essentially static expansion of consciousness ("we shall be *too big* for the Room"), the post-chaise brings in temporality, movement, and communication. As if keeping time with the carriage, he imagines a warm and wide-ranging conversation with his lover.[5]

This article will suggest that the communicative pull of the coach Sterne notes in his *Journal* plays a crucial role in his concurrent fictional travelogue.[6] Throughout the first fifth of *A Sentimental Journey*, Yorick, the novel's cleric-narrator (and Sterne's alterego), shops for a chaise. I argue that the models named in these opening episodes, the *Desobligeant* and the *Vis a vis*, matter as much for the internal and interpersonal experiences they represent as for the distances they can cover.[7] Sterne was by no means the first writer to take an intimate look at the carriage. Well before David Hume and Adam Smith conceived the emotional mechanisms connecting all individuals in society, close encounters on the road had occasioned more concrete forms of protosociological musing in British narrative writing. The arbitrary mingling of travelers in hired vehicles, where a range of differences including gender, rank, religion, profession, or nationality might have to be navigated, well nigh demanded such investigation. Coach conversation achieves an unprecedented coherence, optimism, and figurative significance in Sterne's hands, however, shoring up the novel's projection of its own international public: an entirely approachable sphere in which an English parson might chat as breezily with a French Duke as with a chamber maid.

Before Sterne: Reluctant Familiarities

From the sixteenth-century advent of the coach at the English court until around the time of the publication of *A Sentimental Journey*, the place of the passenger, not the driver, was the honored one.[8] Coaches were distinct from carts after all precisely because their suspension systems (the use of straps, braces, and later, springs between the axle and the carriage body) and their built-in covers made passenger seats more comfortable than ever before.[9] On arrival in England coaches had been merged into an existing culture of pageantry, framing royal and noble occupants as living tableaux or portraits of themselves for subjects to regard in loyal awe. But the vehicle's status was soon troubled. Social mobility became interconnected with a new form of geographic mobility. The demise of sumptuary laws meant that the gentry and wealthy merchants could buy equipages of their own, and as opportunities to travel in hackney- and stage-coaches increased for many others besides, the continual parade of vehicles upset the customary propriety of the street.[10] At whom exactly were passersby looking? Self-styled Water Poet John Taylor gives up his preferred form to rant in prose in *The World Runnes on Wheeles* (1623). He makes the necessary apology: "Princes, Nobilities, and Gentlemen of worth, Offices & Quality, have herein their priviledge . . . [and] may ride as their occasions or pleasures shall indite them, as most meete they should. . . ." Unable to maintain so measured a cadence through the end of the sentence, he continues, "but, when every Gill Turntripe, Mrs. Fumkins, Madame Polecat, and my Lady Trash, Froth the Tapster, Bill the Taylor, Lavender the Broker, Whiff the Tobacco Seller, with their companion Trugs, must be Coach'd . . . I say upon my hallidome, it is a burning shame."[11] The aristocracy merit this luxury but why should common traders raise themselves thus above the crowd? On Taylor's view, such transgression of the coach's ceremonial origins degrades high and low alike.[12]

The mid-seventeenth century brought a significant change to the coach interior which might be understood in relation to the vehicle's shifting status. Originally, most coaches had flaunted elite passengers by orienting them towards the street. The coach "makes people imitate Sea Crabs, in being drawne side-wayes," Taylor had objected.[13] But around the time of the Restoration, the coach took an inward turn: the barge-like structure was superseded by a more compact one in which travelers faced one another.[14] The reorientation retained the exterior visual axes: with the curtains raised passengers could still see landscapes and streetscapes, and see and be seen by passersby, though without giving the former full frontal view. The inward focus also allowed for mutual observation and conversation. Not only did friends and family members face a more intimate, semi-public interaction, so too did strangers.[15]

Cultural historian Wolfgang Schivelbusch notes that the new coach design coincided with a growing culture and discourse of politeness: "The creation of this curious arrangement during the same period that saw the rise of other bourgeois institutions of communication, such as coffee-houses, clubs, newspapers, and theaters, indicates that the coach must be seen as part of that larger configuration."[16] While a brief survey of stage coach scenes by

Delarivier Manley, Richard Steele, Henry Fielding, and Samuel Johnson corroborates Schivelbusch's point in a general way, it also reveals that these increasingly accessible, mobile spaces did not produce civil talk as their inevitable or anodyne effect. Rather, representations of coach travel evince an interest in the conditions of possibility of sociability as such. Unlike coffee-houses, clubs, and theaters, hired vehicles did not provide much in the way of convention or conventional social lubricants for temporary and incidental relationships. At the same time, close-up encounters particularly endowed physiognomy, manners, and diction as signs of difference. Whether or not sundry travelers crossing the city or the country in pursuit of private goals would establish a basis for conversation was a dilemma to be worked out anew in every case. How would anonymous passengers decide where to look and whom to acknowledge? What role should rank play within this transitory intimacy? And how could you even be certain others were who they looked or claimed to be? As William Hogarth's *The Stage Coach, Or the Country Inn Yard* (1747) (fig.1) illustrates, the strangeness of strangers lay not only in the random and unverifiable things they said and did, but in their physical presence as well.

In *Letters Writen* [sic] *by Mrs. Manley* (1696), conversation on the road from London to Exeter comes to consist in sharing stories of heartache, many of which Manley interpolates for the amusement of her friend in the city. Yet these are neither immediately welcome nor inclusive exchanges. Manley defers engaging with others by staring out the window; then throughout the journey she reinforces her connection with the privileged urban milieu she has grudgingly left behind by mocking her fellow travelers. She dismisses the lowest women with a bit of indirect discourse: they "were never so promoted before, and hugely delighted, with what they are pleas'd to call Riding in State."[17] She dubs a merchant's wife, who possesses "all the low, disagreeable Familiarity of People of her Rank," "The Mayoress of Tatness."[18] "She entertain'd us all the Morning with a sorry Love-business about her second Husband; Stuff so impertinent, I remember nothing of it,"[19] Manley writes, with this mental and textual erasure re-erecting the distinctions the merchant's wife has trampled over in presuming to regale her betters. The only passenger of even minimal quality, a baronet's son whom she nicknames "Beaux [sic],"[20] preoccupies her most.

Whereas Manley's *Letters* imply a greater commonality between fellow passengers than the author herself cares to recognize, three later scenes direct their sharpest satire at behaviors that impede the development of social equilibrium on the stage coach. As soon as Mr Spectator's London-bound coach has "jumbled" its occupants "insensibly into some sort of Familiarity,"[21]

Figure 1. William Hogarth's *The Stage Coach, Or the Country Inn Yard* (1747) calls attention to the vehicle's spatial limitations.
Source: Sarah Campbell Blaffer Foundation, Houston, Texas. Reproduced with permission.

a recruiting officer simultaneously propositions both of the female passengers: a nubile heiress named Betty Arable *and* her widowed mother. Their Quaker guardian intervenes, "Friend, Friend, we have hired this Coach in Partnership with thee, to carry us to the great City; we cannot go any other Way. . . . To speak indiscreetly what we are obliged to hear, by being hasped up with thee in this publick Vehicle, is in some Degree assaulting on the high Road."[22] He goes on to preach: "When two such as thee and I meet . . . , thou shoulds't rejoice to see my peaceable Demeanour and I should be glad to see thy Strength and Ability to protect me in it."[23] While the officer's aggression unquestionably needs to be disciplined, only the gentlest twinge of ridicule undercuts the Quaker's vision of moral and physical interdependence. When Joseph Andrews is discovered bleeding in a ditch in the famous scene in Fielding's novel, everyone in the passing carriage reacts according to his or her type. The coachman worries that picking him up will delay the journey and wonders who will pay the beggar's fare; the lady is concerned about her reputation; the gentleman suspects robbery. The beat-up footman is at last rescued because the lawyer fears "some Mischief happening to himself if the Wretch was left behind in that Condition."[24] Only the postillion, who has next to nothing to lose, sympathizes with Joseph and offers him a great coat to cover himself. A hotbed of self-interest, Fielding's heterogeneous stage coach nevertheless proves itself to be capable, willy-nilly, of ethical momentum.[25]

"It was easy to observe the affected elevation of mien with which every one entered . . . ," Samuel Johnson's "Viator" recalls of the beginning of a stage-coach journey in a letter to *The Adventurer*: "we sat silent for a long time, all employed in collecting importance into our faces, and endeavouring to strike reverence and submission into our companions."[26] Highly conscious of their dumb show of upward mobility, anonymous passengers find themselves drawn into a hellish hall of mirrors: "everyone was apparently suspected of endeavoring to impose false appearances upon the rest; all continued with their haughtiness, in hopes to enforce their claims; and all grew every hour more sullen, because they found their representations of themselves without effect." If vision serves double duty here, performing superiority while seeking evidence of its impact, Victor's own gaze assumes a third task, penetrating the layers of pretense in others' performances. His confidence in this skill leads him at last to identify a more sanguine mode of comportment: "Of one of the women only I could make no disadvantageous detection, because she had assumed no character, but accommodated herself to the scene before her, without any struggle for distinction or superiority."[27] Coach conversation more properly begins on this open and neutral ground, Viator implies. As we shall see, Johnson's image of the coach as a social echo chamber will return in Sterne's characterization of this heterogeneous space.

The *Desobligeant*, the Preface, and the Closet

A Sentimental Journey recasts the uneasy sociability of the carriage as a productive tension. At the beginning of his journey, the protoganist, Yorick, lacks not only a means of transportation but also a sense of purpose for his Grand Tour, the written record of which will be the novel itself. Throughout the eighteenth century, travel discourse drew heavily on an empirical logic of personal development: as James Buzard puts it, "If knowledge is rooted in experience and nowhere else, travel instantly gains in importance and desirability. . . . Merely reading about conditions elsewhere was not enough. Those who could travel, *should*."[28] Sterne pokes at this rhetoric of moral and intellectual improvement by suggesting an overlap between the neophyte traveler's internal and external (material) needs throughout the chaise-shopping episodes. Always interested in the permeable intersections between words, things, and metaphors, Sterne brings vehicles themselves into the service of Yorick's budding notions of international travel and travel writing.

Soon after his arrival in Calais, Yorick refuses the petition of an old Franciscan monk, having "predetermined" at first sight "not to give him a single sous" (7). When he then walks out to the coach yard beside his hotel, in his grumpiness he finds himself drawn to a tiny ramshackle chaise: a *Desobligeant* (literally "antisocial"). Getting in, he follows in the footsteps of "many a peripatetic philosopher" (13), composing a Preface in which he expects to classify "the efficient as well as the final causes of travelling" (13). But his deductive logic immediately loops and strains. Categories bump against provisos in his mind. He starts by identifying three distinct motives for travel: "Infirmity of body," "Imbecility of mind," and "Inevitable necessity." Then, ostensibly anxious "to observe the greatest precision and nicety," he muddies things by distinguishing "Simple Travellers" from the rest, arbitrarily switching from motive to type as the term of comparison (14). As if in an effort to reassert some control over the now unwieldy scheme, he next announces that "the whole circle of travellers may be reduced to the following *Heads*." What follows actually increases the number of categories of travelers from four to eleven. If the flimsiness of his construction is not already apparent enough, it is worth noting the odd presentation on the page of the final of these eleven types, along with his confused, incongruously informal explanation:

> And last of all (if you please) The
>
> Sentimental Traveller (meaning thereby myself) who have travell'd, and of which I am now sitting down to give an account—as much out of *Necessity*, and the *besoin de* Voyager, as any one in the class. (15)

Yorick's decision to fashion a new category for himself appears in this context as impetuous and absurd as his line break after "The" and the redundant translation of "out of *Necessity*." He has not adequately distinguished the new class from "Travellers of Necessity." Moreover, he misrepresents his present state of inexperience, adopting the stance of the future Yorick who will "have travell'd" only by the time his book makes its way into readers' hands. From his servant's wry question in the opening lines of the novel—"You have been in France?" (3)—we know that at this point the sum total of Yorick's time on the other side of the Channel consists in the few minutes he has spent in Calais. He has hardly "travell'd." Bracketing this attempt to systematize travellers' motives are speculations on the many obstacles to cross-cultural communication they face. Yorick complains that "from the want of languages, connections, and dependencies, and from the difference in education, customs and habits, we lie under so many impediments in communicating our sensations out of our own sphere, as often amount to a total impossibility" (13). Later he reasons: "Knowledge and improvements are to be got by sailing and posting for that purpose; but whether useful knowledge and real improvements, is all a lottery . . . I am of the opinion, That a man would act as wisely, if he could prevail upon himself, to live contented without [them]" (16). Defeatist dictums with which to launch a Grand Tour.

He alludes to the awkwardness of his Preface immediately upon finishing it. As he exits, he tells the Englishmen whose curiosity has been piqued by the vibrations of the stationary chaise, "It would have been better . . . in a *Vis a Vis*" (17).[29] The *Oxford English Dictionary* gives Sterne's as the first English usage of *Desobligeant* for a single-seater vehicle. (The British had called such a vehicle a Solitaire; later, a Sulky.) Though *vis-à-vis* was not yet in regular use as an adverb or preposition, the coupéd carriage in which two or sometimes three or four passengers sat opposite one another had been called by its French name for several decades (figs. 2 and 3). *Desobligeant* and *Vis a vis* do much more than designate particular coach models, however. These French names for the vehicles loudly invoke the question of stranger sociability satirists had begun investigating on national terrain.[30] Sharing roots with *vision* and *visage* (face), the *Vis a Vis* provides a compact figure against which Yorick's unsatisfying Preface (Pre-face) and his solitude in the run-down carriage might be meaningfully associated with one another in retrospect: both the place and the moment of writing preclude considerable contact with other people, foreign or otherwise.

Yorick employs the *Desobligeant* as a gentleman would his closet, closing its taffeta curtains against distractions so that he can think and write alone. Closets fulfilled a range of personal and private purposes in eighteenth-century households. They accommodated prayers and confidential conferences and housed collections of books or curios; and they continued to be places for solitary study as they had been since the middle ages.[31] Sterne's pointed use of the solo carriage's scornful French name aligns Yorick's initial reflections with the last of these closet functions, and joins an eighteenth-century chorus of censure of learning in elitist isolation. The first on his list of too-insular settings, Mr. Spectator declares, "I shall be ambitious to have it said of me that I have brought Philosophy out of Closets . . . ," before suggesting communal places, such as the club, coffee house, and tea table for reading and discussing his essays.[32] In David Hume's "Of the Study of History" (1748), the closet exemplifies the passionlessness that the historian, concerned with real lives, circumvents: "When a philosopher contemplates characters and

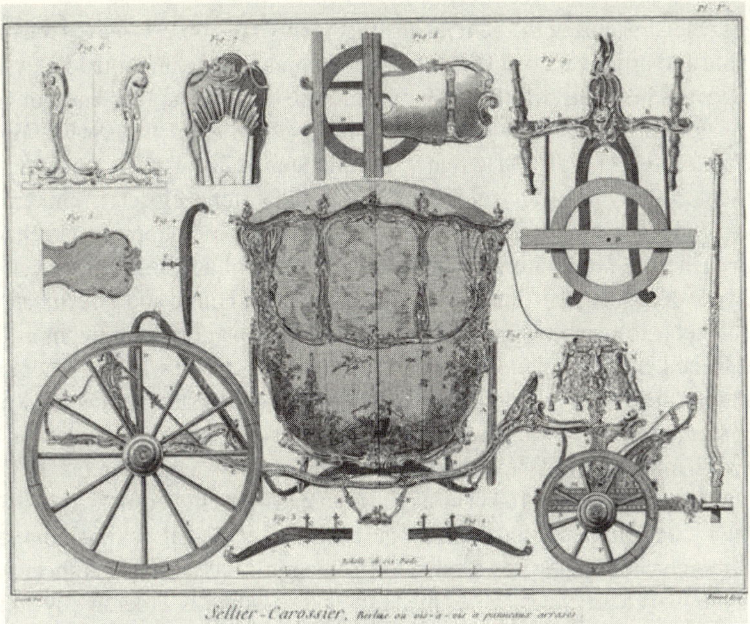

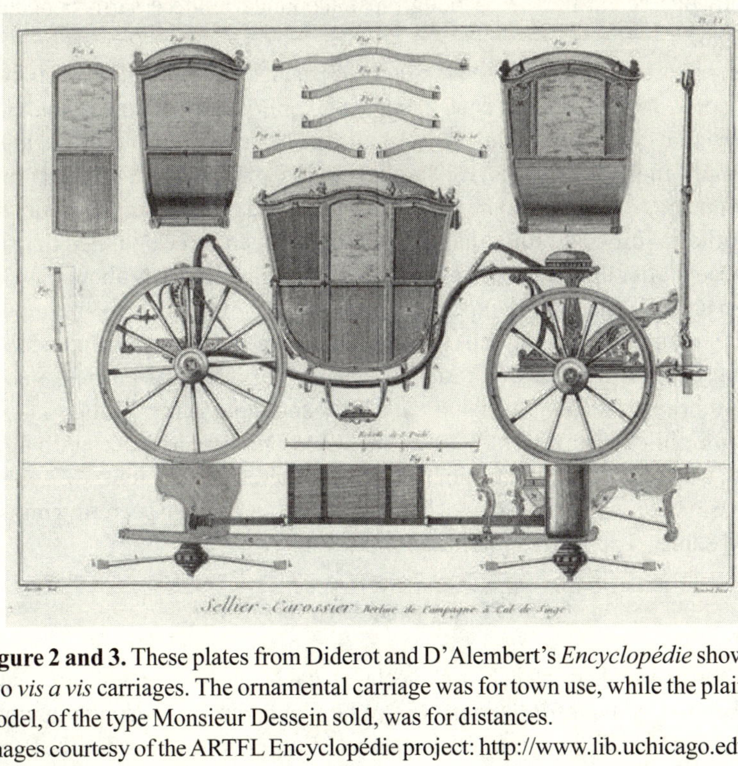

Figure 2 and 3. These plates from Diderot and D'Alembert's *Encyclopédie* show two *vis a vis* carriages. The ornamental carriage was for town use, while the plainer model, of the type Monsieur Dessein sold, was for distances.
Images courtesy of the ARTFL Encyclopédie project: http://www.lib.uchicago.edu/efls/ARTFL/projects/encyc.

manners in his closet, the general abstract view of the objects leaves the mind so cold and unmoved, that the sentiments of nature have no room to play, and he scarce feels the difference between vice and virtue."[33] And Johnson correlates learned privacy with narrow-mindedness when he warns in his *Preface to Shakespeare* (1759), "He that will understand Shakespeare, must not be content to study him in the closet. . . ."[34] Literally alone, closeted thinkers are also psychically alone; reason-obsessed, they are too emotionally detached to apprehend the messy human element in the ethical and aesthetic questions they ponder.[35] Significantly, in the passages from Hume and *The Spectator,* the closet is the architectural *sine qua non* of philosophy. John Lyons argues that René Descartes made the private philosophical as it were by placing an uncommon stress on the location of his reflections. "I stayd alone the whole day, shut up in my Stove [*poêle*], where I had leasure enough to entertain my self with my thoughts," he tells readers of his *Discourse on a Method* (1637),[36] and in the *Meditations* (1641) he explains that his writing room "was dark and quiet, filling completely his needs for the exclusion of all that was not himself."[37] By the eighteenth century an association between closet learning and theoretical analysis had clearly been etched in the social imagination, a metonymy almost parodying a scientific rule, as though spatial boundaries necessarily condensed thought.

Yorick's composition in the *Desobligeant* adapts this conflation of studious solitude with a limited, cold perspective and philosophy's densely analytical form to the context of travel. Yorick calls the system- and axiom-making he attempts there a Preface. He has taken the placement and the title of introductory materials too literally, misconstruing precedence as a reflection of authorial process rather than as a textual convention calculated to orient the reader after the fact of writing.[38] What can he possibly say about traveling given his as yet negligible experience? The setting in which Yorick composes the beginning of his travelogue permits him to evade the temporal paradox his misperception produces. Without particulars Yorick can nevertheless adopt an authoritative stance and make some lofty-sounding generalizations: he can play the philosopher. Sterne's use of the *Desobligeant* as a setting and a figure thus turns on the assumptions of Grand Tour rhetoric. If the journey is meant above all to expand the range of Yorick's experience, then secreting himself away surely represents a false start.

The *Vis a vis* and Lust in Transit

Shortly after leaving it, Yorick declares that he has written himself "out of conceit with the *Desobligeant*"(18). When he begins his second attempt at selecting a vehicle, he spies "another tatter'd *Desobligeant.*" But now he knows better: "notwithstanding it was the exact picture of that which had hit my fancy so much in the coach-yard but an hour before—the very sight of it stirr'd up a disagreeable sensation within me now; and I thought 'twas a churlish beast into whose heart the idea could first enter, to construct such a machine" (32). He does not refer directly to either of the two French coach names again. Significantly, however, the next vehicle Yorick tries, the one he will eventually buy, is the setting of his first foreign flirtation. The artful Monsieur Dessein has ushered an appealing woman whom Yorick has just met, Madame de L***, with him into another chaise, one big enough to seat them both, if only barely. Though it is not necessarily a *Vis a Vis*, this vehicle certainly invites face-to-face contact,[39] and Jonathan Lamb claims its inaugural interchange is the definitive one in the novel, "a situational sentiment at its best, where what is meant is what is being done, and what is being done is what is being said."[40] Yorick doesn't succumb to extremes of any kind here; he doesn't ravish Madame de L*** with embraces or declarations as he imagines a Frenchman would (33). He seduces her slant instead. The best way to make love, Yorick says, is through a "course of small, quiet, attentions, not so pointed as to alarm—nor so vague as to be misunderstood,—with now and then a look of kindness, and little or nothing said upon it—"(34). He finds that understatement, including "quiet attentions" and mild "looks of kindness," communicates best as he observes Madame de L*** coming to enjoy the moment as well. "I solemnly declare you have been making love to me all this while" (34), she blushes. Rather than classifying him as a traveler, the more sociable chaise allows Yorick to learn as he goes along how to think, speak, and act the part by attending and responding to the subtlest of words and gestures.

Yorick's second chaise plays up a bawdy strand in the evolution of carriage sociability. Even prior to its interior reorientation in the seventeenth century, commentators had thought the coach peculiarly well disposed to circulating sexual desire. Single and non-elite women who relied on hired coaches for travel, including girls going into service or for some other reason divorced from their families, were especially targeted, tapping into an ongoing connection between women's mobility and their sexual availability. The link to whoring was especially strong for hackney coaches, and linguistically overdetermined: *hackney* meaning "for hire" or "common" (derived from the Old French *haquenée*) is a homonym of the name of the London borough where there were many brothels. Taylor layers these meanings, depicting coaches as go-betweens: "many times a hired Coachman . . . may man, a brace of . . . [Hackney women] to their places of recreation, and so save them the charge of maintaining a Sir Pandarus or an Apple-squire."[41] Peter Anthony Motteux's opening song for *The Stage-Coach*, the farce he co-wrote with

George Farquhar, adds the joke that erratic shaking of the moving carriage makes female passengers unusally receptive to men's advances:

> Here chance kindly mixes,
> All Sorts and all Sexes,
> More Females than Men;
> We squeeze them, we ease them,
> The Jolting does please them;
> Drive jollily then.[42]

Whitsuntide Holidays (1783) (fig. 4) seems to illustrate Motteux's refrain.

Other erotic associations targeted the public privacy of the coach that was novel for non-elite men as well. Taylor worries about what people hiding inside a coach might do, stressing the difference between the coach and its less secretive, lowbrow cousin: "The Cart is an open transparent Engine, that any man may perceive the plaine honesty of it; there is no part of it within or without, but it is in the continuall view of all men: On the contrary, the Coach is a close hipocrite, for it hath a cover for any Knavery."[43] Furthermore, it "is never unfurnished of a bed and curtaines, with shop windowes of leather to buckle Bawdry up as close in the midst of the street as it were in the Stewes."[44] When Elizabeth Pepys accuses Samuel of being "seen in a hackney-coach with the glasses up with Deb [Willet],"[45] the nature of his offense need not be spelled out.[46]

The erotics of mobile proximity might thus displace the suspicion, snobbery, and self-interest that typically obstructed conversation. Especially for men, the spectatorial possibilities of the coach could be experienced as pleasure, as a melting away of difference or merging with the object of desire. Giacomo Casanova claims to have executed his proudest conquest in a *calash* during a thunderstorm; yet, contriving to sit opposite a new quarry and her officer-boyfriend, he also enjoys the carriage's discreet ocular delights: "my eyes saw her without my having to turn my head to give them that pleasure, which is certainly the greatest a lover can have among those which he cannot be denied."[47] Manley shows that female travelers were not always so thrilled to receive such attention as their male counterparts were to bestow it. In her second letter, she complains of "Beaux," the would-be rake across from her: "I think none was ever so plagu'd with dying Eyes; his are [so] continually in that posture, and my Opposites, that I am forc'd to take a good deal of pains to avoid 'em." He continues to provoke her—"*I vow, this Indifferency does not look natural to you; your eyes promise us much more Fire.*" She silently retorts, "I'll shut 'em . . . for ever rather than such a Fop shall find any thing to like them for—," but he cuts short her internal monologue, "*What! no answer,*

Figure 4. At the center of the crowd riding atop the Greenwich to Charing Cross coach in this print, entitled *Whitsuntide Holidays* (1783), a man gropes the woman beside him and she does not appear to mind.
Source: Guildhall Library Print Room. Reproduced with permission of Guildhall Library, Corporation of London

Madam . . . ; I perceive your Attention by your Silence."[48] Trapped in the coach, Manley cannot escape Beaux's sexual semiotics; and though she remains indifferent to the lowest women, despite herself she does warm a little to her pursuer over the course of the trip. A mutual desiring gaze in a coach was understood to be especially electric. A German satirist described an English stage-coach journey as a multi-sensory frenzy of opportunity for "a dangerous exchange of glances but often also for a scandalous entanglement of legs causing a giggling in both parties and a confusion of souls and thought, so that eventually many an honest young man who only [wants] to travel from London to Oxford [goes] straight to the devil instead…"[49] In this example, visual pleasure combined with physical closeness in the stage coach leads to a kind of cognitive meltdown ("giggling" then "a confusion of souls and thought") that prepares the couple for conversation in the coarsest sense.

As critics have long insisted, Sterne's novel lingers at, but never crosses that line. The reflective charge of Yorick and Madame de L***'s lovemaking delicately engages the coach's notorious reputation. Yorick is planning to ask

Madame de L*** to accompany him to Amiens. The thought has first occurred to him soon after meeting her: "Now where would be the harm . . . if I was to beg of this distressed lady to accept of half my chaise?—and what mighty mischief could ensue?" (28) On articulating the thought, Yorick falls into his own mental trap. The words produce the idea of lust and a physiological response: "Every dirty passion, and bad propensity in my nature, took the alarm, as I stated the proposition—" (28). When Yorick is in the post-chaise with Madame de L***, Monsieur Dessein approaches to announce that the widow's brother has arrived to escort her home (35). The turn of events is "fatal" to Yorick's as yet unstated proposition, but elicits from Madame de L*** the parting words that demonstrate that the thought has nevertheless been conveyed. "I think, said she, looking in my face, I had no evil to apprehend—and . . . had determined to accept [a place in your coach]—If I had—(she stopped a moment)—I believe your good will would have drawn a story from me, which would have made pity the only dangerous thing in the journey" (35). The flash of sentimental fulfillment hinges on its setting: its whiff of lewdness (and the foreclosed though still palpable possibility of Yorick and Madame de L*** navigating that lewdness together) lingers there in the extended pause. The doubled sound and appearance of the name of the intimate coach (*Vis a Vis*) suggests this kind of connection: looking at and listening to one another, they mirror one another's thoughts.

So whereas the *Desobligeant* leaves Yorick alone to speculate, classify, and generalize, the second chaise produces a more fluid relationship to communication and thus to form. In the *Desobligeant*, Yorick predicts that his "travels and his observations will be altogether of a different cast from any of my fore-runners" (15). He wants to define this difference but he decides he had better wait "till [he has] some better grounds for it, than the mere *Novelty of [his] Vehicle*" (15 original emphasis).[50] In this first phase, his book is just a husk, an idea of an idea of a genre. In the post-chaise for two, Yorick clarifies his direction as he talks to a foreign woman he has just met. When he buys the chaise ("I never finished a twelve-guinea bargain so expeditiously in my life" (36), he puns), Yorick confirms that the stuff of his journey and thus of his journal will be conversational minutiae. "I declare, said I, clapping my hands chearily together, that was I in a desart, I would find out wherewith in it to call forth my affections—If I could not do better, I would fasten them upon some sweet myrtle, or seek some melancholy cypress to connect myself to—" (36). He now understands he must avoid the perceptual limitations of his predecessors Smelfungus and Mundungus, each of whom was locked in a vicegrip of self. The former filtered his observations through his bad mood: he "set out with the spleen and jaundice, and every object he pass'd by was discoloured or distorted—" (37); the latter, possessed of "an immense fortune" but overly prudent, "made the whole tour . . . without one generous connection or pleasurable anecdote to tell of; but he had travell'd straight on looking neither to his right hand or his left, lest Love or Pity should seduce him out of his road" (37-8).

Intersubjective Form

Sterne's witty contrast of *Desobligeant* and *Vis a Vis* informs his critique of solitary modes of perceiving, writing, and traveling and their interactive re-invention in *A Sentimental Journey*. In effect Yorick continuously advocates for his own chosen "vehicle" throughout the novel, showing in each gregarious and introspective entry how well his many encounters on the road equip him to breathe life into the grand philosophical questions of his age about the mind, morality, and sentiment. A third set of eighteenth-century spatial associations further clarifies the chaise-shopping episode's parody of introverted learning. Not only was the closet known as a room for thoughtful solitude, but a mechanical version of the closet, the *camera obscura*, had long been in use by philosophers as a metaphor for consciousness itself.[51] For the Cartesian rationalist, the *camera obscura* modeled the way in which the inner light of reason separates what one knows clearly and distinctly from less certain types of knowledge.[52] And, in John Locke's image of the empirical mind, sense impressions and ideas enter reason's domain from without, like light pouring through the window of a dark, empty closet.[53] Recalling these figures, Sterne's *Desobligeant* highlights the radical solitude of the subject of epistemology as he attends to his own mental processes. By contrast, the *Vis a Vis* embodies an idea of learning as reciprocal and of the mind as a dynamic mechanism. We might say that what the *camera obscura* is to the theorist of knowledge, the *Vis a Vis* is to the sentimental novelist.

After the flirtation with Madame de L***, Yorick shares his own carriage only one other time. But actual coaches do shape several interpersonal encounters in *A Sentimental Journey*. In each other's way at the entrance of a Milan concert hall, Yorick and the Marquesina de F*** fall into a courteous *pas-de-deux* before Yorick thinks to stop moving to let the Marquesina pass (77). He follows to apologize and asks if he can escort her to her coach. She consents. "Upon my word, Madame," Yorick says, handing her in, "I made six different efforts to let you go out—" "And I made six different efforts . . . to let you enter—" she replies. When she makes room to allow him to make a "seventh attempt" to enter, Yorick "instantly step[s] in—" (78). The coach abets sexual opportunism again in a later incident: La Fleur asks Yorick for time off "*pour* *faire le galant vis à vis sa maîtresse"* and Yorick observes, "it was the very thing I intended to do myself *vis à vis* Madame de R***—I had retain'd the remise [coach] on purpose for it" (132). He relates to La Fleur's desire to "*faire le galant,*" and the repetition of the relational preposition *vis-à-vis* reminds Yorick of the utility of the coach itself to this aim. On the other hand, the coach is also capable of impeding Yorick's thoughts, such as when he tries to cultivate compassion for a man mourning his dead ass whom he passes on the way to Amiens. A crowd of sympathetic spectators gather around him, but Yorick does not join them: "as I continued sitting in the post-chaise, I could see and hear over their heads" (53). Yorick soon moves on, and though he remains "as candidly disposed to make the best of the worst, as ever wight was" (56), the postillion and the joltings of the vehicle seem to conspire against his attempts to savor the feelings aroused by the grieving man. Looking down rather than looking across (framing a picturesque scene of suffering from a distance) allows for seeing without taking in, reaction without response.[54]

Like metaphors of consciousness in philosophical systems, then, the sociable chaise remains for the most part an implied structure, compelling a giddy and greedy openness to the moment, to movement, and to the possibility of connection rather than the certainty of attachment. This model of cognition is especially useful in mapping the range of Yorick's encounters throughout the novel. One by one, he zeroes in on the people who catch his eye, encouraging them to return his gaze, his words, and sometimes (especially if female) his touch; producing between them a reciprocal zoom whose very intensity and exclusivity ensure it will not last.

Notwithstanding his memorable *rendez-vous* with the grisset, the *fille de chambre*, and Maria in the Moulines (69–75, 121–24, 149–54), I want to conclude by noticing how the *Vis a vis* paradigm shapes two telling encounters with men in the novel. The first of these, in which Yorick converses with an old officer while awaiting a performance at the *Opéra comique*, is, after the episode with Madame de L***, arguably, the novel's clearest illustration of sentimental intersubjectivity in action. When Yorick chances upon the Frenchman, he is reading the program notes through "a large pair of spectacles." On seeing Yorick, he takes off and pockets his glasses, a gesture which Yorick comprehends perfectly: "Translate this into any civilized language in the world— the sense is this: . . .'Here's a poor stranger come into the box—he seems as if he knew nobody; and is never likely, was he to be seven years in Paris, if every man he comes near keeps his spectacles upon his nose—'tis shutting the door of conversation absolutely in his face—'" (76). The English parson responds with a similarly communicative bow. When they finally speak to one another the theme does not change, and the officer concludes with this maxim: "the advantage of travel . . . [is] by seeing a great deal both of men and of manners; it [teaches] us mutual toleration; and mutual toleration . . . [teaches] us mutual love" (84). Yorick cannot identify the source of his pleasure on hearing this: "I thought I loved the man; but I fear I mistook the object—'twas my own way of thinking—the difference was I could not have expressed it half so well" (84). The officer's trite message of tolerance is more striking as a performative than as a constative utterance. Yorick recognizes that something has been gained in his encounter with the officer, but what touches him? His own thought of mutual toleration? The words in which the thought is expressed? Or the man who speaks them? The very problem of attribution attests to the success of the encounter in the opera box: even at the level of cognition it is possible to tell self and other apart.

The second and concluding incident between men I want to consider is an imagined encounter with a Duke. Yorick's journey is in jeopardy because he does not have a passport. Before approaching the Duc de C*** for help in acquiring one at his cabinet at Versailles, Yorick tries to calm his own nerves. Counseling himself to observe carefully, he proceeds to elaborate the process by which he has generated affective connections throughout his journey:

> see Monsieur le Duc's face first— observe what character is written in it; take notice in what posture he stands to hear you—mark the turns and expressions of his body and limbs—And for the tone—the first sound which comes from his lips will give it you—: and from all these together you'll compound an address at once upon the spot, which cannot disgust the Duke— the ingredients are his own, and most likely to go down . . . as if man to man was not equal throughout the whole surface of the globe; and if in the field—why not face to face in the cabinet too? (101)

At the end of this self-instruction, Yorick confuses two radically dissimilar sociopolitical spaces: "man to man" is indeed equal on the battlefield according to an ancient heroic code that couples combatants in violence, but how this localized parity will help him strike a deal within the baroque system of secrets and favorites that governs the Duke's private chambers remains to be seen. "[W]hy not face to face in the cabinet too?" Yorick asks, defiantly naive. The *Vis a vis* seems to be the missing term here, naming both a place where diverse strangers encounter one another and the equalizing mode of perceiving and responding Yorick associates with it. Here Sterne exposes the labor and ideological stakes of Yorick's intersubjective ideal. Taking his own principle of sociability to an extreme, Yorick supposes that in every case attentive proximity can be made to reduce difference, whether of status, nationality, gender, occupation, or age, to tangible elements of conversational style that can be mirrored as soon as they are perceived. Once the "ingredients" of Yorick's conversation match the Duke's, an inherently status-bound relationship will inevitable transform into a more palatable relationship of equals.

Thus Sterne affects to resolve the modern problems of anonymity and stranger sociability with seductive simplicity. If coaches participate in the expansion of infrastructures that increase and speed up the circulation of people and of things (including Sterne's own novels) through Britain, Europe, and beyond, they also offer a pleasing contraction or concentration of interpersonal experience, momentarily dissolving boundaries between self and other which elsewhere prove unyielding.

NOTES

1. Samuel Pepys, *The Diary of Samuel Pepys: Volume 1, Part 2*, ed. Henry Wheatley (New York: MacMillan, 1892): 291.

2. Laurence Sterne, *Continuation of the Bramine's Journal* (1767) in *Works: Volume VI*, eds. Melvyn New and W.G. Day (Gainesville: University of Florida Press, 2002): April 18, 173.

3. Lauren Berlant, "Intimacy: A Special Issue," *Critical Inquiry* 24 (Winter 1998): 281–88, 284, proposes that we might come to view intimacy "as a drive that creates spaces around it through practices" rather than as an aspect of social life firmly and inextricably rooted in stable locations and institutions, narratives, and relationships. The epigraph also comes from page 284.

4. Laurence Sterne, *Letters of Laurence Sterne*, ed. Lewis Perry Curtis (New York: Oxford University Press, 1965): Letter 167, 281.

5. In *Bramine's Journal*: June 22, 206, Sterne tells Eliza, "Ive been as far as York to day with no Soul with me in my Chase but yr Picture—" He plans to make a necklace of the little portrait, so "—it shall be nearer my heart—" (July 9: 220). Eliza translates into Sterne's fictional world in exactly the same form: that is, as a miniature virtual traveling companion around Yorick's neck. Yorick addresses her directly in the first paragraph of the novel. Laurence Sterne, *A Sentimental Journey through France and Italy* in *Works: Volume VI*, eds. Melvyn New and W.G. Day (Gainesville: University of Florida Press, 2002), 3.

6. Appendix E in Gardner Stout, *A Sentimental Journey* (Berkeley: University of California Press, 1967): 322–26, reassesses the alleged irreconcilable sensibilities and styles of Sterne's contemporaneous texts. New and Day point out that *Bramine's Journal* and *A Sentimental Journey* "were intertwined for many months in Sterne's

own mind, and the reading of them should be similarly intertwined in our own" (Sterne, *Works*, xlvi).

7. My argument owes special debts to four critical works. John Dussinger, "'The Glory of Motion': Carriages and Consciousness in the Early Novel" in *The Country Myth: Motifs in the British Novel from Defoe to Smollett* (New York: Peter Lang, 1991): 207–20, 207, suggests that changes in carriage design, horse breeding, and road building in the eighteenth century provided "a material basis for the Age of Sensibilty, when self is felt to be a phenomenon of the nervous system, of the body in motion." Jean-Claude Dupas, *Sterne; Ou, Le vis-à-vis* (Lille: Presses-universitaires de Lille, 1984), invokes the carriage in a discussion of the immediacy of Sterne's authorial presence. Christopher Nagle, "Sterne, Shelley, and Sensibility's Pleasures of Proximity," *ELH* 70.3 (2003): 813–45, 818, underscores the degree to which sensibility focuses on "establishing relationality, not on cultivating the self." And, as I explain at length below, Jonathan Lamb, "The Language of Hartlean Associationism in *A Sentimental Journey*," *Eighteenth-Century Studies* 13 (1980): 285–312, outlines the crucial role played by metaphor in the novel. My essay finds a point of intersection between these arguments, the way in which Sterne weaves together ideas and experiences of mobility and intimacy by characterizing carriages in affective terms.

8. In a story of its origins popularized in early seventeenth-century tracts, the first modern passenger vehicle in England was a gift from a Dutch courtier to Elizabeth I. Transportation scholars usually give a slightly earlier date. Donald Berkebile, *Carriage Terminology: An Historical Dictionary* (Washington: Smithsonian Institute Press, 1978), 94, simply states, "In 1560 but three coaches were known in Paris, and in England the first coaches had been introduced only a few years before."

9. The type of vehicle that came to be known as a *coach*, named for the Hungarian town, Kocs, where they were thought to have first been built, was a wagon redesigned expressly for the pleasure of elite passengers: "to classify suspended and nonsuspended vehicles, as originally developed, is to draw the line between those of aristocratic and utilitarian origin," explains Berkebile, *Carriage Terminology*, 392.

10. G.A.Thrupp, "On Public Carriages" in *The History of Coaches* (1877) (Amsterdam: Meridian, 1969): 97–125, 101–9, explains that some of the discarded vehicles of the nobility were available for hire in London by 1605. Despite Parliament's attempt to limit them to 50 in 1635, there were as many as 300 hackney coaches in the city by 1650; 400 by 1662; and 700 by 1694. After their introduction in 1640, stage coaches (and their routes) also steadily multiplied: by 1775, there were four hundred of them registered for intercity travel in England.

11. John Taylor, *The World Runnes on Wheeles, or, Oddes Betwixt Carts and Coaches* (London: Henry Gosson, 1623), 17.

12. Adopting the persona of censor, Richard Steele protests in a similar vein in Number 144 of *The Tatler: Volume 2* (1709–10), ed. Donald Bond (Oxford: Clarendon Press, 1987): 319–21, 320, "I cannot but admire how Persons, conscious to themselves of no manner of superiority above others, can, out of meer Pride or Laziness expose themselves at this rate to publick View, and put us all upon pronouncing those Three terrible Syllables, Who is that?" Though coaches' exclusive ties to aristocracy had been

severed, their power to call special attention to their occupants, apparently, confusingly, endured. However, they now increasingly conveyed the restlessness and pretensions of upward mobility. Also see the upstart equipages and passengers in John Gay, *Trivia; or, the Art of Walking the Streets of London* (1716) in *The Poetical Works of John Gay*, ed. G.C.Faber (London: Oxford University Press, 1926): 57–87, especially in Book 2, lines 574–90.

13. Taylor, *Wheeles*, 14.

14. Thrupp, *Coaches*, 48, posits that the structural change in coaches "was, no doubt, suggested by the shape of the sedan chair." Sedan chairs carried by footmen had been in use in London since the early seventeenth century.

15. The next crucial changes to carriage design and the culture of the road came with the emergence of driving as a popular recreational activity in the last decades of the eighteenth century. Jeffrey T. Schnapp, "Crash (Speed as Engine of Individuation)," *Modernism/Modernity* 6.1 (1999): 1–49, looks at representations of the owner-driven carriages in the late eighteenth century, especially noticing the ideals of personal autonomy they helped to confirm. I am grateful to Kyoko Takanashi for this and several other sources, and for our ongoing discussion of carriages and eighteenth-century literature.

16. Wolfgang Schivelbusch, *The Railway Journey: The Industrialization of Time and Space in the Nineteenth Century* (1977; English trans. Berkeley: University of California Press, 1986), 74. Schivelbusch, 75, also cites Georg Simmel who, in his *Soziologie* (1908), contended, "Before the development of buses, trains and streetcars in the nineteenth century, people were quite unable to look at each other for minutes or hours at a time, or to be forced to do so, without talking to each other."

17. Delarivier Manley, *Letters Writen* [sic] *by Mrs. Manley* (London: R.B., 1696), 28. Manley's letters were later published as *A Stage-Coach Journey to Exeter. Describing the Humours on the Road, with the Characters and Adventures of the Company* (London: J. Roberts, 1725) by which title they are somewhat better known.

18. Manley, *Letters*, 11.

19. Manley, *Letters*, 27.

20. Manley, *Letters*, 25.

21. Richard Steele, Number 132, *The Spectator: Volume 2* (1711-12), ed. Donald Bond (Oxford: Clarendon Press, 1965): 23–5, 23.

22. Steele, *Spectator*, 23–4.

23. Steele, *Spectator*, 25.

24. Henry Fielding, *Joseph Andrews* (1742), ed. Martin Battestin (Middletown: Wesleyan University Press, 1967), 52.

25. Thomas Keymer, "Readers and Stage-Coaches in Fielding and Sterne," *Notes and Queries* 41.2 (June 1994): 209–11, considers Fielding's frequent use of the coach as a motif of narrative transaction between author and reader. Keymer sees it as an influence on Volume VII of Sterne's *Tristram Shandy*, which recounts Tristram's odd journey through France and in many ways anticipates the second novel.

26. Samuel Johnson, Number 84, *The Adventurer* in *The Idler and The Adventurer*, eds. W. J. Bate, John M. Bullitt, and L.F. Powell (New Haven: Yale University Press, 1963): 406–11, 407.

27. Johnson, *Adventurer*, 410.

28. James Buzard, "The Grand Tour and after (1660–1840)" in *Cambridge Companion to Travel Writing*, eds. Peter Hulme and Tim Youngs (New York: Cambridge University Press, 2002): 37–52, 37.

29. My reading underscores the inconsistencies and pessimism of the Preface in the *Desobligeant*. Conversely, Stout's extensive notes, 78-85 and Appendix E, 326-30, in the University of California edition of *A Sentimental Journey* elucidate the efficacy of the Preface in cataloguing contemporary attitudes toward the Grand Tour and gloss its many allusions, including to Sterne's own sermon on the Prodigal Son which urges intellectual and emotional preparedness for travel.

30. The interplay between these coaches and their narrative context in *A Sentimental Journey* has not gone unnoticed. Dussinger, "Carriages and Consciousness," 212, comments in passing that there is "a metaphysical structure implicit in such names as desobligeant and vis-a-vis . . ." For other critical treatments of these figures, see Lamb, "Associationism," 293; Keymer, "Readers," 210; James Chandler, "Moving Accidents: The Emergence of Sentimental Probability" in *The Age of Cultural Revolutions: Britain and France, 1750–1820*, eds. Colin Jones and Dror Wahrman (Berkeley: University of California Press, 2002): 137–70, especially 153; and George Haggerty, "Amelia's Nose; Or, Sensibility and Its Symptoms," *The Eighteenth Century* 36.2 (1995): 139–56, 141.

31. Though closets connoted closed-mindedness in the critical discourse invested in promoting polite learning, they fared much better elsewhere in eighteenth-century literature and culture. For overviews of the closet's many other cultural roles, see Mark Girouard, *Life in the English Country House: A Social and Architectural History* (New Haven: Yale University Press, 1978); Richard Rambuss, *Closet Devotions* (Durham, NC: Duke University Press, 1998), and Michael McKeon, *The Secret History of Domesticity: Public, Private, and the Division of Knowledge* (Baltimore: Johns Hopkins University Press, 2005).

32. Joseph Addison, Number 10, *The Spectator: Volume 1*, 44.

33. David Hume, "Of the Study of History," *Essays Moral, Political, and Literary*, ed. Eugene F. Miller (Indianapolis: Liberty Classics, 1985), 563–8. 568.

34. Samuel Johnson, "Preface to Shakespeare, 1759" in *Johnson on Shakespeare*, ed. Arthur Sherbo (New Haven: Yale University Press, 1968), 86.

35. John Locke, *Some Thoughts Concerning Education* (1693), eds. Ruth Grant and Nathan Tarcov (New York: Hackett, 1996): 2.A.94, 68, also features the closet in a discussion of the necessity of learning morality *in situ*: "it is not possible now (as perhaps formerly it was) to keep a young gentleman from vice by a total ignorance of it, unless you will all his life mew him up in a closet, and never let him go into company. The longer he is kept thus hoodwink'd, the less he will see when he comes abroad into open daylight." The closet keeps the gentleman-scholar pure, but poorly equips him for dealing with the ethical complexity of "company."

36. John Lyons, "*Camera Obscura*: Image and Imagination in Descartes's *Méditations*" in *Convergences: Rhetoric and Poetic in Seventeenth-Century France*, eds. David Lee Rubin and Mary B. McKinley (Columbus: Ohio State University

Press, 1989), 179–95, 179, cites the original: "Je demeurais tout le jour enfermé seul dans un poêle." The translation above is from the first English edition of *Discourse of a Method* (London: Thomas Newcombe, 1649), 16.

37. Lyons, "*Camera Obscura*,"179.

38. For a different reading of the spiraling temporality of the Preface, see Nagle, "Proximity," 827–8.

39. The question of whether or not the coach Yorick buys is a *Vis a Vis* may be moot: as transportation historians point out, seventeenth- and eighteenth-century carriage names were often used interchangeably. On the other hand, Ralph Straus, *Carriages and Coaches: Their History and their Evolution* (London: Martin Secker, 1912), 172, footnotes his discussion of Sterne with an announcement from *The Gazeteer and New Daily Advertiser* for July 21, 1767, in which a certain Monsieur Dessein, the real-life coach broker and hotelier on whom Sterne's character is based, advertises "a Travelling *Vis-à-Vis* . . . varnished in the newest taste, and covered with an oiled case to preserve it from the weather in travelling, and [requiring] nothing but a new set of wheels to be in perfect repair." Evidently there was some factual basis for Sterne's fictional association of that vehicle and the Calais coach yard.

40. Lamb, "Associationism," 285, defines "sentimental situations" as those in which a word, idea, and interpersonal context fleetingly unite, producing a meaning that oscillates pleasingly between literal and figurative levels. Since *sentiment* is Sterne's crucial key word, it is worth quoting Lamb's illustration of it at length:

> . . .at the end of Slawkenburgius's Tale in *Tristram Shandy* . . . Tristram comes across the strange phrase "the lambent pupilability of slow, low, dry chat." His brain can make nothing of it, but the vibrations round his heart teach him that the sentimental part of this conference between Diego and Julia can be preserved only if their eyebeams stay on a level, and glance neither at the ceiling nor at one another's laps. In this way Tristram can feel he understands it . . . Between . . . cool reasoning . . . and . . . urgent animality . . . there is room for the cardiac vibrations that signal the arrival of sentimental knowledge and the production of sentimental words. The word sentiment . . . is a pun, referring to [this] natural linkage between feeling and thought, gesture and utterance. (285–6)

So sentiment first of all gives a name to a precariously balanced mode of perception; whereas dipping awareness down too low, solely to words, things, or laps, breeds vulgarity or crude literalism, tipping it up too high, to ideas or the ceiling, results in ethereal abstraction or whimsy. Like Diego and Julia's eyebeams, sentiment rests in the nebulous in-between zone. At the same time, it gives a name to the quasi-emotional, quasi-rational *recognition* of this perceptual balance such as when Tristram "can feel he understands" in his heart what "lambent pupilability" means in the context of Diego and Julia's "slow, low, dry chat." Sentiment therefore also signifies meta-sentiment, the awareness of sentiment. Lamb identifies *heart, hand, exchange, situation*, and *volume* as subsidiary key words: they allow for brief fusions between their most tangible (material or physiological) denotations and their most abstract or suggestive connotations.

41. Taylor, *Wheeles*, 8.

42. George Farquhar and Peter Anthony Motteux, *The Stage-Coach* (London: Benjamin Bragg, 1705), 19. First produced on the London stage in 1701 or 1702, the play is a translation of Jean de la Chapelle's *Les Carrosses d'Orléans* (1680).

43. Taylor, *Wheeles*, 13.

44. Taylor, *Wheeles*, 15.

45. Pepys, *Diary*: Volume 8, Part 2, 187.

46. In the decades following the publication of *A Sentimental Journey*, the *Vis a Vis* in particular came to suggest female promiscuity. In the mock-epic poem, "The Vis-a-vis of Berkeley Square; Or, A Wheel off Mrs. W*t*n's Carriage" (London: Murray, Bowen, and Southerne, 1783), 14, a vehicle is both the cause and the effect of the heroine's notoriety as she rides about the city:

> All these [men] have paid for their approach,
> All these have paid to make this Coach,
> This Comet upon Wheels!
> Which, burnish'd as it runs, doth blaze;
> Of all, the wonder and the gaze!

The Mrs. Watson of the poem's title was said to have seduced the Prince of Wales (with the help of her sister) and to own "the smartest vis-a-vis in town." Another well-known courtesan, Agnes Townshend, was known as Vis-a-vis Townshend, despite the fact that she drove herself all over the country in a phaeton. See Horace Bleackley, *Ladies Fair and Frail: Sketches of the Demi-Monde During the Eighteenth Century with Sixteen Illustrations (*London: John Lane, 1909), 282.

47. Giacomo Casanova, *History of My Life: Volumes 3 and 4*, trans. Willard Trask (New York: Harcourt, Brace and World, 1967), 25.

48. Manley, *Letters*, 10.

49. Georg Christophe Lichtenberg, paraphrased in Lázló Tarr, *The History of the Carriage*, trans. Elizabeth Hoch (Budapest: Corvina Press, 1969), 257.

50. Lamb, "Associationism," 293, and Chandler, "Probability," 152, also gloss this metaphor.

51. Jonathan Crary, *Techniques of the Observer: On Vision and Modernity in the Nineteenth Century* (Cambridge, Massachusetts Institute of Technology Press, 1991): 25–66, 29, outlines the extensive influence of the *camera obscura* on ideas of perception throughout the early modern period: "For two centuries it stood as a model, in both rationalist and empiricist thought, of how observation leads to truthful inferences about the world; at the same time the physical incarnation of that model was a widely used means of observing the visible world, an instrument of popular entertainment, of scientific inquiry, and of artistic practice."

52. Lyons, *"Camera Obscura,"* 181.

53. John Locke, *Essay Concerning Human Understanding* (1690), ed. Peter Nidditch (Oxford: Clarendon Press, 1989): 2.11.17, 165 , draws this analogy cautiously: "[M]ethinks, the understanding is not much unlike a closet wholly shut from light with only some little opening left, to let in external visible resemblances, or ideas of things without."

54. While Sterne's ideal shares important premises with moral sense philosophies, Yorick's failed attempt to sympathize from a distance implicitly critiques these theories. In keeping with the empirical separation of subject and object, works such as Adam Smith's *Theory of Moral Sentiments* (1759), ed. Knud Haakonssen (New York: Cambridge University Press, 2002), conceive sympathy as a virtual or parasitic affective structure. Spectators at best experience feelings which parallel those of the agent or "person principally concerned": "Whatever is the passion which arises from any object in the person principally concerned, an *analogous* emotion springs up, at the thought of his situation, in the breast of every attentive spectator," writes Smith. "In every passion of which the mind of man is susceptible, the emotions of the by-stander always correspond to what, *by bringing the case home to himself*, he imagines should be the sentiments of the sufferer" (1.1.1.4, 13 my italics). The payoff of the *Vis a vis* as a paradigm of emotional connection is its immediacy and perfect symmetry: two equal participants play both spectator and agent at once.

Hyperborean Atlantis: Jean-Sylvain Bailly, Madame Blavatsky, and the Nazi Myth

DAN EDELSTEIN

Edward Said's theory of "Orientalism," as a growing chorus of commentators has observed, does not fully account for eighteenth-century representations of the Orient.[1] The Enlightenment certainly had its fair share of prejudiced Europeans, and there are plenty of Orientalist topoi (sultry courtesans, scheming viziers, and of course, oriental despots) cluttering the pages and canvases of eighteenth-century culture. But where are the empires, the colonies? As Joseph Dupleix and Robert Clive learned the hard way, Versailles and London did not begin considering "the Orient" as colonial material until the last quarter of the century.[2] "There was an Orientalism before the empires," Maxime Rodinson reminds us; the eighteenth-century interest in (and uses of) the East can thus not be subsumed under an imperialistic mantle.[3] In her recent study of eighteenth- and nineteenth-century French Orientalism, Madeleine Dobie even went so far as to argue that, "[u]ntil the final quarter of the *nineteenth* century, what we predominantly encounter in Orientalist representation is not a celebration or even a record of conquest and occupation, but a marked aestheticization of both Oriental culture and colonial life."[4] Dobie's study convincingly argues that it is the *non*-colonial Orient that attracts the French/Western gaze, at least until the post-1870 European scramble for empire.[5]

Moreover, eighteenth-century Orientalism was not always derogatory in content.[6] Voltaire's prose works, for instance, resound with praise for Eastern cultures: a Turkish dervish has the final word in *Candide*; the *Lettres d'Amabed* heap scorn on rapacious European missionaries and settlers in India, contrasting them with the virtuous local inhabitants; *La Princesse de Babylone* depicts Voltaire's own version of the Golden Age, on the shores of the Ganges.[7] These laudatory representations of the Orient would be enshrined in his *Essai sur les mœurs et l'esprit des nations* (discussed below), which Raymond Schwab identified as the fountainhead of Indian Orientalism.[8] Tellingly, Said deals only in passing with the eighteenth century, as opposed to Schwab and others, who retrace nineteenth-century Orientalism to its roots in the Enlightenment.[9]

I believe that such a genealogy is indeed requisite, first and foremost to dispel the monist (and ungrounded) characterization of Orientalist studies as the propaganda arm of colonial empires. But there is a darker reason for calling attention to this sincere regard for Eastern cultures, both in the eighteenth century and beyond. As the present paper argues, it is only by acknowledging this initial state of respect that we can grasp how Orientalism was later "recuperated" (in the French sense of the term) in order to authorize some of the vilest Eurocentric ideologies, in particular Nazism. By ignoring this veneration, we overlook both the best and the worst of Occidental attitudes toward the Orient.

The specific act of recuperation that I examine here centers on a key Western representation, which is also a key representation of the West (geographically speaking): the myth of Atlantis. In a series of works on Atlantis, the eighteenth-century astronomer Jean-Sylvain Bailly "orientalized" this Western myth, declaring it not to be an island that once lay between Europe and America, but rather the equally mythical continent of Hyperborea. Jumping ahead a century, this theory inspired Helena Petrovna (a.k.a. "Madame") Blavatsky, a Russian aristocrat, mystic, and international woman of mystery (who co-founded the Theosophical Society in 1875), to weave a Hyperborean Atlantis into her complex mythology, published as *The Secret Doctrine* (1888). In turn, this remythologizing of Bailly's thesis provided the Nazis with the mythical precedent and pretense necessary both to found their ideological platform (as laid out by Alfred Rosenberg in *The Myth of the Twentieth Century*), and to pursue their genocidal programs. Indirectly, though not without his share of blame, Bailly thus lies at the source of a central element in Nazi ideology, one which may be called, following Philippe Lacoue-Labarthe and Jean-Luc Nancy, "the Nazi myth."[10]

To undertake this genealogy of the Nazi myth, we must begin by recalling the anthropological model underlying eighteenth-century Orientalism.[11] This model is best perceived in Voltaire's *Essai sur les mœurs et l'esprit des nations*. In this "universal history," as an earlier version of the *Essai* was entitled, Voltaire rocked the clerical and academic establishment by placing China and India at the head of his chronology, with the Jews well behind.[12] Adding insult to injury, he suggested that the Jews not only succeeded earlier civilizations, but that they *copied* them: "Les Juifs ont tout pris des autres nations."[13] He would also disseminate these heterodox assertions throughout his *Contes*.[14]

What Voltaire intended as a critique of Judeo-Christian primacy was also the result of an anthropological theory, which would later become known as "diffusionism."[15] According to this theory, all cultural inventions and traditions originate from one point (as opposed to arising independently in different places), and spread, or are "diffused," from there. The typical example of cultural diffusion is the Phoenician alphabet: invented by one culture, if not one individual, it was soon adopted by a range of different cultures to transcribe their various languages.

Already in the eighteenth century, however, diffusionism existed in a much more radical form. Rather than mapping cultural inventions back to various loci (for instance, the alphabet to the Phoenicians, pagan gods to Egypt, or gunpowder to the Chinese), radical diffusionists traced *all* cultural inventions back to a single, original locus.[16] Hence, when Voltaire argued that the Jews borrowed their culture from other nations, he was not simply (like other anti-Semites) implying that Jews do not invent anything and only copy others, but was adhering to the strict logic of radical diffusionism. The Jews, as well as every other people that succeeded the Ur-civilization, merely perpetuated a complete cultural system, which they inherited from the primogenitors of human society.[17] At a time when polygenetic theories about the origin of the human race(s) were rampant, radical diffusionism was further bolstered by the notion that only certain select peoples would have had the requisite qualities for inventing culture.[18]

According to Voltaire, these primogenitors of all human knowledge were Indian: "je suis convaincu que tout nous vient des bords du Gange, astronomie, astrologie, métempsycose, &c."[19] This hypothesis was particularly seductive, as it could be extended to the most sophisticated aspects of human culture, namely the sciences. The belief in the super-sophistication of Brahmanic culture grew stronger after Sir William Jones's "discovery" of Sanskrit grammar, but even before the *Asiatic Researches* saw the day, Brahmanism was being hailed as the "origine des sciences" (from the title of Jean-Sylvain

Bailly's 1777 study). In Voltaire's eyes, India superseded Egypt: "Il est bien difficile de dire laquelle des deux nations enseigna l'autre; mais s'il s'agissait de décider entre les Indes et l'Egypte, je croirais toujours les sciences bien plus anciennes dans les Indes…"[20] This substitution of India for Egypt is telling, since throughout most of Antiquity, Egypt was traditionally considered the source of religion and science. India's place of honor was enshrined in the *Encyclopédie* by the chevalier de Jaucourt ("Les Sciences étoient peut-être plus anciennes dans l'*Inde* que dans l'Egypte," *s.v.* "Inde"), and became the dominant opinion during the late Enlightenment: "a wide variety of authors and schools located the birthplace of the entire human race between the Indus and the Ganges."[21]

Radical diffusionism was also underwritten by a myth: the myth of Atlantis. As recounted by Critias (in the Platonic dialogue of the same name), Atlantis had once been home to a highly sophisticated people, who excelled in engineering projects (such as canals, bridges, tunnels, aqueducts) and in war. Having colonized the known world, the Atlanteans shared their technological knowledge with other peoples, before a terrible earthquake pulled their island under the sea. Though remembered only by a few Egyptian priests, they had produced one of the first and finest human civilizations, and had seemingly invented most sciences known to man.[22]

Atlantis remained synonymous with technological perfection throughout European history, and served as a metaphor for scientific gains. At the height of the Renaissance, Sir Francis Bacon celebrated a New *Atlantis*, a sophisticated civilization centered around a scientific academy called "Salomon's House" (named after an Atlantean king Solamona, and not the biblical Solomon, although the confusion is obviously intentional), whose goal was "the knowledge of causes, and secret motions of things; and the enlarging of the bounds of human empire, to the effecting of all things possible."[23] Its scientists had progressed so far towards this goal that they had managed all sorts of engineering feats, from refrigerators and pharmaceuticals to airplanes and submarines. Voltaire would remember this new Atlantis in *Candide*, where the lost civilization of Eldorado contains a "Palais des Sciences" remarkably similar to Salomon's House.[24]

As it perfectly illustrated the theory of radical diffusionism, the myth of Atlantis was easily "naturalized," particularly in the early age of Orientalism.[25] The net result of this naturalization was an "Atlanticizing" of the belief in an Ur-civilization. Rather than vouching for one particular, historical primogenitor of culture (such as Egypt or India), the Atlantis thesis raised the specter of an even older predecessor, which had since disappeared. This hypothesis conformed neatly with the near-universally accepted story of the

Flood, re-emphasized in the eighteenth century by Giambattista Vico and Nicolas Boulanger (in *L'Antiquité dévoilée*). As Pierre Vidal-Naquet has argued, it also allowed the *philosophes* to counter the orthodox account of Genesis, and to present "l'Atlantide comme subsitut de la Palestine [juive] dans l'exégèse de l'histoire."[26] But what exactly was Atlantis, and where was it found? The identification of this proto-Ur-civilization was the project that the astronomer Jean-Sylvain Bailly assigned himself in a series of works, beginning with his 1775 *Histoire de l'astronomie ancienne*, followed by the 1777 *Lettres sur l'origine des sciences*, and finally the 1779 *Lettres sur l'Atlantide*.[27]

Bailly's history of astronomy combines the radical diffusionism of the *Essai sur les mœurs* with the classical *translatio de studii et imperii* trope, soon to become a hallmark of Romantic historiography.[28] "[L]e sceptre des sciences a dû passer d'un peuple à un autre," Bailly claims outright, before invoking a metaphor that would pass into posterity with Hegel's *Philosophy of History*: "leur lumière née dans l'Orient, comme celle du soleil, s'avance ainsi que cet astre vers l'Occident, & dans une révolution très-lente, semble, comme lui, devoir faire le tour du monde."[29] At the dawn of human achievements, however, Bailly did not perceive India, but rather Atlantis: "En examinant les différentes souches du genre humain, on voit que les Atlantes sont la principale & la plus ancienne."[30]

How could Bailly accommodate Voltairean Orientalism with the Occidental myth of Atlantis? He found a very simple solution: he relocated Atlantis to the (north)east. In orthodox Orientalist fashion, Bailly readily conceded that, "le peuple qui tenait jadis le sceptre des sciences dans l'Asie était l'auteur de toutes les idées philosophiques qui ont éclairé le monde."[31] But this people was not Indian, nor was it Voltaire's "Gangarides:" "les peuples de l'Asie ont été *dépositaires*, & non pas inventeurs."[32] Somewhere in Asia there had existed a proto-Indo-European people, who had instructed the other Asian peoples but had since disappeared, only to be remembered in such myths as Atlantis.

It was literally in myths that Bailly sought proof of Atlantis's past existence, and even of its exact location. Myths were in fact the logical place to seek answers to the Atlantis enigma, as they were commonly believed to have originated in the ancient East: "je pense, comme M. de Voltaire, que la philosophie et les fables nous sont venues de l'Orient et des Indes."[33] But what could this collection of grotesque tales possibly reveal about the origins of Atlantis? Had not Voltaire himself declared that, "les plus insensés de tous ont été ceux qui ont voulu trouver un sens à ces fables absurdes, et mettre de la raison dans la folie"?[34] Although he subscribed to these eighteenth-century commonplaces (the *Lettres sur l'Atlantide* refer to mythology as "une vaste idolâtrie"), Bailly was writing in the wake of a scholarly revolution in mythography, brought about by Antoine Court de Gébelin's nine-volume *Monde primitif* (1773–82).[35] This gigantic enterprise, a sort of *Encyclopédie* for the ancient world (as Anne-Marie Mercier-Faivre has suggested), was one of the first eighteenth-century treatises to grant myths considerable cultural value, even going so far as to hail mythology as a "*Discours sacré*."[36] Where philosophes since Pierre Bayle and Bernard le Bovier de Fontenelle had denigrated myths as the product of frightened, pre-logical minds, Court revalorized ancient society by interpreting its gods according to a new hermeneutic code: astronomy.[37] Underlying the manifold branches of mythology, Court argued, were the original sacred symbols of the sun and moon. With the passage of time, these and other cosmic symbols (constellations, planets, comets) were personified and their original referents were forgotten, leaving myths as the corrupt (and corrupting) record of a lost, sublime religion. Knowledge of mythology's true code, however, would allow future mythographers to reconstruct this religion, and to uncover the "sacred discourse" that still lies hidden in myths.

Foregoing the dyadic nature of Court's thesis, Bailly (as Charles Dupuis after him) focused primarily on solar symbols in his reading of mythology, although he concentrated on many of the same mythical figures, notably Hercules: "il n'y a pas lieu de douter qu'Hercule ne soit l'emblème du Soleil."[38] What interested Bailly in these solar myths was their connection to the underworld: Hercules's twelfth and last labor (in the traditional sequence) led him beneath ground to capture Cerberus, just as Persephone, another solar figure, had disappeared underground for half the year. These episodes and others, Bailly surmised, symbolized the complete disappearance of the sun; the inventors of the myth must therefore have lived at a latitude where the sun periodically vanished from the sky. Dismissing earlier theories about the location of Atlantis, Bailly thus reached the surprising conclusion that Atlantis lay near the North Pole, roughly where the Novaya Zemlya archipelago is situated. He proceeded to equate the Atlanteans with the Hyperboreans, the mythical people who lived beyond (*hyper-*) the northern wind (*Boreas*). Little is known about them, except that they worshipped Apollo, the god of the *sun*. Of course, Bailly acknowledged, Hyperborea is uninhabitable today, but in the past, when the climate was different, it had been warmer by the poles. A Hyperborean Atlantis was thus an ideal candidate, in Bailly's eyes, for the original civilization; it was the true Golden Age, too soon abandoned with the cooling of the earth: "l'âge d'or, cette fable séduisante, n'est donc que le souvenir d'une patrie abandonnée, mais toujours chère."[39]

Historians of Atlantis interpretations have a tendency to brush aside Bailly's thesis, claiming that he was simply copying the work of Olof Rudbeck, a Swedish scholar who contended, at the beginning of the eighteenth century, that Atlantis was Sweden.[40] In fact, their two theories bear only a superficial resemblance to one another. Rudbeck's interpretation belongs to the classical tradition of political mythology stretching from Virgil to Ronsard:[41] in his analysis, the myth of Atlantis serves to glorify Swedish pedigree and to authorize its imperialistic pretensions. In Bailly's case, there is no immediate beneficiary of his interpretation: superficially at least, his study pertains to universal history, not to political myth-making. On closer analysis, however, the political import of Bailly's work is perhaps even more potent than Rudbeck's propaganda. As opposed to the Swede, Bailly dissociated Atlantis from the Atlanteans, the place from the people. He thus *mobilized* the myth, tracing its progress from the North Pole through Asia (via Mongolia) down to India, and from there, from East to West. Atlantis became a "floating signifier," an indicator of cultural superiority and originality that could be affixed to any place and people with whom the migrant Atlanteans might have come into contact. By situating their original homeland beyond the scope of empirical inquiry (under the concealing lid of polar ice sheets), he turned the Atlanteans into what would soon become the nineteenth-century myth *par excellence*: the myth of race, and more specifically, of the "white" race's peregrination across the globe.

We can now fully fathom the political thrust of Bailly's gesture: rather than orientalize Atlantis, he Atlanticized the Orient, making a snow-white, northern European people, the Hyperboreans, responsible for the cultural achievements and splendors of the East.[42] He did not deny Oriental achievements: on the contrary, he bent over backwards to concur with Voltaire that Asian civilizations were truly awe-inspiring. But a Hyperborean Atlantis allowed him to credit a European stock with the foundation of these ancient cultures. In this Atlantean version, Orientalism became a means of honoring *Western* accomplishments; the present Enlightenment simply the completion of the Atlantean odyssey.[43] Bailly could therefore amend his initial claim that history moved from East to West like the sun: the real movement of history, he specified in his *Lettres sur l'origine*, was "la marche des sciences du nord vers le midi."[44] This replacement of an East/West opposition for a North/South one served a double role: on the one hand, the better part of the Orient was subsumed under a North that, thanks to the globe's spherical shape, could claim paternity for both Europe and Asia; on the other hand, the representation of a languid, degenerate East was reinforced by commonplaces about the torrid, corrupting climate of the South.[45] The superiority of a civil and civilizing North was now simply self-evident.

Bailly's contribution to the history of Atlantis interpretations was both original and, sadly, very sophisticated. But was it to have any influence? Contemporary reactions were mixed: Georges-Louis Leclerc de Buffon highly praised Bailly's *Histoire de l'astronomie ancienne* in his *Des époques de la nature*, but placed the original cultivated civilization in Tartary (which, according to Bailly, is where the Atlanteans first migrated), and did not so much as mention Atlantis.[46] In his *Histoire philosophique du monde primitif* (1793), Jean-Baptiste Delisle de Sales readily granted the reality of Atlantis, but mocked Bailly (without naming him) for situating it in the far north.[47] By and large, Delisle's attitude seems to have been typical: Bailly succeeded in transferring Atlantis from the realm of myth to that of history, but his own Hyperborean theory found little support. Jules Verne even used the discovery of an Atlantic Atlantis by Captain Nemo, in *20,000 Leagues Under the Sea*, to poke fun at Bailly for having placed it by the North Pole.

There was, however, an important exception to this trend. In 1888, Helena Petrovna Blavatsky published what would become the textbook of the theosophical movement, *The Secret Doctrine*.[48] A series of lengthy glosses and commentaries of an alleged ancient book (consulted by clairvoyance, no less), the *Stanzas of Dzyan*, Blavatsky's text is an anti-Darwinian *Descent of Man* that tells of the rise and fall of seven "root-races" (we are currently on number five, going on six). Each root-race is divided into seven sub-races, and is associated with a different continent—although with continental drift, and the "disappearance" of certain continents, these do not correspond to the ones we know.[49] Unsurprisingly, one of these lost continents is Atlantis. Although writing shortly after Ignatius Donnelly, whose *Atlantis: The Antediluvian World* launched a fin-de-siècle Atlantis craze, Blavatsky did not place Atlantis in-between Europe and America, as Donnelly had, but rather in the far north, near the North Pole.[50] Indeed, in Blavatsky, Bailly had finally found a supporter: she quotes his works extensively (no less than twenty-two times), and credits him with having discovered the truth, or at least part of it, about Atlantis.[51]

Blavatsky also develops to its fullest the racial germ present in Bailly's thesis. Hyperborean Atlantis was home to the Atlanteans, but also saw the emergence of another race, the Aryans: "The Aryan race was born and developed in the far north, though after the sinking of the continent of Atlantis its tribes emigrated further south into Asia."[52] For a long time, the remaining Atlanteans and the Aryans lived together. They brought civilization to India, Egypt, Greece, and Rome, and are the ancestors of the current Europeans.[53]

The Atlanteans transmitted to the Aryans all the known sciences, and even highly sophisticated technologies such as aeronautics ("knowledge of flying in air-vehicles," as Blavatsky puts it). But over time, the Aryan root-race also subdivided. One of the more unfortunate results of this division, Blavatsky writes, was the creation of the Semitic sub-race, "an artificial Aryan race."[54] The Semites were but one of the Aryan sub-races, but she draws strong distinctions between them and the others:

> With the ancient Aryans the hidden meaning was grandiose, sublime, and poetical, however much the external appearance of their symbol may *now* militate against the claim . . . With the Semite, that *stooping* man meant the *fall* of Spirit into matter, and that *fall* and *degradation* were apotheosized by him with the result of dragging Deity down to the level of man.[55]

There is thus an "immense chasm between Aryan and Semitic religious thought," Blavatsky concludes; they belong to "two opposite poles – Sincerity and Concealment . . . Who can ever fathom the paradoxical depths of the Semitic mind?"[56] She further degrades Judaism by describing it as a sex-obsessed and selfish cult: "Judaism, built *solely* on Phallic worship, has become one of the latest creeds in Asia, and theologically a religion of hate and malice toward everyone and everything outside themselves." The true Aryans, by contrast, are "the most metaphysical and spiritual people on earth."[57]

There was of course a strong current of anti-Semitism in Europe at the time Blavatsky was writing, and the unflattering contrast between Aryans and Semites had become routine.[58] To a large extent, then, she was only expressing the mentality of her own period. But she added a new dimension to the standard anti-Semitic discourse: with *The Secret Doctrine*, anti-Semitism now acquired cosmological importance. The Jews suddenly stood in the way of the great pre-ordained progress of the races. There may have to be a battle between Aryans and Semites, as there had been between the Aryans and the last of the Atlanteans.[59] This Aryan/non-Aryan (and specifically Semitic) opposition would become the great historical paradigm of the racist Right, replacing the Marxist historiographic law of class-struggle.[60] Blavatsky also raised the specter of a *new* race, to be chosen from among the most select members of the Aryan root-race. This next race would have even greater powers than the present one, and would truly produce the *Übermenschen* of the future.

With the spread of theosophical ideas, the Hyperborean Atlantis theory attracted more and more supporters.[61] The racist Austrian occultist Jörg Lanz von Liebenfels placed the birthplace of the Aryans in an arctic land called "Arktogäa." In his 1923 *La Vérité sur l'Atlantide*, René-Maurice Gattefossé similarly argued that Atlantis was a polar continent, which, following Bailly, he named Hyperborea. Hermann Wirth, a German ethnologist who would work for the SS Ahnenerbe [Ancestral Heritage] institute, also placed Atlantis in the far North, calling it "Thule"—the mythical name for the capital of the Hyperboreans.[62] And the lost Atlantis figured under this name in Hanns Hörbiger's *Welteislehre* [World Ice Theory], the "German" science that was to become an article of faith under the Nazis.[63]

Blavatsky's Atlanto-Aryans also found supporters in the twentieth century. The Viennese nationalist and occultist Guido von List incorporated her Atlantean genealogy in his own writings on "Ariosophy," and in 1922, Karl Georg Zschaetzsch published a book entitled *Atlantis: die Urheimat der Arier*. The racial differences between Aryans and Semites in these reworkings were often greatly exaggerated: in Lanz von Liebenfels's reformulation of *The Secret Doctrine*, for instance, "the fourth root-race of Atlanteans had divided into pure and bestial sub-species, corresponding to the early anthropoids and the anthropomorphic apes."[64] As these many examples illustrate, the Bailly-Blavatsky hypothesis was given a particularly warm welcome in proto-Nazi Germanic circles.

The role that the Atlantis myth played in the genesis of Nazi ideology can be defined much more precisely than by sampling the period's *mentalité*. To appreciate this role fully, however, we must return briefly to Bailly's time to consider a second political attribute that the Atlantis myth had acquired. This quality derived from the resemblance between Atlantis and another myth, the myth of the Golden Age. As noted above, the two had already been fused by Bailly, who summoned the Golden Age myth as proof of Atlantis's past existence. Although the traditional version of the Golden Age myth seemingly contradicts the Atlantean myth of a super-sophisticated Ur-culture, they nonetheless share a number of features: both describe an ideal form of social organization, and both situate this society at the beginning of human history. The vogue for Indian Orientalism, furthermore, had contributed to merge the two myths. When Voltaire expressed his belief that, "il y a encore un grand païs voisin [de Benarès], où ce qu'on appelle l'âge d'or s'est conservé," he did not have Rousseau's state of nature in mind, but rather his own highly-civilized, Atlantean "Gangarides."[65]

This ready identification of Atlantis with the Golden Age is telling, as the latter myth became, with the French Revolution, a powerful political representation. Not only was the "return of the Golden Age" one of the most common contemporary representations of the historical events underway, but it turned into an ideological blueprint for "regenerating" France and the world.[66] Most importantly for our present concerns, the French Revolution also reversed the temporal dynamics of the Golden Age myth: from representing an irretrievably lost moment of *past* perfection (in the Rousseauist model), it came to stand for an ideal and imminent *future*. Its nostalgic expression was transformed into millenarian promise; the Virgilian version merged the Ovidian one. With the fall of Robespierre, this forward-looking dynamic was accentuated, as the expected return of the Golden Age withdrew into the future—witness the commonplace nineteenth-century lament about how "tout ce qui sera n'est pas encore" (Alfred de Musset). Nevertheless, the myth's millenarian portent was undiminished, and it remained a central tenet of socialist, communist, and anarchist ideologies until the twentieth century.[67]

But the Golden Age myth did not always assume a primitivist form: when Henri de Saint-Simon pronounced his famous phrase, "L'âge d'or du genre humain n'est point derrière nous, il est au-devant," he obviously had a less nostalgic, more Voltairean Golden Age in mind.[68] By the mid-nineteenth century, this vision of a technological future was slowly becoming a reality: in his 1855 *Chants modernes*, Maxime du Camp repeated Saint-Simon's slogan to celebrate the advent of the locomotive. The longed-for Golden Age became Atlanticized: Auguste Villiers de l'Isle-Adam, in a satirical short story about useless modern inventions, sarcastically remarked, "[c]'est à se demander, en un mot, si l'Age d'or ne revient pas."[69] This Atlanticized Golden Age myth did not necessarily lose its revolutionary power: the utopia described in Emile Zola's *Les Quatre évangiles*, for instance, is a sophisticated city, not unlike Voltaire's Eldorado.[70] Tellingly, it was at this time of real technological innovation that the scholarly and popular Atlantis craze took off, with the publication of Donnelly's work. After the Wright brothers perfected their own "knowledge of flying in air-vehicles," Blavatsky's Atlantean Age truly seemed to be returning.

By the early twentieth century, then, the myth of Atlantis had become a hazardous representation, mixing millenarian and racial fantasies. List and Lanz von Liebenfels's theosophical anti-Semitism found a ready reception in both pre- and post-WWI Germany, providing the ideological foundations for the nascent *Germanenorden*. After the war, this para-Masonic and paramilitary organization used the cloak of secrecy surrounding its "Aryan" rituals to plot the assassination of prominent Jewish and republican politicians.[71] It also fed into another pro-Aryan, murderous group—the National Socialist German Worker's Party (N.S.D.A.P.), or Nazi party.

The connection between the Germanenorden and the Nazis arguably passes through one man, the Baron Rudolf von Sebottendorff, although there are many divergent accounts about his role in the genesis of Nazism, and his influence is often exaggerated.[72] What is certain about his involvement is that Sebottendorff founded the Bavarian chapter of the Germanenorden in Munich, in July 1918. He named his chapter the "Thule society," ostensibly to hide its extremist agenda under the benign cover of antiquarian studies, yet as we know "Thule" was not a random choice of name. Indeed, Sebottendorff belonged to the long line of Aryan theosophists, stretching from Blavatsky to Lanz von Lebenfels. And with the Thule society, the myth of a Hyperborean Atlantis became part of the history and ideology of Nazism.

In a mixture that would prove explosive and effective, Sebottendorff's society combined occult speculations with violent political action. During the rapid succession of socialist and Soviet revolutionary governments in post-WWI Munich, the Thule society was at the center of the "white," or reactionary, counter-offensive. Its antiquarian cover may have facilitated this role: while the authorities cracked down on more visible nationalist groups, the Thule society's headquarters at the fancy Vierjahrzeiten Hotel became a haven for the resistance.[73] Throughout the turbulent period between 1918 and 1920, the society thus functioned as an umbrella group for various far-right, paramilitary organizations, communally known as the "Free Corps."

One of the far-right groups that came under the sway of the Thule Society was the German Worker's Party, or D.A.P., soon to become the N.S.D.A.P. under the leadership of Adolf Hitler. The precise connections between the D.A.P. and the Thule society are still debated: Sebottendorff affirmed that it was created by Thule members, but Reginald Phelps has cast doubt on his claims. Whatever the administrative rapport between the two groups may have been, the personal contacts between Thule members and the Nazis are undeniable.[74] As Ian Kershaw observed, the Thule society's "membership list . . . reads like a *Who's Who* of early Nazi sympathizers," and one might add, of future Nazi cadres.[75] Rudolf Hess, Alfred Rosenberg, Dieter Eckart, and Hans Frank (the future governor of Poland), among others, all attended or lectured at Thule society meetings. Anton Drexler, the founder of the D.A.P., frequented Thule meetings, and another Thule adherent, Friedrich Krohn, devised the official emblem of the N.S.D.A.P., the black swastika in a white circle against a red backdrop.[76] Although there are no records of Hitler ever participating in Thule activities, it is most likely that he discussed its Ariosophic theories with his avowed "mentor," Eckart, with his Landsberg prison companion, Hess, or with his Munich companion, Rosenberg.[77] Scholars often invoke Hitler's dismissal of "*völkisch* wandering scholars" in *Mein Kampf* to argue that he paid little heed to mythological and occult theses, but as Jackson Spielvogel and David Redles remark, his private conversations reveal a keen interest in such matters, including the myth of Atlantis.[78]

The real importance of the Atlantis myth in the genesis of Nazism, however, may best be measured in the work of another Thule adherent and future Nazi official, Alfred Rosenberg. Not only was *The Myth of the Twentieth Century* (1930), his major work, the second best-selling book in Nazi Germany (the first, of course, being *Mein Kampf*), but Rosenberg is widely viewed as having exerted a profound influence on Hitler in his formative Munich years.[79] As much as anyone, then, he can be credited with having shaped the Nazi *Weltanschauung* (to employ one of his favored terms) and crystallized Hitler's own anti-Semitic ideas.

The Myth of the Twentieth Century makes very clear that the keystone of this worldview was the myth of a Hyperborean Atlantis. Rosenberg began his lengthy tome by positing the reality of (i.e., by naturalizing) this myth:

> All in all, the old legends of Atlantis may appear in new light. It seems far from impossible that in areas over which the Atlantic waves roll and giant icebergs float, a flourishing continent once rose above the waters and upon it a creative race produced a far-reaching culture and sent its children out into the world as seafarers and warriors. But even if this Atlantis hypothesis should prove untenable, *a prehistoric Nordic cultural center must still be assumed.*[80]

This "prehistoric Nordic cultural center" was indeed the fundamental premise needed to justify all of Rosenberg's subsequent statements about Aryans and Jews. Although rejecting the doctrine of radical diffusionism ("We have long since been forced to abandon the theory of an *identical* origin of myths, art, and religious forms among all peoples"), Rosenberg credits periodical impulses of Nordic-Aryan blood for the rise of successive civilizations across the globe. A primeval Atlantis was thus the prerequisite for exalting the Aryan genius: if the Aryans did not originate in the far North, they could not have both Germanic features and colonized (at different epochs) the entire world. Only by positing a northern Atlantis could Rosenberg declare, as had Bailly, that "the march of world history has radiated from the North over the entire planet."[81] Bailly's use of solar mythology to prove the Nordic origin of Atlantis would also be recuperated to validate Aryan superiority: the cult of the sun, Rosenberg claims, celebrates the "life-renewing, primal creative substance of the world," and figures as such in the very emblem of the Nazi party, the swastika.[82] Atlantis can thus truly be called the foundational myth of Nazism, "the myth of myths," in Lacoue-Labarthe and Nancy's words, that enabled the Aryans to replace the Jews as the chosen people of universal history.[83]

Atlantis was also a myth that encouraged the Nazis in their genocidal projects. In the nineteenth century, anti-Semitic discourses had generally been based on a *hierarchy* of races, with the Aryan race destined to master all others. In this vision, lower races were not destined to be annihilated, but rather enslaved, since a hierarchy requires more than one race. Although the

Nazi final solution can be viewed as a radical extension of nineteenth-century anti-Semitism, it is more plausible that the concept of racial elimination stemmed from Ariosophic theories about a mythical Atlanto-Aryan race.[84] Indeed, the horrors of the Holocaust may lead us to overlook the fact that the extermination of the Jews was part of a vaster racial project whose ultimate goal was the creation of a new superior race. This other half of the Nazi racial fantasy expressed itself with particular cruelty in the eugenic experiments performed in SS laboratories, but was also evident at the highest level of the Nazi party: certain SS officers apparently mutilated themselves in order to achieve biological transfiguration.[85] Nazi attempts to obtain greater psychic powers also reflected contemporary ideas about the Atlanteans, who, according to Rudolf Steiner, possessed "magical, psychic forces."[86] The joint pursuit of creating a race of the future and of destroying a race identified with the past thus betrays a distinctly theosophical vision of racial "evolution," which went well beyond the pseudo-scientific theories of racial purity.

Whether or not Nazi ideology can indeed be summarized as a program for "the eternal return to the continent of Hyperborea," as Angebert suggested,[87] it certainly derived a large degree of its ideological justification, as well as perhaps some of its most vicious ideas, from the myth of an ancient Germanic homeland in the North. The Nazis obtained this myth directly from Madame Blavatsky, whose sinister frauds have long been documented, yet Bailly's own role in this genealogy cannot be passed over. While the myth of Atlantis might have become a late nineteenth-century craze without him, he was nonetheless responsible for designing a Eurocentric Atlantis-model that transferred all the accomplishments of non-Western civilizations onto a white Northern people. Such an interpretation freed Europeans from even paying so much as lip service to the value of other cultures: either the Other in question was simply worthless, as with Judaism, or was a product of Aryan genius, but there was no alternative. Bailly's Atlantis thesis may not have been overtly anti-Semitic (even if his ready agreement with Voltaire suggests an affinity of views on Jews as well), but its ultimate incorporation into Nazi ideology exemplifies how the eighteenth-century myths that informed totalitarianism were less the alleged "myths" of Enlightenment knowledge, than the full-blown mythical narratives about the origins of the Atlantic world.

NOTES

This paper was first presented at the 2004 Boston ASECS conference on a panel entitled "Beyond Orientalism." For its revised version, I am indebted to discussions with the panel's organizer, Alexis Tadié, as well as with the other participants. I would also like to express my gratitude toward the two anonymous reviewers of this essay, who provided very helpful and encouraging criticism, and to the editor of this volume, Jeffrey Ravel.

1. The inadequacy of Said's model for the Enlightenment has been noted by a number of scholars: see for instance J. J. Clarke, *Oriental Enlightenment: The Encounter between Asian and Western Thought* (London: Routledge, 1997), 16–34, and Madeleine Dobie, *Foreign Bodies: Gender, Language, and Culture in French Orientalism* (Stanford: Stanford University Press, 2001), 12–24 and 134. For a review of the controversies provoked by Said's thesis, see A. L. Macfie, *Orientalism* (London: Longman, 2002), 102–47; Fred Dallmayr, *Beyond Orientalism: Essays in Cross-Cultural Encounter* (Albany: SUNY Press, 1996); and Richard King, *Orientalism and Religion: Postcolonial Theory, India and 'The Mystic East'* (London: Routledge, 1999), 82–95. A number of critics have focused on Said's use of the Foucauldian concept of "discourse" (expertly glossed, of course, by Said himself in *Beginnings: Intention and Method* [New York: Columbia University Press, 1975]): see in particular Dennis Porter, "*Orientalism* and its Problems," in *Colonial Discourse and Post-Colonial Theory*, Patrick Williams and Laura Chrisman, eds. (New York: Columbia University Press, 1994); I thank Dorian Bell for this reference. It is also helpful to recall the epistemological gray zones that scholars have identified in Foucault's own definition: see for instance Manfred Frank, "On Foucault's Concept of Discourse," in *Michel Foucault Philosopher*, T. J. Armstrong., trans. (London: Harvester Wheatsheaf, 1992).

2. The East India Company first assumed overt political rule in India in 1765, when it was granted the *diwani* of Bengal, but it was only with the 1784 India Act that the British crown truly became a colonial power in the Asian subcontinent: see Zaheer Baber, *The Science of Empire: Scientific Knowledge, Civilization, and Colonial Rule in India* (Albany: SUNY Press, 1996).

3. Rodinson's *mot* is quoted in Clarke, *Oriental Enlightenment*, 26.

4. *Foreign Bodies*, 21, my italics.

5. For a cultural history of French colonialism, see Raoul Girardet, *L'Idée coloniale en France de 1871 à 1962* (Paris: Hachette, 1972).

6. On the genuine sense of curiosity underpinning sixteenth- and seventeenth-century studies and explorations of the Orient, see Amy Glassner Gordon, "*Autres Mondes, Autres Mœurs*: French Attitudes Towards the Cultures Revealed by the Discoveries," in *Asia and the West: Encounters and Exchanges From the Age of Explorations*, Cyriac K. Pullapilly and Edwin J. Van Kley, eds. (Notre Dame, Ind.: Cross Cultural Publications, 1986).

7. For other French anti-colonial indictments in the eighteenth century, see letter 121 of Montesquieu's *Lettres Persanes* (1721; rpt. edn., Paris: Folio, 2003), Abraham-Hyacinthe Anquetil-Duperron, *Voyage en Inde, 1754–1762: Relation de voyage et préliminaire à la traduction du Zend-Avesta* (1771; rpt. edn., Paris: Ecole française d'Extrême-Orient, 1997), and the abbé Raynal, *Histoire philosophique et politique des établissemens et du commerce des Européens dans les deux Indes* (Amsterdam: n.p., 1770). For a recent study of eighteenth-century European anti-imperialism, see Sankar Muthu, *Enlightenment Against Empire* (Princeton: Princeton University Press, 2003).

8. *La Renaissance orientale* (Paris: Payot, 1950), 152–55.

9. See in particular Léon Poliakov, *The Aryan Myth: A History of Racist and Nationalist Ideas in Europe,* Edmund Howard, trans. (London: Sussex University Press, 1974), 155–82, and Dobie, *Foreign Bodies.* It is noteworthy that Said held Schwab's work in high opinion: see his "Foreword" to the English translation, *The Oriental Renaissance: Europe's Rediscovery of India and the East, 1680–1880,* Gene Patterson-Black and Victor Reinking, trans. (New York: Columbia University Press, 1984).

10. See *Le Mythe nazi* (La Tour d'Aigues: Editions de l'Aube, 1991), or for an abridged English version, "The Fiction of the Political," in Lacoue-Labarthe, *Heidegger, Art, and Politics: The Fiction of the Political,* Chris Turner, trans. (Oxford: Blackwell, 1990).

11. There was, to be sure, a wide array of anthropological theories in the eighteenth century, ranging from Montesquieu's environmentalist "climate theory," outlined in book 14 of *De l'esprit des lois* (1748; rpt. edn., 2 vols., Paris: Garnier, 1973), to the traditionalist "lost revelation theory," found notably in Joseph-François Lafitau, *Mœurs des sauvages ameriquains, comparées aux mœurs des premiers temps* (Paris: Saugrain l'aîné, 1724). But as Orientalism, particularly in its early stages, focused on the spatial and temporal diffusion of culture from an original locus, these theories played a much less prominent role in Orientalist studies. For a general overview of the currents in Enlightenment anthropology, see Michèle Duchet, *Anthropologie et histoire au siècle des Lumières* (1971; rpt. edn., Paris: Albin Michel, 1995) and Marvin Harris, *The Rise of Anthropological Theory: A History of Theories of Culture* (New York: Crowell, 1968), 8–52. For a survey of eighteenth-century representations of primitive society, see *Primitivisme et mythes des origines dans la France des Lumières, 1680–1820,* Chantal Grell and Christian Michel, eds. (Paris: Presses de l'Université de Paris-Sorbonne, 1989). The final chapter of Margaret Hogden's *Early Anthropology in the Sixteenth and Seventeenth Centuries* (Philadelphia: University of Pennsylvania Press, 1964) offers illuminating perspectives on the historicist current that grew increasingly powerful throughout the eighteenth century.

12. On the complex publishing history of the *Essai*, see René Pomeau's "Introduction," in *Essai sur les mœurs et l'esprit des nations*, 2 vols. (Paris: Bordas, 1990). All subsequent page references for the *Essai* are to this edition. On the place of Judaism in Voltaire's philosophy of history, see Bertram Schwarzbach, "Voltaire et ses inversions des 'mythes des origines' juives par une haute critique biblique," in Grell, *Primitivisme et mythes des origines*.

13. *Examen important de milord Bolingbroke,* in *Œuvres complètes de Voltaire / Complete works of Voltaire*, Ulla Kölving, ed., 85 vols. (Geneva: Voltaire Foundation, 1968–), 62: 190. See also the chapter in the *Essai sur les mœurs* entitled, "Si les Juifs ont enseigné les autres nations, ou s'ils ont été enseignés par elles" (1:177–80), that leaves no doubt as to which hypothesis Voltaire favors.

14. See notably the discussions of universal chronology in *La Princesse de Babylone*, 506–7, and *Les Lettres d'Amabed*, 540; page references for Voltaire's fictional works are to *Romans et contes* (Paris: Garnier Flammarion, 1966). Voltaire's anti-Semitism is also prevalent in the *Contes*: in *Les Oreilles du comte de Chesterfield*, for instance, mention is made of "la misérable petite nation juive, grossière *imitatrice* de tous ses voisins" (683, my italics); and elsewhere Voltaire refers to "ces animaux féroces appelés *Juifs*" (*Histoire de Jenni*, 650). On Voltaire's anti-Semitism, see Peter Gay, *The Party of Humanity: Essays in the French Enlightenment* (New York: Knopf, 1971), 97–108. Ronald Schechter takes a more nuanced view in his *Obstinate Hebrews: Representations of Jews in France, 1715–1815* (Berkeley: University of California Press, 2003), concluding that, "Ultimately Voltaire gave a contradictory account of the Jews" (53).

15. "Diffusionism" is the name given to a number of related anthropological theories in vogue in the early-twentieth century. On its history and different meanings, see Harris, *Rise of Anthropological Theory*, 373–92. As Margaret Hogden points out, however, diffusionism dates back, if not in name, then at least in concept, to the Middle Ages, where it can be found in the Christian notion that cultural diversity results from the corruption of an original Adamic state (*Early Anthropology*, 269).

16. This form of radical diffusionism would become known as "heliocentrism," in reference to the hypothesis of Sir Grafton Elliot Smith and William J. Perry, that Egyptian civilization (with its worship of the sun) lay at the source of all cultures.

17. Voltaire placed two limits to this theory. First, he acknowledged that humans could add to this cultural foundation through discoveries of their own (see in particular the speech, echoing Voltaire's own *Lettres philosophiques*, by the English Milord *Whatthen* in *La Princesse de Babylone*: "Nous avons arraché plus de secrets à la nature dans l'espace de cent années que le genre humain n'en avait découvert dans la multitude des siècles," 489). Second, he limited this theory to *human* institutions: in an even more radical form (corresponding in fact to Biblical Scripture), it could extend to plants and animals as well. The wise Phoenix in *La Princesse de Babylone* denounces this version in a proto-Darwinian passage: "Je ne puis croire que les renards d'Albion, les marmottes des Alpes, et les loups de la Gaule, viennent de mon pays [Gangarides]; de même je ne crois pas que les sapins et les chênes de vos contrées descendent des palmiers et des cocotiers des Indes" (506). On the racial (and racist) implications of this line of thought, see the following note.

18. Voltaire, for instance, extended his proto-Darwinism to human races as well: "Plus je réfléchis sur la couleur de ces peuples, sur le glossement dont ils se servent pour se faire entendre. . . plus je suis convaincu que cette race [africaine] ne peut avoir la même origine que nous" (*Les Lettres d'Amabed, etc.*, 537). On Voltaire's polygenetic beliefs, see Poliakov, *Aryan Myth*, 175–76.

19. In Bailly, *Lettres sur l'origine des sciences et sur celle des peuples d'Asie. Adressées à M. de Voltaire par M. Bailly & précédées de quelques lettres de M. de Voltaire à l'Auteur* (Paris: Debure, 1777), 4. The same idea is expressed in his *Essai sur les mœurs*: "portez votre vue sur l'Orient, berceau de tous les arts, et qui a tout donné à l'Occident," 1: 197, and in *La Princesse de Babylone*, where the "Gangarides" are described as the primal, but not primitive, culture.

20. *Essai sur les mœurs*, 1: 232.

21. Poliakov, *Aryan Myth*, 188. In the two decades before the French Revolution, however, Egypt would briefly regain the upper hand in the contest for the Ur-civilization, as can be seen in the works of Court de Gébelin, Charles Dupuis, and Nicolas de Bonneville. But with the steady flow of Sanskrit translations into Western Europe, the Indian hypothesis soon retook center stage.

22. This last point is not entirely clear in Plato: see L. Sprague de Camp, *Lost Continents: The Atlantis Theme in History, Science, and Literature* (New York: Dover, 1970), 41. For those, however, who championed the heliocentric version of diffusionism, it was definitely a prime attribute of Atlantis, as the above quote by Voltaire ("tout nous vient des bords du Gange") illustrates. In the nineteenth century, this originality remained a defining feature: see for instance Ignatius Donnelly, *Atlantis: The Antediluvian World* (1882; rpt. edn., New York: Dover, 1976), for whom it constitutes one of his initial theses concerning Atlantis.

23. *New Atlantis* (1626; rpt. edn., in *Ideal Commonwealths*, Henry Morley, ed. [New York: Colonial Press, 1901]), 19.

24. In Antiquity, Atlantis had traditionally been situated beyond the Herculean pillars (i.e., the Strait of Gibraltar) in the *Atlantic* Ocean. For this reason, when the New World was discovered, there was a strong tendency in Atlantis research to identify America as this lost island (see de Camp, *Lost Continents*, 28). Hence, Bacon places his New Atlantis in America, just as Voltaire's El Dorado is in South America (albeit for other mythological reasons as well). Bacon's text also fascinated Condorcet, who left a *Fragment sur l'Atlantide, ou efforts combinés de l'espèce humaine pour le progrès des sciences*, outlining his plans for a revamped academy of sciences—plans which would later provide the blueprint for the Institut National. See Keith Baker, *Condorcet: From Natural Philosophy to Social Mathematics* (Chicago: University of Chicago Press, 1975) and Roger Hahn, *The Anatomy of a Scientific Institution: The Paris Academy of Sciences, 1666–1803* (Berkeley: University of California Press, 1971), 286–312.

25. I am using "naturalized" here in the sense defined by Barthes in *Mythologies* (1957; Annette Lavers, trans., New York: Hill and Wang, 1984), that is, to present a cultural representation as a natural fact (129). This naturalization is also evident in Delisle de Sales: "il est impossible d'avoir des doutes raisonnables sur l'existence de l'Atlantide," *Histoire philosophique du monde primitif*, 7 vols. (Paris: n.p., 1793), 6: 159.

26. "Hérodote et l'Atlantide," *Quaderni di Storia* 16 (1982): 32. While I wholeheartedly agree with Vidal-Naquet's interpretation, we will see that for Bailly the Atlantis myth served less to address theological concerns (regarding a "chosen people"), than biological, racial, and cultural ones. For two other recent histories of Atlantis

interpretations that complement de Camp's *Lost Continents* and Vidal-Naquet's articles, see Richard Ellis, *Imagining Atlantis* (New York: Knopf, 1998) and Chantal Foucrier, *Le Mythe littéraire de l'Atlantide (1800–1939)* (Grenoble: ELLUG, 2004).

27. An exhaustive study of Jean-Sylvain Bailly's work and turbulent life can be found in Edwin B. Smith, "Jean-Sylvain Bailly: Astronomer, Mystic, Revolutionary, 1736–1793," *Transactions of the American Philosophical Society* 44 (1954): 425–538. On Bailly's Atlantis research, see Chantal Grell, *L'Histoire entre érudition et philosophie: étude sur la connaissance historique à l'âge des Lumières* (Paris: PUF, 1993), 116–20. The full bibliographical references for the two Bailly texts not yet cited are: *Histoire de l'astronomie ancienne, depuis son origine jusqu'à l'établissement de l'école d'Alexandrie* (Paris: Debure, 1775) and *Lettres sur l'Atlantide de Platon et sur l'ancienne Histoire de l'Asie* (1779; rpt. edn., Paris: Debure, 1805).

28. For the early-modern history of this Roman conceit, see Hogden, *Early Anthropology*, 462. She also draws attention to the progressive epistemological movement "from hierarchy to history" in eighteenth-century social and natural historiography.

29. *Histoire de l'astronomie ancienne*, 3.

30. *Histoire de l'astronomie ancienne*, 7.

31. *Lettres sur l'origine des sciences*, 205.

32. *Lettres sur l'origine des sciences*, 194, my italics.

33. *Lettres sur l'Atlantide*, 4.

34. *Essai sur les mœurs*, 1: 18. For an overview of eighteenth-century theories about mythology, see Frank Manuel, *The Eighteenth Century Confronts the Gods* (Cambridge: Harvard University Press, 1959); *The Rise of Modern Mythology, 1680–1860*, Burton Feldman and Robert Richardson, eds. (Bloomington: Indiana University Press, 2000); Jean Deshayes, "De l'abbé Pluche au citoyen Dupuis: à la recherche de la clef des fables," *Studies on Voltaire and the Eighteenth Century* 24 (1963): 457–86; Jean Starobinski, "Le mythe au XVIIIe siècle," *Critique* 366 (1977): 975–97; and Grell, *L'Histoire entre érudition et philosophie*, 111–22.

35. On Court's life and work, see Anne-Marie Mercier-Faivre, *Un Supplément à l'"Encyclopédie:" Le "Monde Primitif" d'Antoine Court de Gébelin* (Paris: Champion, 1999); see also Grell, *Histoire entre érudition et philosophie*, 116–20.

36. *Monde Primitif, analysé et comparé avec le monde moderne, considéré dans son génie allégorique et dans les allégories auxquelles conduisit ce génie . . .* 9 vols. (Paris: Chez l'auteur, 1773–82), 1: 68.

37. This hypothesis was not entirely new, having already been suggested by Macrobius in book 1 of the *Saturnalia*, and revived by Noël-Antoine Pluche, in his *Histoire du ciel où l'on recherche l'origine de l'idolâtrie et les méprises de la philosophie. . .* 2 vols. (Paris: Vve Estienne, 1740). In Court's case, however, it is more likely that it was derived from the Masonic use of solar and lunar symbols (as evidenced, for instance, in *The Magic Flute*). On Court's Masonic ties, see Charles Porset, *Les Philalèthes et les convents de Paris: une politique de la folie* (Paris: Champion, 1996), 263 n 13, and Mercier-Faivre, *Supplément à l'"Encyclopédie."*

38. *Lettres sur l'Atlantide*, 115. Bailly would later express reservations with Court's astronomic system, in his posthumous *Essai sur les fables, et sur leur histoire*, 2 vols. (Paris: Debure, An VII [1798]); this text is presented as a series of letters, all dated 1782. Bailly falls back here on Nicolas Freret's belief in mythology's multiple origins: "Je ne puis croire que tous les secrets de l'antiquité soient renfermés sous une clef [. . .] les fables doivent avoir plusieurs sources," 32. For Freret's theory, see the *Encyclopédie* article on "mythologie," signed by Jaucourt, who lifted it from a *Mémoire* Freret had presented at the *Académie des inscriptions et des belles-lettres* (see Feldman, *Rise of Modern Mythology*, 94).

39. *Lettres sur l'origine des sciences*, 103; see also 95.

40. Rudbeck's thesis was proposed in *Atlantica*. On the resemblances between Rudbeck's and Bailly's theories, see Pierre Vidal-Naquet, "L'Atlantide et les nations," in *Représentations de l'origine* (Ste-Clotilde: Presses de l'Université de la Réunion, 1988), 16–18, and de Camp, who claims that "Rudbeck's work incited the French astronomer Bailly . . . to compose an even more extreme origin for Atlantis" (*Lost Continents*, 178).

41. To this tradition, one can add Francis Gilford, a contributor to Jones's *Asiatic Researches*, who attempted to prove that Britain was the lost Atlantis (or the Hindi "White Isles"), on the basis of Sanskrit documents that his suppliers had forged: see Joscelyn Godwin, *The Theosophical Enlightenment* (Albany: SUNY Press, 1994), 17.

42. As one of the anonymous reviewers of this essay rightly pointed out, Bailly was in this respect repeating the commonplace practice of characterizing attractive exotic Others as biologically white. Voltaire commonly resorted to this practice, notably in *L'Ingénu* and in *La Princesse de Babylone*, where Amazan, the noble Gangarides shepherd, is described as having "[de] longs cheveux *blonds*," 452, my italics.

43. See the *Lettres sur l'origine des sciences*, 207.

44. *Lettres sur l'origine des sciences*, 225.

45. The political and philosophical value of this North/South opposition had been stressed by Montesquieu, notably in *De l'esprit des lois*; tellingly, however, Montesquieu distinguished between a European North and an Asian North (see for instance 299–300 [book 17, chapter 5]). It took the idea of a polar North, i.e., the Hyperborean Atlantis, to unify the North into a single geographical-racial entity.

46. *Des époques de la nature* (Paris: Imprimerie Royale, 1778), 232. As Edwin Smith notes, Bailly distances himself in the *Lettres sur l'Atlantide* from earlier claims that the Atlanteans had developed a sophisticated civilization while still in Hyperborea, and suggests instead that they developed their flourishing civilization after having migrated to Asia ("Jean-Sylvain Bailly," 474). It takes Smith's attentive reading, however, to note this argumentative shift, and one wonders if it would have registered with his contemporary audience.

47. *Histoire philosophique*, 6: 160. Delisle had already written about Atlantis in the first volumes of his *Histoire nouvelle de tous les peuples* (Paris: n.p., 1779–85). It should be noted that in 1793, Bailly was a persona non grata, awaiting execution by the Terrorist government for having authorized, as mayor of Paris, the 1791 Champ de

Mars massacre. On Bailly's important role during the French Revolution (he notably presided over the Jeu de Paume oath), see Edwin Smith, "Jean-Sylvain Bailly."

48. The online version of *The Secret Doctrine: The Synthesis of Science, Religion, and Philosophy*, 2 vols., (London: Theosophical Publishing Society, 1888) has the enormous benefit of containing a thorough index; it can be found at http://www.theosociety.org/pasadena/sd/sd-hp.htm [2005, March 20]. For a study of Blavatsky's Orientalist sources, see Denis Vidal, "Max Müller and the Theosophists," in *Orientalism and Anthropology: From Max Müller to Louis Dumont* (Pondicherry: Institut français de Pondichéry, 1997); on her racial theories, see Peter Washington, *Madame Blavatsky's Baboon: A History of the Mystics, Mediums, and Misfits Who Brought Spiritualism to America* (New York: Schocken Books, 1995). Bailly's thesis also lived on in William Fairfield Warren (a president of Boston University), *Paradise Found: The Cradle of the Human Race at the North Pole; A Study of the Prehistoric World* (Boston: Houghton, Mifflin And Co., 1885).

49. On the geographical implications of theosophy, see Sumathi Ramaswamy, "Catastrophic Catastrophes: Mapping the Lost Continent of Lemuria," *Representations* 67 (1999): 92–129. Lemuria was another "lost continent" in theosophy, generally placed in the Indian Ocean: see for instance K. Browning, *Lemuria and Atlantis: Two Lost Continents* (1924).

50. *The Secret Doctrine* is nothing if not confusing: Blavatsky distinguishes between Hyperborea (land of the second root-race), Lemuria (land of the third), and Atlantis (land of the fourth), but nonetheless calls the latter "Hyperborean Atlantis" (2: 770 n). It would appear that the initial Hyperborea broke up, and that Lemuria and Atlantis were formed out of its fragments. Complicating matters further, however, she describes the Hyperboreans as a sub-race of the Atlanteans (2: 774).

51. See notably *Secret Doctrine*, 2: 742. She also borrows Bailly's explanation for how life near the pole could be possible: "The secret books inform us that *the climate has changed in those regions more than once* since the first men inhabited those now almost inaccessible latitudes. They were a paradise before they became hell" (2: 773, her italics).

52. *Secret Doctrine*, 2: 768. Donnelly had already claimed that Atlantis was the homeland of the Aryans (*Atlantis*, 2).

53. *Secret Doctrine*, 2: 436 and 1: 425.

54. *Secret Doctrine*, 2: 471 n.

55. *Secret Doctrine*, 2: 469–70.

56. *Secret Doctrine*, 1: 383.

57. *Secret Doctrine*, 2: 470–71.

58. See Poliakov, *Aryan Myth*; see also George L. Mosse, *Toward the Final Solution: A History of European Racism* (Madison: University of Wisconsin Press, 1978).

59. See for instance *Secret Doctrine*, 2: 384.

60. This new historical paradigm is explicitly expressed in Alfred Rosenberg's *The Myth of the Twentieth Century* (Munich, 1930; Vivian Bird, trans., Torrance, CA: Noontide Press, 1982). In his introduction, he writes that, "[h]istory and the task of the future no longer signify the struggle of class against class or the conflict between

one church dogma and another, but the settlement between blood and blood, race and race, people and people" (xlix). In a more occult vein, this opposition was also central to Lanz von Lebenfels's doctrine of "Theozoology," where the Aryan/non-Aryan (primarily Semitic) struggle becomes a cosmological, Manichean battle between good and evil: see Nicolas Goodrick-Clarke, *The Occult Roots of Nazism: Secret Aryan Cults and Their Influence on Nazi Ideology* (New York: New York University Press, 1985), 91. Lanz's relation to Nazism will be discussed below.

61. The early twentieth century saw a flurry of works on Atlantis, not all of which adopted Blavatsky's racial or geographical conclusions: see for instance Pierre Benoît's novel *L'Atlantide* (Paris: Albin Michel, 1919), which places the lost continent in the Atlas mountains; Leo Frobenius's ethnographic works, most notably *Atlantis: Volksmärchen und Volksdichtungen Afrikas*, 12 vols. (Jena: Diederichs, 1921–28), which argues that the Yoruba people are the descendants of the Atlanteans; as well as Antonin Artaud, *Les Tarahumaras* (1936–47; rpt. edn., Paris: Folio, 1971), in which Artaud claims to have witnessed "au fond de la Sierra Tarahumara, le rite des rois de l'Atlantide tel que Platon le décrit" (93).

62. "Ultima Thule," as Seneca called it (in *Medea*), was considered in Antiquity to be the northernmost extremity of the world, home to the Hyperboreans. Wirth's major work was *Der Aufgang der Menschheit: Untersuchung zur Geschichte der Religion, Symbolik, und Schrift der Atlantisch-nordischen Rasse*, 2 vols. (Jena: Diederich 1928–34). He fell out with Himmler and Rosenberg with the onset of WWII. On Wirth, see de Camp, *Lost Continents*, 86, and Elizabeth Tumasonis, "Bernhard Hoetger's Tree of Life: German Expressionism and Racial Ideology," *Art Journal* 51 (1992): 85.

63. On Hörbiger, see de Camp, *Lost Continents*, 86–7, who mistakenly claims that the Nazis rejected the *Welteislehre*; on its role in Nazi ideology, see Dusty Sklar, *Gods and Beasts: The Nazis and the Occult* (New York: Crowell, 1977), 75, and Gerald Suster, *Hitler: The Occult Messiah* (New York: St. Martin's Press, 1981), 167. As with many books on Nazi occultism, these two should be consulted with skepticism, as they list few sources for their material. Their claims concerning the Nazi fascination with Hörbiger, however, are substantiated by Hitler himself: "I'm quite well inclined to accept the cosmic theories of Hörbiger," *Hitler's Secret Conversations, 1941–44*, Norman Cameron and R.H. Stevens, trans., (New York: Signet Books, 1953), 204.

64. See Goodrick-Clarke, *Occult Roots of Nazism*, 102 (and for Guido von List, 53). Lanz's anti-Semitic journal *Ostara*, which Hitler most likely read in Vienna, regularly portrayed in comic-book fashion battles between ape-like Jews and Aryan knights. For a list of other pro- or proto-Nazi authors who relocated Atlantis in the far north, see Goodrick-Clarke, *Black Sun: Aryan Cults, Esoteric Nazism and the Politics of Identity* (New York: New York University Press, 2002).

65. For the Voltaire quote, see Bailly, *Lettres sur l'origine*, 6. The equivalency between these two myths was recognized by Bailly's Romantic close-contemporaries: Blake, for instance, refers to Atlantis as "the Golden World" (in *America*, plate 10, l.7), and Novalis similarly amalgamates the two in *Heinrich von Ofterdingen* (at the end of chapter 4).

66. Hannah Arendt famously drew attention to the power of the Golden Age myth in *On Revolution* (New York: Compass Books, 1965). See also Mona Ozouf, *Festivals and the French Revolution*, Alan Sheridan, trans. (Cambridge: Harvard University Press, 1988), 274. Robespierre's forging of a political mythology based on the Golden Age myth was the subject of my dissertation, *Restoring the Golden Age: Mythology in Revolutionary Ideologies and Culture* (Ph.D. diss, University of Pennsylvania, 2004).

67. See Raoul Girardet, *Mythes et mythologies politiques* (Paris: Seuil, 1986), 97–138, although I would take issue with his Jungian interpretation of myth.

68. This quote first appeared at the end of *De la réorganisation de la société européenne* (Paris: Égron, 1814), 112; it later became the slogan of the Saint-Simonian journal, *Le Producteur.* As Frank Manuel points out (in *The New World of Henri Saint-Simon* [Cambridge: Harvard University Press, 1956], 124), Saint-Simon exhibited a great familiarity with Bacon's *New Atlantis* in his own project for a scientific utopia: see his *Lettres d'un citoyen de Genève* (n.p. [Paris], n.d. [1803]), which call for the creation of a "conseil de Newton," 4.

69. *L'appareil pour l'analyse chimique du dernier soupir*, in *Œuvres complètes,* Alan Raitt and Pierre-Georges Castex, eds., 2 vols. (Paris: Pléiade, 1986), 1: 668.

70. Already in Etienne Cabet's Golden Age of Icaria, there were more factories than in Britain: see *Voyage et aventures de Lord William Carisdall en Icarie* (Paris: H. Souverain, 1840), 2. His narrative lists a number of other Atlantean features: "nulle part on ne voit autant d'*immenses machines*; on y *voyage en ballons*, et les *fêtes aériennes* qui s'y donnent effacent la magnificence des fêtes terrestres les plus brillants," 4, my italics.

71. See Goodrick-Clarke, *Occult Roots of Nazism*, 133.

72. Particularly among the more popular sources for Nazism's occult origins: see Louis Pauwels and Jacques Bergier's best seller, *The Morning of the Magicians*, Rollo Myers, trans. (New York: Stein and Day, 1963), or Jean-Michel Angebert's *The Occult and the Third Reich: The Mystical Origins of Nazism and the Search for the Holy Grail*, Lewis A. M. Sumberg, trans. (New York: MacMillan, 1974), as well as Sklar, *Gods and Beasts*, and Suster, *Hitler*. But these authors rely heavily on Sebottendorff's own account of his involvement (related in *Bevor Hitler Kam* [Munich: Grassinger, 1933]), which Reginald Phelps has shown to be only tangentially true, at best: see "'Before Hitler Came:' Thule Society and Germanen Order," *Journal of Modern History* 35 (1963): 245–61. Aside from Phelp's article, the best scholarly account I have found of Sebottendorff's activities is Goodrick-Clarke, *Occult Roots of Nazism*, 135–152.

73. George Franz, "Munich: Birthplace and Center of the National Socialist German Workers' Party," *The Journal of Modern History* 29 (1957): 326.

74. Such as the *Münchener Beobachter und Sportblatt*, a newspaper owned by Sebottendorff, and which soon became an official mouthpiece of the Nazi party (under the new name, *Völkischer Beobachter*). Phelps calls attention to the ideological similarities between this paper's editorial agenda and the Nazi party platform: "On May 31 [1919], the paper announced a *völkisch*, anticapitalist antisemitic program of

twelve points, resembling considerably the twenty-five points of the NSDAP proclaimed by Hitler in February 1920" ("'Before Hitler Came,'" 255).

75. *Hitler: 1889–1936, Hubris* (New York: Norton, 1998), 138–39.

76. See Goodrich-Clarke, *Occult Roots of Nazism*, 151. The swastika also figured in the Thule society's heraldic device, but it was an extremely common symbol in theosophical circles. On Drexler's ties to Thule, see Franz, "Munich," 28. It is not surprising that the memberships for these two groups would by and large have been different, as they targeted different social circles. The Thule society had a relatively upper class, even aristocratic membership: one of its members was a Prince of Thurn und Taxis, who was among the seven hostages murdered by the Reds during the counter-revolution in April 1919. This event, which shocked the world at the time, is largely credited with having fueled the extreme-right trend in Munich. It also precipitated Sebottendorff's departure from the Thule society.

77. The conclusion of *Mein Kampf* pays great homage to Eckart; Hitler's book was in large part dictated to Hess. On Rosenberg, see below. The likelihood of such conversations is all the greater because Hitler was undoubtedly acquainted with Lanz von Liebenfels's Ariosophic theories while in Vienna; not only does solid historical evidence point in this direction (see Goodrick-Clarke, *Occult Roots of Nazism*, 194–96), but Hitler himself claimed to have acquired his anti-Semitic views at that time: see the second chapter of *Mein Kampf* (1925; Ralph Manheim, trans., New York: Houghton, 1971).

78. Although in public Hitler often denounced those who "know National Socialism only from hearsay and therefore [. . .] begin their thematic research with some mythical Atlantean civilization" (Tumasonis, "Bernhard Hoetger's Tree of Life," 89), his table talk reveals a keen interest in these selfsame inquiries. On one occasion, Hitler spoke of the "Greek legend [in which] there is a civilisation known as 'pre-lunar,' and we can see in the legend an allusion to the empire of the lands of Atlantis that sank into the ocean" (*Hitler's Secret Conversations*, 67). Elsewhere, he added that,

> Legend cannot be extracted from the void [. . .] Nothing prevents us from supposing—and I believe, even, that *it would be to our interest to do so*—that mythology is a reflection of things that have existed and of which humanity has retained a vague memory. In all human traditions, whether oral or written, one finds mention of a huge cosmic disaster [. . .] In my view, the thing is explicable only by the hypothesis of a disaster that completely destroyed a humanity which already possessed a high degree of civilisation (203-4, my italics).

This highly sophisticated Ur-civilization, as we shall see, was the same Nordic Atlantis that Rosenberg praises in *The Myth of the Twentieth Century.* For more examples of Hitler's private/public contradictions regarding the mythological elements in Nazi ideology, see Tumasonis, "Bernhard Hoetger's Tree of Life." Jackson Spielvogel and David Redles's article, "Hitler's Racial Ideology: Content and Occult Sources," *Simon Wiesenthal Annual* 3 (1986), was published online at http://motlc.wiesenthal.com/resources/books/annual3/chap09.html [consulted 20 March 2005].

79. For a balanced study of Rosenberg's relations with Hitler, see Robert Cecil, *The Myth of the Master Race: Alfred Rosenberg and Nazi Ideology* (New York: Dodd, Mead & Co., 1972), 30–34. Cecil notes that Rosenberg was generally considered Hitler's *éminence grise* until the latter's imprisonment in 1925 (45). Although Rosenberg's star would fade with the rise of other Nazi luminaries such as Josef Goebbels, he remained among the top echelons of the Nazi party until the bitter end, and was one of the few Nazi leaders executed at Nuremberg. On Rosenberg's conception of "myth," see Lacoue-Labarthe and Nancy, *Mythe nazi*.

80. *Myth of the Twentieth Century*, 4, my italics.

81. *Myth of the Twentieth Century*, 7, and for the preceding quote, 4.

82. *Myth of the Twentieth Century*, 5 and 435.

83. *Mythe nazi*, 57.

84. Lanz von Liebenfels openly spoke about the need to "liquidate" the Jews: see Jackson Spielvogel and David Redles, "Hitler's Racial Ideology." In *Toward the Final Solution*, George Mosse argues in favor of the opposite hypothesis, namely that the Holocaust was only the logical conclusion of nineteenth-century anti-Semitism, an interpretation which I find overly teleological. Ernst Cassirer examines the connection between Gobineau's racial theories and Nazi "political myth" in *The Myth of the State* (1946; rpt. edn. New Haven: Yale University Press, 1974).

85. Jean-Michel Angebert [the conjoined penname Jean Angelini and Michel Bertrand] recounts how the "Knights of Poseidon," an SS unit, experimented with castration and "plasticizing of the thoracic cavity" to obtain superhuman powers (*Occult and the Third Reich*, 265 n 9). Unfortunately, he/they do(es) not back this claim up with any sources. If this anecdote is true, however, it would shed light on the "mytho-logic" behind Nazi experiments: according to Plato, Atlantis was the land Poseidon received when the gods divided up the earth (*Critias*, 113 c). Blavatsky also made Poseidon the tutelary god of the Atlanteans, and by extension, of the Aryans: "Though Zeus reigns over the Fourth Race, it is Poseidon who rules, and who is the true key to the triad of the Kronid Brothers and to our *human* races. Poseidon and Nereus *are one*: the former the ruler or spirit of Atlantis before the beginning of its submersion, the latter, after. Neptune is the titanic strength of the *living* race; Nereus, its spirit reincarnated in the subsequent Fifth or Aryan Race" (*Secret Doctrine*, 2: 766).

86. In *Atlantis: The Fate of a Lost Land and its Secret Knowledge*, Christian von Armin, trans. (Forrest Row: Sophia Books, 2001), 34. This subject is given considerable press in popular accounts of Nazi occultism, but Spielvogel and Redles (among others) have demonstrated how it was indeed a central motif in Hitler's own thought. Himmler's grandiose plans for a future SS state similarly involved the psychic improvement of the Aryan race (see Goodrick-Clarke, *Occults Roots of Nazism*, 203, and in a less scholarly vein, Sklar, *Gods and Beasts*, 84–102). Novels such as Bulwer-Lytton's *The Coming Race* (Edinburgh: n.p., 1871), about an underground Atlantean population that had gained control of the *Vril*, or "life force," or Edmund Kiß's Atlantean novel series (discussed in Goorich-Clarke, *Black Sun*, 131–33) also fed into these occult *Übermensch* fantasies.

87. *Occult and the Third Reich*, 230.

Contributors to Volume 35

Mark Blackwell is Associate Professor of English and Chair of the English Department at the University of Hartford. He has recently published articles on Dryden, Cleland, Radcliffe, and Austen, and his essay on live-tooth transplantation won the 2004-05 Clifford Prize. His article on Burke's *Philosophical Enquiry* will soon appear in *Philological Quarterly*, and he is currently editing a collection of essays entitled *The Secret Life of Things: Animals, Objects, and It-Narratives in Eighteenth-Century England.*

Carol Blum is past President of the American Society for Eighteenth-Century Studies. Her most recent book, *Strength in Numbers, Population, Reproduction and Power in Eighteenth-Century France*, was published by The Johns Hopkins University Press in 2002.

Danielle Bobker is a doctoral candidate in English at Rutgers University, currently completing a dissertation on intimate spaces and the social imagination in eighteenth-century British writing.

Robert G Dimit is Associate Director of the John W. Draper Interdisciplinary Master's Program in Humanities and Social Thought at New York University. He holds a Ph.D. in comparative literature and is the author of "European 'Emotion' before the Invention of Emotions: The Passions of the Mind," forthcoming in *Emotions in Early Modern Europe and Colonial North America*, and several articles on early modern emotion forthcoming in the *Enzyklopädie der Neuzeit* (Stuttgart; Weimar: J.B. Metzler).

Madeleine Dobie is Associate Professor of French and Francophone Studies at Columbia University. She is the author of *Foreign Bodies: Gender, Language and Culture in French Orientalism* (Stanford University Press, 2001), and of articles on eighteenth-century literature, literature and colonialism, and francophone literature. She is currently working on a book titled *Trading Places: Colonialism, Slavery, and Eighteenth-Century French Culture*.

Dianne Dugaw is Professor of English at the University of Oregon. Her books include *'Deep Play': John Gay & the Invention of Modernity* (University of Delaware Press, 2001); *The Anglo-American Ballad*, editor (Garland Publishing, 1995); and *Warrior Women and Popular Balladry, 1650–1850* (Cambridge University Press, 1989; pbk ed., University of Chicago Press, 1996) for which she has recorded a CD, *Dangerous Examples: Fighting & Sailing Women in Song* (cdbaby.com/dugaw). She has written articles on eighteenth–century literature and culture, Anglo-American folklore, and women's and gender studies.

Fraser Easton is Associate Professor of English at the University of Waterloo. His recent publications include "Cosmopolitical Economy: Exchangeable Value and National Development in Adam Smith and Maria Edgeworth" in *Studies in Romanticism* and "Gender's Two Bodies: Women Warriors, Female Husbands, and Plebeian Life" in *Past and Present*. The present article is part of a larger project, supported by a SSHRC Standard Research Grant, on sexual identity and social hierarchy from Defoe to Burney.

Dan Edelstein is Assistant Professor in the Department of French and Italian at Stanford University. He most recently published "Between Myth and History: Michelet, Levi-Strauss, Barthes and the Structural Analysis of Myth" in *Clio*. He is currently working on a book that examines the role of natural right, antiquarianism, and the golden age myth in the politics and culture of the Terror.

Madelyn Gutwirth, Emerita Professor of French and Women's Studies at West Chester University and Former Research Associate at the Alice Paul Research Center for the Study of Women, University of Pennsylvania, is author of *Madame de Staël, Novelist: The Emergence of the Artist as Woman*, (University of Illinois Press,1979) and *The Twilight of the Goddesses: Women and Representation in the French Revolutionary Era* (Rutgers University Press, 1992), and editor, with John P. Spielman and Marcel M. Gutwirth of *Sources et Reflets de l'Histoire de France*, (Oxford University Press, 1972) and, with Avriel H. Goldberger and Karyna Szmurlo, *Germaine de Staël: Crossing the Borders*, (Rutgers University Press, 1991).

Ryan Patrick Hanley is Assistant Professor of Political Science at Marquette University. His research focuses on the history of political thought with a special emphasis on the Scottish Enlightenment, and his recent articles have appeared in the *Review of Politics*, *History of Political Thought*, and the

American Political Science Review. With Robert Wokler he is coeditor of *The Enlightenment: Critical Concepts*, forthcoming from Routledge, and is also currently at work on his first book, *Adam Smith's Apology*.

Katharine Ann Jensen is Associate Professor of French Studies at Louisiana State University. She is author of *Writing Love: Letters, Women, and the Novel in France, 1605–1776* (Southern Illinois University Press, 1995) and co-editor, with Faith E. Beasley, of *Approaches to Teaching Lafayette's* The Princess of Clèves (Modern Language Association Press, 1998). She is currently writing a book, *Ambitious Mothers, Determined Daughters: Subjects in Search of Recognition in Writings by French Women, from Mme. de Sévigné to Colette*. She was co-chair of the ASECS Women's Caucus from 2001–2004.

Ellen Malenas is a doctoral candidate in English literature at the University of Virginia. Her dissertation examines the representation of reform ideologies in the gothic and non-gothic writing of such authors as Horace Walpole, Matthew Lewis, Charlotte Smith, and William Godwin.

Sarah Maza is Jane Long Professor in the Arts and Sciences and Professor of History at Northwestern University and specializes in eighteenth-century French social and cultural history. Her most recent book is *The Myth of the French Bourgeoisie: An Essay on the Social Imaginary 1750–1850* (Harvard University Press, 2003).

Amanda Powell is Senior Instructor of Spanish/Latin American literature and literary translation at the University of Oregon. Her translations of poetry and prose appear in *Untold Sisters: Hispanic Nuns in Their Own Works* (New Mexico, 1989). She has edited and translated *The Answer/ La Respuesta* by Sor Juana Inés de la Cruz (with Electa Arenal; the Feminist Press, 1994); *A Wild Country Out in the Garden: The Spiritual Journals of a Colonial Mexican Nun* (with Kathleen A. Myers; Indiana University Press, 1999); and *Book for the Hour of Recreation*, a "protofeminist" defense of Saint Teresa of Avila by María Salazar (with Alison Weber; University of Chicago, 2002). She has written on sixteenth and seventeenth century Spanish and Colonial Latin American women writers, convent writings, and sapphic lyric.

Vanessa Smith is an ARC Queen Elizabeth II Fellow in the School of English, Art History, Film and Media at the University of Sydney. She is the author of *Literary Culture and the Pacific: Nineteenth-Century Textual Encounters*

(1998) and co-editor of *Exploration and Exchange: A South Seas Anthology 1680–1900* (2000) and *Islands in History and Representation* (2003). She is currently writing a book on friendship and cross-cultural encounter in the long eighteenth century.

Joanna Stalnaker is Assistant Professor of French at Columbia University. She has published articles on Buffon and Mercier, and is currently working on a book on the theory and practice of description during the French Enlightenment. Another article on Mercier, entitled "L'écriture du moi dans *Le Nouveau Paris*," is forthcoming in no. 58 of the *Cahiers de l'Association internationale des études françaises*.

Karyna Szmurlo, Professor of French at Clemson University, has published on eighteenth– and nineteenth–century women writers, the French Revolution, and modern literature. Her research is strongly interdisciplinary, combining history, feminist theory, philosophy of language, and the arts. She is the editor of *The Novel's Seductions: Staël's* Corinne *in Critical Inquiry* (Bucknell University Press, 1999), Staël's bibliographer in *A Critical Bibliography of French Literature*, ed. David Baguley (Syracuse University Press,1993), and coeditor of *Germaine de Staël: Crossing the Borders* (Rutgers University Press, 1991).

Anne C. Vila teaches French at the University of Wisconsin-Madison. She is the author of *Enlightenment and Pathology: Sensibility in the Literature and Medicine of Eighteenth-Century France* (The Johns Hopkins University Press, 1998) and is currently writing a book entitled *Singular Beings: Passions and Pathologies of the Scholar in France, 1700-1840.*

Janet Whatley is Professor of French at the University of Vermont. Her published work includes articles on Marivaux, Diderot, Isabelle de Charrière, and Suzanne Necker, as well as essays on Colette and Marguerite Yourcenar. She has also written on French Renaissance texts of the New World encounters. Her translations include Jean de Léry's *Histoire d'un voyage fait en la terre du Brésil* (University of California Press, 1990) and *There Are No Letters Like Yours: The Correspondence of Isabelle de Charrière and Constant d'Hermenches* (University of Nebraska Press, 2000).

Editorial Readers for Volume Thirty-Five

KATHERINE AASLESTAD / History / West Virginia University
MISTY ANDERSON / English / University of Tennessee
WILDA ANDERSON / French / Johns Hopkins University
HARRIETTE ANDREADIS / English / Texas A&M University
DAVID BAULCH / English / University of West Florida
KATE BENNETT / English / University of Cambridge
ELIZABETH BOHLS / English / University of Oregon
THEODORE BRAUN / French / University of Delaware
GREGORY S. BROWN / History / University of Nevada, Las Vegas
TREVOR BURNARD / American Studies / University of Sussex
KATHRYN BURNS / History / University of North Carolina
DAVID BYWATERS / English / Northern Illinois University
JILL CAMPBELL / English / Yale University
MARK E. CANUEL / English / University of Illinois, Chicago
DANIEL CAREY / English / National University of Ireland, Galway
JILL CASID / Visual Culture / University of Wisconsin-Madison
MARIE-HELENE CHABUT / French / Lehigh University
LISA CODY / History / Claremont McKenna College
SARAH R. COHEN / Art History / SUNY, Albany
ABBY COYKENDALL / English / Eastern Michigan University
ANNE COTTERILL / English / Washington University in St. Louis
DONALD CRUICKSHANK / Spanish / University College, Dublin
MADELEINE DOBIE / French / Columbia University
LEIGH EICKE / English / Grand Valley State University
MATTHEW ERLIN / German / Washington University in St. Louis
NICOLE EUSTACE / History / New York University
LYNN FESTA / English / Harvard University
MARILYN FRANCUS / English / West Virginia University
TOM FURNISS / English / University of Strathclyde
ELIZABETH GARRELS / Spanish / Massachusetts Institute of Technology
ERIC GIDAL / English / University of Iowa
AMANDA GILROY / English / University of Groningen
LISA JANE GRAHAM / History / Haverford College
HARRIET GUEST / Centre for Eighteenth-Century Studies / York University
GEORGE HAGGERTY / English / University of California, Riverside

JEROME S. HANDLER / Virginia Foundation for the Humanities
JULIE C. HAYES / French / Richmond University
ELISABETH J. HEARD / English / St. Louis University
DONNA HEILAND / The Teagle Foundation
CARLA HESSE / History / University of California, Berkeley
CHARLES HASKELL HINNANT / English / University of Missouri-Columbia
JEFF HORN / History / Manhattan College
HEIDI HUTNER / English / SUNY Stony Brook
KRISTINE IBSEN / Spanish / University of Notre Dame
CATHERINE INGRASSIA / English / Virginia Commonwealth University
CHRISTOPHER M. JOHNS / Art History / Vanderbilt University
DOROTHY JOHNSON / Art History / University of Iowa
COLIN JONES / History / Warwick University
STEVEN KALE / History / Washington State University
KATHRYN KING / English / University of Montevallo
MATTHEW J. KINSERVIK / English / University of Delaware
ANNA KLOBUCKA / Portuguese / University of Massachusetts, Dartmouth
MARK LEDBURY / French / Clark Institute for Art
KATE LEVIN / English / Barnard College
ANTOINE LILTI / History / École Normale Supérieure
MARY LINDEMANN / History / University of Miami
DEVONEY LOOSER / English / University of Missouri-Columbia
CYNTHIA LOWENTHAL / English / Tulane University
DEIDRE LYNCH / English / Indiana University
CATRIONA MACLEOD / German / University of Pennsylvania
JEAN MARSDEN / English / University of Connecticut
ROBERT MAYER / English / Oklahoma State University
HEATHER NATHANS / Theater / University of Maryland, College Park
MAXIMILLIAN NOVAK / English / UCLA
JOHN O'BRIEN / English / University of Virginia
JOHN C. O'NEAL / French / Hamilton College
DANNY O'QUINN / English and Theatre Studies / University of Guelph
GIULIA PACINI / French / College of William and Mary
HARRY C. PAYNE / History / Woodward Academy
JENNIFER PHILIPS / French / Hamilton College
JULIE ANN PLAX / Art History / University of Arizona
DANIEL PURDY / German / Pennsylvania State University
JOHN RENWICK / French / University of Edinburgh

JOHN RICHARDSON / English / National University of Singapore
DONNA J. RILLING / History / SUNY Stony Brook
HARRIET RITVO / History / Massachusetts Institute of Technology
PAT ROGERS / English / University of Southern Florida
SOPHIA ROSENFELD / History / University of Virginia
ANA RUEDA / Spanish / University of Kentucky
TED RUML / English / California State University, San Bernardino
ELENA RUSSO / French / Johns Hopkins University
STEPHAN K. SCHINDLER / German / Washington University in St. Louis
HARRY E. SHAW / English / Cornell University
ANDREW SHIFFLETT / English / University of South Carolina
GEOFFREY SILL / English / Rutgers University
JUDITH SLAGLE / English / East Tennessee State University
JOANNA STALNAKER / French / Columbia University
JULIE A. STORME / French / Saint Mary's College
KRISTINA STRAUB / English / Carnegie-Mellon University
WILLIAM B. TAYLOR / History / University of California, Berkeley
BETH FOWKES TOBIN / English / Arizona State University
T. ROBERT TRAVERS / History / Harvard University
CYNTHIA TRUANT / History / University of California, San Diego
STÉPHANE VAN DAMME / History / CNRS (Paris)
SHERRY VELASCO / Spanish / University of Kentucky
BLAKEY VERMEULE / English / Northwestern University
NICOLE VON GERMETEN / History / Oregon State University
TIMOTHY WALKER / History / University of Massachusetts, Dartmouth
CYNTHIA WALL / English / University of Virginia
MIRIAM WALLACE / English / New College of Florida
DORA WEINER / History and Medicine / UCLA
EARLA A. WILPUTTE / English / St. Francis Xavier University
ALOK YADAV / English / George Mason University

ASECS Executive Board 2005–2006

President: **Sarah Maza**, Professor of History, Northwestern University
First-Vice President: **Felicity Nussbaum**, Professor of English, University of California, Los Angeles
Second-Vice President: **Bernadette Fort**, Professor of French and Italian, Northwestern University
Past President: **Margaret Anne Doody**, Professor of English, University of Notre Dame
Treasurer: **William F. Edmiston**, Professor of French, University of South Carolina
Executive Director: **Byron R. Wells**, Professor of Romance Languages, Wake Forest University

Members-at-Large
Helen Deutsch, Professor of English, University of California, Los Angeles
Isobel Grundy, Professor of English, University of Alberta
Christopher M.S. Johns, Professor of Art History, Vanderbilt University
Ann B. (Rusty) Shteir, Professor of Humanities and Women's Studies, York University
Beth Wright, Professor of Art History, University of Texas at Arlington
Larry Wolff, Professor of History, Boston College

Administrative Office
Office Manager: **Vickie Cutting**, Wake Forest University

For information about the
American Society for Eighteenth-Century Studies, please contact:
ASECS
P.O. Box 7867
Wake Forest University
Winston-Salem, NC 27109-7867
Telephone: (336) 727-4694
Fax: (336) 727-4697
E-mail: asecs@wfu.edu
Web Site: http://asecs.press.jhu.edu

American Society for Eighteenth-Century Studies
Patron Members 2005–2006

Hans Adler
Shane Agin
Stanford Anderson
Mark S. Auburn
Paula Backscheider
James G. Basker
Barbara Becker-Cantarino
Barbara Benedict
Oliver Berghof
Kevin Binfield
Theodore E.D. Braun
Fritz Breithaupt
Peter M. Briggs
Jane Brown
Morris Brownell
Martine W. Brownley
Michael Burden
Joseph A. Byrnes
Susan Carlile
Vincent Carretta
Julie Choi
Michael Conlon
Brian A. Connery
E. Heckendorn Cook
Kevin L. Cope
Margaret Mary Daley
Marlies K. Danziger
Jenny Davidson
Joan DeJean
Margaret Anne Doody
Julia Douthwaite
William F. Edmiston
Frank H. Ellis
Roger J. Fechner
Christopher Flynn
Riikka Forsstrom
Bernadette Fort
Christopher Fox
Charles Gobin
Scott Gordon
Sayre Greenfield
Monika Greenleaf
Joan R. Gundersen
Phyllis Guskin
Susan Gustafson
Knud Haakonssen
Mark Haag
Wolfgang Haase
Martha Hamilton-Phillips
Phillip Harth
Donald M. Hassler
Robert D. Hume
Lynn A. Hunt
J. Paul Hunter
Malcolm Jack
Margaret C. Jacob
Regina Mary Janes
Annibel Jenkins
George Justice
Gary Kates
Shirley Strum Kenny
Charles A. Knight
Jocelyne Kolb
David H. Koss
Thomas W. Krise
Susan Lanser
J. Patrick Lee
Meredith Lee
Nancy M. Lee-Riffe
Elizabeth Liebman
Loretta Lindgren Voorhees
Devoney Looser
Steven Walton Lynn
Robert P. MacCubbin
Elizabeth Mansfield
Sarah Maza
Marie E. McAllister
Christie McDonald
George C. McElroy
Alan T. McKenzie
James C. McKusick
Donald C. Mell Jr.
John H. Middendorf
Dennis Moore
Anja Mueller-Muth
Yvonne Noble
Mary Ann O'Donnell
John H. O'Neill
Frank Palmeri
Virginia J. Peacock
Ruth Perry
Jane Perry-Camp
Stuart Peterfreund
R.G. Peterson
J.G. Pocock
Todd Porterfield
John Valdimir Price II
Ruben D. Quintero
Ralph W. Rader
John Radner
Clifford Ramsey
Kirk Rasmussen
Gary Richardson
John Richetti
Betty Rizzo
Raymond Rizzo
James Rosenheim
Roseann Runte
Elizabeth Samet
J.T. Scanlan
Steven D. Scherwatzky
Harold Schiffman
Volker Schroder
Richard Sher
Eleanor F. Shevlin
Kazuko Shimizu
Craig A. Simmons
Douglas Smith
Robert Louis Smith
David Sorkin
Barbara Stafford
Susan Staves
Masashi Suzuki
Mika Suzuki
Ruud N.W.M. Teeuwen
Randolph Trumbach
Linda Troost
Bertil Van Boer
David F. Venturo
Joachim Von der Thusen
Howard D. Weinbrot
Byron R. Wells
Betty E. White
J. Edmund White
Lance Wilcox
James A. Winn
Karin E. Wolfe
Servanne Woodward
James Woolley
Karin Wurst
William Zachs
Lisa Zeitz

Sponsoring Members 2005–2006

Janet Aikins
Paul Alkon
Misty Anderson
Joseph F. Bartolomeo
R. Bernasconi
Mark Bisesi
Mark Blackwell
Carol Blum
Thomas F. Bonnell
Martha F. Bowden
Leo Braudy
Fredrick Burwick
Chester F. Chapin
Noel Chevalier
Andrew H. Clark
Stephen P. Clarke
Brian Corman
Patricia Craddock
Marlies K. Danzier
Pierre Deguise
Robert DeMaria
Judith Dorn
John Ebey
A.C. Elias, Jr.
Antoinette Emch-Deriaz
Robert A. Erickson
Liisa Erickson
Bim Erlenkotter
Clarissa C. Erwin
Daniel Timothy Erwin
David Fairer
Polly S. Fields
Robert Folkenflik
Vivian Folkenflik
Brandon Brame Fortune
Anita Guerrini
Basil Guy
Roger Hahn
Elisabeth Harries
Karsten Harries
Julie C. Hayes
Daniel Heartz
Ruth Hill
Adrienne D. Hytier
Catherine Ingrassia
Sarah Jordan
Issac Kramnick
Colby H. Kullman
Joan Landes
John E. Larkin, Jr.
Lawrence Lipking
April London
Steven Walton Lynn
Robert Markley
John McCarthy
R.W. McHenry
Heather McPherson
Linda E. Merians
Patricia H. Michaelson
Ellen G. Miles
Kathryn Montgomery
Maureen E. Mulvihill
Jessica Munns
Felicity Nussbaum
Douglas Lane Patey
J. G. A. Pocock
Suzanne L. Pucci
Walter E. Rex
Larry L. Reynolds
Alvaro Ribeiro SJ
John Richetti
Albert J. Rivero
Wendy Wassyng Roworth
Treadwell Ruml
Peter Sabor
Mona Scheuermann
Beverly Schneller
Barbara B. Schnorrenberg
William Schrader
Ann B. Shteir
Frank Shuffelton
Craig Simmons
Julia Simons
John Sitter
Henry Slosser
Douglas Smith
Jeffrey Smitten
Dennis Todd
Daniel D. Townsend
Raymond D. Tumbleson
Deborah M. Valenze
Charles Vallely
Peter Wagner
Larry Wolff
Myron D. Yeager

Institutional Members 2005–06

American Antiquarian Society
Arizona State University
Brown University,
  John Carter Brown Library
College of the Holy Cross,
  Dinand Library
Colonial Williamsburg Foundation
  John D. Rockefeller, Jr. Library
Emory University
  Woodruff Library
Florida Atlantic University
  Wimberly Library
Folger Institute
Fordham University
  History Department
Fordham University Library
Indiana University,
  Kokomo Library
Johns Hopkins University,
  Milton Eisenhower Library
McMaster University Library
Metropolitan Museum of Art
  Thomas J. Watson Library
National Taiwan Normal University
  Library
National Taiwan University
  Branch Library
Niedersaechsische Staats.
  Universitaets-Bibliothek
Newberry Library
Northwestern University Library
Ohio State University Libraries
Omohundro Institute for Early American
  History - *Kellock Library*
Rutgers University, *Alexander Library*
Smith College, *Neilson Library*
Smithsonian Institute, *AA/PG Library*
Stanford University, *Green Library*
State University of New York Binghamton
  Bartle Library
Sydney University
  Fisher Library
Thomas Jefferson Memorial Foundation
  Research Center
University of California, Irvine,
  Science Library
University of California, Santa Barbara
  Division of Humanities & Fine Arts
University of Evansville Library
University of Kansas Library
University of Kentucky, *Young Library*
University of North Carolina,
  Davis Library
University of Notre Dame Library
University of Pennsylvania Libraries
University of Rochester Library
University of Texas at Austin
  General Library
University of Tulsa, *McFarlin Library*
University of Victoria, *McPherson Library*
University of Wisconsin,
  English Department
Utrecht Universiteit
  Letterenbibliotheek
Waddesdon Manor Collection Department
Washington University, *Olin Library*
William Andrews Clark Memorial Library
Yale Center for British Art,
  Reference Library
Yale University Library

Index

Every effort has been made to include references to all identifiable persons living before or during the long eighteenth century, as well as to often cited twentieth-century critics and commentators, and to provide a selective listing of relevant concepts and keywords. Readers may also wish to consult the endnotes of each essay for more comprehensive information.

H

I

J

K

L

M

O

P